THE REMINISCENCES OF A MARINE
JOHN A. LEJEUNE

General Lejeune.

THE REMINISCENCES OF A
MARINE

by

MAJOR GENERAL
JOHN A. LEJEUNE

UNITED STATES MARINE CORPS

★ ★

Illustrated with Official and Personal Photographs

PHILADELPHIA
DORRANCE AND **COMPANY**
Publishers

PREFACE

It is all but impossible to designate one person as the "greatest" representative of an institution. For example, one simply cannot select the finest baseball player or the best doctor who ever lived. So, too, naming a single Marine as the greatest of all time would surely lead to angry rebuttal by those who would argue — and rightly so — for a different and equally deserving competitor.

But if a search backward were made through the illustrious history of the United States Marine Corps, looking for that one personification of greatest, Major General John A. Lejeune would certainly attract universal support. Combat leader, scholar, thinker, educator, innovator — all these describe the man who became the thirteenth Commandant of the Marine Corps and served as such for nine years during the 1920's.

Besides the many "firsts" of his distinguished thirty-nine year career, Lejeune can perhaps best be described as the man who charted the course of the Corps in the 20th century.

It is interesting to note in General Lejeune's "Reminiscences" that while on sea duty in 1897 as a first lieutenant in command of the Marine Detachment of the *U.S.S. Cincinnati,* he advanced the concept that Marines serving in detachments aboard combatant naval vessels were not necessary as a police force. Instead, they should be used to provide the Navy with an efficient expeditonary force for the conduct of such operations ashore as required to successfully execute a naval campaign. Forty years later this concept became a reality in the establishment of our current Fleet Marine Forces.

As a senior officer, General Lejeune made readiness and the development of amphibious warfare doctrines his principal objectives. Under his direction, studies were undertaken at the Marine Corps Schools from which our current doctrine evolved. Amphibious vehicles were developed and tested in frequent landing exercises conducted in the Caribbean. As a result, when World War II erupted, the Marine Corps was prepared to successfully carry out its missions in the seizure of vital bases in the Pacific. Today's powerful air-ground Marine Amphibious Force can trace its origin to the vision of John A. Lejeune.

General Lejeune was also a strong supporter of the Marine Corps Schools. He firmly believed that every Marine officer should be educated in the tactical and strategical concepts of the military profession.

As the first Marine officer to become a student at the Army War College, General Lejeune gained the reputation as one of the most competent students who had ever taken the course of instruction. It was largely by the success he attained while at the War College, and the friendships he made with several Army officers, who in World War I were in positions of authority in the American Expeditionary Force in France, that General Lejeune was assigned to command the 2nd U.S. Army Division. This division, composed of the 3rd Infantry and 4th Marine Brigades, established a combat record second to none. In the crucial battle for Blanc Mont Ridge, General Lejeune's ingenious assignment of the zones of action of his two brigades enabled them to bypass a strong defensive position in the Hindenburg Line. Likewise, in the operations of the 2nd Division in the Argonne Forest, General Lejeune's employment of his troops in several night attacks which bypassed German front line units contributed materially to the division's success in the final stages of the war.

When General Lejeune became Commandant of the Marine Corps in 1920, he undertook to raise the professional military standards of the Corps. The curriculum of the Marine Corps Schools was improved by assignment to the staff of officers who had served in combat in France during World War I. He also directed that a study of past amphibious operations be made from which our modern amphibious doctrine evolved.

But it was in the halls of Congress that General Lejeune made major contributions to the future stature of the Marine Corps. By his dynamic personality and complete frankness in presentations before Congressional committees, he gained the confidence and esteem of committee members and was able to establish the Marine Corps in a firm foundation as the country's force in readiness. This was demonstrated in the 1920's by Marine Expeditionary Brigades being deployed on brief notice to Nicaragua and China for the protection of United States interests in each of these turbulent countries.

General Lejeune also improved the morale of the Corps by promoting a "teacher-pupil" approach in relationships between officers and enlisted personnel. His efforts were rewarded by the admiration and respect received from all Marines who served under him while Commandant.

Although it would be a mistake to label General Lejeune as the greatest Marine (and he would vehemently deny this title) he should be recognized and given full credit for his many lasting contributions to the Marine Corps.

That Marines today may profit by General Lejeune's accomplishments, the Marine Corps Association which was founded by him at Guantanamo Bay, Cuba, 25 April 1913, has republished in its Heritage Library Series this book. I recommend *The Reminiscences of a Marine* to all officers and staff NCO's serving in the Corps today. It will apprise them of the problems faced and successfully overcome by General Lejeune during his career.

LEMUEL C. SHEPHERD, Jr.
General, USMC (Ret)
Aide to General Lejeune
1920 to 1922

DEDICATED TO

the officers and enlisted men of the Marine Corps, the Navy and the Army, with whom I have served. Devotion to duty, unswerving loyalty, fine courage and unselfish patriotism have been their dominant characteristics. I ask for them and for their successors the sympathetic appreciation of their fellow countrymen.

CONTENTS

ILLUSTRATIONS

ILLUSTRATIONS

FOREWORD

My wife, my sister, my three daughters and a number of my friends for several years have urged me persistently to write a book which would contain my memoirs or reminiscences. Until very recently I successfully resisted their urging.

My lines of resistance were three-fold. First of all, I insisted that I had no literary ability; second, that I had done nothing worth recording on the printed page; and third, that no publisher might be found who could be induced to place my work before the public. My first two defensive positions were broken through by the loving faith in my ability on the part of the members of my family. They scorned the thought that I could not do what other men had done and insisted that my life story would be of great interest, not only to them and to my grandchildren, but to many others as well. So I finally fell back into my third defensive position, which I felt to be impregnable. That position afforded me security until a short while ago when, to my amazement, it was penetrated by a surprise attack from an unexpected quarter.

In plain English, Gordon Dorrance of Philadelphia came to Washington and made me an offer to publish the book if I would write it. He brushed aside with a wave of his hand my statement that I never had written a book or anything else for publication, and that I was more than doubtful of my ability to write a book that any one would read. Finally, yielding to his insistence, I agreed to take the matter under consideration, and then completely succumbed to home pressure, which was redoubled in strength when I mentioned Major Dorrance's call. The above is my alibi and I here set it forth in extenuation.

The next question to be settled was the title of the

book. Many names were suggested, such as "The Memoirs of General Lejeune," "Forty Years a Marine" and a number of others. I myself decided on "The Reminiscences of a Marine" because it is my intention to draw on my memory for many of the incidents which will fill the ensuing pages. My memory, however, will be fortified and supplemented by certain papers I have in my possession and by the letters that I have written to my wife both before and after our marriage, for she has kept them all. When absent from home, rarely, if ever, did I fail even in the midst of storm or battle to put my innermost thoughts in a daily letter to her. These letters are too sacred to publish, but I shall draw on them to refresh my memory.

In concluding this Foreword I feel impelled to make full confession to the effect that whatever success I may have achieved as a man has been due to the beneficent influence of a deeply religious and most loving mother, a father of great nobility of character, a truly devoted sister, and a wife who has been always unselfish and always loving; and that whatever military success I have achieved has been due to the fidelity, the loyalty, the devotion to duty and the courage of the officers and men with whom I have been associated since that day that I entered the service more than forty-five years ago.

I salute them, whether they be among the living or the dead.

My friends, the anchor is aweigh, the sails are set and the ship, carrying a cargo of hope, is sailing out of the harbor toward the unknown sea. I ask your good wishes for a favoring breeze, a smooth sea, and a safe and happy voyage.

JOHN A. LEJEUNE.

Washington, D. C.

I

MY FOREFATHERS

E VERY man is indebted to his forefathers. I realize that I cannot repay the great debt of gratitude that I owe to my father and my mother, and in a less degree to those who preceded them, but I shall at least make the attempt to express briefly the reverence that I feel for them and my pride in the fact that they were honorable, faithful, courageous and duty-loving people.

All of my original American ancestors emigrated from France and the British Isles and settled on this continent during the Colonial period of American history.

What is written here regarding my father's forebears was told me by him. He personally remembered his great-grandfather Lejeune who, together with two brothers, emigrated in early youth from the section of France known as La Bretagne, or Brittany. They settled in Nova Scotia some years before the French-Indian War of 1756. Early in that war, a British military expedition occupied Acadia, and the French settlers, except those who left for other parts of Canada, were taken into captivity and sent by ship into exile. These exiles for the most part found their way to the Bayou Têche country in southern Louisiana and many of their descendants still live in that district. The story of their sufferings and their exile is simply and beautifully told in Longfellow's "Evangeline."

An incident in my own life illustrates the influence of a man's ancestors on him. A short while after entering the Naval Academy, I was accosted by an upper-classman named Berry who was engaged in the pleasing pastime of running "plebes," as the members of the fourth class there always have been called. After learning that I was from Louisiana, he asked me if I had read "Evangeline." I replied that I had. He then instructed me to learn it by heart and to be ready to recite it when called on by him to do so. He was most emphatic and made it clear that he would regard it as a very heinous offense if I failed to comply with his instructions. Accordingly, I spent many weary hours in the effort to memorize "Evangeline." When he next sought me out he demanded that I recite the poem. I had learned a part of it and repeated a couple of pages very successfully. He then said he had listened long enough and told me that, thereafter, whenever any upper classman asked me my name, I should reply "Gabriel LaJeunesse." Gabriel was the lover of Evangeline and his wanderings in search of her are described by Longfellow. The similarity of meaning of LaJeunesse and Lejeune, the translation of the former being "the youth" and of the latter "the young," appealed to him, and as a result of his facetiousness my classmates promptly adopted Gabriel or "Gabe" as my nickname, and continue to use it to this day.

The Lejeune brothers left their home upon the advance of the British, going to Quebec where they joined the Canadian army and took part in the campaign. Upon the defeat of Montcalm on the Plains of Abraham and the fall of Quebec, they journeyed up the St. Lawrence River and across the Great Lakes, joining other *couriers des bois* or pioneers, and after several years of wandering finally sailed down the Mississippi River with twenty other Frenchmen to Louisiana where they settled in the Fausse Rivière district in the Parish of Pointe

Mr. and Mrs. Ovide Lejeune, 1859.

Coupée, about thirty miles south of the place where I was born.

My father, in telling me the story, said our old ancestor lived to the great age of 105 years and was in full possession of his faculties and hale and hearty up to the day of his death. On that day, the old gentleman complained of the toothache and rode on horseback to the nearest doctor. His tooth was pulled, and on his way home he fell from his horse and died from the loss of blood incident to the pulling of his tooth. I am the only living male descendent by the name of Lejeune of this sturdy pioneer, and I thank him for the heritage of a sound constitution and the love of the simple life and the great outdoors which he transmitted to my father and to me.

My father's mother belonged to the Lemoine family which emigrated from France and settled in Canada and Louisiana in early Colonial days. My sister bears the name of her grandmother, Augustine Lemoine.

My father was born in 1820 and was given the name of Ovide. He had no recollection of his father, who died in 1823, but remembered his mother with great affection. After a long period of illness she died, leaving her only child, my father, an orphan at the age of eight. Being without any near relatives, he was sent to the Jesuit School at Cape Girardeau, Missouri, when still a small boy.

He inherited some property from his parents, and after several attempts at going to school he took up the life of a sugar planter. He was very successful in his chosen vocation and became a wealthy man according to the standards of the ante-bellum period.

He was generous, kind, gentle as a woman, but the most fearless man I have ever known. His temper was a fiery one, but it cooled as quickly as it flamed, and he nursed no malice or hate in his heart for any man. He loved his fellow-man and it was but natural that in early manhood he should have affiliated himself with the Masonic lodge in his neighborhood. At that time, Masonry in the United States had not come under the ban of the Roman Catholic Church. He was a faithful, loyal Mason, and when the edict of the Church was issued requiring all Catholics to sever their Masonic affiliations or suffer excommunication, he elected to remain a Mason.

He was thirty-six years old when he first met my mother, a lovely girl of sixteen, just out of school. He had bought a plantation about thirty miles north of his birthplace in a section called Raccourci. Among his near neighbors were Dr. and Mrs. John G. Archer, the uncle and aunt of my mother, and it was while she was on a visit to them that this scion of a French Roman Catholic family, the product of an altogether different environment from hers, a tall, erect, black-haired, black-eyed, handsome Louisiana Frenchman, was at once attracted by the gentle, fair-haired, blue-eyed girl who had been reared under the strictest Presbyterian influences.

My mother's maiden name was Laura Archer Turpin and she was descended from the Turpin and Archer families of Maryland. Her Turpin ancestors, according to family tradition, were originally French Huguenots who left France and settled in England. My ancestor, Solomon Turpin, emigrated to America in the first half of the eighteenth century, and settled on the eastern shore of Maryland.

My great-grandfather moved from Maryland to the territory of Mississippi in 1808, settling first near Washington, the then capital, where my grandfather, Joseph A. Turpin, was born in 1816. After graduating from the University of Virginia, he married Laura Archer, of Harford County, Maryland.

They made their home in Jefferson County, near Natchez, Mississippi, where my grandfather engaged in the planting of cotton. Both were devout Presbyterians, my grandfather saying to me not long before he died that he believed implicitly in the doctrines of election and predestination, and that any man or woman who ever felt the working of the Holy Spirit in his or her heart was predestined to be saved, as the omnipotent God would not make an unavailing or unsuccessful effort to save the soul of any one. It was a very comforting belief for him and in spite of poverty and sorrow during his old age he spent his last years in perfect serenity of spirit. His life's companion, my grandmother, was a veritable saint on earth, and it was a benediction to have known her.

She belonged to the Archer family of Harford County, Maryland. Robert Archer and his widowed mother emigrated in 1710 from their old home near Londonderry in the north of Ireland. They were known as Scotch-Irish people.

The most noted member of the Archer family was Dr. John Archer, the grandson of Robert. Dr. John Archer received his advanced education at Nassau Hall, Princeton, New Jersey. He then studied medicine at the old City College of Philadelphia, he and nine others constituting the first class of Americans to pursue their studies at a medical school in this country. Upon graduation the diplomas were delivered alphabetically, and he therefore received the first M.D. diploma ever issued in the Colonies. He established himself in practice in Harford County, naming his home Medical Hall. Dr. Archer found time also to take an active part in military and civic affairs. He was an ardent supporter of Thomas Jefferson and in 1797 was elector-at-large on the Jefferson ticket and served two terms in Congress as a Jeffersonian Democrat.

His youngest son, Stevenson, my great-grandfather, graduated at Princeton University and then took up the study of law, spending the remainder of his life in practice and as a judge. He was also active politically as a Democrat, serving in the state legislature and in Congress. He also served twenty-one years as chief judge of the Circuit Court of Appeals comprising Baltimore and Harford Counties, and when the end of his useful life came he was Chief Justice of the Maryland Court of Appeals.

His wife, Pamelia B. Hays, of Harford County, was a woman of strong character and unusual business ability.

It was to this home, Medical Hall, that my mother, at the age of four, was brought in order that she might be given the best opportunities for education, as the neighborhood in which her mother and father lived was devoid of schools. After graduating she returned to the home of her parents in Mississippi, a stranger among her own people.

Shortly afterward she paid a brief visit to Dr. and Mrs. Archer and met my father, leaving a lasting impression on his memory. Nearly two years later she again visited her aunt and uncle, and my father at once began to pay her devoted attention. My aunt often told me the story and of how she and her husband placed every obstacle in the way of courtship, being fearful lest they would be blamed by my grandfather for permitting a man unknown to him to pay court to his daughter. The inevitable happened, however, and they were married in the Presbyterian Church near my mother's home.

The year following their marriage there came the excitement of the political campaign which resulted in the election of Lincoln, the secession of the southern states and Civil War. My father voted against secession, but when it was an assured fact, although over forty years of age, he immediately raised a troop of cavalry, spending $10,000 of his own money in equipping it, and was assigned with his troop to the 2nd Louisiana Regiment of Cavalry, leaving my mother with her infant daughter alone on his plantation. His service was in the Army of the Tennessee. My mother's three brothers served in the same army, one of them, White Turpin, being killed at the battle of Franklin, Tennessee, near the close of the Civil War.

II

BOYHOOD AND COLLEGE DAYS

I WAS born January 10, 1867, on my father's cotton plantation, "Old Hickory," in the district known as Raccourci, Pointe Coupee Parish, Louisiana. Their names refer to the fact that the Mississippi River had changed its channel there, cutting off a point of land, and shortening its course materially. The former bed of the river was known as "Old River," and formed a beautiful lake some twenty miles long and a mile wide which was not connected with the main river channel except during high water. "Old Hickory" was located a short distance from "Old River" and some three miles from the Mississippi.

I was named John Archer for my great uncle, Doctor John Archer, who attended my mother at my birth Uncle John, his wife, Aunt Sarah, and two of their three sons, John and William, lived at Longwood, about one mile away. The other son, Stevenson, lived in Maryland. They and my father, mother and sister were devoted to one another, and the memory of my boyhood days is filled with recollections of incidents connected with them.

I arrived in the world at a very depressing period in the family history. My father had become bankrupt, and a short while after my birth his home and everything that he owned were sold. The family was homeless and penniless. My father accepted employment as the manager of a sugar plantation near his birthplace, where he was employed for several years. He received practically no salary, but supplies were advanced him by the merchant who financed the plantation which, together with what was raised on the place, furnished us with sufficient food. Clothing was limited to actual necessities, luxuries did not exist so far as we were concerned, and money was unknown.   My earliest recollections cluster about this place, as we lived there until I was five years old.

In the Fall of 1871, my father repurchased his former home, "Old Hickory," by assuming the very heavy mortgage which it bore.   We moved back to our old plantation early in January, 1872, and my father began the hopeless struggle to pay off the mortgage which he had assumed.

As was customary then, he worked the place on shares. Supplies were issued to the hands as a charge against their share of the crop.   All purchases were made on credit from a New Orleans commission merchant, to whom all the cotton raised was shipped.   He sold it on commission, and at the end of the year accounts were settled.   Owing to the high prices charged for supplies, the inefficiency of the laborers, and the low price of cotton, a bare existence for the farmer and his hands was about all that could be expected.

My father and my mother were never idle.   They toiled unceasingly.   My father was up at crack of dawn to rouse the hands with his conch shell which he blew lustily, and if they did not appear promptly, he supplemented the blasts of the conch by calling each one by name.   He attended to everything on the place, visiting the fields several times each day, managing the ginning and pressing of the cotton and the grinding of the corn, and personally keeping the accounts.   In spite of all his efforts, however, he was compelled finally to give up the major part of his plantation, retaining only the homestead consisting of about seventy-five acres, including the yard and the buildings.

My mother was equally indefatigable.   In addition to her many household duties, she gave my sister lessons on the piano and educated her.

When I attained the age of seven, my mother began to teach me, as there were no schools in the entire neighborhood or parish.   When the neighbors learned that my mother was teaching me, they begged her to teach their children also. This she consented to do chiefly because of her desire to be of service to the people of the community, but partly also because of the need of the small sum which was paid her.

My mother's influence for good among the people both old and young was incalculable and her school soon became the social center of the community. My aunt, Mrs. Archer, was of great help to her in the social activities of the school, freely giving her time and her remarkable executive ability to the creation of a community spirit and to teaching the young people deportment, dancing, mass singing and the dramatic art. Entertainments of many kinds were held, such as amateur theatricals, May Day festivals and dances. My aunt personally supervised the rehearsals, planned the costumes, acted as stage director and was the general manager of all the entertainments, my mother and sister acting as her assistants.

Religious as well as secular instruction formed an important part of the school curriculum. My Mother was entirely free from all forms of religious intolerance or bigotry. She taught the Protestant children their catechisms, and with the approval of the Catholic priest of the near-by church she prepared the Catholic children for their confirmation and first communion and on his visitations was complimented by the Archbishop on the thorough manner in which she had instructed them.

She was greatly beloved by all the children and by their parents as well, and her memory is so deeply reverenced by those who knew her as to make me feel that her spirit still lingers in the community as an influence for good.

The only Protestant church in the country was situated in the village of Williamsport, about eight miles from "Old Hickory" plantation. It was the Episcopal Church of St. Stephen's, a beautiful little country church built of brick. Here the Protestants of all denominations gathered together each Sunday to worship God, and here my mother and sister were confirmed.

My mother never failed to attend church services when it was physically possible to travel over the villainous roads. In the winter time it was necessary frequently to resort to a four-mule team to haul the wagon through the quagmire which, through custom, was called a road. Often my sister and I rode on horseback to church, following the path on the top of the levee which protected the farms from overflow by the mighty torrent which poured down to the Gulf of Mexico from the great basin between the Rocky and the Allegheny Mountains.

The people dwelling behind the levees lived in constant fear of an overflow. The delight and joy which men usually find in the coming of Spring were changed to anxiety and dread in the hearts of the people of the Louisiana lowlands. Everyone anxiously watched the rising of the waters and read the reports of the approach of the crest of the flood with constant foreboding.

The people who lived behind the levees had to rely on themselves almost entirely in the years of carpet-bag government, as little or no assistance was given them by the state. This failure on the part of the state to make proper effort to protect its citizens from the devastation of overflow was another one of the many evidences of post-war reconstruction and the misgovernment which accompanied it.

No Louisianian whose memory extends to all or a part of the ten-year period preceding 1877, can fail to have vivid recollection of the corruption, and the failure to function, of the state and local governments during that time. A combination of "carpet-baggers," native white "scalawags," and ignorant blacks filled the offices, drew their salaries, and either did nothing or worse than nothing for those who would not join them in misgoverning the state.

In our section the local officials, including those sworn to enforce the laws and prosecute criminals, did not perform their functions. There was no such thing as justice, and no serious effort was made by them to protect the people or their property from the criminal element of the population. Robbery and stealing were prevalent. Cattle, hogs and sheep were killed by night marauders

who, after removing a quarter or a joint for home con-
sumption, left the remainder of the carcasses to be eaten
by vultures. We lost fourteen head of cattle in the
Spring of one year in this way.

It is not surprising, therefore, that the decent white
men should have organized themselves for self-protec-
tion and to secure the blessings of peace and tranquillity
for their families.

In Pointe Coupée Parish the organization did not take
the form of a Ku Klux Klan, as was the case in many of
the Southern states. Instead, in our community a local
Vigilance Committee was organized which, although it
did not form a part of a larger organization, nevertheless worked in harmony with other similar committees
in near-by communities and parishes. My father was the
captain of the Vigilance Committee and was ably assisted
by several young lieutenants, among them Dr. William
B. Archer, a son of my uncle and aunt, Dr. and Mrs.
John Archer. He was an unusually gifted and attractive
young man and possessed a dauntless, daring and chiv-
alrous spirit which made him a natural leader of men.
The blacks outnumbered the whites, however, by about
twenty-five to one and, chafing under the control exercised over them, they conspired to exterminate the white
men and to take possession of their property.

One Sunday night about ten o'clock my cousin, Dr.
William Archer, was riding on top of the levee from our
house where he had been spending the evening to his
home about a mile away, when without warning fire was
opened on him from behind each of six great cottonwood
trees only a few yards away. His horse, panic-stricken,
jumped from the levee to the road, the saddle-girth broke,
and my cousin fell to the ground. He was unarmed, but
although his coat and hat were riddled with bullets he
was unhurt by the firing or the fall and ran to the nearest
house to give the alarm. An investigation was begun at
once and the details of the conspiracy were soon learned.
The plan had been to murder the leaders during the preceding night, beginning with my father, who was to

be roused from his sleep and called out of doors to look out for the cattle, when five or six men were to fire on him from concealed positions. The plan failed because two or three gentlemen spent the night with us and the conspirators did not dare to make the attack that night. It was postponed accordingly until the following evening, but due to the failure to kill my cousin and to the prompt action taken, the would-be assassins became frightened and hid themselves.

The plan also provided for the assassinations to be followed by the immediate uprising of thousands of blacks. As soon as the plan was learned, messengers were sent far and wide for all white men to assemble in a woods about one mile from our home on the following Tuesday morning. Monday was an anxious day; the men were busily engaged in conferences and in preparations to crush the uprising, and to the boys fell the task of guarding the homes.

Tuesday morning at dawn the clans began to gather and the road was crowded with armed men on horseback going to the rendezvous. Grim-visaged men they were —farmers, storekeepers, laborers, lumbermen, men of all types and from all walks of life. Literally thousands of them appeared. The conspirators were overawed and the uprising did not take place. Instead, five of the six men who had attempted to murder my cousin were arrested, tried by a jury, convicted, sentenced and executed on the day that the assembly took place. It was a terrible, distressing and never to be forgotten incident, but the effect was salutary and lasting. No similar disturbance has ever since occurred in that community.

It was darkest before the dawn, however, as a few months after the events I have just described took place, the election of November, 1876, was held. In this election the Democratic candidates for the state offices received a large majority of the votes cast, and although their opponents were inaugurated and assumed office, it was only for a brief period of time. President Hayes, after his inauguration, issued orders for the withdrawal of the United States troops from participation in the internal affairs of the state. The military guard was relieved from duty at the state capitol in New Orleans. General Nichols, who had lost an arm, a leg and an eye during the Civil War, was seated as Governor and the members of the legislature who had received the majority of the votes in their districts were declared elected. A constitutional convention was then called, which drafted a new constitution and legalized the acts of the Nichols state government.

As soon as the state government was reorganized and ready to function, my father completely disbanded the Vigilance Committee, saying that such an organization had no appropriate place in a state whose government was in the hands of the people.

I have briefly described some of the incidents connected with the reconstruction period in order to indicate the difficult conditions under which the people lived and to demonstrate the indisputable fact that it is impossible, except by the use of military force, to maintain a backward race in power over a superior race. To attempt to do so was not only unwise, but was the cause of much ill will, sorrow and suffering. The wounds caused by reconstruction required a much longer time in which to heal than did those resulting from the war between the states.

My studies were necessarily interrupted to some extent by tasks which had to be performed, so my mother, imbued as she was with the conviction that a good education was the best legacy that could be left to a child, arranged to send me to the boarding school of her uncle, James Archer, who had opened a few years before a private school for a small number of boys at his home place, "Oakwood," about twelve miles from Natchez, Mississippi.

I left home early in January, 1880, when I was just thirteen, making my debuté in the outside world. I went by river steamboat to Natchez, where I spent the night with my relatives, the Chamberlains, and the next morning I completed the journey by rail. It was my first ride on a train, and the first time, too, I had been away from my mother. I suffered the keenest pangs of homesickness which were accentuated by my intense bashfulness or diffidence. To be with strangers was torture. This trait or defect remained with me for many years, causing me much discomfort of mind and depriving me of the enjoyment of a great deal of innocent pleasure. Realizing fully the handicap under which I labored, I finally managed to overcome it, but it was a slow and painful process.

To return to the subject of my school days at "Oakwood," it is sufficient to say that life there was dull and monotonous, but tempered by the kindness and affection of Aunt Mary, the wife of Uncle James, and of Cousin Olivia, their daughter. "Oakwood" was a most attractive home in an isolated location, and one saw other people only very occasionally, as when we drove in the old family carriage to Natchez, where the Chamberlains never failed to make me feel that I was one of the family.

On one of these journeys to Natchez there occurred the outstanding event of the two years I spent at Oakwood. The U. S. S. *Alliance,* which was making a so-called good-will cruise up the Mississippi River, had come to an anchor at Natchez and my uncle decided to take his scholars on board that ship for educational and patriotic purposes. We drove to the wharf boat and embarked in one of the ship's twelve-oared cutters manned by stalwart sailors. The family coachman, a body servant of Uncle James, accompanied us. The ride in the cutter gave us a thrill. The river was high and swift, but the sturdy, well-trained crew easily breasted the current with powerful, clock-like strokes, and a perfect landing was made alongside the gangway. My uncle, closely followed by his colored servant and ourselves, started up the ladder when the officer on duty stopped us by saying to my uncle, "You and the boys can come on board, but the colored man cannot do so and will have to go back ashore." My Uncle James, who was a very distinguished

looking man, drew himself up to his full height and replied, "Where I go, he goes, and where he cannot go, I
do not go.   Good afternoon, Sir!" and, much to our
chagrin, he turned about and started down the ladder,
telling us to get back in the boat.   The officer hastily conferred with superior authority and then called down to
the boat that all of the party could come on board.   When
we reached the top of the companionway, he explained
that the officers were giving a dance that afternoon to
the beauty and chivalry of Natchez and vicinity, and that
his orders were to permit only the invited guests to come
on board so as not to overcrowd the ship, but that an
exception had been made in behalf of my uncle's vener-
able looking attendant.   The *Alliance* was beautifully
decorated with flags and was spotlessly clean.   The
decks, the guns, the paintwork, the brass, the yards, the
masts, the awnings and the rigging were immaculate, as
were the sailors, the marines, and the officers in their
resplendent uniforms.   As we looked about us, taking
count of everything we saw, we were thrilled through
and through, especially when we turned our eyes towards
our glorious flag flying to the breeze at the peak.   We
remained on board for an hour or two, visiting every part
of the ship and watching the dancing on the quarterdeck.
I noticed that one of the officers was dressed in a different uniform from the others, wearing sky blue trousers
instead of dark blue, and a braided blouse instead of a
double-breasted frock coat carrying two rows of brass
buttons.   I asked the sailor who was acting as my guide
who the officer was, and he replied that it was the Marine
officer of the ship.   In after years I came to know him
well and had the honor of serving under his command.
He was First Lieutenant George F. Elliott, for seven
years the Commandant of the Marine Corps, and now
living in Washington, D. C., as a Major General on the
retired list.
  We went ashore with our minds filled with thoughts of
the ship, the crew, the far-away ports they had visited,
and the strange peoples they had seen, but somehow it

never once occurred to me that the hand of fate was beckoning me to take the path which would lead me away from home across the trackless oceans and to far countries, but always under the inspiration and guidance of the beautiful flag—that symbol of the united nation which it would be my good fortune to serve, in calm or in storm, in peace or in war, during nearly all the remaining years of my life.

Although I progressed rapidly in my studies under Uncle James' wise and skilful tutelage, I concluded, as my second year drew to a close, that life there was too secluded, and that I needed contact with a large number of boys and the opportunity to see something of the great world in which I would have to struggle for a livelihood. As soon as I went home I told my father and mother of my conclusion and they both agreed that it was wise.

After inquiry, it was decided to send me to the Louisiana State University at Baton Rouge, the capital city of the state. From Raccourci to Baton Rouge was a short trip by steamboat, and early in September, 1881, my father took me there and entered me in the upper preparatory class. Owing to the lack of schools in Louisiana during the Civil War and the twelve-year period following, it was necessary for nearly all the boys entering the University to receive a part of their preparatory training there. I was fortunate in being sufficiently far advanced at fourteen to enter the upper instead of the lower preparatory class.

The school had been founded a short while before the Civil War, its first President being William Tecumseh Sherman, then an unknown former Army officer, but whose fame as a great military commander soon became world wide. Colonel David F. Boyd had been Sherman's assistant in the earliest days of the school, and after the Civil War was ended he returned to it, and devoted nearly all the remainder of his life to re-establishing, maintaining, and building it up. Sherman had made it a military school, and so it continued to be, all the students being termed Cadets, and all being required to wear the Cadet uniform, which was like that of the Virginia Military Institute, except the cap, which was blue in honor of the founder of the school.

When I entered the University, Colonel William P. Johnston, the son of General Albert Sidney Johnston, was the President, Colonel David F. Boyd, a very positive character, being in disfavor with the then existing state administration. Soon after I left the University, Colonel Boyd was reappointed, Colonel Johnston having been appointed President of Tulane University.

The buildings eventually became inadequate and a beautiful group of buildings was constructed on high ground overlooking the river just below the city of Baton Rouge. In April, 1926, I was present at the dedication of the new University buildings and made an address before the members of the Alumni Association and other friends of the old school.

It was at the University that I acquired the rudiments of military training, as we were instructed daily in close order drill up to and including the School of the Battalion, and in the ceremonies of Dress Parade and Guard Mounting, following with almost religious punctilio the rules and regulations prescribed in Upton's Military Tactics. The company officers and non-commissioned officers were required to be experts in drill and devoted considerable time to the study of Upton's incomparable manual. I attained the exalted rank of Second Lieutenant during my third and last year at the University, and proudly wore my shoulder straps when I went home for the Christmas holidays.

My experience at the University was not only of great benefit to me from the standpoint of mental training and education, but was of even greater advantage because of the physical training, the discipline, and the habits of military obedience and military command which were inculcated there. I am confident that several years at a first-class military school or college would be of incalculable value to every American boy in fitting him to engage in life's arduous struggle and in preparing him

John A. Lejeune, Naval Cadet,
U. S. Navy, 1886.

Cadet John Archer Lejeune,
Louisiana State University, 1882.

to perform the duties of American citizenship in time of peace.

For a number of years, my father had frequently discussed the possibility of my going to the United States Military Academy at West Point. He had acquired a very high opinion of that institution by reason of the sterling character and splendid military ability displayed by the great military leaders on both sides in the Civil War. In fact, I was taught to revere them and above all to regard General Robert E. Lee as being the embodiment of the noblest qualities of which human nature is capable. General Lee's lofty character as displayed in war, under the humiliation of defeat, and in the years that followed the surrender at Appomatox, had a far-reaching and lasting effect on the soldiers of the Confederacy and on the generation of young men which succeeded them.

So it came about that when I had attained the required age, my father took steps to secure me an appointment.

Our Congressman, Judge E. T. Lewis, informed him, however, that there was no vacancy at West Point, but that one had just occurred at the Naval Academy, and offered the appointment to me. I unhesitatingly accepted it, because after all the chief reason for my willingness to go to West Point was to lift the heavy financial burden of my education from the shoulders of my parents.

It was early in April, 1884, that I received notice of my appointment to the Naval Academy. I promptly resigned from the University, being then near the end of the Sophomore year, and went home, where I spent a month in self-preparation for the entrance examination and in association with the dear ones in the home in which there dwelt thrift, wisdom, unselfishness, love and, therefore, happiness.

III

THE NAVAL ACADEMY, 1884-1888

THERE was then only one member of the family connection in the Navy. He was Medical Director
Lewis J. Williams, who had retired from active duty several years before and was living in Baltimore. He had
married my mother's aunt, Harriet Archer. Aunt Hallie,
as we called her, had died a number of years before, but
her husband continued his interest in her relatives. My
mother wrote to him telling him of my appointment and
asking him for information about the Naval Academy.
He at once replied, expressing great interest in the matter of my future career in the Navy, and insisting on my
going to his home in Baltimore, saying that he would
accompany me to Annapolis and see that I was properly
installed.

My father, in our conversations, frequently referred
to the obligation of service which I would assume when
I became identified with the Navy. He impressed on me
the fact that I was about to become an officer of the
United States Government, that I would owe the Government my undivided allegiance, and that it would be my
duty to serve it honorably and faithfully in peace, and
to defend it loyally and courageously in war against its
enemies, both foreign and domestic. His words were
stored away in my memory and they have often recurred
to my mind during the more than forty-four years that
have elapsed since I entered the service of the United
States.

The days at home passed by as rapidly as if they were
winged and the hour of departure on my journey, to
what seemed to me then to be another and a distant world,
soon arrived. I never can forget the mingled feelings of
homesickness and anticipation which came into my heart

as I stood on the deck of the river steamboat and waved good-bye to father, mother, sister and friends as they watched me from the river bank.

Two or three days were given up to visiting friends and sightseeing in New Orleans, and then I took the train for Baltimore.

I arrived there on time and, following the directions given me, easily found my way to Dr. Williams' house on Preston Street.

At the appointed time, Dr. Williams and I proceeded via Odenton and the Annapolis & Elkridge Railway to the quaint old capital city of Maryland. On our arrival we went to the Superintendent's office to register and to report officially. We were ushered into the presence of Captain F. M. Ramsey, the then Superintendent. He was a very handsome and distinguished looking man, but when he sized me up with his cold, blue eyes, I felt chilled to the marrow, and hoped that I might never be brought before him to answer for any misconduct on my part.

After a courteous greeting and a brief conversation we left his office, and I registered my name and home address in the great volume in the office of the Secretary, Mr. Chase.

Before registering, I looked at the several pages of names of my future classmates, and seeing that many of them hailed from cities and large towns, I was a little diffident about entering the name of the obscure post office which constituted my home address, but my mind was relieved when I read the name and address just above mine. It was "C. B. Williams, Strawberry Point, Iowa." I then unhesitatingly wrote down "Raccourci P. O., Louisiana" just after my own name.

The candidates did not have long to wait, and in a comparatively few days were informed as to the result of the examinations and the successful ones passed from freedom into restraint, or so it seemed to most of us; but it was a restraint which had a real objective and a definite purpose.

It is a real joy to turn my thoughts back to those early

days when one's heart was being fastened to other hearts by the rivets of steel which have withstood the ravages of time, and which are as sound and strong today as they were when, fresh from the heat of the furnace, they were first driven home.   Entrance to the Naval Academy, therefore, not only involved the beginning of a career, but the creation of new and lasting friendships as well. From both points of view, it marked the beginning of a new volume in one's life history, the ending of the individualistic conception of life, and the beginning of the life of service to the Government, our people, and the nation.   Henceforth, while clinging with the strongest kind of sentimental attachment to the locality in which I was born and bred, I became before all else a citizen and a servant of America.

These thoughts were the product of a gradual growth and development.   They did not at once spring into being. In fact, my first thoughts, after taking the oath to support the Constitution and receiving instruction concerning the very practical things that I was to do, were to admit to myself that a "plebe" was a very humble and unimportant person who was lucky to be permitted to enter, even on sufferance, the sacred precincts of the Naval Academy where there dwelt the exalted personages known as "upper classmen."   Our first duty tended to increase the feeling of humility.   It was to go to the Cadet Store and draw a great variety of necessary articles which we rolled up in a blanket and carried about a quarter of a mile to the *U. S. S. Santee,* an old sailing ship, which was fast in the mud alongside the dock, and which was used as a temporary barracks or dormitory for the "plebes."

We slept and lived on board the *Santee,* but marched back and forth to the so-called New Quarters about a mile away for our meals.   We were a motley crowd. The only article of Naval Academy uniform we wore was the blue cap minus the gold cord.   We had been measured for our blue uniforms, but some days were required in which to complete them.   My classmates

wore every known variety of civilian clothing, from a
sack suit to a Prince Albert coat of the vintage of many
years before. Personally, I was the most unfortunate of
all, because I was arrayed in my gray uniform, having
decided that it would be foolishly extravagant to purchase
a civilian suit which I could not wear after I entered the
Academy. Fortunately, I had removed the second lieutenant's shoulder straps before leaving home, but the uniform itself made me very conspicuous, so that when we
"broke ranks" after arriving at the New Quarters, some
ten or fifteen minutes before mess formation, I always
received a great deal more than my fair share of attention from the upper classmen. For this reason the other
"plebes" in nearly all instances kept away from me and I
was left to bear the brunt of my popularity alone. On
one occasion, however, I looked up and there stood one
of my classmates just as close to me as possible. He
said, "I am going to stand by you. I like the color of
your uniform." He was a young man of huge frame,
powerful physique, and with a look of kindness, courage
and affection shining in his fine blue eyes. He was Carlo
Bonaparte Brittain, of the little mountain town of Pine-
ville, Kentucky. From that moment we became fast
friends, and my affection for him has continued unabated
to this day. He died on board the Flagship of the Atlantic Fleet at Guantanamo Bay, Cuba, about seven years
ago. He was then a Rear Admiral and the Chief of
Staff of the Fleet. A nobler spirit than his I never have
known.

So much attention was paid me by the upper classmen
that it was observed by the officer in charge, and one evening an order was received on the *Santee* to send me
under escort to report to the office in charge. When my
escort, Naval Cadet Harry G. Carpenter, a turn-back, and
I reached the New Quarters, we were ushered into the
office. The officer said to me sternly, "I saw several upper classmen surrounding you and apparently 'running'
you just before supper formation, among them Mr. Griswold. I direct you to repeat to me in full just what they

said to you." I replied that I didn't know Mr. Griswold. He then asked me if I could identify him. I stated in reply, with perfect truthfulness, that I could not identify any of the upper classmen who had spoken to me, as there had been so many of them, and that I couldn't remember anything specific that any of them had said, but that nothing had been said which was humiliating to me, or to which I could properly take exception. This was the substance of the interview, which lasted some ten or fifteen minutes. On our way back to the *Santee*, Carpenter described it with a good many trimmings to several groups of upper classmen that we met. The incident passed from my mind until the following October, when, one evening, five or six members of the Class of '86 entered my room. They were in a fierce mood and gave every indication of being on a hazing expedition. They hadn't been on the practice cruise with us, their class— the second—having spent the summer at the Naval Academy, as was then the custom, and they had just returned from their September leave. Consequently, I had no recollection of ever having seen any of them before. The first question asked was my name. I answered, "Gabriel LaJeunnesse," which the reader will recall had been given me by Berry, a member of the same class. One of them—a six-footer—said, "Don't get funny, Mister. There isn't any plebe by that name. What is your real name?" I replied, "Lejeune, Sir." He said, "Aren't you the plebe that the officer in charge, Lieutenant Manney, sent for last spring and asked if Mr. Griswold hadn't been 'running' you?" I answered that I was. He said, "I am Mr. Griswold," and, turning to his classmates he said, "This plebe saved me from being court-martialed; he is my friend, and he is exempt from running or hazing by any member of the class of '86." They then wished me goodnight, left the room, and continued their activities at the expense of some of my less fortunate classmates living in near-by rooms.

As my mind reverts to the plebe year at the Naval Academy, I have no recollection of any serious form of

hazing being inflicted on me, or any 'running' to which
I could make valid objection.   While still a candidate, I
had been told by Volney O. Chase—a member of the
class of 1885, who was from Louisiana and who had received a letter from Jastremski, my predecessor, who
had himself been dismissed for hazing, asking him to look
out for me—that I should submit to the ordinary 'running' to which all plebes were subjected, but that I should
not brook any treatment which, in my judgment, was
such that a gentleman could not properly submit to it.   He
also very kindly offered his advice and help whenever
I felt that I needed it, and told me that I should not hesitate to call on him for it.   Throughout my career in the
service, I have never ceased to be grateful to him, and
as the years passed by I came more and more to admire
him.

My class technically continued to occupy the lowly
position of the plebe class until after graduation of the
first class (1885), but the members of my class felt that
they actually ceased to be "plebes" when the new fourth
class entered, about three weeks before graduation.
There was room for disagreement on this subject during
the period between the two dates.   I for one, however,
was thoroughly convinced of the soundness of our contention and determined not to submit to any form of running or hazing during the few days remaining before we
became entitled officially to be designated as third classmen.   One morning after breakfast, my determination
was put to a severe test.   Accompanied by several classmates I was walking along the brick walk leading from
the front steps of the then New Quarters to Maryland
Avenue.   On our left there was a group of third classmen
(1887) going in the same direction, and one of them,
by the name of Cash, said something to me in a rather
peremptory manner which I didn't hear distinctly, but
which I understood to be an order "to square my cap."
I paid no attention to him, whereupon he stepped up to
me and took hold of my cap.   I had been brought up to
consider that my person was sacred, and that the laying

hold of or touching it in an unfriendly manner was an indignity which should be resented. My indignation at his act, combined with my determination to assert my belief that I was no longer a "plebe," caused me to strike him a light blow on the chest as a fair warning that a fight was on. As I did so, I stepped back, and as the terrace just behind me was very slippery from the heavy dew, I slipped and fell. Immediately my opponent was astride my prostrate form and struck me a blow in my left eye. I struggled to my feet and resumed the fight, during which I succeeded in landing a heavy blow just above his left eye. We were promptly separated by the bystanders but, unfortunately, the little unpleasantness occurred immediately in front of the office of the officer in charge who happened to be looking out of his window at the time. We were called before him and severely reprimanded for our conduct. Cash explained that he had told me that the sweat band of my cap was ripped and hanging down below the cap and, as I didn't seem to understand him, he had reached over in a perfectly friendly way to adjust it, when, to his amazement, I struck him, thus precipitating the bout. I explain my misunderstanding of the purport of his words and his act. The officer in charge then required us to shake hands and to express to each other that no hard feelings remained. I thought the incident was closed, but the next morning when the Report of the Day was published, we learned that we were on the report for "Ungentlemanly conduct, fighting in Academy grounds." I put in a statement to the Commandant, explaining the affair in detail and closing it with the remark that, under the circumstances, I did not feel that either one of us was guilty of ungentlemanly conduct, but that, on the contrary, it would have been ungentlemanly if I had failed to resent actively what, through a misunderstanding, I had considered to be an unwarranted act; and that certainly it would have been ungentlemanly for my opponent to have failed to take up the challenge by returning my blow. The report was changed to "Improper conduct," and three demerits were awarded instead of the much larger number that we would otherwise have received and, what was of much greater importance, the words "ungentlemanly conduct" were erased from my record. I have described this incident in detail because it was the only fight in which I took part during my four years at the Academy, and because it illustrates to some extent the code which was in vogue among us.

I must, however, take up again the thread of my narrative and return to the *Santee,* where we learned the then first duties of a sailor, which were: to rig a hammock, to climb into it with facility, to sleep in it securely, and to lash it in shipshape manner in the morning when the boatswain's shrill pipe, followed by his hoarse voice shouting, "All hands! Up all hammocks," roused us from our sleep, and caused us to dress hastily, lash our hammocks, and carry them to the nettings. Ships' hammocks were then to me an abomination and still are to this day. However, I am glad to say that they are gradually being relegated to the discard and that "standee" bunks are being substituted for them on board the larger vessels of the Navy.

Our comparatively brief stay on the *Santee* was signalized by an inspection of the ship by President Chester A. Arthur on the occasion of his visit to the Naval Academy to attend the graduation exercises. We plebes were properly awed as we stood in line and watched him. It was my first opportunity to see a President, and I remember his appearance distinctly. He was a man of distinguished appearance and was immaculately dressed in the fashion of the day.

Almost immediately after the President's visit, we packed up our belongings and were transferred to the U. S. S. *Constellation* which, with the U. S. S. *Dale,* was utilized for the summer practice cruise of the naval cadets. When we embarked we could sing with feeling and with truth, "We are in the Navy now." It was a hard, rough, three months experience, an experience which the present-day midshipmen could not possibly visualize or comprehend. To begin with, we swung and had our mess on the berth deck under the most crowded conditions, and when the airports were closed, as they always were at sea, there was no ventilation except from a windsail or two which were thrust down the hatches from the spar (upper) deck. The crew was quartered just above us on the gun deck, where the old 9-inch, smooth-bore, muzzle-loading, cast iron guns looked savagely out of the gunports at real or imaginary enemies as the case might be. Above the spar deck towered the three lofty masts with squared yards and bent sails in readiness to get under way. There was no such thing as refrigeration on board, or ice. We drank the almost tepid, dark-brown water which was obtained from the lake of the Dismal Swamp near Norfolk, Virginia, and which was discolored partly by the rust of the ship's iron water tanks and partly by the myriad of juniper berries which fell into the lake and which were supposed to impart to its waters some peculiar virtue not possessed by water drawn from less fortunate localities. Our food, after a day or two at sea, consisted of the customary sea fare. Salt meat, especially salt beef (called by the sailors "salt horse"), salt fish, hard tack, baked beans, and other similar deep sea dishes constituted an important part of our daily fare. Hard work by night as well as by day, however, gave us ravenous appetites, after seasickness was overcome, and our quarrel was less with the quality of the food than with the infrequency of the meals, as the hours which elapsed between the three meals per diem seemed interminable. Neither was there any difficulty with sleep on my part, although I preferred the soft side of a plank on deck, with a coil of rope for a pillow, to the hot, stuffy berth deck to which we were supposed to repair when our four-hour night watches on deck were ended. We stood watch and watch, and besides spent our daylight hours both on and off watch in practical seamanship and drills. Going aloft to furl, loose, or reef sail at sea, and to cross or send down the light yards in port, not to speak of hauling on the hal-

liards, the braces, and the sheets, etc., the hoisting of
boats, and the manning of the capstan bars, the "cat,"
and the "fish," developed us physically to such an extent
that by the end of the plebe practice cruise we were as
hard as nails and had become inured to the rough life
of the sailorman at sea.

Having given a brief outline of some of the hardships
which we experienced on the practice cruise, and their
effects, I should wish to describe some of the impressions
which were made on my mind, by the unaccustomed environment in which we lived.   First of all, there was the
impression of beauty which I felt vividly as I watched
the *Dale* make sail, get under weigh, and move out to sea
under full sail accompanied by the *Constellation*.   A very
fresh breeze was blowing and a choppy sea was running
as we headed out between the Capes.   The sails fairly
glistened in the bright sunshine and the *Dale* appeared a
thing alive and the embodiment of grace.   Thrilled by the
attractive scene, I went aloft to the main top to obtain a
more perfect view of the harbor, the Capes, the shipping,
and the broad expanse of the ocean.   Becoming drowsy
from the motion of the ship, I stretched myself out on
the coils of rope and went to sleep.   My sleep must have
continued for several hours, because when I awoke the
land had disappeared, and for the first time in my life I
visualized the horizon as the circumference of a circle
where the sky and the ocean meet, and was able to comprehend the loneliness of the sea, for within the confines
of that circle no object but the distant *Dale* was visible.
The wind had increased in force and I noticed that a
decided change had taken place in the motion of the ship.
A heavy sea was running and the ship pitched and rolled
in a most fantastic and uncomfortable manner.   I had
queer, sinking feelings, and a headache which made me
realize that seasickness had laid hold of me.   I, at once,
began to lay down from aloft, and squeezed the rigging
during my descent until the tar ran out.   When I reached
the deck, I found that a number of my classmates had

already paid their tribute to Neptune from the lee gangway, and it was not long before I joined them there.

During the night, the wind became a severe gale and by morning nearly all sail had been furled or close reefed. The storm staysail, close reefed foresail, and main topsail were all the sail we carried. The scene was awe-inspiring. Great, mountainous seas, whipped by the gale, came rolling toward us, and often even over us, and it seemed impossible that the ship could live. I saw no symptoms of fear, however, among any of the plebes, but I am of the opinion that it was the drug of nausea rather than any exceptional courage which made us indifferent to our fate. We lay on the deck in a stupor except when a loud call from the inner man drove us hastily to the lee gangway. With the cessation of the storm and the quieting of the sea, we quickly recovered our health and spirits, not to speak of our ravenous appetites, and made up for the meals we had missed.

Throughout the remainder of the twenty-five days in which we cruised before we entered the harbor of Portsmouth, New Hampshire, we enjoyed fine weather and had opportunity, especially in the night watches, to make the acquaintance of some of the "old salts" who constituted the crew. They were to us the most interesting human beings imaginable. They told us many remarkable stories of their adventures in far away parts of the world, and described their voyages on the Seven Seas. They were rough, seafaring men who had come in contact with the waifs and strays of humanity in the seaports of the world, but concealed in their bosoms were the tenderest and most generous of hearts and an innate refinement, or whatever one might call it, which prevented them from telling us anything defiling. In fact, they always respected our youth and inexperience. I especially remember the captain of the forecastle. He was older than most, and a typical seaman of the old days. We often gathered about him in the evening watches to listen to his stories, which were interlarded, not with oaths, as might be supposed, but with sound advice. He described pitfalls that we should avoid and drew on his own experience to warn us against the harpies which were to be found ashore in seaport towns. His earnest face is before me as I write.

When we reached Portsmouth and the ship was made spick and span, the crew were given "liberty," and at its expiration our kind old friend was absent over leave. One evening, five or six days later, we found him on the country road outside of Kittery, stupefied from indulgence in hard liquor, and we carried him aboard ship. After his recovery, and when we had gone to sea on the return voyage, he again occupied his accustomed seat on the forecastle chest, and we gathered around him as was our custom. One of the crowd, more forward than the rest of us, asked him to explain his conduct when ashore. He was most penitent and apologetic, but finally said, "You see, it's this way. When I am sober, I am so and so, Captain of the Forecastle, Sir; but when I have had a few drinks, I am Admiral so and so, of the U. S. Navy, Sir." Perhaps that explains to some extent the weakness of some otherwise splendid men in and out of the service.

On our return to Annapolis, all except the plebes were granted leave during the month of September to go home. We spent that month on the *Santee* hard at work drilling and receiving practical instruction. This monotonous grind, however, was lightened by the pleasing duty of welcoming on board the September plebes, about half of our class of ninety-odd cadets having entered during that month. For the sake of the reputation of the class, the May plebes considered it essential that the September arrivals should be properly broken in and taught to conduct themselves in the most approved plebe manner. We felt proud of our work and quite important until the return of the upper classmen, when we reverted to our former humble status.

The scholastic year began on October first, and we soon found that only by the hardest kind of work could we keep up with the procession. The class was divided into sections of ten, and the instructors gave us undivided attention for an hour in each subject each day. There was no way for one to camouflage his ignorance. Each of us had to know his lessons and satisfactorily pass the monthly and semi-annual examinations, or be "bilged," as it was expressed in the Naval Academy vernacular. The slaughter was great, and only thirty-five out of the original ninety-five members of my class received diplomas at the end of the four years' course. Each year at the Academy closely resembled the others, except that we became more important and assumed added responsibilities as we advanced. Especially was this the case when we ceased to be plebes and became third classmen. Our hearts then rejoiced because the period of servitude, as it were, had ended and we could enter into the exalted estate of upper classmen.

Other unforgettable periods were the home leaves. There is no joy in a boy's life which can equal the joy he feels when he returns home at the end of his third class practice cruise. It is a holy joy, too, because his happiness is shared by the home folks, and above all by his mother and father. All too short was that first leave at home, and poignant was the grief at parting.

On my return to the Academy, I found that Edward L. Beach, of Minneapolis, Minnesota, and I were to be roommates. We roomed together for the remaining three years of our stay at the Academy and never during that time did we have a quarrel or a serious disagreement. Our friendship, which became stronger as each month passed away, has remained unbroken throughout the forty years which have elapsed since graduation day.

That day, of course, was the most momentous of all the days we spent at the Academy. It marked an epoch in the lives of the thirty-five graduates. Our diplomas were presented to us by the Secretary of the Navy, William C. Whitney, who enjoyed an immense popularity among the cadets. As he arose to make the annual address, he was cheered and applauded so vociferously that it seemed impossible to restore sufficient order to enable him to proceed, and when he concluded his address the applause was intensified. It was manifest to all that he was the most popular of all the men who had appeared before us on similar occasions.

Certain officers, too, were especially well beloved. After the graduation exercises were over, the Class of 1888, as was the custom, formed outside the Chapel and gave three cheers for those who were left behind and, in addition, and in accord with the prearranged plan, three cheers were given to two officers of the Academy Staff whom we admired and loved to an unusual degree. They have long since joined the great ship's company on the other shore, so there can be no harm in mentioning their names. They were Lieutenants William P. Potter and Charles E. Colahan, U. S. Navy. No finer men ever wore the uniform of the United States.

Of the thirty-five members of the Class of 1888 who received diplomas, five resigned immediately in order to enter civil life. They were Curtis D. Wilbur, Louis J. Anderson, Stuart W. Cramer, Samuel J. Aiken, and Moses D. Monroe. Wilbur settled in California, studied law, and finally became the Chief Justice of the Supreme Court of that state. He was holding that position when he was appointed Secretary of the Navy by President Coolidge. In the latter capacity he has been able to renew his association with those of his classmates who are still in the service, as well as with many others who were at the Academy during part of our sojourn there. Those of his classmates who are privileged to serve with him at this time (September, 1928) are Charles F. Hughes, formerly Commander-in-Chief of the United States Fleet, and now Chief of Naval Operations; Admiral Henry A. Wiley, Commander-in-Chief of the United States Fleet; Rear Admiral Ashley H. Robertson, formerly Commander of the Scouting Fleet, and now Commandant of the Naval Base, San Diego, California; Rear Admiral Samuel S. Robison, formerly Commander-in-Chief of the United States Fleet, and now Superintendent of the Naval Academy; Major General Eli K.

Cole,* Commanding General of the Marine Corps Department of the Pacific; and Major General John A. Lejeune, Commandant of the U. S. Marine Corps.

In concluding this chapter, I deem it appropriate to summarize briefly my impressions concerning the efficiency of the Academy as a training school for young officers. In the first place, the system of education was thorough and was conducted in a most conscientious and able manner by the instructors. The discipline was severe, but salutary, and I observed little favoritism there, our class standing being determined by the ability and the application displayed by each one of us. My first class practice cruise was an exception to the rule, however, and a number of my classmates felt that they were discriminated against in the marks awarded by some of the officers, and in the recommendations which they made for the appointment of cadet officers. Lieutenant Leutze, the Executive Officer on that cruise, was a notable exception, however. While very exacting and strict, he was altogether just and encouraged all of us by his fair treatment.

A defect in the conduct of the Academy which I observed was the fact that it impressed me as being a great machine. I missed the human appeal. Only once during the four years was my class as a whole addressed by an officer, and that was just before graduation, when Commander Sigsbee gave us a very practical talk containing much good advice concerning our future conduct as officers. I believe that the counsel of officers of experience would have had great weight with us and that we would have responded more readily to the exercise of leadership than to a system based chiefly on compulsion. In spite of these defects, however, it was a fine old school, and those of us who were fortunate enough to go through the mill owe it a great debt of gratitude.

---

* Died July 4, 1929.

Class of 1888, U. S. Naval Academy.
Photograph taken 1886, around **Tecumseh.**

IV

TWO YEARS' CRUISE AS A NAVAL CADET

AT the time of my graduation from the Naval Academy, a post-graduate course was required, consisting of a cruise of approximately two years' duration on board a naval vessel attached to one of the stations to which the U. S. Naval forces were then assigned. Upon completion of this cruise, the members of the class were again assembled at the Naval Academy where they were given an examination, the final class standing being determined not only by the marks received during the Academy course proper, but by the marks received on the final examination and on the two years' cruise as well, the Academy work counting three-fourths and the final examination plus cruise reports counting one-fourth.

Class standing was of vital importance to us at that time, as for several years the number of vacancies in the line of the Navy, the Engineer Corps and the Marine Corps had been sufficient to provide places for only a part of each class, the remainder being honorably discharged at the expiration of the six years' course with one year's pay ($950). This system, however, had the good effect of stimulating our interest in the duties on board ship and of causing us to continue our studies during the cruise.

Stafford, Cole, Wiley and I applied for the *U.S.S. Mohican,* which we learned would arrive at Mare Island for repairs about August first. It must be confessed that the probability of being permitted to remain at home on waiting orders until that date had something to do with our decision, and there was much rejoicing on our part when we were informed that our requests for duty on board the *Mohican* were approved, especially as we received orders to proceed to our homes and there await further instructions.

Graduation day was a happy day.

A glowing sense of freedom filled my heart as I walked out of the main gate, dressed in a new civilian suit, and with my orders and all the money due me in my pocket. I lost but little time leaving Annapolis, going first to Bel Air, Maryland, to pay a brief visit to my Great Uncle Stevenson Archer and his wife, Aunt Blanche. Their home, a beautiful place called Hazel Dell, was located a short distance from Bel Air. During my few days' stay with them I had the opportunity of making the acquaintance of my other kinsfolk in Bel Air and vicinity. Among them were Cousin Steve Williams and his wife, Cousin Allie, Cousin George VanBibber and his wife, Cousin Adele.

My brief visit ended, I took the train for home and there, for the last time, our little family, consisting of father, mother, sister and myself were reunited. Every incident connected with that quiet, uneventful summer constitutes a sacred memory. I never saw my father again, as he departed this life in December, 1899, dying of pneumonia which followed an attack of influenza contracted during the epidemic of that disease which swept over the United States in the autumn and winter of that year. My father and I were inseparable companions, and apart from brief visits to Uncle Stevy Turpin and his family and to some of my friends who lived within reach of a day's drive, I did but little else than spend my time with him and my mother and sister.

Horseback rides and fishing trips were my chief diversions. On one occasion my sister and I attended an all-day political barbecue and listened to two of the ablest speeches I have ever heard. They were delivered by Charles Parlange and Edward D. White in behalf of the candidacy of General Nichols for the governorship. He was the anti-lottery candidate and he and the two speakers were stirring up the people of the state to overthrow the so-called lottery ring and destroy what they termed the unholy alliance between it and the state political machine. History tells us that they were successful in their efforts, and that Mr. White afterwards became a United States Senator from Louisiana and the Chief Justice of the United States Supreme Court.

I talked much to my father about leaving the service and taking up some other occupation or profession. He advised me strongly not to resign at that time, saying that I ought to take advantage of the opportunity to see something of the world, thereby broadening my mind; and that after two years on board ship I would be better able to determine whether or not I desired to make the Navy my life vocation. I agreed that his advice was sound, but decided to save a part of my pay each month, which savings, added to the year's pay I would receive if I elected to leave the service at the end of the six year course, would go far toward enabling me to get a start in civil life.

After being at home about six weeks, I read in the Army and Navy paper to which I subscribed that the *Mohican* had arrived at the Mare Island navy yard for extensive repairs, and each day thereafter I expected my orders to arrive. Over a month elapsed, however, before they came, and it was a sad parting when, before daylight, my father and I left our house on our twenty-five mile drive to Ravenswood Station where I was to board the Texas-Pacific-El Paso train to which the through sleeper for San Francisco was attached. During our drive we discussed many subjects, my father becoming more and more serious as we approached our destination. Finally he said, with deep feeling, "My son, I do not expect to see you again. I have had this thought throughout the months you have been at home and do not seem to be able to throw it off." I endeavored to reassure him, telling him that he was much stronger and more vigorous than most men of his age (68 years), and that I felt sure he had many years of activity and good health still ahead of him. He persisted, however, in the belief that his end was not far distant and said, "I have mentioned this because I want to talk seriously with you before you go out into a strange environment where the restraining influences of the Naval Academy and of your mother and father will be lacking. For many years I had no church affiliations and gave but little thought to religion. During recent years, however, I have been slowly but steadily forced to the conviction that a religion which has produced a woman of such beautiful character as your mother must be a good religion. Now, my son, hold fast to the religion which your mother has taught you, and do not forget her love, her precepts, or her example."

We reached Ravenswood in ample time for the train, and I can see my father's face now and hear his voice, which was broken with emotion, as he said to me just as the train moved out, "Good-bye, my dear son; good-bye."

My mind was filled with serious thoughts for a while, but I was young—just past twenty-one—physically powerful, and constitutionally light-hearted, so it was not surprising that my thoughts in time reverted to eager anticipation of the adventures ahead, or that my responsibilities should sit very lightly on my shoulders. In fact, I was filled with the joy of living. I am glad to say, however, that in a few years I began to realize that there was a serious side to life, that duty should come before pleasure, and that every man owed a debt to corps and country which it was his highest privilege to pay.

The first night on the train, at about midnight, I

awoke suddenly from a sound sleep and saw a man standing by my berth with a bull's-eye lantern in his hand and the light turned on my face. My first thought was that the train was in the hands of bandits, but he explained that he was a Texas quarantine officer and wanted information in regard to my name, residence, the station at which I boarded the train, my destination, etc. I gave him the information he desired and, after showing him my railway ticket in corroboration, he filled out a health certificate which he handed me. I soon learned that it was reported that yellow fever had broken out in New Orleans and that all passengers from that city would be required to be interned in the adjacent quarantine camp. It was an unhappy and tearful group of men, women and children that left the train in the midst of the black darkness of midnight and fearfully entered the camp where they were to be placed in quarantine. It is characteristic of the time that it should have developed in a few days that the report of the yellow fever outbreak was a false alarm, and that the resulting panic and quarantine were, therefore, entirely unnecessary.

Fortunately, such incidents do not now occur, as yellow fever no longer exists in the world. The discovery of its transmission from sick to well by the bite of the stegomyia mosquito made it possible for a world-wide sanitary campaign to stamp out the disease which had been one of the most terrible scourges which ever afflicted mankind.

After leaving the fertile fields of Texas, days were spent in crossing the arid desert country which then extended from southwestern Texas to southern California. Suddenly, one evening just before sunset, we burst into a beautiful irrigated valley and were enraptured by the sight of apparently unending orchards, vineyards and gardens. Verily, water is man's greatest blessing, and brings more joy into his heart than all the wines whose praises have been sung in prose and poem from time immemorial.

I lingered but a few hours in San Francisco before proceeding to Mare Island, where I reported for duty on board the *Mohican* which was lying along side the dock, undergoing extensive repairs. In fact, the ship was so torn to pieces that the crew was unable to live on board but was quartered on the old Receiving Ship *Independence,* a relic of the days when the sea power of the nations of the world was upheld by frigates and line-of-battle ships built of wood and propelled by sail. However, as late as 1888 America still maintained a fleet of wooden steamers with auxiliary sail power; or perhaps it would be nearly as correct to describe the fleet as consisting of wooden sailing vessels with auxiliary steam power and carrying useless iron smooth-bore guns.

In the years following the Civil War our country had fallen from its proud position of being the greatest sea power on the planet to that of being one of the least powerful, for while our fleet deteriorated the nations of Europe had substituted steel ships for wooden ones, and their flags were then proudly floating from the mastheads of great battleships, powerful cruisers and speedy torpedo boats. To such a state of decay had indifference to national defense and an unwise policy of false economy on the part of our political leaders brought the American Navy, which moreover had been first in the world, but a few years before, to create, build and employ in battle the ironclad or all-metal ship which spelled the doom of the wooden men-of-war. America had profited little by her then inventiveness. During the same period, the American merchant marine had nearly vanished from the seas, and the American flag was but seldom seen in the harbors of the world. It was a humiliating era in America's history for those Americans who went down to the

sea in ships, and who came into contact with the
armadas and the argosies of the nations of the Old
World.

Fortunately, during the decade of the 'eighties the
defenseless condition of our coasts and the pitiful
state of inferiority of our fleet aroused a strong
public opinion which made its influence felt on our
government, with the result that a beginning was
made on a program involving the construction of
a modern fleet. First, gunboats and light cruisers
were built, then armored cruisers, battleships and
destroyers. Such progress in the development of
our sea power took place that by the outbreak of
the Spanish-American War, our combat fleet consisted of two armored cruisers, five battleships, and
a considerable number of light cruisers, gunboats
and destroyers.

The record made by the Navy in that brief struggle was so brilliant, and the vast effect of sea power
was so manifest that the steady expansion of the
Navy, both in ships and personnel, became a popular national policy, with the result that by the close
of the World War our country once again occupied
the proud position of naval superiority, its fleet
surpassing in strength even that of Great Britain,
erstwhile "Mistress of the Seas."

In 1921, at the Washington Limitation of Naval
Armaments Conference, our government voluntarily
surrendered its naval supremacy, and in lieu thereof
assumed the obligation of maintaining a fleet equal
in strength to that of Great Britain, but superior
to that of all the other great world powers except
Russia and Germany, which did not participate in
the Conference. The agreement reached in the Conference, and the obligation growing out of that
agreement, involve a sacred responsibility not only
to our own people but to the people of the weaker
nations of North and South America as well, as our
government is charged, not alone with the duty of

providing for the security of its own citizens at home, abroad, or on the seven seas, but, under the terms of the Monroe Doctrine, it must needs protect the people of the republics to the south of us from invasion and from the annexation or occupation of all or any part of their territory by any power located beyond the seas.

With reference to national security, it is a far cry from the bright days of 1928 to the dark and gloomy days of 1888. Then not only was our country without any fighting ships worthy of the name, but the strength of its naval personnel was pitifully weak. The total naval enlisted force consisted of 7,500 seamen and apprentices, and 2,000 marines! The number of officers was correspondingly small and their situation was a sad one. Men grew old in the lower grades and there seemed to be no prospect of advancement. For instance, in the Marine Corps, all the field officers and a large proportion of the captains were over fifty years of age, and a similar condition existed in the line and in the staff corps of the Navy. It is not necessary to elaborate on the results which such a system produced.

Trips to San Francisco, with social activities at the navy yard and in Vallejo, constituted our occupation when off duty. I made a determined effort to overcome my diffidence, with fairly good success, and greatly enjoyed the friendly association with the families of officers and other friends and soon decided that Navy life was much more enjoyable than I had anticipated it would be during my four long years at the Naval Academy.

On January 14, 1889, a bomb exploded in the form of telegraphic orders for a number of the officers of the *Mohican,* including Naval Cadets Stafford, Wiley and myself. These orders involved our transfer to the *Vandalia,* which was fitting out at Mare Island and was nearly ready for sea. We exchanged duty with corresponding officers of the *Vandalia* whose tours of sea duty had nearly expired. At the same time instructions were received for the *Vandalia* to sail at the earliest practicable date for Apia, Samoan Islands. The cause of these orders was described at length and very conspicuously in the daily newspapers, which also stated that the Flagship *Trenton*, with Rear Admiral Kimberly on board, would proceed from Panama to the same destination for the purpose of affording protection to American interests which appeared to be jeopardized in that part of the world by the activities of the German squadron and the German diplomatic representative in connection with the government of the Samoan Islands.

That group of islands and the Hawaiian Islands were the only inhabited islands of any importance in the Pacific Ocean which had not already passed under the control of one of the great European or Asiatic powers. Germany appeared to be endeavoring to gain control of the Samoan group. A few officials of the State and Navy Departments and officers of the Navy who had cruised in the South Pacific were aware that trouble had been brewing for some years in that far away group. The name meant little, however, to the average person, and popular interest in the diplomatic game being played there in which unknown South Sea Islanders were the pawns, had not hitherto been awakened.

Briefly, that game appeared to involve a dispute between rival claimants for the kingship of the islands. In reality it involved the success or failure of the German effort to obtain commercial and political control of one of the two little Polynesian kingdoms which still retained their independence.

A tense situation continued until December, 1888, when the climax came. The forces of Mataafa, several thousand strong, surrounded Apia and the adjacent German plantations. It was charged that his men trespassed on German holdings and carried away fruit, cocoanuts, etc., to add to their scanty commissary supplies. Probably this accusation was correct. At any rate, it was decided to take punitive measures, and before daylight a landing force from the cruisers proceeded in boats via the small channel inside the reefs and landed at the nearest point to the German plantation houses, which were a mile or two in the interior. Under cover of darkness, the landing force occupied the plantation houses and patrols were sent out. The patrols came into contact with Mataafa's forces, firing was begun, and for the first time in the history of the Samoans a battle ensued between their warriors and an armed force of white men. After several hours desultory firing, the Germans retired to the beach and returned to their ships. They suffered heavily, their casualties being about forty-five per cent of their total force of one hundred and sixty men. In the excitement that ensued, it was claimed that one of the many American flags that flew on buildings ashore was desecrated by the Germans. A correspondent of the New York *World* was in Samoa at the time and sent a sensational account of the tragedy, in which the flag incident was stressed. The *World* published the despatch in full, as did all the other daily newspapers. Great excitement prevailed and our proud, sympathetic and sensitive people demanded that prompt and decisive action be taken.

Thus it came about that the *Vandalia* hurriedly sailed from Mare Island and the *Trenton* from Panama, for the purpose of protecting American interests in far-off Samoa, and I had my first experience of the most fascinating side of Navy life—the unexpected orders, the excitement, the hustling, bustling hurly-burly, the farewells to friends, the sudden departure —often for an unknown destination, and the speculation as to what it was all about and as to what was going to happen. It is events such as these which add the bright colors to pictures of life in the Navy and Marine Corps.

Two days after the orders arrived the *Vandalia,* with a new crew, with her bunkers filled with coal, and with all necessary stores on board, cast off the lines which secured her to the navy yard dock and steamed slowly down the channel towards the Golden Gate.

Cheers resounded from everywhere. A great crowd on the dock, the crews of the other ships, and a large gathering on the waterfront of Vallejo waved and cheered again and again. All the way down the bay from passing steamers the demonstration continued. The newspapers devoted columns of space to the sailing of the *Vandalia* and its connection with the international controversy in faraway Samoa, and the youngsters on board felt they were like Crusaders of the olden time, and that on their shoulders rested the proud duty of protecting the interests of their country and of defending the lives and the liberty of the Samoans.

Our voyage to Honolulu was uneventful and the days were spent in stationing and training the crew. It fell to my lot to command the 6-inch pivot gun which was mounted on the forecastle. It was manned by Marines, and for the first time in my career I came into close relationship with the enlisted men of that branch of the service. The Marine detachment was divided, the major part being detailed as sharpshooters and the remainder as the gun crew. The Marine officer, First Lieutenant F. E. Sutton, preferred to command the sharpshooter group.

He gave me sound advice on how to handle Marines and emphasized the importance of giving my orders to the Sergeant who acted as gun captain, rather than to the individual men, and then to hold him responsible for the execution of the orders. I found that this sound military system worked most satisfactorily and that the gun's crew soon functioned like clockwork. This system, I learned in after years, was the foundation on which the efficiency of the Marine Corps was built, and its result was the development of a reliable, trustworthy and faithful corps of noncommissioned officers. No doubt my experiences with the Marines on the *Vandalia* had something to do with the decision which I ultimately made to apply for a commission in the Marine Corps at the end of my six years' course as a Naval Cadet.

Our first port of call was Honolulu, the pearl in the "Paradise of the Pacific" as the Hawaiian Islands were then and still are called. We sailed under a cloudless sky the day of our arrival in the archipelago and at dawn we sighted Mauna Loa on the Island of Hawaii at a distance of one hundred miles and, later on, the great mountain mass of Oahu came into view. As we neared the southern coast of the island, we sighted Diamond Head, the beautiful, extinct volcano which appears to stand watchful guard over the approach to Honolulu from the east. It seems, somehow, to have almost a sacred significance to Hawaiians, who greet its appearance with shouts of joy in somewhat the same way as do Japanese travelers when Fujiyama becomes visible to their straining eyes.

As we rounded Diamond Head and approached the harbor entrance, an entrancing scene was spread out before our eyes. Lying at the foot of the great mountain bulwark was a lovely plain, dotted with houses all nestling in the midst of tropical foliage. It was our first glimpse of a foreign land and our first visit to the tropics, and we experienced a never to be forgotten thrill. I should have said a series of thrills, because, as the vista unfolded, the thrill was repeated over and over again, as indeed it was when we went ashore and saw close-up the unaccustomed scenes and heard the not to be understood chatter of the cosmopolitan population.

The glamour of romance hung about these islands,

too, as the traditions of the native people and their historical record were all blended into a fascinating story; and besides, the island group constituted a kingdom of which Kalakaua was the King, and we looked forward with eager expectation to seeing a real, live King. Our wish was granted sooner than we anticipated. A short while after the ship was moored, two or three of us went ashore and found our way to the Royal Hawaiian Hotel. We walked into the large billiard hall, at one end of which was an American bar. Leaning against the bar were several white men and a tall, fine-looking man of swarthy or brown complexion, immaculately dressed in a white flannel suit. We had no idea who he was and were slightly curious, as he was a striking looking man. Presently our curiosity was relieved. The busy bartender had completed his task and as he placed the finished product on the bar the host of the occasion handed a glass to the man to whom I have just referred, bowing courteously and saying, "This is your Majesty's." And so we caught our first glimpse of royalty.

The next day the Captain and officers were presented officially to the King by the American Minister. The King received us in the throne-room and conducted himself with much dignity during the ceremony. He relaxed somewhat, however, as we joined him in drinking to the health of the President and as we drank the return toast to "His Majesty, the King of Hawaii."

Our stay in Honolulu was brief and in a day or two we began the last voyage of the good ship *Vandalia*. We sailed in a smooth sea and nothing occurred to cause any forebodings except the solitary incident of the ship's black cat which, becoming venturesome, fell overboard and was drowned. There was much grief among the crew and some superstitious fears were aroused as to the safety of the ship, but the incident was soon forgotten in the excitement caused by the preparations being made for the expected visit of King Neptune and his court on the day the equator was to be crossed. This is a time-honored ceremony in the Navy, having been handed down from the British Navy, and tracing its origin to remote antiquity.

At dusk, the evening before the great event, a powerful voice from over the side was heard, hailing the ship. It shouted, "Ship ahoy! What ship is that which dares to encroach on the domain of His Majesty, King Neptune, the ruler of the seas?" The officer of the deck answered, "The United States Ship *Vandalia,* Captain Schoonmaker, commanding, bound from Honolulu to Apia." The voice replied, "Inform Captain Schoonmaker that His Majesty, accompanied by his retinue, will board the ship tomorrow morning and make inquiry as to the members of the crew who have never received his royal authority to cruise in his dominions." The three Naval Cadets, many of the Marines, the apprentices, the landsmen, and all the others who had never crossed the line before were much disturbed over the prespect of the visit and their ears were filled with lurid descriptions of the punishment that was to be meted out to them.

The next morning, shortly after eight o'clock, the ship was again hailed, and upon the invitation of the Captain, King Neptune and his retinue appeared on board, proceeded to the mainmast and there were received by Captain Schoonmaker and Lieutenant J. W. Carlin, the Executive Officer. The King and his party were clothed in costumes that were original to say the least. The King wore a royal robe, was adorned with a heavy hempen beard, carried a trident, and wore a crown. The Queen—a tall, slender sailor—was arrayed in what was deemed the most appropriate fashion, wore long, golden curls, and had her cheeks brilliantly rouged. The retinue was clad in the most bizarre manner that their ingenuity could devise.

The King outlined his plans briefly to the Captain, and then we heard him say in a deep, sepulchral voice, "I am informed that there are three young officers on board who have never been initiated into the mysteries of the sea." The Captain admitted the correctness of his information and called us to the mast to make our peace as best we could. The King, in a ferocious manner, said to us, "How dare you encroach on our domains without authority?" We apologized humbly for our heinous offense and asked meekly if a gift of two dozen bottles of good American beer from each of us would appease his wrath. The King consulted the Queen and then announced more peaceably that it would; and so it came about that we were exempted from having to submit to the far from pleasant initiation ceremonies.

These were promptly begun. The tank, consisting of a large tarpaulin secured between the break of the forecastle and the bridge, had been rigged and pumped full of salt water during the morning watch, and the other necessary paraphernalia appeared as if by magic. The barber's chair, the huge wooden razor, and the bucket of slush were in readiness; the dolphins, sea urchins and polliwogs took their places in the tank; the barber stood in readiness and his assistants stood by; and the King, the Queen and their aides occupied positions whence they could view the proceedings clearly. The first victim was forcibly produced, his face, mouth and eyes were properly lathered with the slush, he was shaved with one stroke by the barber, and was then shoved head over heels into the tank where he was none too gently handled and repeatedly ducked. Victim after victim followed in rapid succession and the initiation exercises proceeded amid shouts of laughter and shrieks of merriment from the old salts who had qualified on previous voyages and were now enjoying the discomfiture of their less fortunate shipmates. The Naval Cadets congratulated themselves on their escape and voted unanimously to make their tribute three dozen bottles of Milwaukee's best instead of two dozen each in accordance with their original offer. This voluntary action of ours was discreetly conveyed to the King and served to clinch the exemption which we were fearful might be withdrawn.

At last the ceremony was ended. Neptune and his motley crew disappeared and then as if by magic reappeared in the steerage clothed in normal garb, to receive our tribute. They had certainly earned it, and doubtless they enjoyed it.

We arrived off the harbor of Apia the forenoon of February 22nd, and at noon fired the national salute of twenty-one guns in honor of the birthday of George Washington. We then headed for the entrance to the harbor. It was a typical day for that latitude in that season of the year—heavy rain, followed by the intense heat of the blazing sun and great humidity, and that followed in turn by another downpour. We found the harbor to be of the prevailing tropical island type, a wide-neck bottle in shape, and bounded on all sides except at the neck by jagged coral reefs. There was a boat channel along the shore inside the reef, an opening in the reef to the landing place, and a narrow stretch of sand beach at the mouth of the Vasigano River where the fresh water interfered with the coral formation.

We entered the harbor from the northward, the opening in the reef being in the direction of the northeast-northwest quadrant. In the harbor there lay at anchor the antiquated U.S.S. *Nipsic,* the modern British cruiser *Calliope,* the German squadron consisting of the cruiser *Olga* and the gunboats *Adler* and *Eber,* and a number of sailing trading craft. In addition, the harbor was thickly dotted with native canoes, each equipped with an outrigger, and oc-

U. S. S. **Constellation.**

U. S. S. **Cincinnati.**

cupied by two or three Samoans dressed or undressed, depending on the viewpoint of the spectator, in their seagoing costumes, paddling out to meet the ship and singing a strangely familiar air which turned out to be "Upi de i da," a very old popular song which, we were told, they had learned from American sailors. It was a picturesque scene which greeted our eyes—the mountains, covered with a dense tropical forest, the sprawling town of low-pitched frame houses lying along the shore, the native thatched shacks in the background, the ships at anchor, the jagged, cruel looking reefs, and a hundred or more native canoes. Slowly and more slowly the good ship steamed, and when the selected place was reached the engine was stopped, then reversed, and in obedience to the shouted order of the Executive Officer, the starboard anchor was let go, the chain was paid out and secured, and the *Vandalia* lay quietly at anchor in the haven which she would never leave.

Several of us went ashore in the evening after dinner and met at the boat-landing some of the officers of the U.S.S. *Nipsic,* among them being Ensign Hilary P. Jones. I mention this fact because during that evening was begun the friendship between Jones and myself which has continued unbroken until today. In fact, my admiration and affection for him have increased as each year has passed by, and I know of no finer character or more gallant gentleman than Rear Admiral Jones. His distinguished services to the Navy and to our country are a matter of public knowledge and, therefore, need not be recounted here.

The officers of the *Nipsic* acted as our hosts and took us in charge for the evening, taking us to call, among others, on Seuamanu Tafa, the chief of the Samoan clan of Apia and vicinity. He was a splendid physical specimen and his countenance bore evidence of his possession of the noble qualities which characterized many of the chiefs of the Samoans.

As a special mark of good will, a Kava party was arranged for our entertainment. It was held in a large native shack of which the gravel or pebble floor was covered with finely woven mats. In the center was a large hardwood bowl, brilliantly polished and the interior delicately stained by its frequent use on similar occasions. Around the bowl were seated on the mats a bevy of Samoan maidens, appropriately costumed in native dress. First, with great ceremony, the proper measure of water was poured in the bowl, and then each maiden began preparing the national drink by chewing a fragment of the root of the Kava plant which, when thoroughly masticated, was deposited in the bowl. Additional fragments underwent the same process while the maidens deftly strained the solid particles from the bowl by means of long wisps of cocoanut fiber which they gracefully dipped into the liquid in the bowl and, after withdrawing them, washed and squeezed them dry. This process was continually repeated. While the ceremony was in progress, our *Nipsic* friends told us that should we refuse the drink our Samoan hosts would be mortally offended and their feelings hurt. I was trying hard to screw up my courage to the sticking point in the interest of international good will when my mind was relieved by seeing another bowl of Kava in preparation in the foreign way. There was no ceremony connected with its concoction, large cocoanut graters being used in lieu of the pearly teeth of the maidens, and after being properly stirred it was poured through a strainer into beautifully polished cocoanut shells which were the national drinking cups. The maidens then ceremoniously served us with the foreign variety and our Samoan hosts with the real article and we quaffed the drink as a pledge of friendship and good will.

A most attractive, light-hearted, hospitable people they were. They showed every evidence of good will towards us and in the few words of English that they had learned they expressed undying gratitude to Americans generally, and with childlike trustfulness showed perfect confidence in the ability of the American Admiral who was soon to arrive to settle all their difficulties and to relieve them of German interference in their affairs.

We learned from the *Nipsic* officers that while the situation ashore was very strained, there had been no active hostilities since the tragic events of December, which I have already briefly narrated. Tamasesi, the German puppet king, with a small force, was still holding his stronghold; German sailors were garrisoning their section of the town; American Marines from the *Nipsic* were guarding the United States Consulate; and Mataafa and his armed force surrounded Apia and were in occupation of the remainder of the Island.

In a few days the U.S.S. *Trenton,* flying the flag of Rear Admiral Lewis A. Kimberly, arrived and anchored in the outer harbor near its entrance. Salutes were fired and the customary formal visits were exchanged. While the relations between the American and British officers were very cordial and friendly, as indeed they have always been during my years of service afloat and ashore, we had had no contacts with the German officers except those of an official nature since our arrival at Apia, and the same conditions continued after the *Trenton's* arrival.

The term "watchful waiting" seems best to describe the situation, which continued to be very tense, but without apparent change until the greatest of all powers intervened and with one wave of His puissant hand banished ill will, hatred and malice from the hearts of all the peoples concerned, and substituted for them grief, sympathy and brotherly love.

I refer to the manifestation of omnipotence in the form of the hurricane which brought disaster to the ships at anchor in the harbor of Apia, and to its effect on the minds and hearts of the people of the Samoan Islands, Germany, and the United States.

Ample warning was given of the approach of a severe storm. On March 14th the barometer fell steadily and it was the common opinion that we were in for a serious tropical disturbance. During the night fires were started under all boilers, and the next morning, March 15th, preparations were made to ride out the approaching gale. Topgallant masts were sent down and secured on deck, lower yards were sent down and lashed, topmasts were housed, boats secured for sea, and all sail except fore and aft sail was unbent.

During the day the barometer continued to fall and the clouds were dark and lowering. Heavy rains, interspersed with frequent variable wind squalls followed by periods of dead calm, also indicated that nature was preparing itself for a formidable destructive effort.

At about 4 P. M. the storm burst, with the wind blowing a gale from the northward. As the hours passed, the wind gradually increased in violence until it attained the force of a hurricane and shifted its direction towards the northeast. Very soon great ocean waves came rolling into the harbor and over the reefs, causing currents of such strength as to make it impossible to hold the ship's head to wind and sea.

That evening the officers and men had their last meal on board the *Vandalia;* at dinner everyone was in his accustomed good spirits. Storms are part of the everyday life of the sailor and stimulate rather than depress his mental activity. Frequent struggles with the titanic forces of nature and with the hazards and perils of the sea make the sailor bold, dauntless and resourceful; so that it is not surprising to find that the pages of history are filled with the daring deeds and the heroic exploits of the men who have sailed the Seven Seas in the prosecution of the pursuits of peace or of the enterprises of war. After dinner and the customary evening conversation, those of us who were not on duty turned in, but not to sleep, as the sound of the gale, the violent pitching and rolling of the ship, and the creaking and groaning of its timbers served to banish slumber.

At midnight I took the four-hour watch on the forecastle, relieving Naval Cadet Wiley. He turned over his orders to me briefly, the tenor of which was for me to keep a sharp lookout ahead and on each bow, and to lower a canvas covered lantern over the bow every ten or fifteen minutes so as to take a look at the anchor chains and report by messenger to the Officer of the Deck, Ensign John H. Gibbons, the direction they were tending. Both bower anchors were down with about forty-five fathoms on each chain, but there was an elbow in the hawse caused by the shifts of wind before the final blow began.

It was the darkest night I ever experienced. Literally, it was impossible to see one's hand before one's face. The wind was blowing with terrific force, the rain was falling in blinding sheets, and a very heavy sea was running. A short while after I went on watch, the ship began to drag and we commenced to steam up to our anchors. We had but one sheet anchor, and its stock had been broken in a hard blow which had occurred about a week or ten days before. This anchor was held in reserve as long as possible, in expectation of the wind coming out from west of north, but was finally let go under the personal direction of Lieutenant Carlin about 2 A. M., as near the weather reef as possible.

It was the longest four hours I ever spent. I stood in the eyes of the ship, straining my eyes in the endeavor to penetrate the darkness, and periodically lowering the lantern over the bow and sending my report to Gibbons. At about 3.30 A. M., just after I had sent the messenger on his usual errand, a tremendous sea came over the bow and hurled me across the deck. I thought at first that I was overboard, as my hands could find nothing to grasp, and the sea which had come on board was so deep that I could not reach the deck with my feet. In a few moments, however, I came up against the starboard fore rigging, struggled to my feet, and made the best of my way back in the darkness to my post of duty. During the remainder of the watch several waves washed over me, but I was prepared for them as I made a line fast around my waist and, in addition, kept a firm grasp on the pin rail.

Promptly at 4 A. M. I was relieved by Stafford, and went below, undressed, and to bed. I greatly enjoyed the comfortable warmth of the dry blankets for a half hour or so, when "All hands" were called and I hurriedly slipped on my blue uniform coat and trousers and went on deck. There I found that owing to the constant shipping of heavy seas it had been decided to batten down the hatches to keep the water from going down below and putting out the fires. With considerable difficulty we got the hatch gratings in place, covered them over with the tarpaulins, and carefully secured them. I then went up on the forecastle to see how Stafford was getting along.

Dawn had come, and I found him crouched down behind the rail, as sea after sea in rapid succession was coming on board. In between the seas we looked about the harbor as best we could. Huge waves, whipped about by the blinding force of the wind, and running irregularly owing to the effect of the swiftness of the opposing currents and the smashing action of the reefs, made the harbor a veritable cauldron. The ships had dragged their anchors during the night and all had changed their positions. We were directly in the hawse of the *Calliope;* the *Trenton* was holding her own right manfully near the entrance to the harbor; the *Nipsic* and *Olga* were closer to the beach and nearer to each other; the *Adler* was periously near the lee reef; the *Eber* was nowhere to be seen; and some of the sailing craft had gone on the reefs. We guessed the fate of the *Eber* and learned afterwards that at early dawn she had been broken to pieces on the reef and all of her six officers and sixty-six men had been lost except Lieutenant Gaedeke and four sailors who were rescued by the Samoans with whom they had lately been at war. These heroic Samoans had forgotten the oppression to which they had been subjected and had risked their own lives to save the lives of their former enemies.

In a short while the Officer of the Deck notified Stafford that he was relieved from standing watch, as daylight made it unnecessary, and then, too, there was the constant danger from the heavy seas that were coming over the bow. We started aft together and stopped at the break of the forecastle to look about the harbor, and there witnessed a most remarkable and awe-inspiring sight. The *Adler* had dragged her anchors until she was very near the reef on the western side of the harbor. She was lying broadside to the reef, when suddenly she was picked up by a huge wave, carried bodily on top of the reef and, as the wave receded, she slowly heeled over and lay on her side some thirty or forty feet from the edge of the reef, with her keel towards the sea. The waves broke angrily but harmlessly against the hull, and the crew, except twenty men who were drowned when she capsized, remained safely on board until the storm was over.

We soon sensed the fact that our engines had slowed down and that the *Vandalia* was dragging her anchors, and went aft to find out what was wrong. As we climbed the ladder to the poop deck we saw the great ram bow of the *Calliope* rising and falling with the waves, so close aboard on the starboard side that it seemed to be inevitable that the *Vandalia* would be cut in two. We had unavoidably drifted down on the *Calliope,* and her Captain, magnificent seaman and brave man that he was, made the decision to put to sea. He slipped his moorings and so maneuvered that both ships were saved from immediate destruction. It was a touch and go affair, however. First, her jibboom struck our forecastle deck a severe blow and was broken off; then, as she dropped aft, our starboard boats were torn from their davits; and finally her bow rammed and smashed our starboard quarter gallery. We were in extreme jeopardy, and the few minutes that elapsed until we were assured that the *Calliope* had cleared us and was heading for the open sea seemed interminable. Our hearts were filled with gratitude because of our escape, and then again stood still as we watched the fight for life that the *Calliope* was making. In clearing us she had been compelled to approach to a dangerous proximity to the lee reef, and in steaming out of the harbor it was necessary to hug the reef closely in order to avoid a collision with the *Trenton,* while breasting the terrific sea and steaming into the teeth of the hurricane. Her progress was agonizingly slow, and destruction confronted her as she barely avoided collision with the *Trenton* which lay near-by, helpless by reason of flooded fire rooms and broken rudder, but as we gazed, she gained headway, she cleared the *Trenton's* stern, she avoided the reefs, she made the open sea, she won the fight.

The *Trenton's* crew gave her three hearty cheers as she went clear and moved slowly but surely out of the harbor. Those cheers, I am sure, will resound down the ages, and the memory of them will always bring the warmth of brotherly affection to the hearts of all British and American seamen.

Our eyes did not linger long on the *Calliope* and the *Trenton,* however, as the *Vandalia* continued to drag her anchors and soon her stern was close to the reefs. It seemed that the crisis had come. We drifted astern until not more than twenty feet separated us from the jagged wall of coral rock which was exposed to view as each wave receded. We were in the outer harbor, and to strike the reef there meant not only the destruction of the ship, but probably the loss of every life on board. Fortunately, the trouble in the fireroom had been overcome by the skillful hands of courageous men, the steam pressure in the boilers had begun to rise, the revolutions of the propellers to increase in velocity, and the ship moved slowly away from the reef. Feeling, however, that the danger of going on the outer reef was still imminent, it was decided to make every effort to get the ship into the inner harbor. In doing so, we passed between the *Olga* and the lee reef, with but a few feet to spare on either hand. To avoid fouling the *Olga's* ground tackle, we slipped the sheet chain and, in order to clear the ship herself, we veered chain on both bower anchors. After going clear of the *Olga,* strenuous exertions were made to bring the ship head to wind, but without avail, and the stern took the inner point of the reef at 10.45 A. M.

The engines were kept going until it was evident that we were hard and fast aground. They were then stopped, safety valves opened, and the engine and fire-room force called on deck. The ship's head swung slowly to starboard, she began to fill and settle, and the rail was soon awash, the seas sweeping over her at a height of fifteen feet or more above the rail. We were within two hundred yards of the shore and near the *Nipsic* which had been beached near the mouth of the Vasigano River some time before, after a collision with the *Olga* in which the *Nipsic's* smokestack was struck by the *Olga's* head-booms and had fallen to the deck. The officers and crew of the *Nipsic,* with the exception of seven men who were drowned, had reached the shore in safety by means of a hawser which had been got ashore with the aid of the Samoans, whose nautical skill, physical endurance and high courage stood out pre-eminently in the saving of human lives.

It seemed at first that we had reached a place of safety, as, owing to our proximity to the beach and to the lee made by the ship, we thought it would not be difficult to reach the shore by swimming. In fact, a number of the officers and men made preparations to swim ashore. Gibbons said to me that he and Wiley had talked the matter over and had concluded that the ship would probably either go to pieces, or else we would soon have to take to the rigging, and that it was the part of wisdom to attempt the swim now before becoming exhausted in the struggle with the waves. As he spoke, I saw Wiley, stripped of all his clothes, going out on the starboard main yardarm, the yard having been rested on the hammock nettings and there secured in place. I got ready to follow him, removing my coat and trousers, which I afterwards greatly regretted doing. In a moment he was overboard and swimming strongly towards the shore. The current, however, was running swiftly seaward and carried Wiley under the port quarter of the *Nipsic,* where he grasped the boatfall and attempted to climb on board. A huge wave swept him from our sight, and we feared he was lost. We afterwards learned that he had been rescued by Seumanu Tafa and his gallant men who, seeing him at the mercy of the current, had formed a chain of men, the outer one of whom had barely been able to grasp him as he floated by, and had brought him ashore. He was unconscious and nearly drowned but, after much hard work, was resuscitated. While swimming a piece of wreckage had struck him a severe blow on the head which had rendered him unconscious.

About this time E. M. Hammar, seaman, and one of the most powerful swimmers on the ship, volunteered to carry a line ashore, but was swept back against the ship and killed. A powerful fireman, of Greek extraction, however, swam to the *Nipsic* and succeeded in climbing on board. With his assistance a line was got on board her, but more were drowned than saved in the effort to reach the *Nipsic*. Other men attempted to swim ashore, but so many were swept out to sea by the current that the remainder, including Gibbons and myself, decided to stay by the ship.

In a short while the ship was being boarded every few seconds by huge waves that swept over the poop deck with great violence. A number of officers and men who had gathered on the poop tried to find some slight shelter behind the weather rail, grasping whatever was available; others stood to leeward of the mizzen mast holding on to the running gear that was belayed to the belaying pins around the mast. I was with the last-named group, close by Paymaster Arms and Pay Clerk Roche. Each sea that came over us was deeper and more powerful than its predecessor, and swept us from our feet and across the deck, the lines slipping through our hands. The first of this group to go overboard and to death was Paymaster Arms. He was an elderly man and of not very vigorous physique. As we struggled to our feet, I missed him and asked Pay Clerk Roche about him. He said, simply, "He is gone; he was too weak to hold on longer." I replied, "I am going to take to the rigging. Why don't you do so also?" I leaped for the starboard rigging and was barely clear of the deck when a great roller came on board and crushed me painfully against the iron ratlines. I looked to leeward and there I saw Roche struggling in the water. He was a very large man and was fully dressed. He was carried under the stern of the *Nipsic,* and there made a feeble effort to take hold of the Jacob's-ladder which was hanging over the stern, but having failed to reach it, he turned face upwards and sank beneath the waves.

I observed that Captain Schoonmaker, Lieutenant Carlin, First Lieutenant Sutton of the Marines, and a number of sailors were still lying behind the port rail on the poop deck. Captain Schoonmaker was not very strong and had been hurt by a fall the night before. Carlin stayed close beside him with one arm around him. After an unusually heavy sea had washed over them, Carlin evidently decided to try and get the Captain up in the rigging. He left his side and, standing in the rigging, reached out his hand for him. The Captain made an effort to join him, and although he was assisted by a sailor, he was too weak to do so. He was carried overboard by the next wave and was not seen again. Carlin leaped to his rescue, but the same wave carried him partly down the opening in the deck where the cabin skylight had been. He made a desperate struggle to extricate himself and finally was successful owing to his powerful physique and great strength. I can see him now in my mind's eye as distinctly as I did then. He was without a stitch of clothing and his body was torn and gashed as he slowly but surely climbed back on deck in spite of the onrush of the waves, and made his way safely to the port rigging.

Lieutenant Sutton, I could plainly see, was fast weakening. He too was unable to take to the rigging, as he was suffering from a neuritis of the right shoulder which almost paralyzed his arm. A sailor lay beside him and held him tightly, but a huge green sea carried Sutton across the deck and partly over the side. For a moment he was seen struggling to climb back on board, when the following wave tore loose his hold and swept him into the maelstrom. I saw him as he sank, lying face upwards, with his eyes turned towards the sky, and a look of peaceful resignation on his face.

The faces of many of our men as they drowned are vividly borne in my memory and are as distinct today as they were the day they died. None had the look of agony, but all seemed to be at peace. Perhaps it is true that "there is an angel up aloft who takes care of poor Jack."

Everyone remaining on board finally took refuge in the tops and in the rigging. The larger portion of the crew was forward, some eight or ten were in the main top, and the remainder on the mizzen top grating and in the mizzen rigging. For us it had become a question of physical endurance, provided the masts continued to stand. The planking of the poop deck was soon ripped from its fastenings by the upward pressure of the seas which were forced into the cabin, and the mast worked ominously each time it was struck by the wall of water which charged resistlessly over the ship again and again. I stayed in the rigging for hours, with my legs thrust between the shrouds and resting on the ratlines, and holding on with both arms around the shrouds. My bare legs were lacerated and bleeding, as were my arms and breast as each pounding wave tightened the rigging to the uttermost and, as the wave passed on, the rigging sprang back to its normal tension. They were hours of physical torture, with every lacerated spot burning like fire from the effects of the salt water, and my mouth and throat parched and raw from the same cause. Utter weariness, too, overtook me, and I felt very strongly the urge to let go and take the slight chance of swimming ashore. The thought, however, of the grief of the loved ones at home buoyed me up and strengthened my resolution to fight it out to the end. Finally I decided to try the Jacob's-ladder which hung up and down the mizzen mast. I climbed inside the rigging and swung over to the ladder, being helped in doing so by Glynn, a coal passer, who occupied the part of the ladder just below the top grating. As it was necessary to stand on a round of the ladder, I was relieved of the acute pain caused by the constant tearing of the flesh by the ratlines, but this produced another danger. I was overcome with drowsiness. In spite of the howling of the gale, the roar of the sea, and the thrashing back and forth of the Jacob's-ladder, I could not throw off the lassitude and the weariness. I went to sleep standing and was in the act of falling when Glynn caught hold of me and shook me violently until I awoke. He then lashed me to the Jacob's-ladder in the manner in which he had already lashed himself, and stood careful guard over me. Night, however, was beginning to drop her pall of darkness upon us. The force of the wind and the power of the sea were increasing, the mast worked more and more, and it seemed impossible that we could survive. My prayer for mother, father and sister rose upward to the Mercy Seat. Grim death stood close by and gazed searchingly into my eyes. Suddenly there was a cry from many throats, "The *Trenton!* The *Trenton!*" That stout ship, which had drifted nearer during the afternoon, suddenly bore down upon us and it appeared that our destruction was inevitable; that the port side would be crushed and the masts go by the board seemed certain. She was handled, though, by the master hand of a great mariner, Admiral Kimberly. Her starboard quarter struck gently just abaft the foremast; a line was made fast to our foremast and her bow hauled in. We could hear the boatswain's pipe, the music of the band, the shout of cheery voices, the stamp of many feet as the ship was swung alongside. In the midst of death we were in life. Quickly everyone forward was helped on board, then the occupants of the main top reached safety just before the mainmast fell, and as her stern came abreast the mizzen rigging our people made the best of their way on board. I swung over to the port Jacob's-ladder, then to the inside of the port rigging, climbed outside and leaped into the waiting arms of the men standing on the *Trenton's* deck, clearing the rigging a brief time before the mast crashed to the deck.

I stood at the rail for some minutes looking searchingly at the *Vandalia* to see if any of our crew were still on board. I saw a group of the *Trenton's* men removing an injured man from the tangle of the mizzen rigging, and another being taken on board from the vicinity of the mainmast. Then I went below, and the first person I met was Chaplain McAlister who, pitying my nakedness, provided me with a pair of woolen civilian trousers and a clerical vest. The next good Samaritan I saw was the Admiral's Chinese steward who handed me a good, stiff drink of gin which, although it scalded my mouth, throat and stomach, which were raw from swallowing so much salt water, sent a delicious, tingling sensation to every nook and cranny of my body and produced a comfortable warmth from the tips of my fingers to the ends of my toes. The steward also gave me some canned fish which, being soft, I was able to swallow, but I failed on the hardtack. In fact, for several days I could eat nothing but soft food.

I was told to go into the Admiral's cabin. There I was welcomed by Lieutenant Carlin, Lieutenant Abraham E. Culver, Ensign John H. Gibbons, Lieutenant Frank R. Heath, Lieutenant John C. Wilson, Dr. Frederick J. B. Cordeiro, Stafford, and Passed Assistant Engineer Harrie Webster, who had stood watch in the engine and firerooms continuously from 5 P. M. of the 15th to 11 A. M. of the 16th, when all hands were ordered on deck. The fate of Chief Engineer Greene, Ensign Ripley, Surgeon Harvey, and Naval Cadet Wiley was still in doubt. During the night Dr. Harvey was found on the upper deck sleeping the sleep of utter exhaustion. His health was permanently injured by the exposure and the physical strain which he had undergone, and he died a year or two later.

The excitement incident to our transfer to the *Trenton* soon disappeared and in spite of reports by the *Trenton's* officers that the storm and sea were raging with unabated fury, that the berth deck was flooded, that the ship was pounding fiercely against the *Vandalia's* hulk and the outlying spurs of the reef, and that the situation was very grave, we fell asleep. We were waked at sunrise with the glorious news that the storm was over; that owing to a shift of the wind during the morning hours the violence of the sea had materially lessened, and that the crew was being taken ashore by boat. We hurried on deck and there we saw the most beautiful of Sunday mornings. The sky was cloudless and the great orb of the sun was shining brightly just above the horizon. A hawser had been got ashore with the aid of the Samoans and the officers and men on shore, and a boat was ferrying the survivors to the beach. The sea was still rough and the utmost skill was required to make the passage safely through the surf, but as we neared the beach we were greeted by shouts of welcome and the willing hands of our Samoan friends who carried us bodily ashore. We learned at once the joyful news that Ripley, Wiley, Chief Engineer Greene and many others had been saved, but our joy was chastened by the sad chronicle of the lost.

The bodies of many of our dead already had been found and it became our loving duty to give them fitting burial and to patrol the beach in a search for others. This patrolling continued unremittingly and a large proportion of our dead were found, among them Captain Schoonmaker, who was buried on high ground overlooking the bay in the beautiful garden of Captain Hamilton, the harbor pilot, a loyal American and a true friend of the Samoan people.

Living conditions on shore were, of course, very congested, as accommodations had to be found for the crews of the American and German ships. The town of Apia was divided between the two nations, and in the American section a provost guard of Marines under the command of Captain R. W. Huntington was detailed and the strictest discipline was enforced. The *Nipsic's* crew re-embarked and the salvaging of property on board the *Trenton* and *Vandalia* was begun immediately. The diving operations were carried out by the Samoans under the direction of their Chief in a remarkably efficient manner. These people seemed to be almost amphibious in their nature, being apparently as much at home in the water as on the land.

There was then no telegraphic communication between the Samoan Islands and the outside world. In fact the only regular mail communication was by steamers making monthly trips each way between San Francisco and Sydney, Australia, and stopping en route at Honolulu, at sea off the east end of the Island of Tutuila of the Samoan group, and at Auckland, New Zealand. An officer of the *Vandalia* was sent by the southbound steamer to New Zealand with instructions to charter a ship to carry the crews of the *Trenton* and *Vandalia* to the United States. On arrival at Auckland he sent the cablegram to the Navy Department which contained the first news of the catastrophe and which gave the names of the dead. Its effect was electrical, and almost immediately steps were taken by the governments of Great Britain, Germany and the United States to settle the Samoan dispute peaceably with the result that a conference was soon in session at

Berlin which reached an agreement concerning the questions at issue.

The northbound steamer was due off Tutuila the latter part of March. It was necessary that the seven Naval Cadets of the *Trenton* should be sent home by that steamer if they were to arrive at the Naval Academy in time for their final examinations, as they belonged to the Class of 1887. Lieutenant Carlin, who had succeeded to the command of the survivors of the *Vandalia,* concluded that Stafford, Wiley and I should also return to the United States so that we could be assigned to another ship and continue our sea duty. He recommended accordingly, and Admiral Kimberly so ordered. Fortunately, an American trading schooner, the *Equator,* arrived at Apia a few days after the hurricane from Pango Pango, the land-locked harbor of Tutuila Island, where she had found refuge during the storm, and she was engaged to furnish passage for the ten Naval Cadets to meet the steamer. Our voyage of eighty miles was soon completed, and after a day or two of waiting we boarded the S. S. *Alameda,* which, in obedience to the request of Admiral Kimberly, proceeded to Apia and, although already crowded to capacity, took on board thirty sick and injured officers and men.

It was with mingled feelings of joy and sadness that we began our journey homeward, joy because we would soon be within reach of the dear ones there, sadness because we were leaving our living shipmates behind, and because of the grief we felt for the families of the gallant men who had laid down their lives in the service of their country just as truly and just as heroically as if they had died in battle. While the ship steamed on her course to the northward, we stood on deck and gazed at the Island of Upolu until it disappeared from view behind the clouds which seemed always to hover over it, and then turned our faces and our thoughts toward the homeland.

About two weeks later, we arrived at San Francisco. A large number of press correspondents boarded the steamer at quarantine and we were beset with their insistent questions in regard to the details of the hurricane and the causes of the disaster. It was a new experience for me as I never before had been interviewed by a representative of a newspaper. I declined to answer any of their questions, however, for the very good reason that upon leaving Apia I had been entrusted by Admiral Kimberly with a package containing the official written reports and a telegram for the Secretary of the Navy, and was instructed to proceed immediately to the Mare Island Navy Yard upon arrival in San Francisco for the purpose of turning over the package to Rear Admiral Benham, the Commandant, and was cautioned that, as a bearer of important despatches, it would be improper for me to give advance information to the press.

The *Vandalia* Naval Cadets were a shabby looking crowd when they landed from the steamer. We found that the Inspectors of Customs had been instructed to give us the freedom of the port, which seemed like a good joke to us, as our only luggage consisted of a few suits of underwear, two or three shirts, some socks, a suit or two of pajamas, a toothbrush, and a comb and brush. These were made up in small bundles which we carried ashore in our hands. I then equipped myself as quickly as possible with some presentable clothing and caught the first train for Vallejo Junction and Mare Island. I called at the Commandant's house, but was told that he had gone out to dinner and that I would find him at the quarters of Medical Director Hudson.

On my way to the Naval Hospital, I met Civil Engineer and Mrs. Walcott, who insisted on my taking dinner with them, and I accepted, subject to the delay in reporting to Admiral Benham with the despatches. At Dr. Hudson's quarters I found the guests about to go in to dinner, but as soon as I was released by Admiral Benham they surrounded me and I was the target for innumerable questions. Mrs. Hudson, however, soon came to my rescue and, taking me aside, she said that she had intended inviting me to stay to dinner, but that Mrs.

Forney, the wife of Colonel Forney of the Marines, had become very superstitious, and on counting the guests had found that there would be thirteen at the table if I remained, so she had offered to go home in order to bring the number down to twelve. I at once relieved the situation by replying that I had already accepted an invitation to dinner.

Mrs. Hudson then told me, at length, the story of Mrs. Forney's remarkable dream which had caused her to become very superstitious. In brief, the story was to the effect that at about the time the *Vandalia* was wrecked, Mrs. Forney had had a vivid dream, indicating that a calamity had happened to the ship—just what was not clear—but she plainly saw numbers of men struggling in the sea, yet recognized only one of them, who, having ceased to struggle, turned face upward for a moment and sank beneath the waves. The face was unmistakably that of Lieutenant Sutton. The dream was so vivid that she described it in detail to a number of her friends the next day, and when the news of what really had happened finally came by cable, she was prostrated and became intensely superstitious. When I told Mrs. Hudson that Lieutenant Sutton actually died in the way she described, I could see that she was much affected, as indeed were all those who knew of the dream and the strange coincidence.

The Cadets were assigned temporarily to the Receiving Ship *Independence* pending the receipt of orders from the Navy Department. They arrived in a week or two, and in obedience thereto we reported for duty on board the *Adams* which was fitting out for a new cruise. A few weeks later the officers and men of the *Trenton* and *Vandalia* arrived from Samoa and some of them were detailed for duty on board the *Adams*. We caught but a fleeting glimpse of Lieutenant Carlin, as he went East to Washington for the purpose of securing legislation to reimburse us for our losses and to straighten out our accounts. It was characteristic of him to be everlastingly on the job of looking out for his subordinates. He was a wonderful man—physically powerful, forceful, strong-willed and absolutely fearless, but light-hearted, kind, generous, and very human. He was a man intended by nature to be a leader of men, and they loved him and followed him gladly. He was successful in his efforts in our behalf, and Congress, at its next session, passed the desired legislation.

The *Adams* finally sailed in June for Honolulu and we expected to make an extended stay there. However, within a week or two after our arrival orders were received from Admiral Kimberly, who had remained at Apia, to proceed at once to that place. Our captain, Commander Woodward, who kept in close touch with the American Minister, was informed by him that it was imperative that the *Adams* should remain at Honolulu until a relieving ship should arrive, as a revolution was brewing and it was of vital importance that we should not abandon the field to the three British cruisers which were the only other war vessels in the Hawaiian Islands. Our commanding officer therefore decided to postpone the date of sailing.

Fortunately for him, the so-called revolution took place exactly as scheduled. About four o'clock one morning, a small Kanaka boy came on board with a note addressed to our Captain. As I was the Captain's clerk, the Officer of the Deck called me to deliver the note to the Captain. The latter instructed me to open it and read it to him. It was written with a lead pencil on a soiled piece of paper and was not enclosed in an envelope. The note was very brief and to the point. It was as follows: "Dear Captain Woodward: A revolution has broken out and the rebels are in possession of my palace. I have taken refuge in my boathouse. What shall I do? (Signed) KALAKAUA, Rex."

The Captain instructed me to prepare a reply for his signature, stating in effect that he would be glad to give the King a safe asylum on board the *Adams*. When the note was ready, it was handed to the Kanaka boy, who paddled away in his canoe to the King's boathouse, a few hundred yards away.   The King did not take advantage of the invitation, however, but remained at the boathouse with the royal barge, manned by its Kanaka crew in readiness to shove off.

Communication with the American Minister was at once established, and soon the Marine Detachment. under the command of Lieutenant Doyen, was sent ashore to guard the legation where many of the American and other foreign women and children were assembled.   The British ships were making an inter-island cruise at the time, and the *Adams* was the only man-of-war in the harbor.   Reports from ashore indicated that the revolutionists had failed to gain possession of the palace proper and that it was still held by the palace guard, but that they had captured all the outbuildings in the palace grounds and two or three cannon with which they had opened fire on the opera house which, together with a church also commanding the palace grounds, had been occupied by the local militia.   Intermittent artillery and rifle fire could be heard plainly from the ship.   Presently an excited messenger came on board bringing the news that the militia was out of proper ammunition, as the stock on hand was of different caliber from that of the rifles, and urgently requesting a loan of cartridges.   The request was complied with, the Captain sending 40,000 rounds ashore.

Late in the afternoon, fearing a more general uprising at night, the ship's battalion of sailors was landed and proudly marched through the principal streets around the palace grounds to the accompaniment of drum and trumpet.   The men were billeted in warehouses and arrangements were made to patrol the streets during the night.   In the meantime, the militia had gotten hold of some hand-grenades and had bombed the rebels out of their buildings, and all of them who had not escaped came out, surrendered, and were confined in the city jail, among them the leader, Mr. Wilcox, a highly educated resident, who afterwards represented the Territory of Hawaii as its delegate in the Congress of the United States.   By the next morning the dove of peace completely resumed her sway, the ship's landing force returned on board, and the King reoccupied his palace.

A few days later, the *Nipsic* arrived under convoy of the U. S. S. *Alert*. The *Nipsic* was hauled up on the marine railway for repairs and became the object of a great deal of curiosity, especially the ingenious jury rudder which had been constructed by the crew to replace the rudder which had been broken to pieces when the ship was beached.

Our Captain immediately made preparations for sea and sailed for Apia within a couple of days after the arrival of the *Nipsic* and *Alert*. Captain Woodward was in poor health and he worried a great deal as to the manner of his reception by Admiral Kimberly. He knew the Admiral to be a stern man who exacted from his subordinates an implicit obedience to his orders, so I spent a large part of my spare time during the passage to Apia in the preparation of a letter to the Admiral setting forth the Captain's reasons for his failure to obey the Admiral's orders more promptly and describing in full the events of the twenty-four hour revolution. I had to rewrite this letter several times before it suited the Captain, but finally he approved the draft as submitted and signed it. Incidentally, the position of Captain's clerk was a sinecure in those good old pre-typewriter days. Official correspondence was kept at a minimum, and an official letter either sent or received constituted an episode of some moment.

When we arrived at Apia, the Captain was sick in bed and I was sent ashore with his letter to the Admiral as soon as the *Adams* arrived in the harbor. I found that the Admiral was quartered in the residence of Mr. Moore, an American merchant, which actually was the second story of Mr. Moore's general store. The Admiral had retained his Flag Secretary, Lieutenant Merriam, and his Flag Lieutenant, Lieutenant Rittenhouse, and his barge's crew of sailors. I was announced by the orderly and, upon entering, I at once explained that the Captain was ill, but that the Executive Officer would come ashore to call as soon as the ship was moored, and that I had been instructed to hand the Captain's report to the Admiral. He was plainly very angry, and I feared an explosion, but he restrained himself and proceeded to read the letter. As he read each page, he handed it to Lieutenant Merriam. I could see that the Admiral was becoming mollified as he read, but I was not prepared to hear him come vigorously and caustically to our defense, as he did when his Secretary made some sarcastic remarks about the Captain's illness and his clerk being sent as a substitute.

The Admiral further stated that he had signalled to the *Adams* to be prepared to get under way at once, and handed me a letter for delivery to the Captain which contained his instructions with reference to our new mission. I asked permission to return to the ship, and he replied, "You can walk with me. I am going down the street." He asked questions about the officers and men of his ships who had returned home and about the *Nipsic,* and spoke of the salvage operations on the *Trenton* being completed, but never said a word about the *Adams'* delayed arrival, the contents of the letter I had handed him, or the new mission of the *Adams.* When we reached a point opposite the landing, he said good-bye. I saluted and went back to the ship. He never said a word to the Captain or to anyone else connected with the *Adams* about the failure to obey his orders promptly, nor did he write a line on the subject. I have described my interview with him in detail as it seems to illustrate a phase of the character of this great seaman.

The anchor was hove short when I reached the ship and we were soon outside and heading for Pango Pango harbor, where the store-ship *Monongahela* lay at anchor. When clear of the harbor, the lines were cast off, the *Monongahela* made sail and we returned to Apia. The next day, the sound of guns firing the signal of distress was heard and in the midst of a terrific downpour of rain we went out to search for the *Monongahela.* Fortunately, the rain ceased in time and we found her becalmed in dangerous proximity to the reef, and, taking her in tow, we returned with her to Apia. There short work was made of loading the guns, etc., and again we took her in tow and wished her good-bye, as with all sails set she headed for God's country, as the sailors call "the land of the free and the home of the brave."

Then, and not until then, did Admiral Kimberly decide to leave Apia, and we put him on board the next northbound steamer. The ensuing month Captain Woodward was sent home sick, and we settled down to a long and dreary stay in the Samoan Islands, alternating between Apia and Pango Pango, going to the latter place whenever a falling barometer indicated a possible storm.

In December we learned that the U. S. S. *Iroquois* was en route to relieve us, proceeding via the Gilbert and Marshall Islands. We expected her to arrive by Christmas, and day after day the horizon was closely watched and every sail that appeared caused a fluttering of our hearts, but we had disappointment after disappointment. Weeks passed by without any news whatever of her whereabouts. Her fate was becoming a mystery of the sea. Finally, it was learned that her engine had been so badly damaged that it could not be repaired, and that she had turned back under sail from the vicinity of the Marshall Islands in the endeavor to make Honolulu, but was driven to the westward of the Hawaiian Islands by easterly gales, and then headed up for San Francisco. Failing to make that harbor, her course was set for Puget Sound where she finally arrived late in the month of March, completely out of coal, and with the crew living on short rations and with a very scant supply of drinking water on board.

The recollection of the constant scanning of the horizon to seaward and the excitement caused by the appearance of a sail or the smoke of an incoming steamer, recalls to my mind the fact that the Samoans gave to all white people the name of "Papalangii," meaning "the people who appeared in the sky." The most noted of the Papalangii who arrived at Apia during the stay of the

Adams were Mr. and Mrs. Robert Louis Stevenson on their yacht.   Mr. Stevenson, who was suffering from tuberculosis, had cruised the world over in search of health and a place in which to establish his abode.   He chose a fairly high spot on the side of the mountain which dominated the harbor and the town.   There he proceeded to build and furnish a home which he called "Vailima"; there he spent the remaining years of his life, and near-by, on the mountain top, he lies buried. We came to know him well, and his face and figure are before me now as I write. A frail bit of humanity he was, weighing between eighty and ninety pounds, and with arms and legs that were veritable pipestems.   We met him first ashore and then, after repeated urging, he came on board to luncheon, and we soon learned what an indomitable spirit dwelt in the frail body, and that the burning fire of genius lit up and illumined his face.

I will not attempt to narrate the future course of events in connection with the Samoan troubles, but will bring to an end the Samoan part of my story by recording the fact that, about March, 1890, we were put on the northbound steamer with orders to proceed to the Naval Academy for final examination.

At Annapolis we took off our coats and went to work. Hard study was essential, as we had lost our books in the ship-wreck and did not replace them until we arrived at Annapolis.

Owing to the unexciting time we had enjoyed while on board the *Adams,* I was able to prepare a very complete and somewhat interesting cruise journal and navigation notes which included every conceivable kind of sight as well as a compass deviation table and dygogram. Then, too, my marks on the final examination were high, so that I materially improved my class standing, going up from twelfth place to sixth.   This was very gratifying to me, as I thought that no doubt could exist as to my assignment to the Marine Corps, for which I had applied, naming the line of the Navy as my second choice.

I often have been asked for my reasons for applying

for the Marine Corps, and this seems as good a place as any in which to record them. I arrived at my choice chiefly by a process of elimination. First of all, I promptly eliminated the Engineer Corps, because I had no bent for mechanical engineering. The choice between the line of the Navy and the Marine Corps was much more difficult to arrive at, and I gave much thought to the subject and weighed the pros and cons with great care. For instance, I liked going to sea occasionally, but not for the greater part of my life; I preferred the military to the naval side of my profession; I foresaw that the sail as a means of propulsion and the old-fashioned sailor would soon become extinct and be replaced more and more by machinery and more and more by men skilled in engineering; and last and most important of all, I realized that whatever ability I had lay in the direction of handling and controlling men rather than in the direction of handling and controlling machinery. From my own standpoint, therefore, the Marine Corps seemed to possess more advantages and less disadvantages than did the other branches of the naval service, and I made my decision accordingly.

As soon as the examinations were over, I became very impatient to start for home, for I had constantly pictured to myself the great sorrow and the poignant grief of my mother and sister because of my dear father's death from pneumonia in the month of December, and I knew how they yearned to see me. My mother, however, unselfish and self-sacrificing woman that she always was, had written to me suggesting that I pay a brief visit to our kinfolk in Bel Air before going home, because of the distressing events which had recently taken place there. I reluctantly decided to carry out my mother's suggestion and to postpone for a few days our family reunion. I also decided, why I do not know, to leave my trunk in Annapolis and return there for it instead of checking it to Baltimore and leaving it at the station until I should start on my journey home.

Although seemingly unimportant, these two decisions

had a potent and far-reaching influence on the whole of my after life.

NOTE: If any reader of this chapter has become interested in the Samoan people, it is suggested that he read the book by Robert Louis Stevenson, entitled *"A Foot-Note to History—Eight Years of Trouble in Samoa."*

V

I BECOME A MARINE AND GET MARRIED

I RETURNED to Annapolis after a two-day stay in Bel Air and found my classmate, George Hayward, at Mrs. Aspold's. After greeting me, he drew a long face and said in a very serious manner, "Gabe, I have bad news for you. The Academic Board has recommended your assignment to the Engineer Corps." He could give me no information beyond the bald statement which I have just quoted.

I was bitterly disappointed and intensely indignant, my indignation being stronger even than my disappointment, because I felt very keenly the sting of injustice. I had worked hard for six years and had succeeded in obtaining a class standing sufficiently high to warrant the belief that I was justly entitled to be assigned to the corps or branch which I had requested. My indignation was further stimulated by the fact that while my wishes had been completely ignored, the wishes of my juniors in class standing had, in nearly all instances, been granted.

I therefore immediately came to the determination to do everything honorable in my power to overturn the decision of the Academic Board in my case. Hayward and I spent the evening discussing the subject and mapping out a plan of campaign. I decided that, first of all, I would endeavor to induce the members of the Academic Board to change their decision, and early the next morning I called on my good friends, Lieutenant and Mrs. E. K. Moore, to obtain the benefit of their advice. They advised me to see Commander Asa Walker and Chief Engineer Milligan, two members of the Board, which I promptly did, and learned that Hayward's information was correct. I exhausted every argument I could think of in the endeavor to secure their support of a proposal to have the Board reconsider its action at a meeting to be held that day.   I also told them that if the assignment were not changed, the action of the Board would be tantamount to forcing me out of the service, as I would resign as soon as I could find other employment in civil life.

They were non-committal and held out no hope of favorable action, but each advised me to see Professor Hendrickson, the head of the Department of Mathematics.   Professor Hendrickson was a "fixture" at the Naval Academy, a man of great ability and force of character, and an exceedingly influential member of the Board.   My interview with him was fruitless.   He explained that Commodore Melville, the Engineer-in-Chief of the Navy, had insisted that all of the four Naval Cadets to be appointed to his Corps should not be chosen from the lower part of the class, and that as there were twenty-four vacancies in the three branches to be filled, the Board had divided the upper twenty-four members of the class into four blocks, and had selected one from each block for the Engineer Corps, and that I had been selected from the upper block of six.   Evidently he was the author of the plan and was committed against making any changes in the assignments.

As a last resort, I called on the Superintendent, Captain W. T. Sampson.   He listened to my plea attentively and then said calmly and dispassionately that the Board had made the appointment for the following reasons: first, they deemed it important to assign graduates of ability to the Engineer Corps; second, I was the only member of the upper block who had not applied for the Line as first choice; and third, because the Board considered that I stood too high in the class to be assigned to the Marine Corps.   He further intimated that there was no probability that the Board would make any change in its action.   I left his office depressed but more determined than ever to continue the fight until it was won.

I returned to my boarding house to get my baggage, intending to go at once to Washington, and there found a letter from Senator Randall Gibson, of Louisiana, congratulating me on completing the six years' course so satisfactorily, stating that he wanted me to consider his home in Washington as a part of Louisiana, and insisting on my calling on him when I passed through Washington.

I immediately took the train for Washington, but upon arrival I went at once to the Navy Department to appeal to Commodore Ramsey, the Chief of the Bureau of Navigation, who had the Naval Academy under his jurisdiction, as I felt it to be incumbent on me to conform to the Navy's code scrupulously by appealing to the next higher authority. My interview with him was of about the same tenor as that with the Superintendent. He expressed his personal sympathy for me, but stated that he could do nothing to assist me as the decision of the Academic Board was final and could not be altered even by the Secretary of the Navy. He added the advice not to attempt in any way to influence the Secretary in my behalf, as my efforts would prove unavailing and the only result would be to worry the Secretary.

I then called on Senator Chandler and found my classmate, Stickney, there. He had been found physically unfit for a commission by reason of defective eyesight, which he said had been brought on by hard study and was temporary in its nature. He desired assignment to the Engineer Corps, and in the conference between Senator Chandler, "Sec" Chandler, Stickney and myself it was decided that Stickney would apply for appointment to fill the vacancy in the Engineer Corps for which I had been designated, and that Senator Chandler would coöperate with Senator Gibson, if necessary, in securing my assignment to the Marine Corps. Senator Chandler told me that he had already spoken to Senator Gibson concerning me, and advised me to call on him at once. This I did, and found him alone in his library. I spent the evening in conversation with him and found him to be a most delightful gentleman, and the most cultivated, intellectual and interesting man I had hitherto known.

He listened patiently to the recital of my story and was indignant because of the arbitrary and unjust treatment of which he considered I had been the victim. He called up the Secretary of the Navy, Mr. Tracy, on the telephone and made an appointment to see him at the Navy Department at ten o'clock the next morning, and told me he felt certain that the Secretary, after hearing my case, would right the wrong which was in process of being done me. He then talked on many topics, among them his experiences in the Civil War and in politics, and his impressions of many noted men at home and abroad with whom he had been associated. I was fascinated and entranced and listened attentively until the clock struck eleven, when I reluctantly said good-night and went to the rooms where several of my classmates had taken up their quarters, and where a bed was in readiness for me.

I was at Senator Gibson's residence bright and early the next morning and accompanied him to the Navy Department. As soon as we entered the ante-room we were shown in to the Secretary's office. The Senator introduced me to Secretary Tracy as a survivor of the Samoan hurricane and as a representative of his French-speaking Louisiana constituents. He then very briefly, but very forcibly, stated my case, and Mr. Tracy said: "The young man can have anything within my power to give him," and asked me what assignment I desired. I told him I wanted the Marine Corps. He rang for Commodore Ramsey, and when the latter came in, he said, "Commodore, I want this young man assigned to the Marine Corps." The Commodore made a note of the Secretary's directions and the interview was ended.

I was very grateful and very jubilant.

I took the through train south and not long thereafter I was at my old home. It was a sad homecoming though, as my joy at being with my mother and sister was quickly changed to grief. I missed the physical presence of my father at every turn; I missed the sound of his voice; I missed his affection and his companionship. It was the first break in our little family, and my

Mrs. John A. Lejeune, 1897.

mother felt most keenly the absence of the strong arm
on which she had leaned for more than thirty years, and
the separation from the brave, the true, the loving heart
of the man who had cherished her, protected her and
idolized her during all the years of their married life.
Our home could never again be the same. His face and
form, however, have always remained in my mind's eye,
and are as clear and distinct to me as I write these lines
as they were forty years ago when he was still alive.
This statement applies with equal force to the memory
of my precious mother. Most vivid of all, however, is
the sense of their spiritual presence, and the consciousness
of their unending, unselfish love and of their protecting
influence. During all the years that have elapsed since
their death, the feeling that their souls—their spirits—
are still alive and are still watching over me and mine has
become a profound conviction, and I need no argument
to demonstrate to my inner consciousness that after death,
the spirit—the personality—continues to live. Strange
as it may seem, this conviction of conscious life after
death has grown stronger instead of weaker as the years
have gone by.

We paid a brief visit to the home of Uncle Stevy
Turpin and Aunt Salome to see them, their children, my
grandfather and grandmother who lived with them, and
Stanley, my uncle's son by his first wife. Stanley had
been raised by my mother and father and we were devoted to him and he to us. A short while thereafter we
left home for Mont Eagle, Tennessee, where we planned
to spend the two months of my vacation, stopping
en route at Natchez and at Uncle Archer Turpin's plantation home in Tensas Parish, Louisiana. He and his
wife, Aunt Fannie, had a family of twelve children and,
although poor, they were the most cheerful, happy people
I ever have known. Crowded as they were, a warm welcome was always waiting for those they loved. I also
spent the day with Aunt Emily and Uncle Scott, who
lived at Sicily Island, Louisiana. Their daughter,
Laura—a lovely girl—had been educated by my mother

and has always been deeply attached to the members of our family. Aunt Emily, although nearly ninety, is still alive and in unusually vigorous health for a person of her age.

Our visits ended, we took the train for Mont Eagle. There we were with Aunt Ellie and Uncle Steele Drake, my mother's invalid sister, Aunt Rebecca, who lived with them, and the Drake children, Joseph, Ruth, Katie, Nell, Winbourn and Laura.

Mont Eagle is situated on the Cumberland Plateau at an altitude of over 2,000 feet, and its cool air was a delightful change from the summer heat and humidity of the Louisiana lowlands. Mont Eagle was the head-quarters of the Southern Chautauqua Association which occupied extensive grounds in which about two thousand people lived in cottages and boarding houses during the summer months in full enjoyment of the mental and spiritual refreshment which characterizes that wonderful educational institution. We lived in the hotel just outside the grounds, but paid daily visits to the amphitheater and to the Drake cottage.

The days were winged and soon the end of August came, bringing with it the necessity of proceeding to New York to report for duty as a Second Lieutenant of Marines at the Marine Barracks, Navy Yard, Brooklyn. There the five newly commissioned Second Lieutenants assembled for a two months' course of instruction so that we might be initiated into the mysteries of the new branch of the naval service which we had joined.

Major Robert W. Huntington was our immediate commanding officer, and Captain Richard Wallach our instructor. Captain Wallach was a very painstaking and conscientious instructor, and the brief course under his guidance was of great value to me in after years, especially as I had no opportunity to attend a military school until 1909, when I went to the Army War College.

Just prior to the expiration of the two months' course, we were directed to inform the Colonel Commandant as to our choice of stations. This we did, but with one exception none of us received orders in accordance with our requests. Stafford and I had applied for Philadelphia, but he was ordered to Boston and I to Norfolk, while Ingate, who had requested Washington or Annapolis, was sent to Philadelphia. Whatever the reason for ignoring our requests might have been, my orders to Norfolk instead of Philadelphia exercised a profound influence on my whole future and brought me great happiness and much joy. I had no premonition to that effect, however, and was much amused when the wife of one of the officers said that it was a common saying, based on experience, that a young officer going to duty at Norfolk would either become a drunkard or get married. I expressed with cocksureness the prediction that I would be an exception to the rule, as I was certain that I would not become a drunkard, and had fully decided that I should never marry. *"L'homme propose et Dieu dispose,"* is an old French proverb, and we learned at the Naval Academy, from Robertson's story of *le jeune Alexis de Latour,* that proverbs are generally true.

Upon reporting at the Marine Barracks, Navy Yard, Norfolk, I took up the routine of duty. The barracks was a wretched wooden building, containing, in addition to the mess hall, kitchen, etc., one big squad room in which all the men slept in two-storied iron bunks. Sacks stuffed with straw constituted all that the government furnished in the way of bedding, and barracks chairs were the only articles of furniture. The ration cost only about fourteen cents per man per diem and was insufficient in quantity and there was but little variety, the supper, for instance, being limited to bread and coffee, with molasses, or a slice of cheese, or bologna sausage. The pay table provided for $25 per month for the Sergeant Major and First Sergeants, $18 for Sergeants, $15 for Corporals, and $13 for Privates. There was only one Sergeant Major in the Marine Corps, and no Quartermaster or Gunnery Sergeants.

The quality of the men was astonishingly good under the circumstances. Although a large majority were foreign-born, many never having been naturalized, they were nevertheless intensely loyal to the Marine Corps and to the flag under which they served. It mattered not whether they were American born citizens, or immigrants from the Emerald Isle, the states of the German Empire, or other Old World nations, they always stood ready to defend Corps and Country against all their enemies and opposers whomsoever and they were worthy of the motto of their Corps—*Semper Fidelis*. At various times, I learned much of the practical side of the duties of a Marine officer, especially those relating to handling men, from such splendid old-timers as First Sergeants John Rice (English), Richard Evans (American), Barchewitz (German) and Daniel Reardon (Irish), and Sergeant Major John Quick (American). Perhaps of all the Marines I ever knew, Quick approached more nearly the perfect type of noncommissioned officer. A calm, forceful, intelligent, loyal and courageous man he was. I never knew him to raise his voice, lose his temper, or use profane language, and yet he exacted and obtained prompt and explicit obedience from all persons subject to his orders.

Attached to the ships at the Yard were several classmates and other friends, so I went on board to see them quite frequently. This was especially the case with the *Atlanta*. One afternoon, after I had been in Portsmouth for two or three weeks, I was in the junior officers' messroom of that ship when I heard the sound of feminine voices and laughter outside, and, sensing the fact that a party was about to take place, I hastily said good-bye and, starting for the door to make my escape, I almost bumped into a winsome young lady who was leading the way into the room. Everybody laughed at my discomfiture, and I was introduced to Miss Ellie Murdaugh and her sisters, Miss Marion Murdaugh, Miss Georgie Murdaugh, and Mrs. Thomas A. Bain. This was my debut in Portsmouth society and it was executed in accordance with the prearranged plan of my friends who had, in inviting me on board, carefully refrained from letting me know that I would meet a group of charming and lovely young ladies. I was immediately attracted to Miss Ellie with her light-brown curls, her smiling face, her animated conversation, and the expression of innocent coquetry in her eyes; while her friendliness of manner made me feel perfectly at ease for the first time in my life when with a young lady and caused me to attach myself to her during the afternoon and to take passage with her in the steam launch which carried the young ladies to the foot of High Street when the party was over. Thus was the romance of my life begun, and although during the eleven months I lived in Portsmouth I met all the young ladies of that city and of Norfolk as well, my devotion to Miss Ellie grew ever stronger. It was a gay and happy period of my life. Everyone treated me as if I had grown up in the community and was a life-long friend. Dancing was the chief amusement, and with the weekly dances on the receiving ship *Franklin* where Captain and Mrs. McGlensey and their daughter were the most hospitable of hosts, the frequent Navy Yard hops, the entertainment of the Portsmouth Casino and the Norfolk Shakespeare Club, the very popular Norfolk Germans, and the numerous informal parties ashore and afloat, my life when off duty was one continuous round of gaiety and pleasure.

Miss Ellie was a most elusive young lady, a care-free, laughing, bewitching damsel, who seemed not to esteem one admirer more than another. Many were the heart pangs I suffered, and often was I visited by the green-eyed monster, jealousy. In a few weeks I found two congenial spirits, Heber Cassell and Tom Moore, who were paying court to Miss Marion and Miss Georgie. We became fast friends and constant companions, calling in unison on the three sisters, trying to anticipate all others in our invitations, and endeavoring to monopolize their society. Tom Moore, in spite of much persistence, was unsuccessful in his suit, while Heber Cassel finally won the prize for which he had striven faithfully for many years.

My orders to the U. S. S. *Bennington* came unexpectedly at the end of September, 1891, and only three or four days remained before I would have to leave for New York to join the ship and be subject to the uncertainty of a three years' cruise. I determined to come to an understanding with Miss Ellie before leaving, and in order to be "far from the madding crowd" I invited her to go driving with me. I chose the quiet Deep Creek Road and, as we rode along, we talked of the days we had spent together and of the coming separation. Finally, as the sun was setting, I told her of my love and of my hope that she might learn to care for me. After much pursuasion, she did admit that there was a tenderness in her heart for me and that she cared for me more than for any other man. A great happiness filled my soul because I knew that she was as true as she was entrancing, that during my absence she would be faithful and unchanging, and that on my return she would be waiting to welcome me.

Early in December, we sailed for Montevideo, Uruguay, in company with the *Atlanta* and the *Chicago,* the latter flying the flag of Rear Admiral John G. Walker who had been for several years in command of the so-called "White Squadron," comprised of new steel cruisers and gunboats which were painted white instead of black as were the wooden ships on which I had hitherto served.

Again our orders were a surprise, as we had fully expected to make a cruise of three or four months' duration in the West Indies and then to return north for the summer and autumn.

The change in our plans was caused by rather serious friction with the Republic of Chile. In October, a large liberty party from the U. S. S. *Baltimore* while ashore in Valparaiso was set upon and attacked by a mob with the result that several men were killed and some twenty or twenty-five were more or less severely injured. The police either could not or would not afford them protection and, in some instances, were believed to have joined with the mob. It was evident that the trouble was not accidental, but that the mob had been actuated by violent hostility against Americans. This hostility was believed to be due to the feeling that the United States had unduly favored President Balmaceda during the revolution against his authority which had resulted in his defeat and the installation of the revolutionary government. Whatever the cause may have been, the relations between the United States and Chile at once became very strained and a forcible demand for redress was sent by Secretary Blaine to the President of Chile. Although the Chilean Government at once instituted an investigation, no progress was made toward a settlement and a tone of truculence appeared in the communications of the Chilean foreign office with reference to the affair. To further complicate the situation, several shots were fired from hostile persons on shore at the crew of the U. S. S. *Yorktown's* gig which was lying peaceably alongside the dock. It was at this stage of the imbroglio that we sailed, with Montevideo as our announced destination. Our voyage was without important incident, but was varied by brief stops at St. Thomas, Santa Lucia, West Indies, and Bahia, Brazil, for coal.

Two or three weeks after reaching Montevideo, the U. S. S. *Concord* and U. S. S. *Philadelphia* arrived, the latter flying the flag of Rear Admiral Bancroft Gherardi who, being senior to Admiral Walker, assumed command of the combined force which also included the U. S. S. *Essex* and *Yantic* which had previously constituted the U. S. naval force on the South Atlantic Station. Their military value was about nil.

We remained at anchor in the rough and stormy Rio de la Plata while negotiations continued rather acrimoniously between the two governments. Finally, about January 20, 1892, the Chilean government, in response to a stern demand for immediate action, made the *amende honorable,* apologizing for the indignity suffered by our men, and offering to place the adjudication of all questions in dispute in the hands of the U. S. Supreme Court or of an arbitration commission. Our government expressed itself as being fully satisfied and once more the dogs of war resumed their peaceful appearance and mission.

The controversy having been settled, the *Philadelphia* and *Concord* returned to the North Atlantic Station of which Admiral Gherardi was commander-in-chief, leaving Admiral Walker in command of the U. S. naval force on the South Atlantic Station. The squadron visited Maldonado, Uruguay, where small arms target practice was held. The country about Maldonado is a sandy, desolate waste, but at that time was literally swarming with birds of the quail or partridge species, and the bird hunters had rare sport slaughtering them without the assistance of bird dogs. "Doc" Norton, a classmate on board the *Atlanta,* announcing that he would hunt only in the most approved fashion, borrowed the fine pointer dog of the British Consul, a Scotchman, who prized it as his most cherished possession. After an absence of two days, "Doc" returned without the dog which had fallen a victim to Doc's prowess as a marksman. The loss of the dog almost created an international episode, but the affair was finally settled peaceably at the expense of a heavy drain on Doc's exchequer.

The squadron also visited the city of La Plata.

We didn't loiter long about the empty streets of La Plata, but at the first opportunity took the train for Buenos Aires and saw something of that remarkable city which seemed surcharged somehow with energy, vivacity, brightness and enthusiasm.

On our return to Montevideo, the *Chicago* and the *Atlanta* sailed for home, leaving the *Bennington* on the station for what we feared would be a full cruise. We visited Colonia, Uruguay, for landing drills and then proceeded to Buenos Aires as the dock system there was already sufficiently advanced towards completion to permit a comparatively light draught ship, such as was the *Bennington,* to enter it. We lay within a few minutes' walk of the heart of the city and, participating in the gaieties of that gay town, managed to spend two or three weeks very pleasantly.

Suddenly the curtain was rung up on the second act of the play and to our amazement and our joy the scene had shifted from the pampas of Argentine and Uruguay to the ports and cities of the Mediterranean. Once more the magic wand had been waved and our minds were filled with visions of the sights and scenes of the Old World concerning which we had read and heard. The Navy Department cablegram directed the *Bennington* to proceed with all despatch to Huelva, Spain, in order to participate there in the celebration of the four hundredth anniversary of the sailing of Columbus on his voyage of discovery from that port, which then bore the name of Palos, an ancient fishing village which had been relegated again to obscurity by the building of the nearby city of Huelva.

A "pampero" however brought us disappointment. This is a wind blowing with great force across the level pampas and down the river, causing such a fall in the level of the river as to make it necessary to close the gates of the docks and to hold all ships there until the storm is over and the river risen to its natural level. On this occasion, there was a fall of nine feet and a delay of two or three days before we could leave port. We then went on our way rejoicing, enthusiasm giving extra power to the strong arms of the firemen and coal passers, and bringing about frequent controversies with the navigator because his daily position reports failed to show that we had gone as far on our way as we had hoped. We chafed at delays caused by rough seas, or by the manana spirit of the coal dealers at our ports of call; and finally we arrived one day late. Columbus, in the person of Captain Concas of the Spanish Navy, had sailed down the Rio Tinto in the caravel *Santa Maria,* and had passed in review the assembled squadrons of the maritime nations of the world which lay at anchor in the outer roads.

Our country was represented by Rear Admiral Benham and the U. S. S. *Newark,* who, on our arrival, directed the *Bennington* to proceed up the river and anchor in the inner harbor with the other smaller vessels. On shore, the beautiful Hotel Cristobal Colon was placed at the disposal of the officers and we were treated royally. The hotel was built around an entire city block and surrounded a beautiful inner court or garden. We sat in the garden and were served with afternoon tea, champagne, or anything else we desired. At night the whole city was illuminated, and a ball was given at which the Queen Regent was present and graciously received all the guests.

Our stay at Huelva ended, the squadrons proceeded to Cadiz and were there sumptuously entertained, and then we sailed for Genoa, Italy, stopping en route at Gibraltar, Barcelona and Toulon. Everything was novel and enchanting, each place having its own special attractions and providing a different variety of interesting experiences.

At Genoa, the birthplace of Columbus, there was a series of fêtes which eclipsed anything of the kind I have ever seen. King Umberto, or Humbert, and the Queen honored the city by their presence and danced the quadrille at the grand ball given by the Dutchess of Pallavicini, Admiral Benham having the Queen for his partner. During our stay, the King visited the flagships of all the nations, being rowed from ship to ship in the huge royal barge. As he left the shore, the fortress fired a salute of twenty-one guns with the royal standard hoisted. This was returned by each ship.

Each ship fired the national salute when the King arrived on board and again when he left the ship, each salute being returned gun for gun. The harbor offered a brilliant spectacle, the Italian fleet and some forty foreign vessels being moored side by side to the mole, and all were gaily dressed in flags. The crews in immaculate white and the officers and Marines in special full dress were drawn up to welcome the King. When he boarded the *Newark,* he was escorted down the line of officers by the Admiral and was introduced to each officer by Lieutenant Bernadou who acted as interpreter. The King made some pleasant or humorous remark to each one. For instance, to a very stout officer he said, "They must feed you very well in the American Navy," and to me he said, on hearing my name, "Ah, Monsieur, vous serez toujours jeune."   (Ah, Sir, you will be always young.) The *Newark* was one of the last ships visited and our Admiral, knowing that the King would be tired and thirsty, decided to violate court etiquette and invite the King to partake of some refreshments. To the amazement but delight of his staff, the King gladly assented and all quenched their thirst in sparkling champagne and refreshed the inner man with the delicious repast which Admiral Benham had provided.

The great mariner's birthday was indeed gloriously and gorgeously celebrated, but as soon as the King and Royal party left Genoa, the ships sailed for other ports, the *Bennington* going to Ville Franche for small arms target practice on a French army range. Monte Carlo and Nice, which were but a few miles from our anchorage, afforded ample opportunity for pleasure of which those of us who were off duty took advantage in the evening hours.

Barcelona was our next port of call, and there we took charge of the caravels *Niña* and *Pinta* which had been constructed by our government. We took the caravels in tow and proceeded with them to Huelva where the four hundredth anniversary of the discovery of America was celebrated with great pomp and circumstance. The scene at La Rabida and on the Rio Tinto could never be forgotten. The old convent or monastery had been restored, and the Queen Regent, the little King Alfonso, and his two little sisters, the Princesses of Asturia, were seated on a great throne erected out of doors overlooking the river; on the plain a large military escort of all arms was drawn up and a vast concourse of people was assembled. On the river, the three caravels, flying standards and banners which were exact reproductions of those flown in 1492, lay at anchor and the officers and crew of the *Santa Maria* were arrayed in reproductions of the court costumes and regalia worn by Columbus and his followers.   Amid a blare of hundreds of trumpets and the roar of many pulsating drums, the Queen arose and presented to the highest dignitary of the Church a scroll which he read and by the terms of which La Rabida, rebuilt and restored, was returned to the religious order which had owned it four hundred years before.   Columbus and his officers then made profound obeisance to the Queen and moved slowly down the stone steps which led to the landing place, embarked in a medieval barge and rowed out to the *Santa Maria,* while hundreds of guns and cannon, afloat and ashore, thundered out the most formidable salute I had ever listened to.

The celebration over, we proceeded to Cadiz where we spent several months in fitting out the *Nina* and *Pinta* for the voyage across the Atlantic and in endeavoring to make them manageable under sail.

In February, 1893, the *Newark* and the *Bennington* sailed for Havana, via the Canary Islands, each towing a caravel, where, thanks to good weather, we arrived with the caravels intact and where we turned them over to the Spanish authorities under conditions resembling the remarkable fête staged at Huelva.   They there passed under the command of Columbus (Captain Concas) who had sailed the *Santa Maria* across the Atlantic from the Canary Islands.

At last we were temporarily free of Columbus and the caravels, and headed for Hampton Roads.   We did not stop at Hampton Roads, but proceeded direct to the Navy Yard to paint and otherwise prepare the ship for the naval review which was soon to take place.   I lost no time in making my way from the Navy Yard to the great old house on the corner of Crawford and London Streets where I had spent so many happy hours in the company of Miss Ellie.   To my great joy, I found her unchanged, even though I knew from her letters that she had been the gayest of the gay and had had many harmless flirtations with very good friends of mine who had tried hard to take the place of the absent friend; for in those days, as in all other days and now, anything was fair in love and war.

It was a blissful week, and at its end, we joined the Fleet at Hampton Roads and were instructed that all our spare time was to be spent in entertaining the officers of the foreign ships which were rapidly gathering there.

It wasn't much of a fête by comparison with what we had seen in Spain and Italy, but the old Hygeia Hotel at Fortress Monroe was gay with lovely American girls and there was no doubt in our minds as to the superiority of our home girls over their European sisters in beauty, grace, vivacity and charm. The ballroom was a brilliant sight, filled as it was with lovely women and officers in full dress uniform. The famous bar of the Hygeia too was never so well patronized; it was literally lined with thirsty warriors, the foreign officers being loud in their praise of American mint juleps and the other delicious concoctions which the team of expert bar-tenders knew so well how to compound. The chief entertainments were dinners, each American ship being assigned two foreign ships to dine and wine, all of which they returned and reciprocated.

We felt quite disappointed though when the Spanish squadron appeared with the caravels in tow. No special honors were shown to the modern Columbus and his crews. There was no dressing of ships, no booming of cannon in his honor, no manning of the rail, no ceremony. To our matter-of-fact Americans, he was just Captain Concas, who had done a good job in sailing a medieval looking craft across the Atlantic.

On the date fixed, the combined fleets got under way and steamed in formation to New York, anchoring in the Hudson off Riverside Park. The river was soon a mass of boats of every description and the display continued throughout our stay, especially at night, when the ships were illuminated. The international parade on shore brought millions to the stands, the sidewalks and the windows. Cosmopolitan, polyglot New York turned out *en masse* to see the representatives of the nations of the world.

The naval review was terminated by a visit of the foreign officers to the Chicago Exposition as the guests of the railways and the Exposition, our governmental authorities being too completely inoculated with the economy virus to expend more than a small proportion of the liberal appropriation made by Congress for entertainment, the remainder being either returned to the Treasury, or spent in painting and making necessary emergency repairs to our ships in preparation for the review.

After a brief New England cruise, the *Bennington* was ordered to the New York Navy Yard for an extensive overhaul preliminary to a foreign cruise; there our commanding officer was relieved by Commander Charles M. Thomas, and in all my forty-five years of service I have never seen a more complete or rapid transformation in a ship or a shore command. In a week the little *Bennington* had become a happy home for officers and men alike. Commander Thomas was a taut Captain too, but somehow he instantaneously captured the imaginations and the hearts of his subordinates so that it was a joy to work for him and we strove mightily for a word of commendation from him.

My mother and sister joined me in New York and it did my heart good to see my dear mother's enjoyment of some of the great city's pleasures. Surely she needed and richly deserved a rest from her labors and I finally was able to secure her promise that she would give up her school and rely to a greater extent on me for her support. At the end of July I was detached and, in accordance with my request, I was again assigned to the Norfolk Yard, reporting there for duty after a month's leave spent at Mont Eagle, Tennessee, with my mother.

I went to duty at Portsmouth, Virginia, with the full determination of getting married during my tour of duty there, provided I could succeed in pursuading my very elusive lady love to give up her care-free, sheltered home life for the gypsy life of a Marine.

It was not long before I was generally recognized as the probable future husband of Miss Ellie and was treated with all the kindness and hospitality which Virginians show to their friends and especially to their kinfolk. I came to know intimately all the members of Miss Ellie's family. It was a large family, even for those days. Besides her parents, Judge and Mrs. Murdaugh, it then consisted of nine children, Marion, Georgie, Ellie, Bessie, Johnnie, Willie, Joe, Claude, who had married Fleet Wilson, and Eugenia, who had married Tom Bain. The oldest son, James, I never knew, as he had died several years before I went to Portsmouth. Four other children had died very young. Judge Murdaugh, a splendid type of the old-fashioned Virginia gentleman, had been most fortunate in the choice of his wife, a famous beauty, who had become the most devoted and the most unselfish of mothers. I was accepted and adopted too by all the many relations and intimates of the family and was, in other words, in process of becoming a member of the clan.

In August, 1895, I went to Bel Air, Maryland, with my mother for a few days' visit, and while there a telegram from Miss Ellie was handed me telling me the crushing news that her brother, Willie, had been killed in the wreck of an electric car on his way to Ocean View. He was a beautiful boy of seventeen or eighteen, and his nature was even more lovely than his face. I returned at once to Portsmouth and there I found a family completely prostrate and crushed with grief. No words could console Miss Ellie, who idolized her brother and whose heart was bleeding because of his untimely end.

A few weeks later, I gently but firmly urged that our wedding day should not be postponed and sought the help of Miss Ellie's sister, Mrs. Bain. Eventually, my gentle persistence combined with her assistance resulted in success, and the twenty-third of October was set apart as our wedding day, the day that was to be the happiest and the most sacred of my life.

We were married in the afternoon, at four o'clock, in the parlor of the old house. Only our families, our relatives, and a few friends were present. Ellie wore a simple but lovely white crêpe dress and was exquisitely beautiful. It was a solemn service, my heart was filled with sacred tenderness and love, and my will was set like flint in the resolve to be true and loyal and loving to my wife during all the years of our lives. We went away together, blissfully happy, on our wedding journey to New York and Niagara Falls, and a short while after our return we rented a small house and furnished it gradually, taking our meals at Cousin Mary Cross' until our dining room and kitchen were ready. It was an exciting day in our lives when the cook was installed and we sat down to our first meal at home. I thought it was the best dinner I had ever eaten and that everything in our little home was perfection.

On the 18th of August, 1896, at seven o'clock in the morning, the greatest of all great events occurred. A child was born into the world, and that child was Ellie's and mine. I sat in the adjoining room alone, as my mother and sister had gone to market, when Mrs. Murdaugh came in with a bundle in her arms which she handed to me, saying, "Here is your beautiful little girl." What a wonderfully tender feeling fills one's heart when he sees his first-born child. I can never forget the emotions that surged within me as I looked at her lovely black head, her wide open eyes, her perfectly formed body, the little hands and feet, and as gently and as deftly as I could, I cradled this little living human being in my arms. I at once named her Ellie Murdaugh, for her mother. What a wonderful baby she was in our eyes, more beautiful, more intelligent, more attractive than any other baby that had ever lived in the world. Needless to say, she greatly changed our mode of life. A "mammie" was obtained who assumed a very dominating position in the family, and everything revolved around

The wreck of the German man-of-war, Adler.

Wrecks of the Trenton *and* Vandalia; *German man-of-war* Olga *ashore.*

the baby.   A more loving, attentive, or faithful mother was never had by any baby in the world, and little Ellie, now herself the mother of two children, is the ideal mother too.

CHAPTER VI

THE SPANISH-AMERICAN WAR

K NOWING that I would become due for sea duty in the summer of 1897, I arranged, so I thought, for my assignment to the battleship *Maine,* but was ordered to the cruiser *Cincinnati* instead.

I reported on board the *Cincinnati* at the New York Navy Yard on August 1st and found the ship in the hands of navy yard working men who were fitting it out for a three years' cruise. The month of August went by rapidly and at its end we had the new crew and the new marine detachment on board, and intensive training was necessary in order to get them into shape before sailing. It was far from a light-hearted group of officers on board early in September when we sailed. Nearly all were married and three years away from our families was a big slice to be taken out of our lives.

Before leaving New York, I made inquiry of the Executive Officer as to the guns the Marines would man, and he replied that it was not the intention to assign them to any part of the battery. I earnestly urged him to reconsider the decision, but without success. I then put my views in writing in a letter addressed to the Commanding Officer in which I presented the case as forcibly as I was capable of doing, and stated in conclusion that I greatly desired an increase of duties instead of a decrease. I handed the letter to the Executive Officer, who, after a conference with Captain Chester, informed me that my request for guns was approved and furthermore that the Captain would detail me to duty as the Intelligence Officer of the ship and to serve on his staff as Squadron Intelligence Officer after he assumed command of the United States Naval Forces on the South Atlantic Station.

During the years preceding the Spanish-American War

there was much agitation on the part of a group of naval officers, of which Lieutenant Fullam was the leading spirit, in advocacy of the policy of withdrawing the Marines from the vessels of the Navy, which meant, in my judgment, the ultimate abolition of the Marine Corps. Manifestly the best way to defeat the advocates of that policy was to so build up and maintain the efficiency of the Corps and to make it of such great usefulness to the Navy as to cause far-seeing and broad-minded naval officers to oppose its abolition and to favor its growth and development.   This was the thought I had in mind during my cruise on the *Cincinnati* and the thought which I have clung to throughout my career.   Gradually it has become recognized that while Marines are not necessary as a police force on board ship, yet their service afloat is necessary in order to provide the Navy with an efficient expeditionary force habituated to ship life, accustomed to being governed by Navy laws and regulations, and officered by a personnel whose members have been closely associated with the officers of the Navy officially and unofficially throughout their entire naval careers.   Duty on board the combat ships of the fleet is not only the best, but is practically the only means by which these eminently desirable results can be attained.

There is a wide and important field of usefulness for a military force with the characteristics of the Marine Corps.   I refer to the field occupied by the expeditionary force, which accompanies the fleet in its overseas campaigns, for the conduct of such shore operations as are required for the expeditious and successful prosecution of the naval campaign.   The operations of such an expeditionary force are extraordinarily difficult and hazardous and require unusually skilful and resolute leadership, and troops which are especially trained for the accomplishment of their mission

The retention of that field of usefulness by the Marine Corps is dependent on its efficiency.   In the hands of its officers, therefore, rests its future.   If they allow the Corps to deteriorate, its mission as the Navy's expeditionary force in peace and in war will pass into stronger and more capable hands and the Corps will be marked for extinction.   On the other hand, if by dint of united, industrious, intelligent and conscientious performance of duty the efficiency of the Corps be increased and become manifest to all, its future development and growth will be assured.

In this discussion, I have wandered far afield from the business in hand and must return to the *Cincinnati* and her leisurely voyage to South America.   After stopping at Bermuda, Barbados and Pernambuco, we finally arrived at Rio de Janiero where we remained for about one month.   Many writers have attempted to describe the beauty of that marvelous harbor and picturesque city with more or less success, chiefly less, as the supply of adjectives in the English language is insufficient to enable one to paint a real word picture of its mountain peaks, its islands, its gardens, its multi-colored houses, its avenues, its distant mountain ranges, and the ocean which washes its nearby beaches.   Rio has indeed been blessed by nature and now that the plague of yellow fever has disappeared, it will doubtless draw to itself a steadily increasing number of tourists.

Our month there was very stupid, however, as we lived under the strictest sanitary regulations.   There was no liberty for the crew, no leave ashore after sunset for officers, practically no drills on board, no harbor water used for scrubbing decks, no pulling boats used, no laundry sent ashore.   In fact, we ran the gamut of "don'ts." Nowadays, all is different in the tropics.   We have learned by experience that exercise, occupation and recreation are just as necessary for good health and contentment in the tropics as they are in the temperate zones, and that night air may be enjoyed by strangers as well as natives without injurious effects.

Suddenly one day our sleepy existence in Rio was disturbed and all was excitement for a while.   Transports bearing an expeditionary force returning from a successful campaign against a revolting Indian tribe arrived in

the harbor and received an ovation. The harbor and
the docks presented a busy scene; boats, gaily decorated
with flags, ran aimlessly everywhere; there was a great
booming of cannon as the President of the Republic, the
Minister of War, and a large military staff visited the
Commanding General on board his ship to felicitate him
on his victory, and again the cannon boomed as they
landed at the Naval Arsenal. Then something happened, we knew not what, except that there was a turmoil
on shore. Mobs could be seen gathering in the squares,
on the waterfront and in the streets. Troops of cavalry
quickly appeared and began clearing the streets. Rumors
of all descriptions came aboard. In the capacity of Intelligence Officer, I was sent ashore to obtain information. Quiet had been nearly restored. Mounted soldiers,
though, still patrolled the streets and detachments of
mounted and foot soldiers were everywhere to be seen.
I went to the United States Consulate, which was near
the landing, and the Acting Consul, who had been stationed in Rio for many years, said nothing definite would
be known until the "extra" editions of the newspapers
published the official account of the happenings. In a
few minutes we heard the newsboys shouting, and, buy-
ing copies of each newspaper, I began the task of trans-
lating, which I was able to accomplish successfully owing
to the close relationship between the Portuguese language
and those of Spain and France, of which I had some
knowledge. It seems that a soldier on guard in the
Naval Arsenal attempted to assassinate the President
after his return ashore from the transport, and that the
Minister of War, in the endeavor to prevent the assassination, had himself received a serious wound from the
bayonet which was the soldier's weapon. Instantly mobs
had filled the streets, rioting had occurred, and graver
disturbances were feared, but the troops had stood stead-
fast and order had been promptly restored. We also
learned from the press within two or three days that the
affair had been a conspiracy to substitute the Vice President for the President, and that the former, as well as a

large number of members of Congress and other prominent men, fearing arrest, had left the country. Later on it was reported that they were at Buenos Aires in voluntary exile.

The incipient revolution was easily stamped out and Captain Chester and several officers, including myself, were presented by the United States Minister, Mr. Conger, to the President in order to congratulate him on his escape from injury. He received us in the great salon or reception hall of the Imperial Palace. He was an elderly man and of very feeble appearance. As the officers were being introduced I accidentally dropped my black helmet which, striking the stone floor on the brass spike, made a loud report which reverberated in the large hall and, for a moment, caused consternation. The interview ended pleasantly enough, but the thought was in my mind that being President of a Latin American republic was a rather nerve-wracking occupation.

While at Rio, I was able to obtain a full description of the *Almirante Barrozo,* built in England for Brazil, which was sent to the Navy Department as an intelligence report and which we were informed was of value in connection with the purchase of the two sister ships for our Navy which received the names of the *New Orleans* and the *Albany.* In fact, I spent a large part of my time in intelligence work which not only afforded me occupation of interest, but resulted in the receipt of a number of commendatory letters signed by the Assistant Secretary of the Navy, Theodore Roosevelt.

Early in December we sailed for my old stamping ground, Montevideo, proceeding thence to Buenos Aires for the Christmas holidays, and returning to Montevideo early in January. Captain Chester then began working on plans for an extensive cruise on the station which would involve a visit to all Brazilian ports by at least one of the ships of the squadron, and then a cruise on both coasts of Africa.

One morning, however, Mr. Bottini, the Comprador, came on board with a long cipher cablegram which produced an intense state of excitement. Instructions were given to get up steam at once and it was made known that we would sail for Buenos Aires as soon as ready for the purpose of docking the ship in order to clean and paint her hull, and orders to have coal and supplies in readiness to put on board on our return were given to Mr. Bottini. We had learned from press despatches that the relations between our government and Spain were steadily becoming more strained owing to the indignation of our people because of the long drawn out Cuban insurrection and the alleged atrocities of the Spanish troops, especially with reference to the reconcentration policy of Captain-General Weyler; and there were frequent protests by the Spanish government in regard to filibustering expeditions and the shipment of arms and ammunition to the Cuban insurgents, which even the greatest vigilance on the part of the United States authorities could not altogether prevent. The friction and ill-feeling culminated in riots in Havana early in January, 1898, which appeared to be directed against Americans, and the American Consul General, Fitzhugh Lee. At any rate, the *Maine* was ordered to Havana in order to afford protection or at least an asylum for Americans in case their lives should become endangered. We therefore assumed rightly that the cipher cablegram was in reference to the Spanish-American embroglio, and that it contained directions governing our movements.

Upon arrival at Buenos Aires we learned with considerable perturbation that before the ship could be docked the removal of all shell and other ammunition was required, and that the lighter on which it was placed would be towed out in the river and anchored until after the ship should come out of dock. The presence of a Spanish gunboat alongside the adjacent pier and the manifest sympathy of the people of Buenos Aires for Spain added to our worries. An armed guard of Marines, in charge of a Sergeant of courage and determination, was put on board the ammunition lighter and we felt that it would be secure. Nevertheless, while the ship was in dock it was the part of wisdom to be on our guard and to avoid anything like a broil between our men and the people of the city. I talked to the Marines concerning the situation and appealed to their *esprit de corps* and their patriotism. Their performance of duty and their conduct were most praiseworthy and impressed the naval officers on board most favorably, especially as some of the crew took advantage of the opportunities to procure cognac and other varieties of hard liquor from the many native bootleggers who hung around the ship. We were greatly relieved in mind when we had left the dock, reloaded our ammunition, and sailed for Montevideo. The loading of coal and supplies at Montevideo detained us but a short while, and within twenty-four hours we were on our way down the Rio de la Plata to an unknown destination, the announcement having been made that we were leaving for a cruise and drills in conjunction with the gunboat *Castine* which had already sailed, and the *Wilmington,* which was en route to the station.

Within a day or two we learned that we had been notified to proceed to the northern limits of the station and there await orders. Our movements, however, were shrouded in secrecy to such an extent that our mail continued to go to Montevideo for some months, and much of it was over a year old when received.

Para, situated on the Amazon River about one hundred miles from its mouth, was our final destination, but on arriving there no shore leave was allowed as both yellow fever and smallpox were prevalent in the city. Lying about two degrees south of the equator, it is not surprising that the climate was abominable, being characterized by heat, humidity and frequent tropical downpours of rain.

While at Para, the bombshell burst. A general courtmartial was in session, of which Lieutenant Charles J. Badger, the navigator, was the President, and I the Judge Advocate. During the trial the orderly delivered a message to Lieutenant Badger to the effect that the Captain wished to see him at once. The court took an informal recess until his return, a few minutes later. When he came into the courtroom he said, "Gentlemen, very grave and very serious news has been received. The battleship *Maine* has been blown up and destroyed in Havana harbor. There was heavy loss of life. Confidentially, it is my personal opinion that this means war."

A few hours later, a cablegram arrived stating that owing to the unhealthful conditions at Para, the *Cincinnati* and *Castine* were authorized to proceed to Barbados and take station there temporarily. On arrival we found the *Wilmington* had already reached there, and the South Atlantic Squadron, therefore, was complete.

The full power trial of the *Cincinnati* was not successful. The boilers were in poor shape, owing to leaky tubes, and the fire-rooms were man-killers owing to their terrible heat. This condition had been apparent throughout the cruise and there were frequent heat prostrations among the fire-room force. The Chief Engineer recommended that the ship go north to a navy yard for repairs and alterations, which it was estimated would take about one month. Lieutenant Badger strongly concurred in his views. The eagerness of the commanding officer for active service, and his fear lest the war would break during the absence of the ship from the theatre of operations, caused him to disapprove the recommendation.

Near the end of March we were ordered to Port Antonio, Jamaica, and thence to Key West, Florida, the center of naval activity and the concentration point for the fleet. As we approached and entered the harbor, we were thrilled by the busy and stirring panorama spread out before our eyes. The Flagship *New York* and the battleships were anchored outside the reef, while in the inner harbor were the cruisers, gunboats, destroyers, tugs, and a myriad of small boats plying back and forth from ship to shore and from ship to ship. It was the end of March, and the interest of the fleet and of the nation was centered on the proceedings of the court of inquiry which was then still investigating the destruction of the *Maine*. At that time, divers under the supervision of Naval Constructor Powelson were making a careful and minute examination of the ship's hull. Newspapermen were everywhere and the streets of Key West were filled with officers, sailors, marines, reporters and other civilian visitors. All the talk was of the probable findings of the court of inquiry and their effect on public opinion. The vast majority of the newspapers of the country appeared to be clamoring for war. The word "war" was on every one's lips.

Key West was poorly equipped to serve as a base for the fleet, in fact, it lacked all the essential facilities except one storehouse. All supplies, including coal and even water for the fleet, had to be transported by sea from Tampa. Yet its situation was such that there was no escape from the dilemma. Inexorable logic made it the base, and it was up to the government to do the best it could towards improvising the necessary facilities.

Jack Dayton—who had married Ellie's cousin, Nancy Reid—and I concluded that, war or no war, it would be a wonderful thing if our families could come to Key West and join the little colony of Navy wives who had assembled there. Our Captain thought it likely that we would leave Key West in a few days and take station in the Virgin Islands to be in readiness to scout for Cervera's fleet, which was known to be in the Canary Islands. We suggested to Nancy and Ellie that they endeavor to find out at the Navy Department what the probabilities were of our remaining at Key West, and if favorable, to lose no time in joining us. They had no difficulty in obtaining the desired information through the assistance of Judge Leigh R. Watts, of Portsmouth, who was assured by the Department that it was altogether probable that the *Cincinnati* would remain at Key West for some weeks. They therefore telegraphed us that they were leaving for Key West, via Tampa, and giving us the date of their arrival. It was their first long journey and to them it was a thrilling adventure. The night before their arrival, it was the *Cincinnati's* turn to patrol outside the battleships, and the steamer came in before we had returned. They were prepared for the contingency, however, and when we finally got ashore we found them at the Key West Hotel. We moved them to a very nice boarding house in a quiet part of the town where Mrs. Cornwell of the Navy and her daughter were boarding. Their stay of nearly two weeks was an inexpressibly happy one for us, even though shore leave for the officers was greatly curtailed. War, with all its uncertainties, was imminent and there was in our minds the ever present but carefully concealed thought that perhaps this might be our last reunion.

As each day passed, it appeared more probable that President McKinley would be unable to resist the popular clamor for war, and this probability became a practical certainty when it was made known that the court of inquiry had found that the destruction of the *Maine* had been caused by the explosion of an external submarine mine, and that its explosion had detonated one or more of the ship's magazines with disastrous results. The war fever spread rapidly, and cries of "Remember the *Maine!*" were heard from one end of the country to the other. It has always been thus. Men and women are controlled by their emotions rather than by the cold light of reason, and as long as this is the case, a modern Peter the Hermit can readily bring about a modern crusade, and the fallacy as well as the folly of pacifism be demonstrated over and over again.

Diplomatic notes were feverishly exchanged, but without avail, as the American people had decreed that there should be war. Finally, the President proclaimed the establishment of a pacific blockade of Cuban ports, and the fleet sailed at daylight one April day from Key West to blockade Havana. It was a picture to stir one's soul to its depths. A great armada composed of every class of combat ships then known to man (an armored cruiser, battleships, monitors, light cruisers, gunboats, destroyers, tugs, auxiliaries), laden with men whose hearts were aglow with patriotism and filled with the determination to maintain the prestige and the honor of the glorious flag

which fluttered from the masthead of every ship, was
steaming towards an unknown destiny.

Our progress was slow, but before sunset we arrived
off Havana, and then the *New York* hoisted the signal,
"Disregard the movements of the Flagship," and moved
off at full speed in the direction of a column of black
smoke which we plainly saw on the horizon.   It was a
Spanish liner, with a valuable cargo on board, and if
captured would have been a rich prize, as prize money
was still being paid in those days.   She made good her
escape, however, and during the night the Flagship returned empty handed.   The great aggregation of ships
lay off Havana with lights out, and we watched the night
through until dawn.

In the morning, on signal from the Flagship, the
monitor *Puritan,* the *Cincinnati,* the *Wilmington* and a
destroyer or two proceeded towards Matanzas to establish
a blockade of that port.   While en route we sighted a
large cruiser close in shore heading west.   It was impossible at first to make her out, but as she drew nearer
she seemed to possess many of the characteristics of the
Oquendo class of Spanish armored cruisers.   Each ship
headed towards the stranger and beat to general quarters.
On the *Cincinnati* the enthusiasm was intense, and preparation for battle proceeded with the speed of lightning.
We had landed at Key West nearly everything that was
movable, but had retained the mess chests for the crew
and a few other similar articles.   These were marked
"U. S. S. *Cincinnati*—To be thrown overboard."   So
overboard they went, thereby causing not only a great
deal of discomfort to the crew, but much anxiety to our
families as well, for some of the material drifted ashore
and was picked up, causing the Spanish authorities to
report that the *Cincinnati* had been wrecked off the north
coast of Cuba and that a great deal of the wreckage had
been found on the beach.   This report was cabled to the
United States and published broadcast in the newspapers.
There were other casualties on this occasion.   Although
the greater part of the wooden bulkheads in the ward-

room and elsewhere had been removed and replaced by canvas screens to minimize injuries from splinters, a few were still allowed to remain, with the understanding that they would be removed in the event of battle. Among these were the bulkheads of the Chief Engineer's office. When the cruiser was sighted, the carpenter assaulted these bulkheads with an axe, demolishing them completely, also the Chief Engineer's gold watch which was hanging on a hook inside the office. The Chief Engineer, a veteran of the Civil War, was greatly displeased by the carpenter's exhibition of energy and expressed himself quite forcibly on the subject. But he should have expected as much. There is no more powerful emotion known to man than that which permeates every fiber of his being when first he goes into battle. The most civilized, highly cultured man is in this respect no different from the most primitive, the most savage of the inhabitants of this earth of ours. Some superhuman power seems to grip him and to spur him onward into the vortex, the maelstrom of destruction which men call battle.

On this occasion, to the tremendous disappointment of every one on board, the battle did not materialize, as on our approach to the cruiser a breeze sprang up and her colors, which had been hanging limp, straightened out and were recognized as those of Italy, while the ship herself was easily identified as one of a well-known group of Italian cruisers. It is impossible to imagine the letdown feeling we all had, when we turned away from the pursuit and resumed our course.

On arrival off Matanzas, blockade stations were assigned both by night and by day, and we were cautioned to exercise great care in screening all lights. For a ship to show a light other than the authorized secret, code-identifying light under the prescribed conditions and circumstances was regarded as one of the most heinous offenses man or ship could commit. All stood watch and watch on deck, and the part of each gun's crew whose watch on deck it was, lay down by their guns in readiness to jump immediately to their stations. Guns were loaded, with breech-blocks open as a safety precaution, and ammunition was kept on deck. I spread my poncho and blankets on the poop deck near the marine gun crews and slept there each night during the war when at sea and off watch. The deck was made of very hard planks, but I preferred them to my comfortable bunk, partly because of my desire to be with my men, and partly because of the stifling heat below, with all air ports closed, no artificial ventilation, and fires under all boilers.

Blockade duty was a very trying experience for all classes of ships, but especially so for the small destroyers or torpedo boats like those we then had. This was the case even in normal weather, while in rough weather conditions on board the destroyers became intolerable. Knowing this, Captain Harrington of the *Puritan,* the senior officer present, directed Lieutenant William L. Rodgers to take soundings in an area near the shore and under the lee of high ground, with the view of learning whether it would be suitable for use as an anchorage for the destroyers in the event of bad weather. While engaged in taking the soundings, a concealed battery on shore opened fire on the destroyer. He continued, however, to take the soundings in an orderly and deliberate manner until he had completed his task, and then steamed out to report the result. A number of shells were fired at the destroyer, but none took effect. The crew of the *Cincinnati* were in a tremendous state of excitement and spontaneously gave three resounding cheers to Lieutenant Rodgers and his gallant crew as they passed by. This was April 27th, and the shells fired by the Spanish battery on that occasion were, I believe, the first hostile shots fired by either side during the war.

Report of the incident was made immediately to the Commander-in-Chief, and on the following day, April 28th, the Flagship joined the blockading force and directed by signal that fire be opened on the Spanish batteries located on the western side of the harbor entrance. The fire was conducted at a range of about 4,500 yards, and was promptly returned by the forts. The enemy shells fell short but made an uncanny din as they hurtled through the air, in fact, we continued to hear the sound for an appreciable time after the shells splashed in the sea. It was a novel experience for nearly all of us, as never before had we been shot at by cannon.   Our men were remarkably calm and cool, however, and served and fired their guns with deliberation and with careful aim.   This brief engagement assumed an important place in history because it was the first battle of the war.

Blockade duty was ordinarily, however, far from exciting and every unusual incident was a matter of interest. For instance, a few nights after the bombardment of Matanzas, we heard the sound of rapid fire from the direction of the *Puritan*.   Some ten or fifteen shots from what appeared to be a one-pounder gun were fired, and then there was complete silence.   The *Puritan* did not communicate the cause of the firing that night or the next morning until finally Captain Chester's curiosity got the better of him and he sent me over to the *Puritan* to ask for instructions in regard to the disposition to be made of a Spanish Army officer we had picked up in a fishing smack.   Captain Chester, in giving me my orders, added a final word to the effect that I was to ask Captain Harrington casually what was the cause of the firing.   I did this with considerable trepidation as I had learned Captain Harrington's characteristics well during the two years he had been Commandant of Cadets while I was at the Naval Academy, and I feared a rather severe reaction.   To my surprise, he smiled and said, "Tell Captain Chester that an over-zealous young officer thought he saw something close by and opened fire on it, but it turned out to be a false alarm."   Several years afterward I spoke of the incident to then Lieutenant Spencer Wood, who had commanded the destroyer *DuPont* during the war. He replied that it happened to be the *DuPont,* and that never before or since had the *DuPont* made such a burst of speed, as the shells struck all around her.   The Spanish officer claimed to be on the way to Havana to see his sick wife who was about to give birth to their eighth child, so, tempering war with mercy, he was put ashore near Havana after undergoing an examination on the Flagship.

It was not long before our boilers were in such bad shape that we could only make five or six knots an hour. Tube after tube blew out, and the ship was in an almost helpless condition. The Commanding Officer called a survey on the boilers and the board found the ship unfit, in her then condition, for active service and recommended that she proceed at once to a navy yard for overhaul and repair. The Captain very reluctantly approved the report of the board. The next day orders were received for the *Cincinnati* to return to Key West for coal and then to proceed to Norfolk Navy Yard for necessary repairs.

On arriving at Key West it was decided that emergency repairs to the boilers were necessary before undertaking the voyage to the Norfolk Navy Yard, and navy yard workmen who had been sent to Key West from northern yards were therefore put to work immediately. In the meantime, the war had taken on a more exciting phase, several events of epochal importance having occurred during our absence on the Cuban blockade.

In the first place, Congress had passed a resolution declaring that a state of war existed between the Kingdom of Spain and the Republic of the United States of America, whereupon Cervera's fleet had sailed westward across the Atlantic towards an unknown destination, causing a feverish state of activity on the part of our Navy and a tense state of excitement on the part of the public. In the meantime, popular imagination had been fired and popular enthusiasm aroused to an unprecedented degree by the astounding news of Dewey's glorious victory on May 1st in Manila Bay, when our Asiatic Fleet under his command, having entered the Bay under cover of darkness, had attacked and completely destroyed the Spanish fleet as it lay at anchor off Cavite. At one bound the thoughts of Americans leaped across the Pacific Ocean and our country lost, never to regain, its insularity, and became a world power. Dewey was acclaimed a superman, the glamor of romance hung about him like a halo, and his name was on the lips of every American.   In the white heat of the furnace of war great reputations are made or unmade and radical changes in popular sentiment are wrought in the twinkling of an eye.

A day or two after our arrival in Key West, Rear Admiral John C. Watson came on board with Captain Chester and it was announced that he had selected the *Cincinnati* as his temporary flagship.   He had no staff with him, consequently it fell to my lot to act as a member of his staff during his stay on board.   I shall never forget my introduction to my new duties.   It was late in the evening when Captain Chester sent for me and told me that he was acting as Chief of Staff, and that the Admiral wanted me to serve as his Flag Secretary for a few days.

I felt it to be a very great honor to be selected to assist the Admiral and to be taken into his confidence.   He was a courtly gentleman of the old school and an officer of distinguished record, having established an outstanding reputation for efficiency and courage while serving as the Executive Officer of Farragut's flagship, the *Hartford,* during the Civil War, especially in the famous battle of Mobile Bay.

Captain Chester took me into his cabin and after I had reported to the Admiral for duty, he invited me to sit down.   It was a very interesting and inspiring evening that I spent with those two gallant gentlemen.   I had never before met Admiral Watson, although, of course, he was well known by reputation to every officer of the naval service, and I was deeply impressed by his courtesy, his kindness and his simplicity—qualities which I have learned to be the attributes of true greatness.   He and Captain Chester were lifelong friends and it was delightful to listen to their intimate, personal conversation and to obtain therefrom an insight into their characters. Their love of country and their pride in the Navy were the dominant notes in their utterances.

In a few days the startling news was received that

Cervera's fleet had been off Martinique and that a Spanish destroyer had stopped there to cable home. Admiral Sampson, with his battleships and monitors, was then off San Juan, Porto Rico, where he had engaged the forts in battle; Commodore Schley was at Hampton Roads with the so-called Flying Squadron; Commander McCalla, with some small cruisers and gunboats, was blockading Cienfuegos, Cuba; and the remaining cruisers and gunboats were blockading Havana and the other northern Cuban ports. The *Cincinnati* and the *Vesuvius* were the only vessels at Key West. They were ordered to proceed at once to the Yucatan Channel to gain touch with Cervera's fleet should it head in that direction from Curacao, to which place it had proceeded from the vicinity of Martinique, and whence it had sailed to the northward after taking on board a small amount of coal. At the same time, Schley sailed for Key West and Sampson moved west to the vicinity of the same place.

The *Cincinnati* and *Vesuvius* engaged in a ceaseless but fruitless vigil for about one week, when at two o'clock one morning a never to be forgotten thrill shot from one ship to the other like an electric shock. Seven lights were sighted just above the horizon. They were in view for a few moments only, and then disappeared simultaneously. About one-half hour later they again flashed and again disappeared. This time they were distinctly nearer and it was evident that they were the signal lights of seven ships cruising in squadron formation and were being utilized to effect changes in course. The lights were seen several times. There were seven lights and there were known to be seven ships in Cervera's fleet—four armored cruisers and three destroyers, the fourth destroyer having taken refuge at San Juan, Porto Rico. Our mission required that prompt information should be sent to Key West if the Spanish Fleet were sighted. The momentous question to be decided was whether or not the ships in the offing were Cervera's ships. The facts could not be determined until daylight. Captain Chester, therefore, made the decision to steam towards Key West until daylight and then to turn about and steam towards the approaching ships. As soon as they could be made out, and if they turned out to be enemy ships, the *Vesuvius* would proceed at full speed—over twenty knots—to Key West with the news, while the *Cincinnati,* making such speed as she could, would engage the enemy. We were confident that in a stern chase the remarkable gunnery efficiency of our men would cause very heavy losses to the enemy ships, and perhaps even decisive results were possible, especially if they should string themselves out by reason of their varying speeds.

These and many other questions we discussed until daylight, and then we could plainly see the smoke of the approaching ships. We headed towards them, and in a little while we made them out. They were the United States ships *Marblehead* and *Nashville* and the other craft constituting Commander McCalla's little squadron which had been blockading Cienfuegos, and which had been ordered back to Key West because of the proximity of the stronger hostile fleet.

Oh! The flatness of that moment! A little while before, we had visions of being the outstanding heroes of the war and of going down in history with John Paul Jones, Decatur, Cushing and the other immortals, and now the exaltation of spirit had vanished even as the early morning mist had disappeared with the rising of the sun.

We continued on our vigil for two or three days longer, when the *Texas,* the *Massachusetts* and the *Brooklyn,* the latter flying the flag of Commodore Schley, were sighted heading south. They stopped when near us and Captain Chester was ordered to report on board the Flagship. After an hour's conference he returned and told us that the Squadron was proceeding to Cienfuegos where it was expected Cervera's fleet would be found, and that he had begged the Commodore to authorize the *Cincinnati* to accompany him, but that permission to do so was refused owing to the fact that the *Cincinnati* was short of coal.

The next morning we started on our return voyage to

Key West as our supply of coal was running short, and met the *Marblehead* off the north coast of Cuba. The two ships stopped and Commander McCalla came on board. The sea was smooth, there was scarcely the vestige of a breeze, the sky was clear, and not a ship was in sight, when suddenly there was a severe explosion. The ship shook from stern to stern. The magazines, the coal bunkers, the storerooms were inspected, but nothing could be found to indicate that an explosion had taken place, or its cause. The *Marblehead* signalled over reporting the explosion and asking if we had felt it and if we knew its cause. It was, and still is, a mystery of the sea.

On our return to Key West we found a busy scene of activity and much uncertainty, as nothing had been heard of the movements of the Spanish Fleet since it had sailed from Curacao. Speculation as to its whereabouts and its plans was rife, and one man's guess was as good as another's. Admiral Sampson had returned from San Juan and his fleet was assembled at Key West. The harbor was full of ships, among them a naval transport with a force of six or seven hundred Marines on board under the command of Lieutenant Colonel Huntington. I was filled with enthusiasm when I saw them drilling on shore, as I had never before seen so many Marines gathered together.

The Marines landed and went into camp along the beach so that the transport could join Admiral Sampson's fleet when it sailed for the north coast of Cuba to be in readiness to meet the hostile fleet should it attempt to reach Havana from the eastward. The Marine officers were thereby tremendously disturbed in mind as they feared that they would be marooned at Key West for the period of the war. Actually everything turned out for the best, as it usually does in the service if one makes the best of the situation. In this case, full advantage was taken of the opportunity for drill and target practice, and at the end of two weeks on shore the efficiency of the battalion was greatly increased and it was thereby enabled to give a good account of itself in the campaign in which it became engaged immediately after it landed at Guantanamo Bay, Cuba, early in June. The fact that this battalion was the first United States force to effect a permanent lodgment on shore in Cuba, and the success of its military operations there, brought the Marine Corps into great prominence and caused the Navy to appreciate more fully its value as an expeditionary force for the performance of the shore operations which always play such an important part in a naval overseas campaign. The increase of the Marine Corps which followed the Spanish-American War was due to the fine record of this battalion, supplemented as it was by the efficiency displayed by the Marine detachments afloat, and by the trying experience of the Asiatic Fleet during the three months which followed the battle of Manila Bay, an experience which Admiral Dewey himself stated would have been obviated by the immediate occupation of the city of Manila had he had at his disposal an expeditionary force of four or five thousand Marines.

These pages, I must not forget, are not intended to contain a history of the war or of the Marine Corps, but rather an account of only such events as came under my personal observation, together with occasional brief excursions into other fields which are connected with the narration of my reminiscences. Let us, therefore, direct our thoughts once more to the good ship *Cincinnati* and to the events in which she participated. Captain Chester eagerly sought and obtained orders to join Admiral Sampson's fleet and we spent several days of watchful but unavailing waiting during which the great aggregation of ships of every class, kind and size then in the Navy, steamed slowly in two columns back and forth in the channel between Cuba and the Bahama Islands. In the meantime, Schley's squadron lay off Cienfuegos until Commander McCalla had communicated with our Cuban allies on shore and had ascertained that Cervera's fleet had not reached that place.

At this stage of the campaign, orders were received from the Navy Department for the *Cincinnati* to proceed without further delay to the Norfolk Navy Yard for overhaul and repairs. This time there was no escape from the fate which had been pursuing us, and after again coaling ship at Key West we sailed for Norfolk, arriving there safely, but with our boilers in a seriously crippled condition. Our disappointment because of our enforced absence from the theatre of operations was somewhat lessened when we learned that our fleet had not met the enemy fleet on the high seas, but that it had reached Santiago where it was securely bottled up, and hope, which springs eternal in the human breast, held up to our view the pleasing picture of our return to Cuban waters in time to participate in the great sea fight which everyone felt sure would be the final culmination of Cervera's reckless dash into the sea area dominated by our fleet.

This hope, however, soon vanished, as events moved swiftly during the month that our ship lay at the navy yard. The Marines landed at Guantanamo Bay; Shafter's army sailed from Tampa and landed near Santiago; the battles of San Juan Hill and El Caney focused the attention of the world temporarily on the trying military situation which followed; Hobson sank the *Merrimac* in the entrance of Santiago harbor; and, finally, Cervera's ships made their dramatic exit from that harbor and met disastrous defeat and complete destruction at the hands of our fleet.

We chafed bitterly because of our enforced inactivity during this critical period, but our enjoyment, too, was great for we were united with those we loved. My little girl brought joy to my heart. She was the brightest and loveliest of children, as indeed she has grown up to be the loveliest of women, and my dear wife, who had been the most pleasure-loving of young ladies, had become the best and most dutiful of mothers. It was a sacred family reunion, too, as my beloved mother was with us for the last time here on earth. The pleasure that dear little Ellie gave her was beautiful to behold and there is imprinted on the tablet of my memory the picture of the happiness in my mother's face as she listened to little Ellie saying, "I love you, Grandma."

A few days after the destruction of Cervera's fleet, the *Cincinnati* sailed for Guantanamo Bay and arrived there on July 15th. There we heard the details of the important events that had taken place. We learned of the surrender of Santiago and the Spanish army which garrisoned it; of the sad physical condition of the troops constituting Shafter's army; and the fact that none of the light cruisers had participated in the defeat of the Spanish fleet, as they were all engaged in blockading Cuban and Porto Rican ports. This last piece of information relieved our minds considerably as it convinced us that even if we hadn't been at Norfolk, we would not have been vouchsafed the honor of forming part of the squadron which had destroyed the naval power of Spain with one smashing blow.

We also learned that a military expedition commanded by Lieutenant General Nelson A. Miles was to invade and occupy the island of Porto Rico in the immediate future. The *Cincinnati* was directed to proceed at once to Cape San Juan, Porto Rico, which had been designated as the rendezvous for the naval vessels and transports of the expedition. When we reached there we found only the monitor *Amphitrite* and a naval tug lying at anchor in the little harbor adjacent to Cape San Juan, the southeastern promontory of the island. The boarding officer from the *Amphitrite* informed Captain Chester that the U. S. S. *Columbia* had been stationed there until a few days before, but had proceeded to the Port of Ponce. He also reported that the *Columbia* had sent her landing force to the town of Fajardo, some three or four miles in the interior, which, after occupying the town, had supplied the friendly inhabitants with arms and ammunition and returned to the ship upon the assurance of the people that they would have no difficulty in holding the town. However, it seems that they had promised more than they could perform as a day or two afterwards a Spanish force of seven or eight hundred men had retaken the town, and the American sympathizers had fled with their families and had taken refuge in the lighthouse and adjacent buildings on Cape San Juan.   The Captain sent for me, and after telling me the story, he stated that he had about decided to land the Marine Detachment (40 men), reinforced by the 3-inch landing gun and its crew of sailors, with the view of re-occupying Fajardo.   I asked and received permission to have Naval Cadet Yancey Williams detailed to accompany me, and he and I at once began preparations for the landing, which I planned to effect after dark so that we might make a surprise attack on Fajardo under cover of darkness.   In the meantime, Captain Chester went to the *Amphitrite* to call on her commanding officer, and on his return, about an hour later, he again sent for me and said that after a conference with Captain Barclay it had been decided that it would be unwise to engage in a mission which, at most, could be only temporarily successful unless a large force were landed to re-enforce it and permanently occupy the town.   It was a disappointed lot of Marines and sailors that heard the news that the order for the landing was "belayed."   All Marines and all sailors are always eager for any kind of adventure and the more difficult and hazardous it is, the better they like it.

That night the refugees at the lighthouse signalled that they were being attacked and the three ships with their secondary batteries opened fire on the approaches to the lighthouse.   This fire was continued off and on all night, the ships taking turns in firing when requested by shore signal to do so.   At daylight the Marine Detachment landed and on reaching the beach was joined by a detachment of sailors from the *Amphitrite* commanded by Junior Lieutenant Volney Chase.   We advanced cautiously through the thickets and woods to the lighthouse, and although the many piles of empty cartridge cases we found indicated that firing of considerable volume had been conducted by a good sized force, we did not encounter a single Spanish soldier.   The refugees said that firing had ceased a short while before daylight and that the attacking force had then withdrawn. We sent the refugees off to the tug and they were taken to the Port of Pence which was in the possession of the United States forces. We then returned to the ship and sailed that afternoon for the Port of Ponce, General Miles having substituted that place for Cape San Juan as the concentration point for the expeditionary force, giving as his reason for so doing the fact that it had been broadcast all over the world that the American forces would land in the vicinity of Fajardo and would therefore advance on San Juan City via the road along the northern coast.

We found the *Massachusetts,* the *Columbia* and several smaller naval vessels at anchor in the harbor, all under the command of Captain F. P. Higginson of the *Massachusetts.* General Miles, after landing a brigade at Guanica, proceeded to the Port of Ponce and preparations were made to land the major part of his force there beginning early the next morning. Under the arrangement effected, the Navy was in control afloat and the Army ashore, the beach being the line of demarcation between the two. Captain Chester was appointed Captain of the Port, Lieutenant Badger the Harbormaster, Surgeon Byrnes the Quarantine or Health Officer, and Lieutenant Hoogewerff in charge of landing operations. All of these officers were attached to the *Cincinnati.*

Early the next morning the landing of troops and supplies was begun and at about 11 A. M. the city of Ponce was occupied without opposition by a brigade. I went ashore early to observe the landing and the advance of our troops and, hiring a *carromata,* or by whatever name the one-horse shay was known in Porto Rico, another officer and I followed the troops into Ponce. We were greeted most enthusiastically, the people evidently believing that we were officers of high rank, so we drove all around town to receive the cheers and plaudits of the populace which we graciously returned by doffing our caps and bowing to the right and left. It was a gay scene; the city was bedecked with bunting and smiling faces were everywhere visible.

That afternoon a steamship flying the Red Cross flag entered the harbor and was boarded by the Health Officer and a representative of the Harbor Master. Conditions on board were very bad. It was an improvised hospital ship and was overcrowded with sick soldiers. There was insufficient medical and nursing personnel on board to care properly for the sick and the Health Officer was unable to determine offhand whether the rash or eruption, which he found on examination to be very prevalent, was due to smallpox or to some other disease, or to lack of sufficient bathing facilities. He, therefore, as a precautionary measure, placed the ship in quarantine and the Harbor Master assigned her a berth outside the other ships. These acts must have caused some consternation on shore, as it seems that the ship was loaded with military stores pertaining to the Engineers and that these stores were needed at once. The Chief of Engineers accordingly reported the circumstances to the Chief of Staff of the Expeditionary Force, who directed the Captain of the ship to move in close to the beach, and authorized the Chief of Engineers to haul down the quarantine flag and to unload his supplies.

These actions naturally had the effect of causing indignation on the part of the responsible Naval officers and the occurrences were reported to Captain Higginson. He, too, was indignant, and directed that, beginning with the following morning and until further orders, no assistance would be given the Army in landing its supplies. These instructions put an effectual stop to landing operations, as the Navy had the only power launches available for towing the loaded barges ashore. This situation continued until about 10 A. M., when General Miles sent his Aide to the *Cincinnati,* to which ship Captain Higginson had repaired. The Aide reported to him and said, "General Miles sends his compliments, Sir, and requests that the landing of the mounts of himself and staff be expedited." Captain Higginson replied, "Give my compliments to General Miles and say to him that when the quarantine flag is again hoisted on that ship over there (pointing her out) and she is returned to the berth assigned to her by the Harbor Master, I will unload his horses." Needless to say, General Miles succumbed, and landing operations were resumed.

General Miles' plan also provided for landing a flanking column at Arroyo, near Guayama, some miles to the eastward of Ponce, with which he hoped to strike to the rear of the Spanish force near Ponce. The *Cincinnati* was designated to accompany the transports and assist in landing operations. The troops were embarked on the *St. Louis* and another vessel of the American Line. The *St. Louis,* commanded by Captain Caspar F. Goodrich, steamed in close to the shore sweeping the beach with her guns, anchored, lowered her boats, and landed her troops in record-breaking time. The other ship lay far outside and had great difficulty in getting the men ashore because of the rough sea. In fact, they did not land for several hours after the men from the *St. Louis* had advanced and taken the town of Guayama, driving in the enemy outposts which opposed their advance. The *Cincinnati* anchored close inshore and again I had the opportunity to go ashore and follow the troops, this time on foot.

The following day, the *Cincinnati* proceeded to San Juan to take over the blockade duty there from the *New Orleans.* Our chief concern was the Spanish destroyer which had taken refuge in San Juan harbor and which we rather expected would make a night foray, but nothing of the kind occurred. One evening, however, we sighted a big passenger steamer heading towards San Juan. She looked like a Fall River boat, as every light appeared to be turned on and as she drew nearer we could see hundreds of soldiers about her decks and in the rigging. She stopped her engines in obedience to our signal and our Navigator, Lieutenant Badger, went on board. When he returned he had an amusing story to tell. It seems the Captain, a merchant marine officer, had received instructions from the War Department to proceed to Cape San Juan. However, the only chart of that part of the world which he had was a general chart of the West Indies on which Porto Rico was represented by a very small spot, and San Juan City was the only San Juan shown thereon. The Captain, therefore, in perfectly good faith, was heading for the harbor of San Juan City, and his ship probably would have been sunk by the guns of the shore fortifications a few minutes later if we had not stopped her. Lieutenant Badger gave him a large scale chart of Porto Rico and directed him to proceed to Cape San Juan as originally intended.

Late one afternoon in August, the officer of the deck observed a signal flying ashore on Morro Point which was made out to be to the effect that the Peace Protocol had been signed and requesting the *Cincinnati* to come in closer and communicate. With every gun loaded and manned, our ship steamed slowly in, exchanging signals meanwhile with the shore station. The Governor General asked that an officer be sent ashore to receive an important communication from General Miles. This was done, the Executive Officer going ashore in the steam launch. On his return, he delivered to the Captain a copy of the message from General Miles which contained the Peace Protocol. The Executive Officer said he had been driven in a carriage between double lines of soldiers and was escorted by a cavalry troop to the Governor General's palace. He had had a very pleasant interview, after which he was escorted back to the dock. He also said that the town was in gala attire and every one seemed delighted over the news that the war was ended.

The *Cincinnati* anchored just outside the harbor, and during the night the *Columbia* informed us officially that hostilities had ended, that the blockade was raised, and that the *Cincinnati* was directed to proceed to St. Thomas to coal ship and await orders there. St. Thomas we enjoyed greatly, as we had an unrestricted run on the beach and the opportunity to take on board some rare old wines at extremely low prices. St. Thomas was then a free port which had lost the greater part of its trade, as it had ceased to be the port of call of several steamship lines. The shops, therefore, were in most instances overstocked, and prices were correspondingly reduced.

From St. Thomas we returned to San Juan to receive the United States-Porto Rican Peace Commission of three members, of which Admiral Schley was one. They lived on board pending the evacuation of Porto Rico by the military forces and Spanish government officials, and moved ashore when our troops occupied the city, and the U. S. Governor General assumed control of the government of the island. We greatly enjoyed our shore leave in what had so recently been a Spanish city and the thrill which shot through us whenever we looked at the Stars and Stripes fluttering to the breeze over the fort and the navy yard and the public buildings. Surely patriotism, pride in the good victory achieved, and a sacred devotion to the flag—the beautiful symbol of our country—are aspirations of too great reality, strength and permanence to be eradicated from the hearts of Americans by the sophistry of pacifism.

Our duty at San Juan ended, we proceeded to Guantanamo Bay. There we found the *Infanta Maria Teresa,* Cervera's flagship, had been salvaged and was being repaired preliminary to being towed to the United States to be exhibited as a war trophy. The *Newark,* the *Vulcan,* the *Hist* and the *Alvarado,* commanded respectively by Captain Goodrich, Lieutenant Commander Ira Harris (a former Naval officer who had returned to the Navy during the war), Lieutenant Lucien Young, and Junior Lieutenant Victor Blue, were in Guantanamo Bay, and all under the command of Admiral Watson. Constructor Hobson, who was still endeavoring to raise the *Cristobal Colon,* was also with the fleet. The *Cincinnati* in a few days went down the coast to inspect the wrecks of the Spanish ships. We went on board each one of them. They must have been veritable infernos when they went ashore, shot to pieces, aflame, and filled with corpses. Even the bravest man must have felt his heart quail within him.   The *Cristobal Colon* alone was uninjured by shell or flame, but, after running ashore, had rolled over on her side and was partly resting on a rocky ledge. As we climbed over her, we felt sure that Hobson would not be able to gain his heart's desire, and that the *Colon* would lie where she fell until broken to pieces by storm and sea.

Returning to Guantanamo Bay, we witnessed the sailing of the *Infanta Maria Teresa* under the command of Lieutenant Commander Ira Harris, accompanied by the *Leonidas* and a tug.   The *Cincinnati* escorted the historic ship as far as Cape Maysi, and after signaling our good wishes for a safe voyage, we returned to Guantanamo to learn a few days later of the gale encountered by the ill-fated vessel and her wreck on one of the Bahama Islands, where her bones still lie.

The remainder of our stay in Cuba was devoted chiefly to small arms target practice, boat drills, drills on shore, and to fishing and hunting.   Deer were plentiful in the surrounding country, and hunting leave was occasionally granted to officers and selected enlisted men.   While a deer was sometimes brought back, it more often happened that the parties returned mosquito bitten, tired and empty-handed, but happy because of their excursion into unknown jungles over strange paths.   On one occasion, the hunting party lost its way and considerable alarm was felt because of its failure to return at the appointed time. This alarm was increased when one of the party came on board and recounted the suffering they had experienced. They had wandered for miles off the trails, cutting their way through the underbrush, were without water or food, physically exhausted and, except himself, unable to continue any farther.   He stated that he had left them on top of a hill near the coast, but several miles away from the Bay.   A conference was held in the cabin and it was first decided that it was best to wait until morning and then to send the *Hist* along the coast to land a party to locate and bring back the men by sea.   Dr. Byrnes, who had served in the Army on the western frontier for several years, was much disturbed, being fearful that the men would become crazed from thirst and wander off into the jungle, as he had known them to do in the arid western country. At this juncture, the cabin orderly, Private Murphy, who had heard the discussion in the cabin, volunteered to go ashore as a member of a rescue party, stating that he had been all through the country hunting, and knew the trails. I went into the cabin and offered to take a detachment of Marines ashore that evening and endeavor to find the three lost men. The plan was approved, and twelve of us, including Private Murphy, left the ship about 9 P. M., taking with us stretchers, water, soup, coffee, lanterns, etc. The hospital steward, who was the man who had brought the news aboard, volunteered to guide us to the spot where he had left the other men. We took the trail he had followed along the cliff. It was rough going and the night was dark, but we finally reached the vicinity of the place where the men were and located them by their answers to our hallos.

It was a strange coincidence that we had unwittingly followed the same route and reached the same hill as did the main column of the Marines in their surprise attack on the Spanish force in camp at Cuzco, at daylight on a June day, an attack which resulted in the complete defeat of the enemy and the cessation of their harassing night sniping at the Marines' camp on McCalla Hill.

We decided to return by the interior trail over the hills which Murphy knew instead of by the more difficult trail which we had followed, and after giving water, nourishment and stimulants to the exhausted but happy hunters, we commenced our homeward journey. It was a rough, rocky and steep path, and our progress was slow, as two of the hunting party had sprained their knees or ankles and had to be carried all the way on stretchers. We returned to the ship just before daylight, much to the relief of those on board, as they feared that perhaps we, too, had lost our way. Our good doctor administered to each of us a stiff noggin of grog, and we slept the sleep of the just despite the numerous sharp cactus needles which we had picked up ashore and which still remained in various parts of our anatomies.

The latter part of my stay in Cuban waters was saddened by very disturbing news concerning my mother's health. She and my sister, after spending the Summer in Maryland and Virginia, had stopped off at Port Gibson, Mississippi, on their way home to visit Uncle Steele and Aunt Ellie Drake. One evening while there she had fallen downstairs and was unconscious for some time. Her left arm, too, was broken, but the most alarming symptoms were the occasional lapses into unconsciousness, followed by hours of profound sleep. However, she seemed to be improving and wrote me a brave, loving letter in which she minimized her injuries and expressed the utmost optimism concerning her speedy recovery. I was greatly worried nevertheless, and chafed over the length of our stay in the West Indies. One December evening, however, a serious accident to the engines made it mandatory that we should go north. The accident occurred as we got under way to get clear of a collier alongside of which we were lying in order to take coal on board. As the engines started to turn over, there was an ominous shock which caused the ship to quiver from one end to the other, and we soon learned that it was caused by the condensation of steam in the low pressure cylinder of one of the engines, which, acting as a water hammer when the engines started, had completely fractured the cylinder's supporting brackets. Temporary repairs were made and the partly disabled ship sailed for Key West a day or two after Christmas. On reaching the Florida straits, Captain Chester decided to go into Havana harbor so as to take part in the transfer of Cuba to United States control on January 1st.

We found several ships at Havana, including a transport with a battalion of Marines on board, all under the command of Rear Admiral B. J. Cromwell. At noon on January 1st, the American flag was hoisted simultaneously over all the public buildings, the naval arsenal, and

Morro Castle. The *Cincinnati* Marines formed a part of the detachment which landed at the naval arsenal and presented arms as the Stars and Stripes were raised and the batteries of the ships and forts thundered their salutes of twenty-one guns. The wreck of the battleship *Maine* was not forgotten, as a party of sailors from one of the ships hoisted the American flag over the hulk. It was a day of national rejoicing. The flag of Spain had been lowered over the last of that proud nation's possessions in the New World, but there was a feeling of sadness, too, as we knew the humiliation the gallant Spaniards felt as the last regiments embarked and sailed for home, leaving us in full possession of their most cherished colony, Cuba, the gem of the Antilles.

On arriving at Havana, I found a telegram awaiting me informing me that my mother was growing worse and was not expected to live more than a few days longer. Captain Chester, who was one of the kindest of men, granted me leave to go home with permission to rejoin the ship at New York. I left Havana on January 1st for Tampa, via Key West, taking passage on an antiquated side-wheel steamer. It was the roughest sea trip I ever made. The old ship rolled tremendously and the waves pounded her paddle boxes so severely that I expected them to be smashed to pieces. At breakfast the next morning, I was the only passenger to appear, and all were much relieved when we arrived at Key West at 10 A. M., sixteen hours having been consumed in going eighty miles. From Tampa I went to Port Gibson, and when I reached Aunt Ellie's they told me that my mother's pure, brave, beautiful spirit had taken flight some days before, and that her body had been taken home and buried in St. Stephen's Churchyard near my father's. I left the next day for home, where I found my sister and Aunt Sarah Archer. It was the saddest period of my life and the sadness has never left my heart, but there is also joy because I know that she is happy and at peace.

My sister and I discussed freely the disposition to be made of our home, and agreed that it would be wise to dispose of it to our friend, Ovide Lacour, who already owned a number of plantations in the vicinity. This she did, and has since lived in Bel Air, Maryland, where she purchased a home adjoining the house of Aunt Blanche Archer.

After spending a few days with my sister, I went to Portsmouth, Virginia, and thence to New York, where Ellie joined me a week or two later. I found the *Cincinnati* preparing to go out of commission, and in February her officers and men were scattered to the four corners of the earth. It was with deep regret that I said good-bye to Captain Chester, the other officers, and the men with whom I had been associated. I was transferred to the *Massachusetts,* which was also at the New York Navy Yard, and it was with much pride that I assumed command of the larger Marine Detachment of a battleship, especially as the Marines manned the 6-inch guns and the two 6-pounders on the main deck, a very important part of the ship's battery.

Our chief concern at this time was the Navy and Marine Corps Personnel Bill. This bill provided for a reorganization of the Navy officer personnel. The Marine Corps section of the bill provided for a Corps of about two hundred and twenty-five officers and six thousand enlisted men, an increase of more than one hundred percentum. It meant for me immediate promotion to the rank of Captain, and a much brighter future and a more important career to which to look forward. That Congress would pass it seemed too good to come true, but it did on March 3, 1899, which has become a red letter day in the history of the Marine Corps.

My tour of duty on the *Massachusetts* was a very agreeable one. It involved a brief cruise to the West Indies and a summer spent on the New England coast, with Newport as the headquarters of the fleet. My wife, accompanied by her sister, Bessie, who had married Dr. Kennedy of the Navy, and our little girl, joined me at Newport, and in the autumn moved to Staten Island when the fleet assembled off Tompkinsville to welcome Admiral Dewey and his flagship, *Olympia,* on his triumphal return to the United States from the Philippine Islands. In all the history of the world, I don't believe any man ever before received a greater ovation than did Admiral Dewey in New York City. Literally speaking, millions of people acclaimed him as the national hero, and cheered themselves hoarse as he drove from Grant's Tomb to the Battery at the head of a brilliant military parade. It was the greatest spectacle I have ever seen except the Victory Parade in Paris on July 14, 1919, and that outpouring of millions was in celebration of a victorious peace, and not as an ovation to any individual.

Later in the Autumn, the *Massachusetts* was used to test Marconi's invention, the wireless telegraph. Sending and receiving sets were installed on board the flagship *New York* and the *Massachusetts,* also ashore at Sandy Hook, and communication between the three stations was maintained without difficulty. As the final and culminating test, the *Massachusetts* went to sea on a dark and rather stormy night, and we stood awe-stricken as we watched messages being accurately exchanged between the two ships until we were forty miles away, and occasional words or letters for twenty more miles, when all communication ceased. What is now commonplace seemed miraculous to us then. The wireless system of communication was adopted by the Navy forthwith and the Navy has never ceased to be in the forefront in its development.

At Christmas time, the *Massachusetts* went to the Navy Yard at New York and after a thorough overhaul was placed in reserve at the Philadelphia Navy Yard in May. My cruise was ended and I was ordered to my home to await orders, as was then the custom. I remained in Louisiana only a few days, returning north with my sister, who was on her way to establish herself in Bel Air. This was my last visit to my old home until after my return from the World War, when I took my wife there and with her visited the places which were so intimately connected with my childhood days.

VII

PENSACOLA AND PANAMA

FOLLOWING the completion of my tour of sea duty, I was detailed as a member of an examining board which held its sessions at the Marine Barracks, Washington, D. C. The Boxer trouble in China was at its height at that time. The marine detachments of the *Oregon* and *Newark* had been sent to Pekin to guard the United States Legation, arriving just in time, as immediately thereafter all the foreign legations were beseiged and the Seymour Naval Relief Expedition, unable to reach Pekin, made good its retreat only after the greatest difficulty. Colonel Meade and Major Waller, with all available Marines in the Philippines, were rushed to Tientsin and an international military force of considerable size was being assembled there preliminary to an advance on Pekin to relieve the legations and to chastise the Chinese government, as the Dowager Empress had adopted a decidedly hostile attitude toward all foreigners, and Chinese government troops had joined in the attack on the Seymour column and had engaged in battle with the international force at Tientsin.

Although more than a year had elapsed since the enactment of the Personnel Law, recruiting of the additional men authorized for the Marine Corps had progressed rather slowly. Consequently, a small provisional battalion of two companies only constituted the Marine Corps force sent from the United States to Tientsin in June, and an additional battalion of four companies followed it in July. It was also planned to send to China other similar battalions as fast as the required number of men became available. Majors Biddle and Dickens commanded the two battalions that actually sailed in June and July, and Major Karmany was selected to command the next battalion to be organized, and he informed me that my name was on the list of the officers to be assigned to his battalion. It failed to materialize, however, as the international force had occupied Pekin before the battalion could be organized. In the meantime, the recruiting service was expanded and an intensive drive was made to stimulate recruiting. All available officers, including myself, were assigned to recruiting duty and I took station first at Boston, Mass., then at Portland, Maine, and finally again at Boston when the curtailment of recruiting incident to the clearing up of the Chinese situation necessitated the closing of a number of offices.

The Boston climate, combined with life in a boarding house, was so injurious to the health of our little girl, who had a severe bronchial attack from which recovery was slow, that on the advice of our physician I applied for duty at a southern post. My request was promptly granted and I was ordered to command the detachment of Marines stationed at the Pensacola, Florida, Navy Yard.

The Navy Yard was then unimportant, isolated and lonely, as very few officers were stationed there, but we greatly enjoyed our stay nevertheless. We made good friends among the Pensacola people and the Army officers and their families at Fort Barrancas.

In Pensacola we enjoyed the outdoor life and balmy air all the year round except for an occasional cold snap in mid-winter, and our little girl soon regained her health. Then, at Pensacola, there came into our family again the greatest of joys; on June 9, 1902, my precious wife gave birth to a sweet little girl. We named her Laura Turpin for my mother and because Laura has always appealed to me as one of the sweetest of names for a lovely little maiden. It was a humid, hot summer following the baby's arrival, and I could see that her mother needed a change, so on my insistence she went home.

I agreed to spend my spare time fishing with my friend, Doctor Tom Kirkpatrick of the Army, who had initiated me into the mysteries of salt water game fishing. We spent many days together at Fort McRae near the entrance of the bay engaged in the most delightful pastimes. We caught sea bass, or red fish as they were locally known, *caballo,* or yellow-tail, gruper, trout, sheepshead, shark, and horse mackerel. The last named are the gamest fish for their size and weight of which I have any knowledge and are of remarkable speed and strength. I have seen them dart twelve or fifteen feet in the air when striking at a school of mullet. What a thrill I had when I hooked my first horse mackerel. It seemed to me I had an automobile going eighty miles an hour on the end of my line.

In September, Pensacola Bay was visited by what was to me a strange variety of fish. As they played in schools, coming frequently to the surface, they glistened like polished silver, so the natives called them silver fish. I learned in a day or two from Dr. Kirkpatrick that they were tarpon, and I determined to try my luck. I went out on the bay in a flat-bottomed skiff with a music boy rowing, and when far enough out I began to troll very slowly, using a live mullet for bait with the hook through his snout in the most approved manner. As quick as a flash there was a strike, the great silver fish leaped into the air, shook himself in the endeavor to throw the hook out of his mouth, and then gave a dash, bringing so sudden a strain on the line that it broke, as owing to my inexperience I kept it too taut. My tarpon was gone, and although I tried again for a while, I had no further luck.

In January, 1903, I was detached and assigned to recruiting duty in New York City pending my assignment to foreign duty.

I remained in New York for only three months, when I was ordered to Marine Corps Headquarters and assigned to duty as Aide to Colonel George C. Reid, the Adjutant and Inspector, who was in charge of the Commandant's office during Major General Heywood's absence on a tour of inspection which took him to the Pacific Coast and to Sitka, Alaska. My close association with

Colonel Reid was an experience of much value to me. He was in many respects a great man and possessed in a remarkable degree an understanding of human nature and the faculty of making friends. He was a strong, but not unbending character, as he was able to visualize the importance of sometimes yielding in non-essentials in order to obtain essentials and had the rare gift of accomplishing his purposes without creating resentments. I learned to admire him as a chief and to love him as a friend.

On General Heywood's return, I was ordered to command the so-called "Floating Battalion" on board the U. S. S. *Panther,* then at Oyster Bay, where the Fleet had assembled to be reviewed by President Roosevelt. It was with a heavy heart that I obeyed my orders, as word had gone out concerning the unhappy situation of that battalion due to the misconception of how it should be handled on the part of the Commanding Officer of the *Panther.* I had served with him on board the *Vandalia* and had no illusions in regard to my being able to induce him to modify his methods.

Soon after joining the ship, I learned that the reports about conditions had not been exaggerated, and furthermore that it was impossible for me to remedy them, as under existing orders the battalion commander had authority only over drills and instruction while on board, and when ashore he was without independent authority, but was completely subordinated to the Commanding Officer of the ship. Officers and men were dissatisfied and discontented, and the relations between the ship's officers and the Marine officers were far from satisfactory either officially or personally. The battalion, however, was a very efficient organization, having been thoroughly trained during the months it had spent in camp ashore on the island of Culebra under the able command of Major H. C. Haines. I decided to make the best of a bad job during the remaining two or three months that we would continue to serve on board the *Panther,* and then endeavor to secure the adoption of a better system when the transfer of the battalion to the *Dixie* should be effected.

On October 22nd, official information was received to the effect that the *Dixie* would arrive at Philadelphia the following morning, and that the Battalion, with its stores, would then immediately embark. We had previously been notified that when the transfer to the *Dixie* should be effected, the complement of the battalion would be increased to four companies of two officers and one hundred men each, together with a small Headquarters Detachment. The *Dixie* arrived from New York as scheduled, with the fourth company on board, and the embarkation of the battalion and its stores was completed by three o'clock in the afternoon.

As late as four o'clock in the afternoon, no one on board had any knowledge of the destination of the ship. At that hour, Captain Delano went to the Commandant's Office and reported that the ship was ready to sail, except for the arrival of the replacements, but that he couldn't very well do so until a destination was assigned. The Commandant called up the Navy Department by telephone and was then given instructions for the *Dixie* to proceed to Guantanamo Bay. Prior to the arrival of these orders, all kinds of rumors were rife among the officers and men, and a correspondent of the New York *Herald,* who was on board, stated to me and several other officers that he was positive that the *Dixie's* destination was the Isthmus of Panama. We guyed him when the Captain returned on board and announced that we would sail at daylight the next morning for Guantanamo Bay. He was unconvinced, however, and reiterated his former statement most emphatically. The evening papers published a despatch from Washington stating that the *Dixie* was proceeding to Guantanamo Bay in order to afford an opportunity for drill so as to lick the replacements into shape. It is certain that they needed the drill badly as the New York company and the men who joined from Philadelphia were nearly all recruits of only a few weeks' service.

On the way to Guantanamo Bay, Lieutenant Com-

mander Braunersreuther, the Executive Officer, after a
thorough discussion, approved the plan I had worked out
for the control of the battalion while on board ship. He
prefaced his remarks by the statement that the Commanding Officer and he were familiar with the situation that
had existed on board the *Panther,* and they were determined to avoid any similar situation arising on the
Dixie, and asked me for suggestions. I replied that the
sole purpose of putting the battalion on board ship was
to have it in readiness for service on shore in the event
of an emergency, and that it should be controlled in such
a way as to bring it to a high state of efficiency and so as
to enable it to pass from ship to shore with as little change
as practicable in its administration. With these ends in
view, I proposed, first, that the Lieutenant and the men
of one company should be detailed to ship's duties exclu-
sively each day; second, that the three companies not
detailed for ship's duties should be available for the intensive training program which I desired to put into
effect; third, that all questions affecting the battalion
should be taken up through me or my office, so that the
interior administration and control of the battalion should
be in the hands of its commander, who would be in a
sense the assistant to the Executive Officer in all matters
connected with the contacts between the marines and the
ship, and would be responsible for the discipline and
efficiency of the battalion and its readiness for emergency
service on shore.

The arrangements made meant that there must be
complete and loyal coöperation on the part of all the
officers, and I impressed on them the vital importance
of their giving me full support on the one hand, and of
their gaining the good will of the ship's officers on the
other; and furthermore, that it was our mission to make
the battalion so efficient and so useful that the officers and
men of the ship would be glad to have it on board and
proud to be connected with it. All this meant unremitting effort on the part of the battalion commander, and
in looking back over my forty-five years' service, the two

months I spent on the *Dixie* stand out as more confining and more exacting than any similar period of my career. It had its compensations, however, inasmuch as our efforts were successful and we did build up and maintain a very efficient organization, and we did gain and retain the good will and the commendation of Rear Admiral Coghlan, Captain Delano, Captain Merriam, the other officers and the enlisted men of the ship.

The arrangement which has just been outlined was put into effect on our way to Guantanamo Bay, and we expected to have ample opportunity while there to take the battalion ashore for drill and target practice, but were unable to land as we sailed the next day for Kingston, Jamaica, in obedience to the Navy Department's instructions. Immediately upon our arrival, we went alongside the dock and began to fill up with coal. About four o'clock in the afternoon, a cablegram in secret code was received, and as soon as it was deciphered orders were issued to stop coaling and to prepare to get under way. At six o'clock we steamed out of Kingston harbor and headed due east for several hours. Captain Delano sent for me in the evening and told me that the ship was en route to Colon, and that he would change course to the southward as soon as the ship was out of sight of Jamaica. He also told me that a revolution was brewing on the Isthmus of Panama and that it was probable that the battalion would be landed on its arrival there.

The *Dixie* reached Colon Harbor about 8 P. M., on November 5, and was met by the U. S. S. *Nashville*. That ship signalled, "Situation on shore very serious. Be prepared to land battalion at once." Commander Hubbard of the *Nashville* came on board as soon as the *Dixie* had come to anchor, and shouted, "Fifty men from the *Nashville* who have been guarding the railway station for some days are in imminent danger of being attacked by about a thousand Colombian troops. You should lose no time in getting ashore." All boats were in the water, loaded with two companies, and on their way ashore under tow of the steam launches in a few

minutes. Colon harbor was then an open roadstead and
a heavy sea was running, making it necessary to proceed
with great care, especially as the night was inky black
owing to the dense, low-hanging clouds from which there
began to fall one of the hardest downpours I ever experienced while we were on our way ashore. On reaching
there, we were informed that the Colombian troops, on
learning that the *Dixie* with a battalion of Marines on
board was in the offing, had decided to return home on
board the Royal Mail Steamer which sailed for Cartagena
as we landed on the dock. We took refuge from the
rain in the railway station, and as everything on shore
had become quiet and peaceful for the time being, Captain Delano and Commander Hubbard, who had accompanied me ashore, together with the *Nashville's* detachment of tired men, went back to their ships. Captain
Delano, before shoving off, gave me the instructions
received from the Navy Department, which were to the
effect that no troops, either Colombian or Panamanian,
would be permitted to land within five miles of the
railway line, or to interfere with the transit of the
Isthmus by rail.

This is perhaps as suitable a place as any other to describe the salient features of the Panama Revolution just
as I learned them from conversations with reliable people
residing on the Isthmus. It will be remembered that the
government of the United States of Colombia had failed
to ratify the treaty providing for the construction of the
Panama Canal by our government. Delay followed delay, and there seemed to be, to say the least, no anxiety
on the part of the Colombian government to expedite the
digging of the canal. The people of the Isthmus were
naturally impatient to have the preliminaries settled so
that work could begin and prosperity replace the poverty
which followed the debacle of the French canal company.
Secret plans were made in Panama to establish its independence, and the support of General Huerta, commanding the so-called Panama Battalion, was secured. At the
critical time, however, to the consternation of the con-

spirators, a transport arrived at Colon from Colombia with a regiment of troops and two of Colombia's leading generals on board. They asked for railway transportation to Panama, but Colonel Shaler, the superintendent of the railway, stated that he was unable to furnish it for the troops as all his passenger and freight cars were on the Pacific side to meet two steamers which had just arrived, but that he would be glad to loan the two generals his private car and a special locomotive to take them to Panama. They accepted, and on arrival there directed General Huerta to form the Panama Battalion for inspection, intending to take command of the troops and put him in confinement, as well as the other leaders of the secession movement. Their plans failed to work out as intended, however, as when they visited the barracks to inspect the troops and to relieve Huerta of his command, they were themselves placed under arrest by Huerta. This incident precipitated the revolution, as the leaders deemed it advisable to take immediate action. This they did by proclaiming the independence of the State of Panama and the establishment of the Republic of Panama. A provisional government was at once organized, with Señor Amador as the first President. At this juncture, the *Dixie* arrived at Colon.

The morning after the Marines landed there, I was informed that a public meeting would be held in the town hall of Colon at 10 o'clock at which important action would be taken. I attended the meeting. Outside of the building a great concourse of people had assembled. I was courteously escorted through the crowd to the entrance and then upstairs into the hall where I found a seat reserved next to the American Consul. Senor Melendez presided over the meeting which he called to order as the clock struck ten. He then read very dramatically a paper declaring that the State of Colon was and of right ought to be a free and independent state, and that it forthwith united itself with the State of Panama to form the Republic of Panama. At the close of the proclamation he shouted loudly, "Viva la Republica de Panama!" The shout was repeated by those in the hall and was taken up by the crowd outside amid much enthusiasm. Senor Melendez, in the proclamation, also stated that he had assumed provisionally the office of Governor of Colon. Copies of the address or proclamation were immediately posted al] over the town and distributed in the form of handbills to the people, so that cries of "Viva Melendez!" were everywhere heard.

When quiet in the hall was somewhat restored, Governor Melendez announced that the national flag of the new Republic would be hoisted from the portico just outside the hall, and invited the Consul and myself to join him in hoisting the flag. Both of us declined on the ground that we were present in the capacity of observers only. The flag was hoisted amid deafening shouts and the click of cameras. The photographs were widely published and showed Major Black, of the Army Engineer Corps, standing in the group on the portico. Major Black was on duty with the U. S. Panama Canal Commission and was stationed at Culebra Cut with Lieutenant Mark Brooks and several civilian assistants, to keep a record of the amount of work done by the French Canal Company subsequent to the date on which the agreement was reached for the sale of the unfinished canal and the equipment to the United States Government. Major Black was an authority on all matters pertaining to the Isthmus and his advice was afterwards of much value to me in connection with the selection of a camping place for the Marine Battalion.

A few hours after the independence of Colon was proclaimed, the Marines returned aboard ship, as Colon had resumed its normal condition of lassitude. The same old police force was continuing the performance of its functions as heretofore, and the railway trains were running freely and without any threats of interruption. In fact, it would be impossible to imagine a more peaceable, orderly and bloodless revolution. Neither was the fear of an early invasion by Colombia very acute, owing to the announcement of the United States that it would not permit any troops to land in the vicinity of the railway.   If landed elsewhere, a long march on almost impassable trails, through almost impenetrable jungles, and over almost insurmountable mountains would be necessary. Nevertheless, our country took no chances of the happening of any untoward events, and within a few days the U. S. S. *Mayflower,* flying the flag of Rear Admiral Coghlan, and several other naval vessels arrived at Colon, and the Pacific Fleet, commanded by Rear Admiral Henry Glass, arrived at Panama.

Pending the establishment of a permanent government in Panama and the negotiation of a treaty with our government providing for the construction of the canal and the protection of the republic, there was a period of inaction.

The drawbacks inherent to a military organization living on board ship, were ameliorated on the *Dixie* because of the kindness and good will shown us by the Captain and the other officers, and we were tremendously distressed when Captain Delano was detached and ordered home to appear before a retiring board because of deafness.   He was greatly beloved by all the officers and enlisted men of the ship, both Navy and Marine Corps, and it was our unanimous verdict that he was the Prince of Captains and that we preferred him, even though he were deaf, to any other Captain that we knew of.   On leaving the ship he gave me a copy of that part of his report which referred to the Marine Battalion.   It was most complimentary and commendatory, and all of us were deeply grateful to him, especially those of us who had served on board the *Panther* and had there dwelt in a different kind of atmosphere from that prevailing on the *Dixie*.

After Captain Delano's departure, there was much discussion and many surmises as to who his successor would be.   There was also some perturbation when Captain Greenleaf Merriam arrived on board.   He was regarded as being very exacting and a rather hard man to get along with.   I feel, however, that I owe it to him to go on record here and now with the statement that so far as I was concerned, I could not have asked for a better Captain. Some time after he had reported on board, we went to Chiriqui Lagoon to coal ship, as it was too rough at Colon to do so. It was an "all hands" job, and the Marines, under the personal supervision of their own officers and through the spirit of competition between the companies, made a really remarkable record. Captain Merriam frequently referred to it in conversation and made a report of it to the Admiral. In fact, he sang our praises on all occasions to such an extent that I was afraid we would be made unpopular with the officers and men of the ship.

However, we were not destined to remain on board very long after our visit to Chiriqui Lagoon, as the *Dixie* was recalled to Colon for the purpose of preparing a camp site for occupation by the Marine Battalion. During our previous stay at Colon, I had made a thorough inquiry into the subject of camp sites. All agreed that the interior was more healthful than either terminus of the railroad, and after making a careful, personal inspection, in company with Lieutenant Ramsey, the Battalion Adjutant, and Dr. Orvis, the Battalion Surgeon, I reported in favor of Emperador, but at the same time I strongly recommended that before occupying it the site be placed in a thoroughly sanitary condition by hired civilian labor. My recommendation was approved by the Admiral, and on our return from Chiriqui Lagoon, the preliminary sanitary work was begun and pushed vigorously to completion. A detachment of Marines, Captain Wirt McCreary, Dr. Orvis, and Captain Burton, the Quartermaster, were transferred to Emperador after two or three of the old French Canal Company's houses had been made fit for habitation. The mechanics went to work repairing all the houses to be occupied, and native laborers were hired to clear the hill of the jungle growth which had covered it since it had been abandoned by the French, and to scrub and disinfect thoroughly the interiors of all the houses; the old French waterworks and pipe line were repaired by machinists sent to camp from the *Dixie;* ditches were dug as drains; kerosene was used on probable mosquito-breeding places; natives were moved out of adjacent houses which were then placed in a sanitary condition; and buildings near the railway were put in shape to be used as storehouses.   I went to camp each morning and returned to the ship each evening so as to keep the Admiral and Captain informed of the progress being made.

After about a week's preliminary work, I reported the camp in readiness for occupancy, and on my request Admiral Coghlan issued written orders detaching the Battalion from the *Dixie* for independent duty on the Isthmus of Panama, and directing it to occupy the French Canal Company's houses at Emperador.   These orders were dated December 12, 1903, and the entire Battalion landed the next day.   These orders solved all the difficulties of administration which had caused so much trouble when the Battalion was ashore from the *Panther.*   The Battalion became a separate unit, and the Admiral my immediate superior in command.

About one week after going into camp at Emperador, an additional battalion, commanded by Major Lucas, which had arrived at Colon on board the *Prairie,* landed and went into camp at Bas Obispo.   Bas Obispo is now covered by Gatun Lake, and the hill I lived on for a year at Emperador was dug away during the construction of the canal.

It was a dismal looking place we occupied, but I had never before been happier professionally than I was the night I moved into a room of an old, dilapidated house on the top of the hill, after tramping up a steep, muddy trail in a heavy downpour of rain.

The rainy season continued with full force throughout the month of December and into January, but the work of making Emperador a healthful and fairly comfortable place of abode continued, every officer and man being busily employed in the task except during the early morning, when drills were held daily.   Early in January the

Dixie returned to Colon, from a trip to Philadelphia, with Brigadier General Elliott, the newly appointed Commandant of the Corps, Lieutenant Colonels Biddle and Waller, a Brigade Staff, and two additional battalions on board. They landed at once, dividing the force between Bas Obispo and Emperador, with Brigade Headquarters at Haute Obispo. Lieutenant Colonel Biddle commanded the First Regiment at Emperador, and Lieutenant Colonel Waller the Second at Bas Obispo. Major Cole and I were assgned to the First Regiment, and Majors Mahoney and Lucas to the Second. It was the first time I had served with a brigade of Marines, and I was glad to be associated with so large a number of our officers and men. The fact that we were under the immediate command of the Commandant was an event of historic importance, as no Commandant had hitherto taken the field in command of troops except Brigadier General Henderson, during the war with the Seminole Indians. General Elliott was a very strenuous commander and kept his brigade actively engaged in drilling, hiking, rifle-shooting and map-making.

Nothing startling of a military nature occurred, although many rumors of prospective attacks and invasions were prevalent. Colombia finally seemed to have accepted the situation, although with bad grace it is true, the treaty between the United States and Panama was ratified, and at last it seemed certain that the canal would be built, as no one doubted the ability of the United States to carry it through to completion, although there was much acrimonious discussion as to the type of canal to be built and the kind of organization best adapted to prosecuting the work economically, successfully, and expeditiously.

The break-up of the Brigade took place the latter part of February, and all the senior officers departed, leaving me once more in command of a separate and detached Marine battalion. The company officers were Captains Little, McCreary, Wallace and Wright, and Lieutenants McCormick, Kensel, Wiltse and Hamilton. Ramsey and

Burton remained with me as members of the Battalion Staff, and Doctors Spratling and Carpenter, two splendid medical officers, joined it on the break-up of the brigade.

Before leaving the Isthmus, General Elliott had informed me that our tour of duty on the Isthmus would be for a period of about one year, and that we could confidently count on being relieved, probably by November first. We therefore proceeded to get settled down for a fairly long stay. The health of the men was still the paramount consideration. Yellow fever, malaria, dysentery, and smallpox were present on the Isthmus, not to mention other diseases of an unmentionable nature. Drinking places, where vile liquor was dispensed, were everywhere; immoral women, many of them diseased, were in evidence; gambling dens were plentiful, and added to it all were the heavy rainfall and its accompanying mud, the dense fogs which visited us nightly, the lack of wholesome diversion, the dense population in our vicinity consisting of West Indian Negroes, the lack of roads, the thick tropical jungle which everywhere surrounded us, and the absence of governmental control of the Canal Zone pending the installation of the United States Governmental machinery.

To protect the men from disease and from the more serious effects of dissipation required discipline of the strictest kind, combined with a careful, detailed explanation of the reasons for the measures taken, close supervision over food and water, the requirement that every man leaving camp should carry with him a canteen filled with water, no liberty after 8 P. M. in the villages along the railway line, no liberty at all in Panama or Colon, screened houses and kitchens, rigid compliance with the order that the men should sleep under mosquito nets, verification that mosquito nets were being used and that men were in their bunks by means of two mosquito net inspections after taps by company officers, liberal bathing facilities and at least one bath per diem for each man, clothes to be scrubbed by the men themselves, scrubbing tables and clotheslines furnished, at least a two-hour early morning drill and hikes each day, rain or shine, muddy or dry, forenoon camp drills and instructions (not perfunctory), parade, review, or heavy marching order inspection at 4 P. M., three days each week, follow-up treatment of malaria attacks until the parasite was eliminated, flannel shirts worn at all times when out of doors to protect the abdomen and to prevent the men from becoming chilled, scrupulous cleanliness of camp, dormitories, kitchens, mess gear, etc., a liberal use of quick lime, etc., etc.

On the other hand, the men were encouraged to engage in athletics and a baseball league was formed, each company having a team, and games taking place four afternoons each week; hunting passes were issued to parties going outside the Canal Zone in charge of officers or reliable non-commissioned officers; men returning from liberty intoxicated, but not creating a disturbance, were not placed in confinement; close attention to duty by officers who lived in the same buildings and under the same conditions practically as the men; a kindly interest by the officers in the personal welfare of each man, and conscientious efforts made to protect the men from vicious and depraved associations.

We had our periods of excitement, too, just often enough to keep up the interest of the men. At first there were rumors of invasion by Colombian troops, when patrols were sent out several days' march into the interior. These expeditions over the trails were greatly enjoyed by the men. On one occasion I received a communication from Admiral Coghlan stating that he had been informed that Colombian troops had landed on the east coast for the purpose of attacking Panama, and directing me to make every effort to determine if the report were correct, and if so, to submit report as to my plans to meet such an emergency. I set out with two or three officers on horseback to make a personal reconnaissance of the trails leading to Panama, going to San Juan and over the old paved roads which had been used continuously since the Conquistadores drove their Indian slaves over mountain ranges and through tangled jungles, each laden like a beast of burden with supplies or gold or silver, or whatever else the conquerors directed. We camped on the banks of the upper reaches of the Chagres River, and took our early morning plunge in its limpid waters to the consternation of the native guides, who said that to bathe in the Chagres meant death from fever. We countered with an explanation that our mosquito nets gave us protection, but they laughed at the idea. In fact, we had a wonderful time, and my report to Admiral Coghlan giving him the desired information brought forth a commendatory letter, couched in such affectionate terms that I have put it away among my choicest possessions.

The arrival in May of the advance guard of the canal builders gave us a thrill. It was a small beginning that had a great ending. Admiral Walker, the Chairman of the Commission, Governor General Davis, Colonel Gorgas of world-wide fame because of his great accomplishments in sanitation, Mr. Wallace, the first Chief Engineer, Colonel LaGarde, the first Director of Ancon Hospital —all these and numerous others were our friends and more or less frequent visitors to Emperador. In fact, our camp was the showplace of the Canal Zone, Colonel Gorgas sending or personally bringing there distinguished visitors from the four corners of the earth to let them see with their own eyes that it was possible for Americans to keep their health, their strength and their energy when domiciled on the Isthmus.

We gave a great blowout on the Fourth of July, inviting several hundred prominent persons to spend the day at camp. We had field sports in the forenoon, when the Panama military band which General Huerta brought with him furnished stirring music, and luncheon in camp. About two hundred dignitaries were entertained at headquarters where there were spread quantities of good food and drink, Dr. Carpenter having spent the better part of several days brewing a wonderful punch. It rained in torrents, so that the baseball game which was on the program for the afternoon did not materialize, but the guests stayed on, the band played, the old house shook because of many dancing feet, and Americans and Panamanians blithely fraternized under the pleasant influence of our delicious punch. The party was voted a great success, and I never saw dear General Gorgas in after years but that he referred to it as one of the most successful parties he had ever attended, both from the standpoint of personal pleasure and international good will.

In the Autumn, we had a real thrill. One Sunday morning I was called on the telephone from Panama by Admiral Goodrich's aide, the Pacific Fleet, under the Admiral's command, having arrived there that morning at dawn. The aide said the Admiral directed that I send part of the Battalion to Panama and be ready to send part to Colon; that there was a serious situation in Panama, and that full information and instruction would be given me when I arrived. I replied that a company would go to Panama by the train due at Emperador in half an hour. Captain Little's company was selected and entrained in heavy marching order. On arriving at Panama, the company was sent to Ancon Hospital where it was quartered in one of the newly constructed hospital buildings, and the Aide took me to the American Consulate where I met Admiral Goodrich. He described the situation to me, saying that a plot to seize the President and spirit him away with the view of installing an opponent in office had been unearthed the evening before. General Huerta had invited the President and the Cabinet to an early morning review of his troops, when it was believed that the proposed seizure was planned to take place. The invitation had been accepted, but only the Minister of War and his staff actually attended the ceremony. He addressed the battalion, stating that, by direction of the President, General Huerta was relieved from his command, that the battalion was disbanded, that its members would receive their discharges and a bounty on personal application at the office of the Minister of War, that they would be given employment by the government, and that the President would be supported by the Pacific Fleet which had just anchored in the harbor of Panama. Admiral Goodrich further stated that General Huerta and the troops had accepted the situation, but that there prevailed an undercurrent of unrest in the city; that the Marines had been brought to Panama to give the President personal protection, but that it was deemed advisable that they should be quartered in the Canal Zone at Ancon rather than in the city of Panama itself.

I suggested the advisability of holding the remaining three companies, with necessary railway transportation, at Emperador in readiness for an immediate move, as there was now no apparent need for any force at Colon. The Admiral approved my suggestion and closed the interview by saying, "You are in command on shore. Make such disposition of your battalion as you deem advisable. If an additional force is needed, I will land the Marines from the Fleet to report to you for duty. If the situation ashore should become very serious, I will send the fleet landing force ashore and I will assume personal command. Establish a signal station and keep me constantly informed of the situation. I will see President Amador and tell him of your presence at Ancon, and of the instructions I have given you. I will say that so far as his personal protection is concerned, I have drawn the sword and placed it at his disposal."

I then arose, saluted the Admiral, and went to Ancon Hospital to make the necessary arrangements to carry out his instructions. The signal station was established and signals were exchanged with the flagship every half hour, and I sent an officer to President Amador's office to make effective plans for prompt communication with him. Three alternative means of communication were provided, viz: Telephone, signal lights from the roof of the President's residence, and mounted men who were members of the President's family. A guard was established and the company was prepared to meet any emergency which might arise at any hour of the day or night. We remained a week at Ancon—a perfectly uneventful week it was; the conduct and bearing of the enlisted men were perfect and drew forth the commendation of General Davis and of Admiral Goodrich. We then returned to Emperador after a thoroughly enjoyable experience and with something interesting to talk about for a while. While at Ancon, I lived with Colonel LaGarde, the director of the Ancon Hospital. He was from Louisiana, too, and had been a cadet at the Louisiana State University, and was of French extraction. We had much in common, therefore, and were most congenial companions.

In October, I received a letter from General Elliott stating that Mr. Taft, the Secretary of War, would visit the Isthmus in November for the purpose of making an inspection, and that the relief of the battalion would not be effected until December. He also directed that I personally report to the Secretary and offer him all the facilities at my disposal. He arrived at Colon on an armored cruiser, and I reported to him aboard ship, and went about the Canal Zone with him during the greater part of his stay ashore. On my urgent invitation, he and his party visited Camp Elliott, as our cantonment at Emperador had been named. It was a steep climb up the hill and the morning sun was very hot, so I provided all the horses we had for the occasion, the largest and strongest horse being assigned to Mr. Taft. He mounted without difficulty and started up the hill, but there was no horse-block or stepping-stone for Mrs. Taft. Quick as a flash, Lieutenant Provence McCormick, who, then my adjutant and who had been detailed to escort Mrs. Taft, got down on his hands and knees in the mud and insisted on her using his back as a stepping-stone. She complied with his request, and since then has frequently referred to the incident and has asked solicitously regarding the handsome, black-eyed boy who accompanied her that morning. Poor fellow! He long since met an untimely fate, but those of us who knew him will still remember his many attractive qualities.

It was an interesting week I spent with Mr. Taft, and it is with much diffidence that I make mention of my observation of his personal traits, but somehow I feel that I cannot refrain from writing here what is in my heart, and that feeling is that for me to have known a man with so great a soul and so noble a character was a privilege for which I shall be exceeding grateful during all the years of my life.

The last few weeks of our tour of duty on the Isthmus were marred by the outbreak of yellow fever among the Americans and other foreigners residing in or near the city of Panama. Hearing of it, I went to Ancon to consult Colonels Gorgas and LaGarde in regard to the precautions to be taken to prevent its spread to the Marine Battalion. Colonel LaGarde told me of the near panic among the uninformed and took me into the hospital building to show the steps that had been taken to demonstrate that yellow fever infection could only be carried by mosquitoes. In the four corners of each large ward, there had been constructed mosquito proof rooms in which lay yellow fever patients in full view of the bedridden sick. At first, the Colonel said, much excitement prevailed, but as the days passed by without any ill effects, their fears had been removed and they accepted the situation placidly and without any outward show of resentment. In a comparatively short time the fever outbreak was stamped out and it proved a blessing in disguise as it demonstrated conclusively that sanitation on a large scale and at great cost was an essential prerequisite to the construction of the canal. As for the Marines, it was decided by Dr. Bell, who was then the Battalion Surgeon, and myself that it was the part of wisdom to clamp the lid down tight during the few remaining days before our departure for home, and to prohibit officers and men from visiting Panama except on duty, and to so arrange our official business that it would seldom be necessary for any one to be sent there for any purpose whatever.

Just before Christmas time, the *Yankee* arrived at Colon with Lieutenant Colonel Thomas N. Wood and a battalion of Marines, the long looked for reliefs, on board. They promptly disembarked, entrained, and arrived at Emperador. My battalion was in readiness to go, and in a few moments we were on our way rejoicing. A smooth sea and a comfortable voyage we had until we arrived at New York, where we were greeted with a snowstorm. That was all in the day's work, however, and very quickly the battalion was disembarked and the men were on their way in detachments to every station on the East Coast. It was with a deep pang of regret that I saw the organization broken up, as I had hoped to the last that it would be kept intact and held in readiness somewhere for emergency expeditionary duty. It was a splendid body of men; men who were physically vigorous, trained to the minute, and of the highest morale. They had gone through the mill with flying colors, and had stood the gaff successfully.

When all were gone, it was my turn to go, so I left for Portsmouth, Virginia, on a month's leave of absence. At last, I was going home. I was going to see my precious family in the house on North Street which my wife had made into a home. She had had many trials while I was away. The making of a home when about to become a mother again was a heavy burden to her, and then came our darling little Ellie's illness with pneumonia that brought terror to my wife's heart and to mine too, when the news came by cable to me at Emperador; and following her convalescence, Eugenia Dickson Lejeune made her debut in the world on St. Valentine's Day, and a lovely valentine she seemed to me when I first saw her in her little carriage in front of the house where my family lived. I couldn't believe my eyes when I saw how grown up she was, as somehow I had continued to visualize her as a tiny baby, and here she was a young lady over ten months old. It was a happy homecoming. Surely, service people deserve to be rewarded for the separations they endure and the sad hearts which they so often have when sorrow or illness comes while the husband is on a far voyage or in a distant clime, and each has to bear the sorrow alone.

VIII

WASHINGTON, THE PHILIPPINES, JAPAN

I ASSUMED command of the Marine Barracks, Washington, D. C., the latter part of January, 1905, relieving Colonel Randolph Dickins. I found the barracks in process of reconstruction. The old buildings on H and 9th Street, S.E., which formerly had been used as offices for the Commandant and the Staff Departments had been torn down and Headquarters, U. S. Marine Corps, had been moved up-town to a building in the vicinity of the Navy Department. New barracks were built and a concert hall for the Marine Band, a guardhouse, and other accessories were constructed.

The old arcade barracks on 8th Street, the "Center House," and the Commandant's House were still standing practically as they were originally built in 1803 and 1804, when Headquarters Marine Corps, the Marine Band and the Headquarters Detachment of Marines were established there subsequent to their removal from Philadelphia to Washington at the time the seat of government was permanently located in the nation's capital city. In 1907 and 1908 the Center House and the Arcade Barracks were torn down, and officers' quarters were built, leaving the Commandant's House as the only building of the original group that is still standing.

President Adams, on the convening of Congress in December, 1802, recommended an appropriation for a marine barracks. This appropriation was authorized on March 3, 1803, the day before President Adams was succeeded by President Jefferson.

President Jefferson took an active interest in the project, and we read in a copy of the *National Intelligencer* of March, 1803, that he and Lieutenant-Colonel Burrows, the then Commandant of the Corps, spent a day riding around the District in order to select a suitable site for the marine barracks. The present site was then selected, and the square purchased for $8,000.

At that time, and until after the conclusion of the War of 1812, Marines were the only military force stationed in the District of Columbia and constituted, to some extent, the household troops of the President; and the Marine Band, from June, 1802, until the present day, has been the official White House band and has played at all the official functions which have taken place there during the administrations of the Chief Executives from President Adams to President Hoover. Countless have been the distinguished men and women of all nationalities who have enjoyed its rendition of the hymns of the nations and the musical works of the great composers.

The Marine Barracks at Washington has witnessed, too, many stirring events in the history of our country. When, in 1814, the nation suffered the humiliation of having its capital occupied by an invading force, which burned its principal public buildings, the barracks escaped as it was utilized by that force as quarters for its headquarters staff and detachment, the commanding officer occupying the Commandant's House. It was from the Barracks, too, that the marine detachments marched to the battlefields of Bladensburg and Bull Run, where the marines acquitted themselves like brave men and gallant gentlemen; and it was from there that the detachment commanded by Lieutenant Israel Green was sent to Harpers Ferry where, acting under the orders of Colonel Robert E. Lee, it captured John Brown and suppressed the futile uprising.

During my incumbency in command of the barracks,

our country had the good fortune to be in a state of profound peace, and consequently the only occasions on which Marines assembled there were for such purposes as participating in the inaugural parade of President Roosevelt on March, 1905.   I commanded a battalion in that parade, and I distinctly remember the impression made on me by President Roosevelt's vibrant personality and the feeling that he was looking me through and through, as I rode by the reviewing stand.

My duty at the barracks was varied by service on expeditionary duty from May to August, 1906.

In conformity with Marine Corps custom, our orders to this duty were of the rush variety, about twenty-four hours being allowed for the assembly at Philadelphia of a battalion of Marines and its embarkation, together with all its stores, on board the U.S.S. *Columbia* for transportation to the Isthmus of Panama.   Its officers and men were drawn from practically every station on the East Coast.   This system of organizing provisional emergency battalions or regiments manifestly had many inherent defects, but there was then no way of avoiding the practice as there was no Marine Corps post equipped to house permanent expeditionary units.   The battalion in this instance was to constitute a part of a regiment, the remaining battalion being stationed at Bas Obispo, Panama, under the command of Major C. G. Long. Colonel J. E. Mahoney was detailed as regimental commander, and he and his staff accompanied the battalion which was under my command.

On arrival at Colon, the battalion was at once landed and proceeded by rail to Bas Obispo, where it occupied buildings formerly belonging to the French Canal Company.   It was then the month of June and the rainy season had set in with the accompanying increase of the mosquito pest, but the men were comfortably housed and we did not anticipate any great difficulty in protecting them from malarial infection.

However, we had been sent to Panama for the purpose of preventing disturbances or uprisings at the approaching election, and Governor Magoon decided that it was important for a part of the regiment to be stationed nearer to the City of Panama than Bas Obispo. He chose Corozal as the site for the camp. Colonel Mahoney urged instead that the men be quartered in screened buildings at Balboa, and pointed out that Corozal was then low and swampy and that proper protection could not be afforded to men living in tents. Colonel Mahoney's recommendations were overruled by Governor Magoon, who insisted on Corozal, with the result that about 95 per cent of the officers and men of regimental and battalion headquarters and the three companies of my battalion which were encamped there became infected with malaria in spite of large prophylactic doses of quinine, and of every possible precaution. We were beset by swarms of infected mosquitoes, and they did their work effectively.

Our presence in close proximity to the city of Panama accomplished the desired result, however, as no serious disorder took place at election time. We preserved order, but we did not supervise the election, with the natural result that the "Ins" stayed in and the "Outs" stayed out.

After about ten days in camp at Corozal, we returned to Bas Obispo, and a few days later re-embarked on the *Columbia* and sailed for Monte Christi, Santo Domingo. On the day of embarkation, the effects of Corozal became evident, and as each day elapsed the number of sick increased greatly. Conditions became serious, as much of the malaria was of the pernicious variety and many of the men became dangerously ill. The ship's medical personnel were unable to cope with the situation, and the ship, upon recommendation of the Captain, was ordered to San Juan, Porto Rico, where a survey of conditions was made by Surgeon Stokes of the Navy, whose drastic recommendations concerning the care of the sick were put into effect by order of the Commandant of the Naval Station who, at the same time, assigned Surgeon St. J. Butler to temporary duty with the battalion.

The *Columbia* then sailed for Boston, and by the time of her arrival there Dr. Butler's untiring and effective efforts had brought about a greatly improved situation, all of the officers and men except about thirty being able to return to their permanent stations upon the disbandment of the battalion. The malarial bugs were only temporarily quiescent, however, as nearly all of us had many recurring attacks before complete cures were effected. In my own case, I had violent chills every two weeks for several months, until finally I placed myself in the hands of Surgeon R. M. Kennedy who prescribed gradually increasing doses of strychnine, arsenic and iron for six days each week, and about sixty grains of quinine on the seventh day. This treatment brought about a complete cure in two months. Dr. Kennedy had married my wife's sister, Bessie, in 1898, and was then on duty at the Naval Dispensary and as assistant White House physician.

I have gone into considerable detail in connection with the malarial infection of the battalion with the view to pointing out the danger involved in the interference with military dispositions by civilian officials. That the shoemaker should stick to his last is a safe rule to follow, especially in dealing with the operations of military forces.

As commanding officer of the barracks, I served under the immediate command of Major General Elliott, the Commandant of the Corps. General Elliott had a fine record of service in the field, having especially distinguished himself in the Spanish-American War at Guantanamo. A splendidly frank and courageous officer, and a kindly, though impulsive, and gallant gentleman he was and is, for he still survives and still retains the deepest personal interest in the welfare of the Corps and its officers and men.

In March, 1907, I was ordered to the Philippine Islands for duty with the Brigade of Marines then stationed there. My wife had not entirely recovered from the effects of a surgical operation, but she nevertheless insisted on accompanying me. Packing up and preparing for the long journey was a trying ordeal for her, but she was ready when the time came and we set forth with our three little girls on March 28th, going by rail to San Francisco, and thence by the Army transport *Sherman* to Manila. Colonel Bellinger, of the Army, who had been our next door neighbor in Washington, was then the Quartermaster in San Francisco. He did everything in his power to make our stay in the earthquake and fire-stricken city a pleasant one, and to facilitate our embarkation on the *Sherman.*

Our voyage to Manila was over smooth seas and was most restful. We stopped at Honolulu and at Guam, and at the latter place were entertained by my old shipmate, Captain Templin Potts, who was Naval Governor. Guam is a beautiful island, but too isolated and too lonely for me to have desired duty there. Manila, on the other hand, is a great city with many attractions and a very desirable living place except for the heat and the typhoons. We reached there at the hottest period of the year, the end of April, and Cavite, where I was assigned to duty, was hotter even than Manila.

Colonel Biddle, the commanding officer of the Marine Brigade during the first year of my service in the Philippines, had his headquarters in Manila. I was intimately associated with him both personally and officially, as he frequently visited us in Cavite, and I frequently went to Manila to see him. His generosity and kindness to our children endeared him to my wife and myself and a warm friendship between us was formed, which included Mrs. Biddle when he surprised his friends the ensuing year by ceasing to be a "confirmed old bachelor." I was the best man at his marriage to Mrs. Adger, and I have always felt that I never did any man a better service than I did in helping him to enter the flowery path of a happy married life.

The calm, peaceful atmosphere of Cavite and Olongapo was disturbed on July 1, 1907, by the arrival of instructions from Washington to fortify the entrance to Subig Bay, utilizing thirty-five naval guns of 3, 4.7 and 6 inch caliber which were parked in the Cavite Navy Yard. Commander Walter McLean, the Commandant of the

Navy Yard, sent for me about seven o'clock in the morning to inform me as to the orders, as it became the duty of the Cavite Marines to move the guns from the ordnance park to the waterfront and load them on barges which were towed out in the bay and placed alongside a supply or fuel ship, on board which the guns were hoisted. The Marines at Olongapo were given the task of unloading them, transporting them to the gun positions on Grande Island and the mainland, digging the gun-pits, putting the mounts in place, mounting the guns and manning them. The work proceeded apace and at Subig Bay it assumed heroic proportions. It was in the midst of the typhoon season, yet by night and by day, in tropical downpours, in storms and typhoons the men landed the guns through heavy seas, hauled them up the steep, slippery inclines, shoveled the mud from the deep gun-pits, handled the heavy timbers, and mounted the guns. Major E. K. Cole, who was in immediate command of the operations, and all the officers and men who gave their energy and their strength to the execution of their task, are entitled to the highest commendation for its expeditious and successful completion, even though hostilities did not materialize and though by the time the guns were mounted and ready for use the excitement had subsided. The friction with the Japanese Empire over the question of the alleged discrimination against its nationals by the State of California was the exciting cause, the aftermath of which was the famous cruise of the United States Fleet around the world.

What a stirring, glorious and never to be forgotten spectacle was the entry of that mighty American armada in Manila Bay, where it stopped for a few days while en route to Japan from Australia. At Manila, as at every port visited by the Fleet, it afforded a convincing ocular demonstration of the power and the might of America, and added immeasurably to the respect with which our nation was regarded. For all peoples, whether they be orientals or occidentals, are far more impressed by an exhibition of power than by the perusal of diplomatic notes. To President Roosevelt was given the ability to realize the effect of such a cruise and the courage to carry it into execution.

Such great events as I have just briefly referred to were exceptional, however, as the greater part of our sojourn in the Philippines was quiet and unexciting. The effect of the climate and the environment was detrimental to the health of my family, so I decided to take them to Baguio, the summer capital, which is located on a plateau in the Benguet mountains. After spending the night with Colonel Biddle, we took the 6 A. M. train for Camp No. 1, the then terminus of the railroad. It was the hottest and dustiest railway journey I have ever experienced, and we were delighted to change from the train at 4 P. M. to an Army spring wagon drawn by mules, by which we proceeded to Twin Peaks where we spent the night. Twin Peaks was in the midst of the mountains at an altitude of about 1,000 feet and seemed like a veritable paradise. The nipa hotel was situated on the bank and partly over a beautiful mountain stream, the huge mountain masses and the lofty peaks were everywhere about us, and a wonderful swimming pool, which had been hollowed out to a great depth by a waterfall, brought me refreshment and invigoration.

Early the next morning, we were on our way to Baguio. The road, a marvelous engineering feat, was a monument to its builder, the late Colonel Kenyon. It climbed up a ravine, frequently crossing from side to side by swinging bridges, and finally, by many sharp curves and zigzags reached the plateau on the mountain top. Camp John Hay, our destination, was then a tent city, only a few frame buildings, such as the messhall and kitchen, having been erected. Captain Hilgard was the presiding genius; he had built and beautified the camp and was its commanding officer, quartermaster and commissary officer. Everyone looked to him for everything. The air was gloriously cool and the view superb. From an altitude of over 5,000 feet we looked down on a scene of surpassing loveliness. Pine forests clothed the higher portions of the mountain range, while the foothills were covered with dense tropical foliage. In four hours we had passed from the torrid to the temperate zone.

It was very damp, however, as the heated, moisture-laden atmosphere was chilled as it blew in over the mountains, causing fogs of great density. Each evening, nevertheless, we gathered around a bonfire and enjoyed the entertainments frequently provided for our benefit by Captain Hilgard, or else entertained ourselves. The war dances of the Igorrotes were the most interesting performances we witnessed. Their costumes, consisting only of the traditional G-string, and the sound of the tom-toms added to the weirdness of the occasion. Brigadier General John J. Pershing, Mrs. Pershing and their children were at Camp John Hay, also Major and Mrs. James G. Harbord, and many other Army people. I first came to know General and Mrs. Pershing at Baguio. Mrs. Pershing was extremely charming and attractive, and the Pershing home was a delightful place to visit. Little did we dream that General Pershing's great happiness would be suddenly changed in a few years to heart-rending sorrow and grief by the calamity which overtook his wife and all of his children except little Warren, the baby we played with at Camp John Hay. I remained a week only at Baguio, as I had promised to return to Manila in time for Colonel Biddle's wedding. I put my house in Cavite at his disposal and he and Mrs. Biddle spent a few days there before sailing for home.

Dr. Carpenter and I messed together and tried to keep each other company while our families were in Baguio, but were glad to return there the latter part of May to bring them back to Cavite. We left Baguio just in time, as a day or two later a prematurely early typhoon destroyed many sections of the road, thereby marooning for two weeks those who had tarried too long at Camp John Hay. Cavite seemed hotter, more humid and more unattractive than ever on our return, and we were anxious to be transferred to Olongapo, as Lieutenant Colonel Mahoney, who had been in command there, had succeeded

Colonel Biddle in command of the Brigade; but our plans came to naught, as Mahoney was invalided home within a few weeks and I became Brigade Commander temporarily.

I fully expected a Colonel to arrive in a month or two, so we continued to live in Cavite, and I went back and forth to Manila every day by boat. My temporary duty as Brigade Commander continued for nearly a year, although each month I heard that a Colonel would be out by the next boat. The Brigade Commander at that time performed his duties under the immediate control of the Commander-in-Chief of the Naval Forces on the Asiatic Station, and occupied a position similar in that respect to that of the Commandant of the Naval Stations Olongapo and Cavite. It was a rather delicate situation, as I was a young Major, while the Commandants during my incumbency were Captain Uriah Harris and Rear Admiral Nazro. Although Rear Admiral Harber, the Commander-in-Chief, was away from Manila Bay a great part of the time, there was not the slightest friction between the Commandants and myself, but, on the contrary, both our official and personal relations were among the most agreeable and the most satisfactory of my whole career. Admiral Harber increased instead of curtailing the authority of the Brigade Commander by leaving many details of administration in his hands, but required of him the closest coöperation and the fullest information. He was an ideal Commander-in-Chief and thoroughly understood and successfully practiced the art of command.

About eleven o'clock one evening a signal message from the Flagship was received, stating that the Emperor of China and the Empress Dowager had died almost simultaneously, and directing me to report on board early the next morning. I was aboard the Flagship before seven o'clock, and at the conference which followed the Admiral asked for my plans in case it should be decided to send a force of Marines to China. I replied that any size force up to the full strength of the

Brigade would be in immediate readiness to go, but that I would reorganize the Brigade tentatively into a regiment of three battalions; that the status of the Brigade Commander and Headquarters would be changed accordingly; and that supplies for one or more companies, a battalion, or the entire regiment would be made ready at the Depot for embarkation.   He approved the plan and directed me to issue the necessary preparatory orders, but China, somehow, drifted along pretty much as before, and finally the Admiral did away with our suspense by revoking the preparatory orders for the embarkation of the Marines.   Peace reigned in China for a few months only, however, and turmoil, revolution, and war have been the lot of the Chinese people almost continuously during the past twenty years, with the result that Marines have frequently been landed at one or more of its ports to afford protection to the lives and property of Americans residing there.

The monotony of life in Cavite, too, was varied by two rather severe earthquake shocks.   One came just at dawn. I was awakened by a continuous roar like distant thunder and jumped out of bed to take a look out of the window. I could scarcely walk across the floor as the house reeled like a ship at sea.   Just as I reached the window, the tiled roof of a large building diagonally across the street slid off, making a resounding crash as it struck the street. The earth tremor soon passed by, and again there was the roar which died out gradually as it receded.   When at a great distance, the so-called drumfire which I listened to so öften during the World War resembled the sound of the earthquake more closely than any other sound I have ever heard.   The roar was unusually distinct, owing to the early morning quiet, and was scarcely in evidence during the second earthquake, which occurred some months later in the early afternoon, at a time when street traffic and other noises were at their height.

Typhoons, too, were not infrequent visitors, and for several days in succession the ladies and children would be confined to their houses because of the high winds and the downpour of rain which partook of the nature of cloudbursts. In between typhoons, especially during the winter months, social life in the Philippines was most enjoyable. Hospitality was universal among Americans residing there, and their front doors were always open as a symbol of the welcome that was within.

Our stay in Cavite wound up with the dengue fever. The entire family had it at practically the same time, the children mildly and my wife and I very severely.

My wife was thin and in a generally run-down condition following the dengue, and after dinner with us one evening in April, 1909, Admiral Harber said to me, "I want you to take your wife and children out of this climate at once, and I direct you to apply for leave tomorrow with permission to go to Japan." I obeyed his instructions and we sailed by the Army transport *Thomas* for Nagasaki, Japan, the latter part of April. We packed up all our belongings in readiness for shipment before leaving, as my tour of foreign duty was completed and I did not intend to take my family back to the Philippines upon the expiration of my leave.

After a pleasant voyage of five days, we arrived off Nagasaki. What an exquisite panorama greeted our eyes as we entered the harbor! Miniature mountains, all marvelously terraced and intensively cultivated, were everywhere. The landscape appeared to be a great checkerboard, as each little terraced field seemed to be of a different shade. The air was deliciously cool and refreshing. Ashore everything was strange and beautiful. The little houses seemed like toy houses, and the rosy cheeked children, and the grown-ups too for that matter, in their Japanese costumes, were like people in a play. The marvelous shops caught the eyes of the ladies and I, for one, wished that I had a fat bank account so I could have indulged my family *ad libitum* in the joy of collecting the beautiful articles exposed for sale. Our children screamed with delight at the sight of the man-drawn jinrikishas which furnished the means of transportation on the city streets and the suburban roads.

Altogether, the days we spent in Nagasaki and elsewhere in Japan were happy days and long to be remembered.

Our destination in Japan, however, was Yokohama, so we took passage on the Pacific Mail Steamer *Manchuria* for that place, going via the Inland Sea of Japan, one of the world's beauty spots, and stopping at Kobe and Shidzuoka. At the last named place we saw Fujiyama, the great snow-capped sacred mountain of Japan, for the first time. It fairly glistened in the rays of the late afternoon sun, and its perfect cone rose up from the midst of what appeared to be a great plain. Entrancingly beautiful is Fujiyama! It was easy to understand the reverence and the love almost reaching adoration which all Japanese people feel for it.

It was but a short voyage from Shidzuoka to Yokohama, and when we arrived there, Fujiyama was still plainly visible, and each clear day during our stay we saw it again and again, and never without a thrill. At Yokohama we had engaged rooms and board at Diana Villa, on the bluff in the quarter of the city occupied by Europeans and Americans. Yokohama itself, while in many respects a foreign city, teemed with Japanese, and many Japanese shops filled with the artistic and beautiful wares of that country lined the streets and drew foreigners within their doors like magnets.

A week after we arrived at Yokohama, Admiral Harber's Flagship, accompanied by a squadron of cruisers, came to an anchor there. I at once went out to call, and the Admiral told me that he had been informed by cable that my relief, Colonel Karmany, had reached Manila and that I need not return there, as in response to his request he had been authorized by the Commandant of the Marine Corps to order me to the United States and to grant me two months' delay en route. We decided to spend the two months sightseeing in Japan, and made side-trips from Yokohama to Kamikura, the home of the great bronze Daibutsu, or Buddha; to Tokyo, the capital city; to Nikko, the shrine city; and to other places of interest. Of all cities we visited in Japan, I give the palm to Nikko.

Nikko is one of the sacred cities of old Nippon, as it is there that the august remains of the mightiest of the Shoguns and the greatest of the Tokugawas lie buried. The Shogun, until the decade of 1860, was the military and therefore the actual ruler of Japan, while the Mikado was the spiritual ruler. The Shogun's capital was Tokyo, or Yeddo as it was formerly called, and the Mikado dwelt in seclusion in his palace at Kioto. All the chiefs of clans spent six months of each year in Yeddo under the watchful eye and in the power of the Shogun, and the Shogun once each year, accompanied by a great array of Samurai, made a pilgrimage to Kioto to do obeisance to the Mikado. Now, the Mikado or Emperor is the military, spiritual and civil ruler of Japan, and he, the most autocratic royal personage in the world, journeys to Nikko at stated intervals to pay reverence to the memory of the great Shogun who governed Japan so gloriously during the early years of the seventeenth century. Nikko is indeed a fitting place for a great warrior to lie at rest. Nestling in the mountains, with lofty peaks and the most beautiful of forests all around and about it, and with a lovely mountain stream dividing it, it seems as if it were the chosen child of nature, and as if man had bedecked nature with the most exquisite expressions of art. A majestic avenue of giant cryptomeria trees about one hundred and fifty years old leads to the north-and-south military highway along the coast, some thirty miles away; a lovely red lacquer bridge leaps across the mountain stream which is used only by the Mikado when he makes his pilgrimage to the shrine; a temple of man's most exquisite handiwork dedicated to the great chieftain who lies sleeping at Nikko, and the peaceful, beautiful grounds surrounding the temple seem to be symbolic of the repose that has come to the soul of the Shogun after many years of strenuous endeavor, warlike enterprise and rigid self-control during his life here on earth.

While we were at Nikko, the annual festival and procession took place.   Priests, maids, boys, men, women, little children and horses, dressed and caparisoned as in the days of the great Shogun, marched by representing scenes and events of which we had no knowledge.   It was quaintly picturesque, and the great height of former Vice-President Fairbanks, whom we saw towering above the crowd, accentuated the fact that the people of Nikko and vicinity seemed to be even smaller in size than the people of other sections of the ancient empire.

On our return to Yokohama from Nikko, I learned definitely that I would be unable to secure accommodations on the Army transport, so that it became necessary to engage passage for my family and myself by a merchant steamer at greatly increased expense.   I selected the *Tenyo Maru,* as that vessel was due to sail on the most convenient date, and we decided to go by rail to Kioto and embark at Kobe, the nearby port.   We found Kioto to be an exceedingly interesting city.   In it were the Mikado's Palace and many other buildings connected with the history of old Japan.   The palace, a single-story building, covered a great area.   Its interior was without decoration and in no respect ornate.   In fact, it was simplicity itself.   The wood used throughout the interior was beautiful, however, and so exquisitely polished that it had the feel of velvet to the touch.   There was no furniture anywhere visible, except the throne, and the guide told us that in the old days the Emperor's home, like that of the other Japanese, was without chairs or beds or any other articles of luxury.

Kioto, too, had many quaint little shops where we saw the artists engaged in creating the most beautiful works of art of all descriptions.   Everything was done by hand with infinite pains, and months were consumed in the manufacture (I use the word in its original sense) of a tiny piece of gold lacquer, or cloisonné, for instance.   The Japanese appeared the most industrious of people.   Seven working days constituted each week, and there was no such thing as the eight-hour day there.

Finally sailing day arrived, and although our sojourn

in Japan had been most delightful we rejoiced in the fact that at last our faces were turned towards home. However, we were to catch one more glimpse of Japan, and that under the most auspicious circumstances. The *Tenyo Maru* stopped at Yokohama for a day or two, and we had the opportunity to see there the beautiful flower festival in honor of the fiftieth anniversary of the signing of the treaty initiated by Commodore Perry of the American Navy, which brought Japan out of its state of complete isolation into contact with the nations of the rest of the world. Each of the principal streets was profusely and artistically decorated with one of the nation's famous flowers, and all most cunningly devised so as to seem to be the handiwork of nature. Arbors of wisteria, cherry trees in full bloom, the iris, the rose, and many other varieties of God's most beautiful gift to man charmed the eyes of strangers no matter where they were turned. The people, too, were in holiday attire, and street players on movable platforms as high as the second story, entertained the happy, laughing throng.

It was a charming memory to carry home, and always since then I have pictured Japan as Yokohama was on its great festival days which, by strange coincidence, were the third, *fourth,* and fifth of July. Our voyage was a pleasant one and filled with the exile's eager anticipation of the happiness which awaits him in the homeland.

The Golden Gate seemed just around the corner from home, and we lost but little time in preliminaries, but were soon on our way across the continent to Washington, to which place I was ordered to proceed.

General Elliott and I discussed the question of my next duty, and after mentioning one or two stations, he referred to the Army War College, stating that General Wotherspoon, the Acting Chief of Staff, had spoken to him about the desirability of sending an officer there. I asked and received his permission to talk to General Wotherspoon about it, who, in our interview, urged me to take advantage of the opportunity, and said that in the event of another war the graduates of the War College would be selected for positions of responsibility and for high command.   He then called up General Elliott on the telephone and requested him to assign me to the College as the Marine Corps representative during the ensuing year.   When he told me that General Elliott had acceded to his request, he added the words, "If you make good at the College, which I am sure you will do, your military future will be assured."

CHAPTER IX

ARMY WAR COLLEGE, NEW YORK, EXPEDITIONARY DUTY

ON the day I reported to Brigadier General Bliss for duty at the Army War College, I learned at once that there was a hard grind ahead of me.

I plunged forthwith into a nightly routine of study, never laying aside my books before midnight, and frequently not until two o'clock in the morning. This intensive application and concentration continued for about six weeks, when I discovered that I had overcome the greatest of my difficulties, and that what had formerly seemed to be insurmountable obstacles had been metamorphosed into hills with gentle slopes which it had become a pleasure to climb.

The close application and the constant concentration was what I needed to systematize my mental reactions and to enable me to think connectedly, logically, clearly and in proper sequence. Above all, the training in quick and accurate thinking produced the ability to formulate sound decisions expeditiously, and what had previously seemed difficult and laborious finally became automatic and instinctive. In this way, one acquires the military technique and, most important of all, sound military judgment without practicing the military art in campaigns and battles, with their accompanying hardship, suffering, danger and death. This so-called applicatory method of instruction was one of Von Moltke's greatest gifts to the military profession.

I became to all intents and purposes an officer of the Army during my stay at the War College and have ever since numbered among my personal friends many of the splendid men who constituted the College Staff or who were members of my class. The friendship of such men as General Wotherspoon, Eben Swift, Hunter Liggett, Fox Connor, Malin Craig, Eli Helmick, John Tillson, and many others who have since attained distinction, has been invaluable to me throughout my military career.

Early in the course, General Wotherspoon succeeded General Bliss as President of the War College. Both were officers of distinguished ability, and both have left their impress on the Army. General Wotherspoon had the rare gift of gaining the enthusiastic coöperation of his associates without apparent effort, and where he led, we followed gladly. He had unusually good judgment, too, and when he instituted a decided change in the course of study, we accepted his views without question. Prior to his tour as President of the College, nearly all problems had been worked out on maps of Germany and of the French-German frontier. He stated that, thereafter, our studies would be directed towards those parts of the world where it was at least possible we might some day be called on to serve. Thenceforth we devoted our attention to the continent of North America and the contiguous islands, to Hawaii and the Philippines, and to other theaters of possible operations. Eight years later, when in command of a division of combat troops, I stood on the very ground the study of which had been discarded, and gazed at the distant spires of Metz. Far-seeing man as General Wotherspoon was, it was beyond his powers or the powers of any man then living to foresee that in December, 1918, the American flag would be flying over the ancient castle of Ehrenbreitstein, and that an American Army, victorious in many pitched battles on the frontiers of France, would march in triumph to the Rhine, cross that historic river where Caesar did, and occupy a bridgehead on its eastern bank.

I mention this incident to indicate to those who read it that there is nothing so uncertain in this world of ours as international relations. What seems certain today becomes uncertain tomorrow, the probable vanishes, the impossible happens and the prognostications of wise men come to naught.

I do not believe in so-called militarism any more than I believe in so-called pacifism.   Both are fallacious; both lead to destruction, but I do believe in being ready to defend what the nation holds so that when good will and international altruism shall have been swept aside by uncontrollable emotion, or when some cunning ruler or rulers decide that the hour has struck to win more power or more land or more wealth, or their nation's place in the sun, or greater mineral resources, we may not be found weak and helpless, but ready like the strong man armed.   It is my honest and unbiased belief that national security cannot be assured except by a fair measure of national military and naval preparedness.

The College program was a delightful one.   It involved, among other things, a three weeks' horseback ride in April over the battlefields of Eastern Virginia, with an accompanying wagon train carrying a camp outfit and other supplies.   Beginning with Fredericksburg, the caravan visited the battlefields of Salem Church, Chancellorsville, The Wilderness, Spottsylvania, North Anna, Totopotomy Creek, Cold Harbor, the theater of operations of the 1862 Peninsular campaign, and finally the remains of the entrenched positions which had been constructed and occupied by the Union and Confederate armies in the vicinity of Petersburg and Richmond during the last months of the Civil War, and in which trench warfare was waged by the contending forces in much the same manner as that which took place on a vastly greater scale in the World War.

Several months before our ride was to begin, we had been instructed to study the campaigns in question, each member of the class paying especial attention to the battles or the military operations which were assigned to him.   Each afternoon during the ride it became the duty of the member of the class to whom had been assigned the phase of the campaign to be discussed the next day, to ride over the battlefield and its approaches in order to locate the positions of the troops, the roads by which they had advanced, and such entrenchments or breastworks as still remained intact.   The following morning, he conducted the party to the battlefield or the theater of operations and described, on the ground where the operations took place, the various phases of the battle or campaign, holding what in these days is termed a critique.   Much discussion was, of course, forthcoming so that our ride was of immense value to us professionally, not to speak of its physical advantages.

In June, we engaged in another horseback excursion, this time combining the working out of tactical problems with the battlefield studies.   Leaving Washington, we proceeded via the battlefields of the first and second battles of Manassas, thence to Winchester and Antietam, and finally to Gettysburg.   The month of July we spent at the large national guard encampment at Gettysburg, having been detailed to assist in the training of the national guard regiments encamped there.   It was very interesting and instructive duty, and as during practically all of our daylight hours we were busily employed out of doors, either on foot or on horseback, we were in the best of condition physically.

August, September and October were devoted chiefly to general staff work, and at the end of the fourteen months of intensive indoor study and active outdoor military exercises, there was unquestionably a marked professional improvement in all of us.

In looking back on my career, it is perfectly apparent to me that the fourteen months at the War College constituted a very marked dividing line in my professional life, and that during the years that have followed the completion of the course I have been conscious that I possessed greater mental power than I before realized, and have felt able to meet successfully any difficulty which might confront me, or to overcome any obstacle which I might find in my path.   For this reason, and because of their many kindnesses, I have the deepest sense of gratitude to General Wotherspoon, the instructing staff, and the members of my class.

I also owe an additional debt of gratitude to General

Wotherspoon for the report he made to General Elliott concerning my work and my qualifications. I will not quote it here owing to its highly commendatory nature; it is sufficient to say that it had a far-reaching effect in giving me a standing among Army officers which stood me in good stead when I arrived in France during the World War, unattached and without a command.

Near the end of October, I received orders assigning me to the command of the Marine Barracks, Navy Yard, Brooklyn, N. Y. From four to five hundred men were stationed there, of whom approximately one hundred and twenty-five were recruits under training. The remainder of the detachment was employed in guarding the Navy Yard and in the customary special duty.

Due partly to the location of the barracks in a district which was plentifully provided with more or less disreputable liquor saloons and dives, there were many disciplinary difficulties to contend with.

One by one, improvements were made, and changes effected.

The practice of excusing all special and extra duty men from reveille and from all drills and military instruction was discontinued, and in lieu thereof, every man in the garrison except the mess-hall and kitchen force was required to fall out for reveille and to participate in the setting up drill and double time which followed it, and all special and extra duty men were required to attend at least one drill period per week. All special privileges in regard to liberty, etc., were withdrawn and all men were treated alike in that regard. Discipline was strictly but justly enforced, and at the same time, the Commanding Officer and the officers, by personal interviews with offenders, were often able to induce them to mend their ways. Improvements in the mess were effected, and a program of entertainments of varied sorts was put into effect. Encouragement was given to athletics, especially to baseball, and every man who was not proficient in swimming was required to take swimming lessons at the Naval Y. M. C. A. under the guidance of the swimming instructor there.

Gradually there was an improvement in conduct and a dimunition in the percentage of desertions. The first year the figure was reduced from nine to seven per centum, and the ensuing year to five per centum. Although much gratified at the progress made, I was not satisfied with the existing conditions. I believed that there was too much idle time, or, as the men expressed it, too much "bunk fatigue," and I therefore finally put into effect a new routine which I had had under consideration for a considerable period.

This routine provided for afternoon military instruction in addition to forenoon drills, and changed liberty call from 11.30 in the morning to 3.30 in the afternoon. Combined with the initiation of the new routine, the importance of preventing the military instruction from becoming perfunctory in its nature was stressed, and the officers were urged to give thought to making it varied and interesting. Nearly all the officers expressed the opinion that the change would cause discontent among the men and that its effect, therefore, would be detrimental so far as their conduct was concerned. To their amazement, there was not one absentee after the next pay day and not one case of intoxication was reported.

I was interested also to learn that an examination of the records for the preceding five years showed that this was the first case of the kind in that period. While in the remaining months that I was on duty at New York this record was not again equalled, there was, nevertheless, a marked falling off in the number of absences without leave and other offenses, and desertions dropped to two and one-half per centum; or in plain English, in three years a reduction from nine desertions for each one hundred men at the Barracks during a year to less than three was effected.

All of our time, however, was not devoted to the solution of these local problems, as one expendition was sent each year to the West Indies and one to Nicaragua during the period 1911 to 1913, both inclusive.

The first of these expeditionary forces embarked at Philadelphia in March, 1911. It consisted of a brigade, made up in the usual way by assembling detachments from all eastern posts at the embarkation point. My first information of the proposed movement was a long distance call from Washington about 10 o'clock one evening. Colonel McCawley, who was on the other end of the line, gave me advance information to the effect that a detachment, consisting of certain officers whom he named and two hundred enlisted men of the various grades, would be transferred to the brigade at Philadelphia the next day, to arrive at its destination not later than noon.

I asked why my name was not included in the list, but he said he did not know. I sent a telegram to Headquarters urgently requesting that I be detailed to duty with the brigade, and then went to work.

It was an all-night party. At eight o'clock the next morning all the details had been completed and the detachment marched to the tug which transported it to Jersey City, where it entrained. Then my disappointment came in the form of a telegram expressing regret that my request for duty with the brigade could not be complied with.

Two days later, I went to Washington and expressed my disappointment to the Commandant and to his assistant, Colonel Cole, in vigorous terms. Both seemed surprised that I should have been so anxious to go, stating that the destination was Guantanamo Bay, and that it was altogether probable that it would remain in camp there for two or three months and then return to the United States without getting a glimpse of Mexico, which was then in a turmoil because of the Madero revolution against the Diaz regime. I then and there went on record as an applicant for duty with every expeditionary force.

Both General Biddle and Colonel Cole promised to act favorably on my request when another emergency should arise. I took this action because I wanted the field experience which could be gained only on expeditionary duty, and because I felt convinced that one's military reputation could be enhanced only through the instrumentality of active service in the field. There was also in my mind the intuitive thought that there might be some time in my career an opportunity for service in some great arena, when my success might well depend on the knowledge and the experience I had previously gained on expeditionary duty.

During the last days of May in the ensuing year (1912), my visit to Washington bore fruit. On this occasion it was a disturbance in eastern Cuba which precipitated the movement of Marines. Colonel Karmany was detailed to command the expeditionary brigade and sailed with the First Regiment to Guantanamo Bay. I was assigned to the Second Regiment, commanded by Colonel J. E. Mahoney. The companies and Headquarters Detachments of the Regiment embarked on board the vessels of the North Atlantic Fleet. The New York Company and myself were assigned to the U. S. S. *Ohio,* commanded by Captain Buchanan, then at anchor off Tompkinsville, Staten Island. The vessels of the Fleet sailed with Key West, Florida, as their destination. After lying at anchor there for several days, I received instructions to report on board the U. S. S. *Minnesota,* Rear Admiral Usher's Flagship, and immediately sailed for Guantanamo Bay.

On reaching there, the Marines were landed, and as soon as I stepped on shore, orders were handed me to embark on the U. S. S. *Culgoa,* with two companies of Marines, and proceed to Santiago and, upon arrival there, to assume command of the Marines stationed in that district. The mission assigned was to protect American mining interests in that vicinity and the lives of the Americans employed there from the depredations and the violence of the insurrectionary bands which were at large throughout that section of Cuba. A large Cuban military force was at the same time engaged in the pursuit of these bands and was making every effort to put an end to the insurrection.

The Marines under my command were distributed as follows: One company, commanded by Captain Manwaring, at El Cuero, an iron mine on the coast some eight miles to the westward of Santiago; one company, commanded by Captain Gulick, at Él Cobre, a copper mine in the interior about nine miles from Santiago and connected with that place by railroad and road; one company, commanded by Captain Delano, at Ocana and at an important railway bridge some ten miles to the eastward of Santiago; one company, plus the detachment from the Naval Station at Guantanamo Bay, commanded by Captain Bearss, at Firmeza and at nearby mines and other important localities; and a small detachment at the ore dock at Santiago.

My duties involved the coördination and supply of these forces, the gathering of information concerning the military and political situation, sending reports at least twice daily to the Brigade Commander, making frequent inspections of the detachments, and coöperating with the Senior Naval Officer in command of the Naval vessels at Santiago and vicinity. I also kept in close touch with the Commander-in-Chief of the Cuban forces, whose headquarters were in Santiago, with the American Consul, and with the Juragua Mining Company. In fact, I lived with Mr. de Berniere Whitaker, the Vice President and General Manager of that Company, who had a comfortable bungalow situated on a hilltop across the bay from the city. Through him I was able to obtain rail or water transportation at any hour of the day or night to all the stations occupied by Marines.

The six weeks I spent at Santiago were by no means quiet weeks. There were frequent alarms and many rumors of impending attacks. For instance, early one morning, while at Firmeza, I received a message from El Cuero in substance as follows: "Camp fired on from both flanks and from front and rear. Firing continued all night. No casualties." I left by rail for Santiago immediately, and thence by tug for El Cuero.   On reaching El Cuero, the *status quo ante* had been resumed, as there were no signs of any armed bands in the vicinity. In the inquiry that I instituted, the information was elicited that unquestionably the camp had been fired on the night before, as several bullet holes through the tents and one or two bullet marks on the trunk of a tree were shown me, but I could find no one who had seen or heard the movements of any part of an attacking force, indicating that the firing had been from a distance.   I instructed the officers that, under similar circumstances, patrols should be sent out to endeavor to locate and engage the hostile force, and that firing from the lines around the camp should be withheld until there was a certainty that the camp actually was being attacked. Some weeks afterwards, it was learned that the firing on the camp was done by employees of the mine on their way home after a Saturday evening spent in the "cantinas" where the contents of their weekly pay envelopes had been exchanged to a great extent for the ardent spirits purveyed there.

Rumors spread like wildfire, and at each repetition are grossly exaggerated, especially in war or insurrection, and by the same token surmises are repeated as facts and dreams as realities.   Care always must be exercised, under such conditions not to be unduly alarmed, as usually there is little or no foundation for the reports brought in by natives, but at the same time one cannot afford to neglect to take reasonable precautions, as occasionally the unexpected might happen and disaster result.

Finally the leader of the insurrection was run down and killed by the Cuban forces.   The chief having been killed, the uprising came to an end and the withdrawal of the Marines from the mines followed soon thereafter.

I was sent via the U. S. S. *Prairie* to Panama, where a Court of Inquiry, of which I was senior member, was convened at Camp Elliott, to investigate a report made by an enlisted man against one of the officers.   I lived with the Commanding Officer, Major Smedley D. Butler, during the time the court was in session. The Canal was practically finished, but not then in use, as the water in Gatun Lake was of less than half the required depth.

The successful completion of the Canal was due to the genius of General Goethals and his assistant engineers, and to the sanitary work of General Gorgas. After floundering along without satisfactory progress in the attempt to build the Canal under the management of a commission, President Roosevelt had solved the problem by appointing General Goethals Chairman of the commission and Chief Engineer, and had vested him with plenary authority. From that moment, success was assured, as successful conduct of all great enterprises requires that there shall be a single, competent head who is entrusted with full power over his subordinates and who can be held responsible for the prosecution of the work by the appointing or electing power.

The Court of Inquiry concluded, I returned to New York by passenger steamer and arrived the last week in July just in time to see a detachment of Marines leave for Philadelphia to form a part of the expeditionary force which sailed the next day for Nicaragua under the command of Colonel Joseph H. Pendleton.

Early in February, 1914, I was again detailed to duty with an expeditionary brigade which was sent to Guantanamo Bay to be in readiness for service in Mexico, where the situation had become more acute then usual. I was assigned to the Second Regiment, commanded by Colonel George Barnett. It was assembled at Philadelphia and embarked on board the Army Transport *Meade*. The *Meade* had been out of commission for several years and was, to put it mildly, in poor condition. Everything appeared to be out of order except the main engines, the boilers and the hull. The deck leaked, the hoisting engines refused to function, the electric lighting plant didn't produce light except occasionally, the rubber airport gaskets had been reduced to punk by age so that many airports leaked, etc., etc. Fortunately, our voyage was over smooth seas and we reached Guantanamo without

the transport being subjected to a real test.   Nevertheless, we were glad to get ashore and in camp on Deer
Point, a familiar spot to Marines in those days.

The two months at Guantanamo were devoted to field
training and to rifle practice.   There were available an
ample terrain, well adapted for training purposes, and
splendid rifle ranges.   I fired the sharpshooter's course
for the last time in my career and succeeded in qualify-
ing, although forty-seven years of age.   The qualifica-
tion course then was more difficult than now, as it included skirmish runs and firing at 800 and 1,000 yards.
I also had special duty as senior member of a board to
draw up a plan for the defense of the Naval Station by
an expeditionary or advanced base force of Marines.
This duty involved a thorough personal reconnaissance
of the surrounding country by the members of the board
and the making of maps by a selected group of officers.
Altogether, it was a useful, if not exciting experience.
Finally, the break came and the brigade was sent home,
disbanded and dispersed.

Our sojourn at the Brooklyn Navy Yard was made
socially very pleasant because of the friends we made
not only among the families stationed at the Yard, but
the civilian residents of Brooklyn as well.   Our friendship with a number of charming people in Brooklyn came
about in an unexpected way.   Immediately after our arrival at the barracks, we begun, as has been our invariable
rule, to look around for a church with which to identify
ourselves.   For several successive Sundays we attended
different churches until finally we went to the Church of
the Messiah.   At the close of the service, some one sitting behind me placed his hand on my shoulder and said,
"Hello! Gabe."   It was Louis Mowbray, a Naval Academy classmate, who left the Academy in our second class
year and had become a successful architect.   He was a
vestryman of the Church of the Messiah, and on his invitation we then and there selected a pew and entered
our girls in the Sunday School.   Mowbray introduced us
to his wife, their two children, Anthony and Virginia,

and to the rector, Dr. St. Clair Hester, and his mother, sister, two daughters and son.   The Mowbrays and the Hesters became our closest personal friends and through them we met many delightful people.   Mowbray was a trustee of Berkeley Institute, an excellent girls' school, and he arranged for our three girls to enter the Institute, with the result that their nearly four years' stay in Brooklyn afforded them much enjoyment.

The latter part of October, 1913, I was greatly astonished by the receipt of a confidential letter from Rear Admiral Victor Blue, the then Chief of the Bureau of Navigation, and probably as close to the Secretary of the Navy as any officer of the service.   He stated, in substance, that Major General Biddle had applied for retirement, that Secretary Daniels was about to take up the question of the appointment of his successor, and that my name was among those under consideration by the Secretary. He further informed me that the Secretary wanted to see me and have a talk with me on the following Tuesday morning at ten o'clock, and suggested that I come to his (Blue's) office and he would introduce me to the Secretary.   I was duly presented to the Secretary and had a half-hour personal interview with him.

My youth and my rank—I was only a Lieutenant Colonel—militated against my appointment at that time, a fortunate circumstance for me, as had I received the appointment I would have missed the greatest experience of my life, and would not have been the commander of the immortal Second Division, A. E. F., during the World War.

The officers most prominently mentioned as successors to General Biddle were Colonels Waller, Karmany and Barnett, the last named being finally selected and appointed as of February 14, 1914.

CHAPTER X

ADVANCED BASE FORCE MANEUVERS ON CULEBRA ISLAND, WEST INDIES—OCCUPATION OF VERA CRUZ, MEXICO

THE General Board of the Navy, prior to the establishment of the office of the Chief of Naval Operations in 1915, was charged with the duty, in conjunction with the Naval War College, of drawing up plans for Fleet maneuvers. In 1913, the plan provided for holding the maneuvers during January, 1912, in the Vièques Sound region, which lies to the eastward of the Island of Porto Rico. It was further planned that the Island of Culebra, which is situated in the region just referred to, should be temporarily occupied and fortified by the Marine Corps Expeditionary or Advance Base Force for use as an advanced base for the Fleet.

That force was to be a small brigade composed of two regiments, the first, or Fixed Defense Regiment, consisting of one battery of navy landing guns, one signal company, one engineer company, one harbor defense mine company, and two batteries of 5-inch navy guns (four guns each); and the second, or Mobile Regiment, consisting of one battery of navy landing guns, one machine gun company, and four rifle companies.

The First Regiment was permanently stationed at the Navy Yard, Philadelphia, and its officers were able to prepare detailed plans for its embarkation and disembarkation and for its part in the defense of the Advanced Base, but the Second Regiment existed only on paper and was to be assembled and organized on the eve of sailing in the customary Marine Corps manner. We had been informed that the Brigade would sail just after New Year's Day—Brigade Headquarters and the First Regiment on the *Hancock,* and the Second Regiment on the *Prairie.*

The Marine Corps, however, played true to form so far as the Second Regiment was concerned, as on the day before Thanksgiving my orders were received directing me to proceed to Philadelphia immediately and assume command of the Second Regiment which was being assembled there. The Regiment embarked on the *Prairie,* together with all of its stores, within twenty-four hours and sailed for the Naval Station, Pensacola, Florida.

Upon reporting to the Navy Department that arrangements had been effected to quarter the Regiment ashore, instructions were issued for it to disembark and occupy the buildings which had been selected, and directing me to assume charge of the entire Navy Reservation which included not only the Navy Yard proper, but also the Naval Hospital and the towns of Warrington and Wolseley.

Our month's stay at the Navy Yard was devoted to military training preliminary to the maneuvers and to improving living conditions there.

While there, the report of the Chief of the Bureau of Yards and Docks on the subject of reopening the station was transmitted to me for consideration and comment, especially with reference to his recommendation that the Navy Yard be reopened to a limited extent only by assigning to duty there a Naval Constructor, a Supply Officer, a Civil Engineer, and a Regiment of Marines, each department to be conducted as a separate unit and independently of the others. My comment was to the effect that the arrangement suggested would result in such a state of military anarchy that the Navy Yard would not be a suitable station for a regiment of Marines. I did, however, recommend that the reservation be turned over to the Marine Corps and stated that it could, at comparatively small expense, be easily prepared for use as a regimental post.

This recommendation was, I then understood, tentatively approved, but during our absence in connection with the Fleet Maneuvers the urgent need of a training station for naval aviators was decided to be the paramount consideration, and the Naval Station was transferred to Naval Aviation, then an infant activity, but which has since become one of the most important and powerful branches of the national defense; and at the Pensacola Navy Yard, have been trained practically all Navy and Marine Corps aviators since 1914.

Pursuant to orders, the Second Regiment re-embarked on board the *Prairie* and sailed for Culebra a day or two after New Year's Day.

It was a crucial period in the history of the Corps and all of us felt that much depended on the success of our efforts.   This belief, I was afterwards reliably informed, was fully justified.   It seems that in a conference held at the Navy Department in the office of the Aid for Operations, Captain Fullam had urged that he be detailed to command the Advanced Base Force, stating that the Marine Corps would never successfully accomplish the very difficult task assigned to it of its own volition, but would have to be driven to do it, and that Rear Admiral Badger, the Commander-in-Chief of the Atlantic Fleet, had vigorously replied that he had never known the Corps to fail in any duty which it undertook, and that it would be an uncalled for humiliation of its officers and men to accede to Captain Fullam's suggestion, and that he would not stand for it.

After-events demonstrated the soundness of his contention.   Both regiments were keyed up to a high pitch of enthusiasm and an intense zeal pervaded the entire force.   Officers and men labored by day and by night, completed their difficult task before the arrival of the Fleet, and acquitted themselves so well during the defense operations which followed as to earn the commendation of the Commander-in-Chief and the other senior officers of the Fleet, among them Captain Sims, who was the Chief Umpire.

We re-embarked and sailed for Pensacola early in

February, and on arrival there, Colonel Barnett, who had been appointed the Commandant of the Corps, was detached and ordered to Washington. Major Neville and I accompanied him, as we were to appear before a board to be examined for promotion to the next higher grades.

On our way north, Colonel Barnett reiterated the statement which he had previously made to me that I would be assigned to duty as the Assistant to the Commandant. I expressed my willingness to accept the detail, but a week later, having in the meantime learned that the Advanced Base Brigade would be held in readiness at Pensacola and New Orleans for possible service in Mexico, I wrote to General Barnett expressing my appreciation of his desire to assign me to duty as Assistant to the Commandant, but telling him also that inasmuch as I had succeeded him, at least temporarily, in command of the Brigade, I could not willingly consent to give up the opportunity which might be forthcoming for active service on shore in Mexico, and asking him not to detach me from duty with troops at that time. He replied that he would comply with my request for the time being, but that when the emergency had passed, he would carry out his original intention.

My letter was written in New York, where I had gone on a week's leave of absence to see my wife and children, as they had continued to occupy my quarters at the Navy Yard during my temporary absence on expeditionary duty in accordance with the Marine Corps practice. To forego duty in Washington where I would have been with my family was a hard decision to make, but I did so with the approval of my wife who, then as always since our marriage, unselfishly put her own wishes in the background whenever they conflicted with what she and I deemed to be the right course for me to follow.

My orders directed me to proceed to New Orleans for the purpose of assuming command of the Advanced Base Brigade, which was then distributed as follows: Brigade Headquarters and First Regiment on board the

U. S. S. *Hancock* at New Orleans, and the Second Regiment ashore at Pensacola with the *Prairie* standing by. A short while after my arrival on board the *Hancock,* the *Prairie* sailed from Pensacola for Vera Cruz, Mexico, with Second Regiment Headquarters and the four rifle companies on board, Lieutenant Colonel Neville having succeeded me as Regimental Commander.

At Vera Cruz, there was in addition Major S. D. Butler's Panama Battalion distributed on board the ships of Rear Admiral Frank F. Fletcher's squadron. That battalion was assigned to the Second Regiment upon the arrival of the *Prairie* at Vera Cruz.

The *Hancock* remained at the New Orleans Navy Yard for some weeks after I reported on board and we chafed because of our inactivity and scanned the newspapers closely for news from Mexico. Finally, on Easter Sunday, orders arrived for the Marines and their stores to be landed at the Navy Yard immediately, preliminary to the sailing of the *Hancock* for Tampico to take American refugees on board for repatriation.

These orders were a sad blow to all of us, but the officers and men worked cheerfully all night and the next day, so that by two o'clock in the afternoon we had about completed our move ashore. Just at this time an urgent message from the Navy Department was received directing the Marines to re-embark with their stores, and the *Hancock* to proceed with despatch to Tampico. Again it was an all night task, but this time zeal and enthusiasm easily mastered fatigue and the desire for sleep, and at an early morning hour officers, men and stores were on board and the *Hancock* was steaming down the Mississippi River and on her way to the scene of excitement and probable military operations.

The splendid morale displayed by the men in the face of what must have seemed to them useless labor was characteristic of Marines. The harder and the more difficult the task assigned to them, the more cheerful and the more enthusiastic they are. Throughout my entire career, I never have known them to fail to meet successfully any emergency or any trying situation with which they have been confronted.

My mind was filled with this thought when the Hancock arrived in the roadstead off the mouth of the Panuco River, and it was the thought which actuated me in the conference with Rear Admiral Mayo which took place immediately after I reported to him on board the U. S. S. *Dolphin* which, together with the *Chester* and the *Des Moines,* was anchored in the Panuco River within a cable length of the custom house wharf at Tampico.   In the outer roads, in addition to the *Hancock,* were the battleship *Minnesota* and several other vessels.

The Tampico incident which a few days before had stirred the people of the United States to a tense state of excitement, involved the arrest of a U. S. Naval officer and two men on some imaginary or trumped up charge, and their removal from a ship's motor boat which lay alongside the customary boat landing. Admiral Mayo demanded and obtained their immediate release, but his further demand for a public apology from the local authorities and the firing of the national salute to the American flag had been refused on the ground that it was an international question which could be settled only by the central government of Mexico.   Admiral Mayo reported the occurrence and his demand to the Navy Department. President Wilson sustained Admiral Mayo's position, and transmitted a peremptory demand that the required action be taken to General Huerta, who had been the provisional President of Mexico since the assassination of President Madero.   President Huerta did not accede to the demand of President Wilson, and Admiral Mayo was, at the time of the *Hancock's* arrival, engaged in the preparation of plans for the occupation of the city of Tampico, by the naval landing force at his disposal.

At the conference on board the *Dolphin,* there were present besides Admiral Mayo, his staff, myself and Lieutenant Powers, my aide, Commander Moffett of the *Chester,* Commander Vogelgesang of the *Des Moines,* Commander Ralph Earle of the *Dolphin,* Major Butler who was on board the *Chester* with two companies of Marines, and Major Harry Lee, the Division Marine Officer. The question of organization and command was first discussed, and Admiral Mayo decided that the combined landing force should be commanded by me and that it should be composed of a brigade of three regiments, the *Hancock's* regiment of Marines commanded by Lieutenant Colonel Long, a regiment of sailors commanded by the Executive Officer of the *Minnesota,* and a mixed force from the ships anchored off the Tempico wharves commanded by Major Butler. A careful study of the city and its environs was then made, and the general plan was prepared in conference and approved by Admiral Mayo.

We began work at once on the necessary field orders and detailed instructions, and the American Consul was sent for in order to inform him of the proposed action. Just after he came on board, we were astounded by the receipt of a radiogram from Rear Admiral Fletcher stating that he intended to seize the custom house wharf at Vera Cruz early the next morning, and directing Admiral Mayo to proceed with despatch with all the vessels under his command to that port.

This information produced a state of consternation, as the Consul felt certain that the landing at Vera Cruz would so antagonize the authorities and the people of Tampico that the lives of the Americans residing there would be in serious jeopardy. Admiral Mayo so reported by radio to Admiral Fletcher and requested a modification of his orders insofar as the *Dolphin* and *Des Moines* were concerned, which vessels he strongly recommended be retained at Tampico as asylums for American refugees. He postponed leaving Tampico until daylight the next morning with the hope of receiving a reply to his message before getting under way. Daylight came, however, without the receipt of further information, and the three ships got under way and steamed down the river to the outer roadstead.

It was not until then that the long expected reply arrived.   It directed the *Minnesota, Hancock* and *Chester* to proceed immediately with full power to Vera Cruz, but authorized Admiral Mayo to remain with the other vessels as requested.   Already, however, the storm had burst, the news of the landing and the fighting at Vera Cruz had been flashed all over Mexico, and Tampico was in a turmoil.   Fortunately for our nationals a British and a German cruiser were at anchor in the Panuco River close to Tampico, and the Americans were offered the privilege of asylum on board those ships.   This they gladly accepted, and apart from the loss of their belongings they escaped without any serious personal injury.

The *Hancock* arrived at her destination after daylight the next morning, and in obedience to signal from the Commander-in-Chief, anchored beyond the vessels of the Atlantic Fleet which were strung out for several miles outside of the Castle of San Juan de Ulloa, which guards the entrance to the inner harbor of Vera Cruz.   As soon as the motor boat was in readiness, Commander Willard, the officers of the Brigade Staff and I proceeded to the Flagship to report in person to Rear Admiral Badger, the Commander-in-Chief.   He and I had been shipmates on board the *Cincinnati,* and his Chief of Staff, Captain C. F. Hughes, was a classmate; I received a warm welcome from both of them.

They briefly outlined the situation and the events which led up to it.   It seems that a German steamer had arrived at Vera Cruz with a large cargo of arms and ammunition on board for delivery to the Huerta government, and that instructions had been received from Washington to seize the custom house so as to prevent the landing of the arms.   In consequence, a brigade of Marines and sailors, commanded by Captain W. R. Rush, and Lieutenant-Colonel W. C. Neville, had been landed on the day before, April 21st, and had occupied the wharf without opposition, General Maas, the Mexican commander, having withdrawn from the city with the organized military force.

There still remained, however, the police force, a

number of stragglers from General Maas' force, the battalion of naval cadets or midshipmen at the Naval Academy, and a great many armed civilians.   These elements of the population opened fire on the Marines and sailors from nearby buildings, and sniping and street fighting ensued, resulting in a number of casualties.   In spite of this fact, the railway yards, the waterfront near the custom house, and the adjacent part of the city had been cleared of opposition and was in the possession of our forces by nightfall.

During the night, the landing force of the main body of the Atlantic Fleet had disembarked immediately after the arrival of the Fleet.   It consisted of a regiment of sailors commanded by Captain E. A. Anderson, and the regiment of Fleet Marines commanded by Lieutenant Colonel A. W. Catlin.   As we stood on the upper deck of the Flagship that morning—April 22nd—we witnessed a scene which stirred us to the very depths of our souls. We saw Captain Anderson's regiment of sailors in column of platoons debouching from a street into the large plaza on the side opposite to the Naval School.   Suddenly an intense fire was opened on our men from the windows of the school buildings.   They scattered to take cover, when suddenly the *Prairie* and the *Chester,* which were at anchor near the shore, opened fire on the school buildings with their 5-inch guns.   The accurate fire of the guns had a magical effect, as the school buildings were quickly vacated by the naval cadets and immediately thereafter fell into the hands of our shore forces.   Commanders Stickney and Moffett, by their quick decisions to turn their guns on the school buildings and the efficient work of the gun crews, brought a speedy termination to what promised to be a serious engagement, and thereby, in all probability, prevented a large casualty list.

Admiral Badger, after a brief conference, directed me to further report on board the *Prairie* to Rear Admiral Fletcher, who had temporarily hoisted his flag on that vessel, and who was in command of the shore forces and the supporting ships.

No time was lost in getting on board the *Prairie,* and after reporting, Admiral Fletcher ordered a signal to be sent to the *Hancock* directing the landing of the Marines on board that vessel.

The interview ended, our party shoved off and went alongside the sea wall at the custom house.   In my eagerness to get ashore, I jumped prematurely and fell overboard between the launch and the sea wall.   Being heavily laden with pistol, binoculars, haversack, canteen, ammunition, etc., I went down like a plummet and had to exert myself considerably to come to the surface.   However, with the assistance of Major Louis Magill and Lieutenant Powers I managed to climb back into the launch without any ill effects except a ducking, which stood me in good stead the remainder of one of the hot days for which Vera Cruz is famous, as the evaporation from my wet clothes kept me cool and comfortable.

After a brief talk with Captain Rush and Lieutenant Colonel Neville, I assumed command of the Marine Corps force and the section of the city which had been assigned to the jurisdiction of the Marines.   Upon the landing of the First Regiment, it was directed to relieve the Second Regiment and to continue the house-to-house inspection for the purpose of seizing all arms and ammunition concealed therein, and the placing under arrest of all men found with arms in their possession.   Colonel Catlin's regiment was detailed to provost duty and on it was placed the responsibility of preserving order within the limits of the Marine Corps sector.   The Second Regiment was quartered in the trainyard, and the First Regiment in a large flour mill.   These two regiments held the defense line which covered the Marine Corps sector of the city, the Second Regiment on the right and the First Regiment on the left.

We had no definite knowledge of the location and plans of General Maas' force, except that it had withdrawn from the city and had retired to the sand hills outside.   Rumors concerning it flew thick and fast; to these I paid no attention.   It was necessary, though, to give consideration to reports from presumably reliable sources, such as American officials. Rather early in the afternoon, one of these reports came to me in the form of a note from the American Consul in which it was stated that reliable information had been received to the effect that General Maas, with six thousand Mexican troops, probably would attack the city during the night. I arranged for a defense line near the outskirts of the city and called attention to the importance of patrolling and alertness. About dusk, another and more alarming note was sent me by the Consul, in which he quoted information he had received from what he claimed to be a thoroughly reliable source. In this note it was averred that General Maas, at the head of a well organized and efficient force of eight thousand men, supported by artillery, was within two or three miles of the City and was even then making preparations for an attack in conjunction with an uprising of the people of Vera Cruz. I directed one company, commanded by Captain Dyer, to cover the approach to our position from the direction of Vergara and Lagarto, and one company, commanded by First-Lieutenant Stone, to establish an outpost on the highway leading into the city from the sand hills, about one-half mile in front of our main position. The guns of the artillery batteries were put in place and contact maintained with the outpost companies.

The men on the defense lines were carefully instructed to refrain from firing except at a well recognized hostile target, and the men within the city were cautioned not to fire their rifles at all, but to use their bayonets should active measures become necessary. These instructions were strictly adhered to, and not a shot was fired by a Marine that night, and no untoward events of any description occurred in the part of the city guarded by Marines.

The following day, Rear Admiral Fletcher moved his headquarters ashore to the Administration Building, and my headquarters were established in a school building. Up to that time, the American flag had not been hoisted over the buildings occupied by the landing force, and the ensuing morning at the daily conference of senior officers held in the Admiral's office he submitted the question for discussion and asked each officer for his opinion. Some favored and some opposed hoisting the flag. I happened to be the last one called on, and I replied, in substance, that the American flag should fly over American troops no matter where they might be located, and I recommended that the national colors be hoisted over his headquarters in the presence of a guard of honor consisting of the Marines and sailors who had landed the first day, and that a national salute of twenty-one guns be fired.

He approved the suggestion, and a few hours later the ceremony took place. A most impressive and memorable ceremony it was and there was scarcely a dry eye among the Americans who participated in it or who witnessed it. President Huerta had declined to hoist and salute the American flag, but we had forcibly seized his principal maritime city and had ourselves wiped out the indignity which had been put upon our country.

In the days that followed there was much uncertainty as to the action to be taken by our Government. The great question to be settled was whether or not a general intervention in Mexico, which would have been tantamount to war, would result from the capture of Vera Cruz. The decision was a momentous one over which we had no control, as it rested in the hands of the administration in Washington. Civilians would make the decision, but if active military operations should take place, I wanted the Marines to be prepared to accompany the Army, the advance guard of which, under the command of Brigadier General Funston, was preparing to sail from Galveston. I therefore directed the Brigade Quartermaster, Major Lemly, to procure all the carts and animals he could find, as we were without transportation of any kind, and also directed the organization of the three companies of artillery into a battalion of artillery under the command of Major Dunlap. He was instructed to convert his battalion into a mobile, mule-drawn force. Requisitions for essential material were transmitted by wireless to Washington and every effort made to place the Marine Brigade in a state of readiness for active service.

General Funston's arrival would, however, mean his assumption of command on shore and the embarkation of the naval forces. In my judgment it was essential for the best interests of the Marine Corps that the Advanced Base Brigade should be detached for active duty with the Army, and that the Marine Detachments should be returned to their ships. I accordingly so recommended. Admiral Badger approved the recommendation and instructed Captain Hughes and myself to draw up a radiogram for transmission to the Navy Department embodying his views. This we did, and before General Funston's arrival the reply approving the plan and containing the President's instructions was received.

Our comrades of the Navy and Marine Corps left us, and we became a part of the Army of Occupation. Temporarily we adopted Army Regulations, Army discipline and Army administration, and temporarily we passed under the command of the distinguished Kansan whose colorful career was well known to all of us.

Personally, I ceased to function as Brigade Commander, but turned the command over to Colonel Mahoney who, with Colonel F. J. Moses, had arrived on a chartered steamer with an additional regiment of Marines. At Mahoney's request I acted as Chief of Staff for a few days so as to give him the opportunity to acquire the requisite information, and was then detailed to my old command, the Second Regiment. Mahoney, a few days later, assumed command of the First Regiment, having been superseded as Brigade Commander by Colonel Waller.

I was putting on my equipment preliminary to leaving Brigade Headquarters for Second Regiment Headquarters a few blocks away, when I heard an excited conversation going on over the telephone concerning a wireless broadcast from the garrison of the city water works at El Tejar, calling for immediate assistance to repel a threatened attack by what purported to be a Mexican force of a thousand men. Colonel Mahoney was instructed by Army headquarters to send all available Marines to El Tejar, and I asked that he send me in command of the force and recommended that the reserve battalions of the First and Second Regiments be directed to proceed immediately to El Tejar, also the Artillery Battalion equipped as infantry. He approved my recommendation and I at once mounted my horse and rode towards Second Regiment Headquarters. Before reaching there I met Major Smedley Butler on the march at the head of his battalion, and as we passed the quarters of the Artillery Battalion and First Regiment the column was joined by their quotas of the composite force, with Major Dunlap at their head.

To reach El Tejar involved a march of about nine miles along the railway track, and we therefore lost no time in boarding a train of freight cars which overtook us and which had on board a large contingent of infantrymen. Major Dunlap's detachment, however, continued by marching as it had already obtained possession of a sufficient number of ponies to provide mounts for a large proportion of its officers and men.

On the arrival of the train, the infantrymen and

Marines were immediately deployed and moved in the direction from which the attack had been expected, but no Mexican force was found to be in the vicinity. Major Butler and I climbed a hill and carefully searched the countryside with our binoculars, but failed to discover any sign of a force of any description. Patrols were sent out in various directions, but with the same futile result.

We learned, after conferring with Major J. H. Russell and the other officers of the garrison, that the broadcast message was sent because of the fact that a Mexican soldier, bearing a flag of truce, had come to an outpost position with a note from his commanding officer which demanded the surrender of the water works, and which further stated that unless his demand was complied with he would attack with his force of about one thousand men at the end of ten minutes. The demand had been refused and dispositions made to meet the attack, but it had not been forthcoming.

The threatened attack on El Tejar remained one of the insoluble mysteries, as no definite information concerning it could be obtained, but it is my belief that it was a piece of bravado on the part of an officer in command of a small mounted detachment which had approached to the vicinity of El Tejar through a near-by woods which screened his detachment from view, not only during its approach, but during its withdrawal as well.

Such occurrences, however, keep up the interest of an occupying force, and prevent it from becoming indifferent and careless. The rapid movement of the troops was a good object lesson too, and produced a feeling of security among the inhabitants of Vera Cruz, who became exceedingly friendly to the officers and men of the Army and Marine Corps who were dwelling among them, even though they were subject to military government and to the jurisdiction of military or provost courts.

The mission of the occupying force was two-fold, involving as it did both the defense of the city from attack by Mexican forces, and the maintenance of law and order among its civilian and military population. To the everlasting credit of the United States, it can be stated with all truthfulness that the people of Vera Cruz had never before experienced a more just and humane government than that given them by General Funston, nor had the laws ever been more impartially or honestly administered.

Peace, justice and honesty reigned in Vera Cruz during the seven months of its occupation by the United States forces. In addition, many important public improvements were accomplished and beneficial sanitary measures were put into effect. Certainly, the Mexican people who came into contact with the Americans of the occupying force lost some of their prejudices.

Much could be written concerning the details of the performance of daily tasks, the preparation of defensive positions, the drills and military exercises, the earnest efforts made to build up and maintain the morale of the troops under very difficult conditions, the sanitary precautions taken, the outpost duty performed by day and by night, the rumors of impending attacks, the northers which visited us, the tropical downpours which flooded us, the insect pests which were our most dangerous enemies, our daily mode of life, and many other matters of more or less interest, but I believe a mere mention of them will suffice, as this book has already taken on larger proportions than I had anticipated.

Our experiences there were, in fact, dwarfed, even in our own minds, by the stupendous events which were taking place in Europe. We watched every move of the opposing armies with the most intense interest, and frequent were the discussions we had over the progress of the war. Sentiment was, of course, divided, some favoring the Allies and some the Central Powers, but gradually sentiment among us crystallized into a belief in the wisdom of President Wilson's policy—a policy which, briefly stated, was America united, America unafraid, America first.

It is not surprising that there was much discussion as to whether our country would be sucked into the terrible maelstrom in which nearly all the European peoples were struggling. Personally, I am and was a fatalist, and I could not cast aside the intuitive belief that there was a grave possibility—in fact, a strong probability—that our country would eventually be engulfed in the European maelstrom. This belief was shared by the thoughtful officers of the regiment which I commanded, and they joined wholeheartedly in the effort which was made to bring the regiment to the highest state of efficiency which our then knowledge of the art of war permitted. This was clearly our most important duty.

Incidentally, the training of troops when intelligently directed is the greatest of morale builders, as they are quick to sense that they are being prepared to meet effectively any emergency that may arise, and after all that is the real reason why the majority of men enlist in the Marine Corps.

Finally, the administration in Washington decided that the hour for withdrawal from Vera Cruz had arrived, and the long looked for embarkation orders were issued about the 15th of November. All supplies having been loaded, the entire force embarked simultaneously on the improvised transports which had been held in readiness for weeks. The orders provided that on the morning of embarkation, the colors should not be hoisted, and that at "zero" hour each regiment should march by a previously designated street to the transport wharf. There was to be no blare of trumpets, no martial music, no cheering, but the march and the embarkation were to be conducted quietly and in complete silence.

The withdrawal of the outposts was so timed that they would reach the dock simultaneously and immediately after the completion of the embarkation of the main body.

The Mexican forces followed the outposts at a fixed distance and, entering the city quietly, moved into the designated barracks or quarters and took up the patrolling of the streets. Carranza, the successor of Huerta as Provisional President, accompanied his troops and established his headquarters on the waterfront in a position of readiness for flight by sea. Pancho Villa was then in possession of Mexico City, having driven Carranza and his government from the capital because of a quarrel between the two chieftains following their joint military success. Some months later the Mexican people, having tired of Villa's vagaries, ousted him from the capital, and Carranza returned to continue his administration under the usual tempestuous conditions.

In fact, it is just as well that we were not required to remain in Vera Cruz until internal peace should be completely established, as under such circumstances we would, in all probability, still be stationed there.

The transports sailed immediately after the embarkation was effected and the vessels carrying the Marines set their course for Cape Henlopen, at the mouth of Delaware Bay. Evidently King Neptune, fearing that we would be weaned from the Navy by our long service with the Army, issued a manifesto to those of his minions who control the sea to still the boisterous winter waves, for our ships sailed over a smooth and smiling sea. Neptune, however, must have had poor liaison with the imps who produce the fogs, as we were held up for hours at Cape Henlopen by a dense fog which caused the Second Regiment's arrival at Philadelphia to be delayed until nearly midnight on December 1st.

It was a clear, balmy evening though, and as the ship was being moored, I saw my dear wife standing on the dock awaiting me. Her bright, smiling face told me as plainly as words could that all was well with her and with our dear ones. The next morning, in obedience to orders, I turned the command of the Regiment over to Lieutenant Colonel Neville, and my wife and I were on our way to New York to pack up our belongings preliminary to changing my permanent station to Washington.

DUTY AS THE ASSISTANT TO THE COMMANDANT OF THE MARINE CORPS

ON January 2, 1915, I assumed the duty of the Assistant to the Commandant, relieving my classmate Colonel Eli K. Cole, who had been assigned to that office by Major General Biddle. General Biddle had recognized the need of a line officer of rank and experience to assist the Commandant in coördinating the various activities at Headquarters, especially with reference to matters pertaining to military training, military education, and equipment of troops, with their organization, distribution, and assembly at embarkation points for expeditionary duty.

The assignment of officers and men to the various ships and stations, and the keeping of rosters for sea and foreign service, likewise required the personal attention of an assistant, while the necessity of preparing war plans, of itself alone, made it mandatory that the Commandant should have the assistance of an officer of the requisite military education and technical knowledge.

To summarize briefly, the growth of the Corps in numbers and in importance, naturally, carried with it the creation and development of an organization at Headquarters, which would be able to assist the Commandant in administering its current affairs efficiently, and in making preparations to meet future eventualities successfully. In other words an Executive Officer, or Chief of Staff, had become a necessity.

Each day new problems came to me for solution,

and unaccustomed difficulties were encountered. To take intelligent action and to make sound decisions necessitated painstaking investigation and much thought.

Nowadays a qualified executive staff would be at my disposal under similar circumstances, but at that time, owing to the lack of sufficient officers in the Corps and to the prejudice which then existed against the employment of additional officers at Headquarters, I, at first, was thrown to a great extent on my own resources except for the faithful and efficient enlisted men who, in addition to their routine clerical work, performed many other tasks which ordinarily would have been assigned to commissioned officers.

Gradually, however, as the burden of my work increased and became heavier than I could bear alone, I sought and obtained the assistance of Captains Thomas Holcomb, Earl Ellis, and Ralph Keyser, the Commandant's very able aides, and we together constituted to all intents and purposes the executive staff, which worked together in the preparation of war plans, and in their execution during the strenuous war and pre-war days until I turned over the duties of my office to my successor.

During the latter part of July, 1915, there came the first test, during my tour of duty at Headquarters, of Marine Corps organization and its arrangements for furnishing supplies to an expeditionary force in an emergency. At nine o'clock one morning, Lieutenant Wilson Brown (Admiral Benson's aide), called me up by telephone and told me to be prepared to send a force of approximately 700 officers and men to Haiti via the U.S.S. *Prairie* from Philadelphia. Haiti was then in a turmoil. The customary semi-annual uprising against the President of Haiti had resulted in the capture of the capital, Port au Prince, by the insurgents. The President, instead of fleeing the country as most of his predecessors had done when the revolutionary army reached the plains of the Cul de Sac (just outside the city), had attempted to overawe his enemies by summarily executing a large number of political prisoners. This infuriated the populace and, feeling that his life was in danger, he took refuge in the French Legation, whence he was forcibly dragged out by the mob and decapitated. His head was fixed upon a pole, ropes were attached to his body, and the mob paraded the streets carrying his head and dragging his body at the head of the procession. Anarchy prevailed; a French man-of-war landed a detachment of sailors to protect the Legation; and there was imminent danger that other nations would intervene to protect their nationals.

Fortunately, the U.S.S. *Montana,* flying the flag of Rear Admiral Caperton, was in near-by waters and within a few hours had arrived at Port au Prince and landed two companies of Marines and the sailor battalion, with Captain Edward L. Beach, U. S. Navy, in command of the joint force. The landing party was at once reinforced by the Marines stationed at Guantanamo Bay. Order was restored in Port au Prince, and the lives and property of the foreigners residing there were no longer in jeopardy. The French sailors returned to their ship, and Admiral Caperton was able to induce the political leaders to select Mr. Dartiguenave, a peaceable citizen of good reputation, as Provisional President instead of one of the revolutionary military leaders. Additional forces, however, were needed to restore peace and tranquility to the remainder of the seaport towns of Haiti, as a state of anarchy everywhere existed, and the people were completely at the mercy of the Cacos—the name given the lawless, semi-bandit military bands which infested and preyed on the country. An additional force of Marines was therefore requested by radio, and it became my duty, when notified by Lieutenant Brown as already narrated, to issue the necessary instructions and to attend to the essential details connected with the sending of the expeditionary force. Owing to the absence of General Barnett on a tour of inspection of Marine Corps stations on the

Pacific Coast, I was Acting Commandant at the time, and therefore carried the responsibility which ordinarily rested on him, as well as the responsibility which normally was my own. However, it proved to be a simple task and was attended to in an hour.

I notified by telephone Colonel Cole, then on duty in command of the Marine Barracks, Annapolis, Maryland, to stand by for orders to expeditionary duty and to proceed immediately to Philadelphia to relieve Lieutenant Colonel Neville in command of the Second Regiment, as the latter was under orders to command the Legation Guard at Peking. I then called up Colonel Waller, who was in command of the Advanced Base or Expeditionary Brigade, at Philadelphia, and informed him of the Department's instructions. He was directed to transfer from the Second Regiment to other organizations all men with less than six months to serve, or who were unfit for field service, and was told that a sufficient number of men from Parris Island who had completed their recruit training would join the Regiment at Hampton Roads when the *Prairie* stopped there en route to Haiti. I then gave verbal instructions to the staff department heads and notified the Bureau of Medicine and Surgery of the proposed movement of troops so that the necessary arrangements could be made for medical personnel and supplies to accompany the expedition. All these verbal instructions were at once confirmed by telegraph or by memoranda, telegraphic orders were sent to a sufficient number of additional officers to bring the Regiment up to its full complement, and telegraphic instructions were sent to Parris Island to transfer the requisite number of men to the Regiment, the movement by rail to be made in time to embark on the *Prairie* immediately upon the arrival of that ship at Hampton Roads. I then reported to the Chief of Naval Operations that all necessary orders for the assembly and embarkation of the Regiment and the loading of its supplies had been issued, and that reports received from Philadelphia indicated that the loading of the ship would be completed within twenty-four hours. There were no unexpected delays, and the *Prairie* sailed from Philadelphia early the next morning.

The retention of the Second Regiment at the Navy Yard, Philadelphia, upon its return from Vera Cruz, and the system of keeping in readiness for loading the requisite expeditionary stores at the Depot of Supplies, Philadelphia, greatly facilitated the movement and did away with the confusion which had formerly characterized the assembly and embarkation of expeditionary forces. Under the efficient management of Colonel McCawley, then the Quartermaster, and of Colonel Radford, then in charge of the Depot of Supplies, the supply of troops had been systematized and placed on a sound business basis. Both of these officers performed service of high value to the Marine Corps and to our country, not only during the World War, but also before its commencement and since its conclusion.

About a week after the sailing of the *Prairie*, Admiral Caperton requested an additional force of Marines, and five hundred men of the First Regiment, under the command of Colonel Theodore P. Kane, were sent from Philadelphia to Haiti by the battleship *Connecticut*, and Colonel Waller and the Brigade Staff sailed on the same ship. The orders directing him to report to Admiral Caperton for duty as the officer detailed to command the U. S. Naval Forces operating ashore in Haiti were approved by the Chief of Naval Operations, and when their revocation was later requested by Admiral Caperton on the ground that they were contrary to the plan of operations he had adopted, which provided for the officer in command of the naval vessel at anchor off each town or place where a detachment of Marines was stationed to exercise command over the shore detachment as well as his own ship, Admiral Benson declined to grant the request, stating that the Department considered it to be very desirable that Colonel Waller, acting under the immediate supervision of the flag officer in chief command, should be vested with authority over all U. S. Naval Forces operating on shore in Haiti.

The wisdom of this decision soon became manifest by reason of the success of the operations against the Cacos, and the rapidity and effectiveness with which the disorderly elements were suppressed in the interior as well as on the sea coast. Haiti was a single theatre of military operations, and in the interests of sound military practice it was essential that the principle of unity of command should be followed there.

The immediate outcome of the operations in Haiti was the negotiation of a treaty providing for the rendering of assistance to Haiti for a term of ten years, with the privilege of continuing the treaty in effect for an additional term of ten years. The treaty also specifically provided for a Haitian Gendarmerie to police the cities, towns and the rural districts, of which the officers should at first be officers and enlisted men of the Marine Corps and Navy, and the enlisted men native Haitians. American sanitary and public works engineers were also to be furnished to the exhausted country, and supervision over custom houses and the national finances would be the care of an American financial adviser. The recruitment, organization and training of the Gendarmeri proceeded apace under the able management of Major Smedley D. Butler, but Congressional authority was needed to enable officers and men of the Marine Corps to serve under and accept compensation from the Haitian Government. An enabling act passed the House of Representatives without delay, but reposed peacefullly in the files of the Senate Committee on Foreign Affairs to which it had been referred. Several efforts to secure consideration of the bill failed to have any effect. Congress was about to take a recess until after the national conventions, and a month's additional delay was in prospect. On the day the recess was to begin, we were stirred by the receipt of a radiogram from Colonel Waller, stating that there had been a jail delivery in Port au Prince; that a large number of revolutionary prisoners, thieves, murderers and other criminals were at large; that there was great unrest in Haiti owing to the failure of Congress to pass the act making the treaty effective, as this fact was being used by the disorderly element as propaganda; and that it was imperative that the bill be passed at once.

It happened to be graduation day at the Naval Academy, and Secretaries Daniels and Roosevelt, Admiral Benson and General Barnett had gone to Annapolis to attend the final exercises. I did not know any of the members of the Senate Foreign Affairs Committee, but, fortunately, Senator Salisbury, of Delaware, was a personal friend of Captain Holcomb, of the same state, and, at my request, Holcomb made an appointment for us to call on him at once. After listening to an explanation of the bill and a statement of the situation in Haiti, he said he would get in touch with the Chairman and arrange to have a meeting of the Committee called at one o'clock that afternoon, and for Holcomb and myself to hold ourselves in readiness to appear before it. Promptly at the hour mentioned, the Committee met. I stated the case briefly and answered the few questions asked. The Committee made a favorable report, the bill was considered by unanimous consent and was passed without debate and without a dissenting vote. It is still in effect and has proved to be extremely beneficial to Haiti and the Haitian people.

It is necessary now to go back to May, 1916, when the good people of the Republic of Santo Domingo, having tired of peace, turned their thoughts to internal dissensions. This was a matter of interest to our Government for a great many reasons. Not only were the large property holdings of our nationals and the nationals of other foreign countries jeopardized by the uprising, but the treaty negotiated by President Roosevelt with Santo Domingo was at stake. That treaty provided, among other things, that the custom houses were to be controlled and supervised by Americans, and that if the Santo Domingan Government should at any time be unable to protect them from domestic foes, the United States would make the necessary arrangements to provide for their protection.

Admiral Caperton, with his ships and a regiment of Marines from Haiti, arrived at Santo Domingo City at the critical moment, and upon being informed by President Jiminez that his forces were not strong enough to engage the revolutionary army in battle successfully, and that in the confusion the custom house would probably be adversely affected, he landed Marines and sailors in the capital city and occupied it.   He then gave notice to the rebels that their forces would not be permitted to enter the capital.   The remainder of the country, however, was in a state of turmoil.   The northern half of the republic was in possession of the revolutionary elements, and they were making headway, too, in southern Santo Domingo. President Jiminez concluded the moment to be an auspicious one for the tender of his resignation and left our people to bear the stigma of intervention.   It was essential though that peace should be restored as the first step towards the establishment of a stable government.   More Marines were requested, and the Fourth Regiment at San Diego, California, was ordered to proceed to New Orleans by rail and embark on a naval transport for service in Santo Domingo.   Small detachments of Marines also were drawn from each post on the East Coast and sent by light cruisers to the scene of activity.

Puerta Plata and Monte Cristi on the north coast, Sanchez on Samana Bay, San Pedro de Macoris and Barahona on the south coast, were occupied by detachments of Marines, in addition to Santo Domingo City, before the arrival of Colonel Pendleton and the Fourth Regiment.   The landing forces were opposed by revolutionary forces of considerable strength, notably at Puerta Plata, where the boats were under heavy fire from the fort and some losses were suffered, including Captain Hirshinger of the Marines.

The Fourth Regiment landed at Monte Cristi and fought its way to Santiago, while smaller columns proceeded to the same destination from Puerta Plata and Sanchez.

The operations conducted by the Marine Corps in Haiti and Santo Domingo not only greatly enhanced its reputation and prestige, but also afforded the finest kind of military training for its officers and men. This service, together with the campaign in Vera Cruz during the preceding year, laid the foundation for the brilliant and heroic services of the Fifth and Sixth Regiments and the Sixth Machine Gun Battalion of Marines in the World War.

My tour of duty as Assistant to the Commandant constituted the busiest two years and eight months of my career up to that time. It would be impossible within the limits of this volume to describe all the events in which I played a part. Probably the most important of these activities prior to our entry in the war was my connection with the Marine Corps Personnel Bill which was incorporated in the Naval Appropriation Bill and became a law in August 29, 1916. A Navy and Marine Personnel Board was convened in the summer of 1915. Its membership consisted of Assistant Secretary Franklin D. Roosevelt, Rear Admirals David W. Taylor and Victor Blue, and Colonel Lauchheimer and myself, with Lieutenant Austin of the Navy as Recorder.

The hearings on the Naval Appropriation Bill were very extensive, continuing daily for three months, but when the Marine Corps section was reached we found the members of the committee to be intensely interested in the plea for a substantial increase in the authorized number of enlisted men, and in the arguments presented in behalf of the proposed personnel legislation. When the hearings were completed, a sub-committee was appointed to draft the bill for submission to the full Committee. The sub-committee, without prior warning, summoned the Commandant to appear before it, and owing to his absence on an inspection trip I appeared in his stead and spent an entire day discussing the personnel features of the bill and answering questions in regard thereto. The item in the bill creating the grade of Brigadier General came in for the greatest amount of discussion, but finally it, together with the other proposals, was agreed to as well as an increase of about 3,000 enlisted men.

The bill passed the House as reported and was referred to the Senate Committee on Naval Affairs. The next morning, Colonel McCawley informed Lauchheimer and myself that Assistant Secretary Roosevelt had told him the evening before that at a White House conference it had been decided to provide for a much larger building program and a considerably greater number of Navy enlisted men than were contained in the House bill, and suggested that the Marine Corps take the matter up at once, as there was no time to lose. It was decided by McCawley, Lauchheimer and me that a telegram be sent to General Barnett at Wakefield, Virginia, informing him of the situation and that I should at once take up the matter with the Navy Department and the Senate Committee. This I did, and in the absence of Secretaries Daniels and Roosevelt, I went to Admiral Benson, who referred me to Admiral Blue. The latter told me he was present at the conference and that the facts were as stated. He further said that the Marine Corps was not mentioned in the conference, probably through inadvertence, and that I would be fully justified in urging a consideration of its needs on the Senate Committee. Fortunately, Senator Tillman, the Chairman, was a close personal friend and I had no difficulty in obtaining an interview with him. While talking to him, Senators Swanson and Lodge entered his office. He directed me to make a statement to the sub-committee, which consisted of the three Senators mentioned. I argued for an increase of Marines to be proportionate to the increase of Navy enlisted men, and endeavored to establish the great need for 17,500 Marines as a peace-time force. The bill as finally reported and passed authorized 75,000 sailors and 15,000 Marines, and included a proviso vesting the President with authority to further increase the enlisted personnel of the Navy by 12,000 and the Marine Corps by 2,400.

The Navy also secured the inclusion in the bill of personnel provisions similar to those relating to the Marine Corps, and in addition, a paragraph establishing a simplified form of promotion by selection combined with the elimination of those not promoted, for the line of the Navy. I have always regretted that the Marine Corps was not included in its scope, as I am profoundly convinced that such a system of promotion is the only sound system, and that promotion by seniority without elimination will ultimately result in a materially lower degree of efficiency, due to lack of incentive, too great age in grade, and the retention on the active list of inferior officers.

The Naval Appropriation Bill which became a law on August 29, 1916, was the culmination of President Wilson's efforts in behalf of a powerful fleet and authorized a larger shipbuilding program than had ever been adopted at any one time by any nation in the world's history. It also contained a great deal of other important legislation and unquestionably represented the longest stride forward ever taken by the American Navy.

I had the good fortune to be present when President Wilson signed the bill, writing Woodrow with one pen and Wilson with the other, and handing them to Congressman Padgett and Senator Tillman. It was a momentous occasion, occurring as it did during the Presidential campaign and in the midst of the most terrible war recorded in history—a war into which Fate had decreed that we should eventually be drawn.

The immediate effect on the Marine Corps of the signing of the Appropriation Bill was the promotion of Colonels Waller, Pendleton, Cole and myself to the rank of Brigadier General of the line, and of Colonels Lauchheimer, Richards and McCawley to the equivalent rank in the staff. The authorized number of enlisted men was increased by 5,000, and the number of commissioned officers from 343 to 600. This involved an active recruiting campaign for enlisted men, the examination for promotion of a great many officers, and the appointment of a large number of second lieutenants. All the distinguished military colleges were called on to recommend recent graduates for commissions.

Next in importance to personnel legislation was the need for the establishment of two stations for the organized expeditionary forces, one on the Atlantic Coast and one on the Pacific Coast.

The Commandant's annual reports for 1915 and 1916 had stressed in emphatic terms the necessity for a base on the East Coast, and urged that immediate action be taken to procure the land to commence the construction of the necessary public works connected therewith. No definite site was suggested, but it was stated that strategic considerations demanded that it be located on Chesapeake Bay, or on one of its tributaries. Secretary Daniels approved the proposition in principle, but postponed the submission of the matter to Congress owing to the very large appropriations that had become mandatory in order to carry out the great program for ships and men which had just been enacted into law. It was further stated in the Commandant's report that the base should not be located within the limits of an active navy yard, as the industrial and other Navy requirements paramount there would probably crowd out the Marine Corps activities, and furthermore that the terrain was insufficient in extent and unsuitable in all other respects for field exercises, rifle and artillery ranges, or field firing.

The selection of the sites for the Marine Corps bases was an important feature of the war plans, as it was evident from even a cursory consideration of the subject that the recruit training stations at Parris Island, South Carolina, and Mare Island, California, must needs be supplemented by stations where the organized Marine Corps forces could be quartered and given advanced training in the art and science of war.

Immediately after the declaration of war a board was appointed which, after visiting several proposed sites, concluded that, all things considered, Quantico, Virginia, came nearer than any other obtainable location to fulfilling the necessary requirements. Its lease was forthwith approved and immediate steps taken to erect and install there the necessary temporary buildings and public utilities, so that by June 1, 1917, the First Battalion of the Fifth Marines was quartered there in tents, and a short while thereafter a portion of the buildings were ready for occupancy.

In the meantime, San Diego, California, had been settled on by the House Naval Committee as the site for the West Coast Base, that city having donated a large tract of land which was supplemented by the government purchase of additional tracts. At San Diego, the buildings were permanent structures, and today it is conceded to be one of the most beautiful military posts in the United States, although the layout of the buildings is not in accord with the best practice, owing to the great distance of one end of the group from the other.

Returning to the period immediately preceding the war, the winter of 1916-1917 was a terrible period for all the combatants. The Western Front had seen terrific carnage and slaughter, combined with much suffering, without either side having been able to end the apparent stalemate. On the Eastern Front the Allied cause had suffered serious reverses. The German and Austrian people felt the pangs of hunger keenly and peace would have been welcomed by both sides, always provided it should bring with it the objectives for which each side was striving. President Wilson's plea for a peace without victory fell on deaf ears. Like two bulldogs, each combatant had fastened his fangs in the other's throat and seemed unable to let go until one or the other should completely lose all powers of resistance. Russia had nearly reached that state, but, by some strange mystery, the fact was unknown to the Central Powers. The German Emperor, like Napoleon, felt the bitterest emnity towards Great Britain, and knowing that the British naval power would continue to be able to prevent an invasion of British territory by the German army, took the fatal step of proclaiming unrestricted submarine warfare against all water-borne commerce entering a so-called war zone which Germany arbitrarily established. It came as a funeral dirge to some and as the blast of a martial trumpet to others.

The evening that the news arrived in Washington, Mrs. Lejeune and I were entertaining Secretary and Mrs. Daniels at dinner at our home at 2008 R Street. Several Naval officers and their wives were also there. While at dinner the telephone rang, the call being for Mr. Daniels. He listened intently and answered by monosyllables only. When he returned to the table the expression on his face was earnest and solemn. He said, simply, that it was a call from the White House; that Germany had proclaimed unrestricted submarine warfare. Dinner was soon over and the men went upstairs to the sitting room to smoke. Mr. Daniels then went more into detail in regard to the message he had received, and closed his remarks with the statement that no one hated or dreaded war more than he did, or loved peace better, but that there sometimes came a situation into the life of a nation when it has to choose between war and a loss of its self-respect. He paused, and then said earnestly, "This is one of those situations. I prefer war to national dishonor."

I knew then there could be no escape from war unless Germany retracted her proclamation, and when diplomatic relations were severed and German officials, acting under instructions from higher authority, endeavored to destroy the German ships which had interned in our harbors, I was completely convinced that Germany would not retract, but would do everything in her power to starve the British people, no matter what the cost might be.

The two months following the severing of diplomatic relations with Germany were full of stirring events. In recalling these events to my mind, it seems as if a great panorama were unfolded. The attempted destruction of the interned German merchant ships by their crews; the Zimmerman note to Mexico urging that nation to declare war on the United States and offering her

Texas and the territory lost by the war of 1848; the cablegram of the German Ambassador at Buenos Aires to his government, suggesting that a certain passenger vessel be sunk without trace; the publication of the story of some of the machinations of the German and Austrian agents in the United States before our entry into the World War; the arming of United States merchant ships and the assignment to them of detachments of Navy personnel to man the guns; the call to the colors of the reserves and retired officers and men; the authorization of the recruiting of 12,000 additional Navy enlisted men and 2,400 additional Marines; the ringing address of President Wilson to Congress advising a declaration of war; and the passage by Congress of the declaration of war against the German Empire.

Step by step the steep mountain was climbed until the summit was reached where, serene and unafraid, the flag was flung to the breeze as a signal to the sons of America that once again they were summoned to battle for God and for the right. Never before had a nation entered a state of war with a cleaner soul or a purer spirit. President Wilson's call to the colors made it plain to all the world that America was prompted by no selfish motives, but, like the knight of old, drew the sword in behalf of freedom, liberty and in defense of the rights of man. It was a mighty crusade and he was the leader of the crusading host. He kept the nation's honor clean and sought only the security, the happiness, and the ultimate peace of the world. Praise, honor and glory will be given to his name by the generations yet unborn.

The people of America, though, were slow to realize that America's part in the war would consist of more than the sending to the Allies of an enormous quantity of supplies and munitions, the loaning to their governments of huge sums of money, and the convoying by the Navy of merchant ships through the submarine infested waters. In fact, many officers in high places were of that opinion. I remember distinctly a conversation

I had on that subject with a senior officer, in **February, 1917.** We were discussing the probable cost of the war, and after enumerating the various items of increased expense for the Navy and Marine Corps, I remarked that, in addition, an Army of at least one million men would probably be organized. He replied, "What in the name of common sense will we do with an army of a million men?" I answered, "It is the duty of any country which sets sail on the stormy sea of international strife to so order its affairs as to be ready for all eventualities." It is a matter of history that an American army of two million men was transported to France before final victory was achieved, and two million more were in training camps at home awaiting transportation.

A few days subsequent to the declaration of war, President Wilson again electrified the country by recommending in an address to Congress the organization, equipment and training of an army of one million and a half men in three increments of five hundred thousand each, the army to be raised by the system which had come to be known as the draft. Only a short while before, I had heard prominent members of Congress state that public sentiment would be in such strong opposition to the draft that it would be hopelesslly defeated if proposed. Yet it was adopted by overwhelming votes in House and Senate and received the unmistakable support of a large majority of our people. It appealed to the public generally as a manly, fair and democratic way of meeting the grave emergency.

The President's suggestions were met by huge appropriations and the granting to him of enormous war powers. The war legislation adopted by Congress constituted the most complete demonstration of the wisdom of the great men who drafted the Constitution. Unquestionably, they had in mind, when the Constitution was written, the determination to avoid the weakness and the feebleness, displayed by the central government during the war of the Revolution, by designating the President as the Commander-in-Chief of the Army and Navy, thereby making it possible for Congress to go to great lengths in strengthening his hands when the safety or the existence of the nation should be at stake.

The Marine Corps problem seemed easy by comparison with the complicated one confronting the Army, but it taxed the resources of the Corps, nevertheless. Thousands of recruits came in almost simultaneously. The accommodations at Parris Island and Mare Island were altogether insufficient, especially at the first named place, where the bulk of the newly enlisted men were sent. Tent cities were established there, and temporary training stations were located at Norfolk and Philadelphia. Deficiencies in clothing at Parris Island caused no suffering, owing to the hot weather; temporary buildings and oyster-shell roads were constructed with the help of the recruits; food in plenty could be obtained, but there was a dearth of cooks. Men who could cook didn't want to admit it, because they had enlisted to fight and not to prepare food for the fighters. All these things were soon adjusted; Parris Island actually accommodated twelve or fifteen thousand men before the war had ended, and Quantico as many more.

The problem of obtaining and training the additional officers was also expeditiously solved. They were drawn from the Marine Corps warrant officers and noncommissioned officers, from the graduates of schools and colleges with military training, from other men with sufficient military experience, and from selected young men in civil life with the requisite educational qualifications. The quota having been filled by June, 1917, it was then directed that thereafter during the period of the war all appointments to commissioned rank should be made from enlisted men. This requirement was made mandatory for the reason that the ranks of the Corps were filled with the finest and the best product of America. The slogan, "First to fight"—a line of the Marines' Hymn—attracted the adventurous, the patriotic and the brave. Its use was the happy thought of Major McLemore, the Officer in Charge of Marine Corps Recruiting.

It is, I believe, well to add that political and social considerations had no weight in the appointment of officers. Merit alone was the governing factor. The Secretary of the Navy did not intervene in behalf of a single individual. He consistently refused to do so.

Mr. Daniels kept the photograph of his son, Josephus, on his desk, so that all who sought special dispensations for their sons or for the sons of their friends could see that his own son was an enlisted man in the Marine Corps. Frequently he sent callers to me with a card of introduction on which was written, "Do for Mr. ————'s son what you did for Josephus." A number of fine lads enlisted under these circumstances.

Early in the war, there was much discussion as to the mission of the Marine Corps in the World War. Almost immediately after the conclusion of the Spanish-American War, the Navy Department had assigned to the Marine Corps the mission of providing an advanced base force to accompany the Fleet for the purpose of seizing, occupying, fortifying and defending the temporary bases required by the Fleet in its overseas operations, and for the purpose also of carrying out the other minor shore operations which might become necessary to enable the Fleet to accomplish its mission, which, in brief, is the securing of the control of the sea. When the United States entered the World War, the Allied fleets had already obtained control of the sea except for the submarine menace. There was no available naval mission, therefore, for an advanced base or expeditionary force. At that time, our officers and men were clamoring for service. Their adventurous spirit could brook no delay. Their thoughts were constantly turned towards France.

Some of us strongly favored the sending of a Marine Corps brigade to France as a messenger or harbinger of good will. This, we believed, was especially desirable, as it was reported that the Army would completely organize and fully train its divisions before sending any troops abroad. I listened to a lecture at the War College in which this course was strongly advocated. Naturally, I had set my heart on commanding the expeditionary brigade, and began casting about for the regimental commanders and staff officers, and actually wrote to Smedley Butler, then in Haiti, to inquire if he would like to go with me in case the plan materialized. He eagerly embraced the prospective opportunity. Our plan, however, did not materialize.

Then the missions from France and Great Britain and all the Allied nations came to Washington. They included Marshall Joffre, M. Viviani, Lord Balfour, and many other noted men. Never shall I forget the faces of Marshall Joffre and Lord Balfour when I first saw them at a reception given to them at the Pan-American Building. Their faces bore the marks of the agony of soul they had endured. They seemed to have walked through the burning, fiery furnace. After speaking to them, I stood and watched them. Their inner souls seemed to be in view. I felt somehow as I gazed at them that there was great need of America, that it would be necessary for us to go to their assistance at once and with great numbers of men and of ships. I told my wife this as we drove home.

Soon, too, we learned of the great gravity of the situation from the attachés of the missions. France was bled white and could not resist much longer without our assistance. England was in grave danger of starvation because of the submarine warfare. Russia was on the brink of an internal explosion which would make that great nation helpless for a time. I heard a lecture by an English authority, delivered to invited officers of the Navy Department in the strictest confidence, in which the lecturer proved conclusively that if the sinking of ships continued at the same rate as in April, 1917, and if the construction of new ships continued at the highest possible rate of speed, Great Britain would be reduced to starvation by December, 1917.

The situation was indeed ominous. Immediate action was necessary to restore the sinking morale of our overseas Allies.   The Elihu Root Mission was sent to Russia, Rear Admiral Glennon, my son-in-law's father, being one of its members.   Destroyers were sent to England. The convoy system of protecting merchant vessels was approved.   President Wilson announced that a war strength division of the Army and a war strength regiment of Marines would be sent to France immediately as the advance guard of the American Expeditionary Force.   General Pershing was detailed as the Commander-in-Chief of the American Expeditionary Force, and he appointed Major (afterwards Major General) James G. Harbord as his Chief of Staff.   General Pershing sailed secretly with some forty other officers for England and thence to France.

There was feverish activity at Marine Corps Headquarters.   We had no organized regiments in the United States, all of our organized forces, except a few small companies, were in Haiti, Santo Domingo, and eastern Cuba.   The plan followed in creating the Fifth Marines was to utilize the small organized companies as the nuclei of the much larger war strength companies.   A number of such companies were brought home from the West Indies, the men taken away being replaced by newly trained recruits.   The first battalion was assembled at Quantico, and the second and third at Philadelphia. Additional officers and noncommissioned officers were assigned to the battalions.   Each company had, as its Captain and one Lieutenant, officers of experience.   The remaining Lieutenants were fresh from college.   Its noncommissioned officers were, to a great extent, oldtimers, but the ranks were filled by young men freshly drawn from Parris Island.   Splendid men they were. Twenty-six hundred in all was the quota.

I went to the Philadelphia Navy Yard early in June with General Barnett to inspect the regiment on the eve of its sailing.   Colonel Doyen was in command, and Majors Turrill, F. M. Wise, and Westcott commanded the battalions.   Lieutenant Colonel Feland, the second in command, had gone to France with General Pershing.

I knew all the senior officers personally and many of the men. It was a magnificent regiment.

We plunged again into work after our day's absence, and a few days later a base, or replacement, battalion of 1,110 officers and men was organized at Quantico under the command of Lieutenant Colonel Hiram I. Bearss for service overseas. It followed soon after the Fifth Regiment and was immediately utilized to bring up that regiment to the new war strength of 3,600 men.

The regiment was not a part of the First Division, but was in addition thereto, and as complete divisions only were being sent to France it was feared that there would be no place for it except in the rear areas, and besides, our officers and men were clamoring for greater opportunity for service overseas. So Secretary Daniels secured the President's approval for a brigade of Marines instead of one regiment to form a part of the A. E. F., and orders were at once issued for the organization of the Sixth Regiment of Marines.

It was assembled at Quantico under the command of Colonel Albertus W. Catlin, with Lieutenant Colonel Harry Lee as second in command, and Majors Holcomb, Sibley and Hughes as battalion commanders. The Sixth Machine Gun Battalion was also assembled there, and Major Edward B. Cole assigned to its command. In organizing these units, a different plan was followed. A sufficient number of noncommissioned officers was detailed to each to provide the complement of Sergeants, Gunnery Sergeants, First Sergeants, Quartermaster Sergeants, and Sergeants Major. The remainder of the men transferred to them were Privates. They were drawn from all stations on the East Coast and from Mare Island, California, as well.

In consequence, the Sixth Regiment had a somewhat different character from the Fifth Regiment. There were very few old-timers. Its early training was, therefore, somewhat more difficult, but it soon found itself, and when the stress of battle came no difference between the two Regiments could be perceived by unprejudiced eyes. Both were unsurpassed. So it was, too, with the Sixth Machine Gun Battalion. No better battalion served in France. Its heroic commander, Major Cole, fell mortally wounded in Belleau Wood in the early days of that struggle, but he left a magnificent battalion as a heritage to the Second Division of which it formed a part.

Coincident with the assembly of the Sixth Marines, it became necessary to organize the Seventh Regiment (1,100 men) for service in Cuba under the command of Colonel M. J. Shaw. Avowedly it was sent to Cuba because of that country's being so well adapted for training purposes. It was mounted immediately after arriving there, and was actually utilized for patrolling and giving protection to the sugar plantations to prevent the destruction of the cane crop by agents of the Central Powers. The Eighth Regiment (1,100 men), under the command of Colonel F. L. Bradman, followed the Seventh to Cuba and was brigaded with the Seventh under the command of Colonel James E. Mahoney.

When the decision was reached to assign a brigade of Marines to the A. E. F., Colonel Charles A. Doyen, then in command of the Fifth Marines, was promoted to Brigadier General and was detailed to command the Fourth Brigade, and Colonel W. C. Neville, then on duty in Peking, China, was detached, ordered home, and thence was directed to proceed to France to command the Fifth Marines.

All of these things having been done, I brought up the subject of my relief from duty at Headquarters and my detail to command the Marine Barracks, Quantico, as the first step towards overseas service. General Barnett reiterated his strong desire to have me remain where I was, and when I insisted on being relieved, he said he didn't have any one in mind to relieve me. I then wrote to Colonel C. G. Long, who was in command of the Marine Barracks, Philadelphia, and told him I wanted a change to duty with troops and, if he were willing, that I would recommend him as my successor. I pointed out, too, the very great importance of the duty

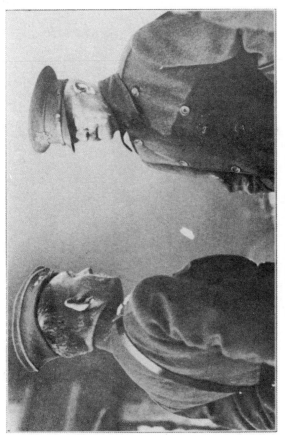

General Pershing and General Lejeune.

and the opportunities it offered. He replied, expressing his willingness to accept the detail.

I then went again to General Barnett and told him I had found a relief and handed him Long's letter. He said, "Long is satisfactory to me, but I don't want you to go. If you are leaving because you feel that you want to be free to work for appointment as my successor as Commandant when my term expires next February, I am perfectly willing for you to stay here and do so." I thanked him, and then said, "General, I do not want to be Commandant during the war. I now have but one desire and that is to go to France, and I am asking now for transfer to duty with troops at Quantico solely for the reason that I want the opportunity to prepare myself for active service with the Marines in France." I further told him that, in my opinion, he ought to continue to serve as Commandant for the period of the war, as it would not be wise to make a change in such an important office in the midst of war.

In a few days I was relieved by Lieutenant Colonel Long and was released from the heavy burden which I had carried for two years and eight months, and was able to spend four or five days with my family before going to Quantico.

Here, I feel, is the place for a brief excursion into other fields, perhaps I should say into gardens of flowers, for it is there that young people wander when in love with each other. Our daughter, Ellie, and Lieutenant James B. Glennon are the young people I refer to. They had been in love with each other since Ellie was a school girl, and their wedding day was April 7th, the day following the declaration of war. They were quietly married in our home, and only the close friends and the relatives of the Glennons and the Lejeunes were present. It was a beautiful wedding, and the bride was the loveliest of all brides except my own. The uncertainty of what the war might bring confronted them and all of those who were present as well. We felt the solemnity of the occasion, and there were but few dry eyes during the

service.   We visualized the many grave possibilities of
war, and our hearts went out to the two young people
who, amidst the sounds of strife, felt that they could face
the perils better if united.

CHAPTER XII

OVERSEAS, VIA QUANTICO

I ASSUMED command of Marine Barracks, Quantico, Virginia, about September 15th, 1917, relieving Colonel A. W. Catlin, who was temporarily acting as Post Commander until the date fixed for his transfer to France with his Regiment (Sixth Marines). Major Hughes' battalion of the Sixth had already sailed when I arrived at Quantico, and the remaining units of the Regiment, as well as the Sixth Machine Gun Battalion, were awaiting orders for their embarkation. The other organized forces then at Quantico were the Eighth Regiment (1,100 men), Colonel Bradman, commanding; the Tenth Regiment (Field Artillery), Colonel Dunlap, commanding; and the permanent post personnel such as the Rifle Range Detachment, Officers' School, and the Headquarters and Supply Detachments.

The Eighth Regiment soon sailed for Cuba, and immediately thereafter the Ninth Regiment (1,100 men) was organized under the command of Colonel L. H. Moses. That regiment sailed for Galveston, Texas, a short while after its organization, where it remained in camp during the remainder of the war, standing by for a quick move to Mexico to protect the oil-fields there in case an emergency requiring its presence should arise. In fact, Mexican oil was of such great importance to the Allied cause that Colonel Mahoney, his Brigade Staff and the Eighth Regiment were transferred later on from Cuba to Galveston.

During the winter months, the Tenth Regiment (Field Artillery) was subdivided and the Eleventh Regiment (Advanced Base Artillery) was formed under the command of Colonel Van Orden, the Tenth again being brought up to full strength by transfers from Parris

Island and other stations. A battalion of the Twelfth Regiment (Heavy Howitzers) under the command of Colonel C. S. Hill was assembled at Quantico in the spring. All artillery units were finally motorized.

The Post Staff was rather heterogeneous, but very efficient, and consisted of Major W. T. Hoadley, Post Adjutant; Major H. L. Roosevelt, Post Quartermaster; Surgeon W. L. Mann, Post Surgeon; Chaplain E. B. Niver, Post Chaplain; Major Earl H. Ellis, Military training; First Lieutenant John H. Craige, Athletic Officer; First Lieutenant Luther Jones, Police Officer; First Lieutenant R. L. Nelson (A-d-C), Intelligence Officer; and in addition the representatives of the Young Men's Christian Association, the Young Women's Christian Association, the Knights of Columbus, and the Red Cross.

Although a sufficient number of barracks buildings to house the personnel were completed, a large amount of construction work still remained to be done, including concrete roads and streets. A great gymnasium building, containing a large assembly hall and other desirable facilities such as the post library, was in process of construction also.

The lack of housing facilities for married officers at Quantico was a serious handicap, as it was necessary for all but a few who obtained rooms at the small hotel there to seek shelter for their families in Fredericksburg, Alexandria, or Washington, and to commute to Quantico. I was one of those who made frequent journeys back and forth to Washington. This custom became very trying during the bitterly cold winter of 1917-1918. I never felt colder weather anywhere. The Potomac River was frozen over and the ice was so thick that many of the great 14-inch shell fired from the Naval Proving Ground at Indian Head ricochetted on the ice and finally came to rest opposite Quantico. Frequently the men would walk out on the ice, haul them ashore, and place them on the company streets as ornaments, or perhaps as grim reminders of what they would have to contend with in battle.

The men were keyed up to a high pitch of enthusiasm, and it was a wonderful inspiration to be in contact with them. I was ably assisted in morale work by Chaplain Niver, Lieutenant Craige, and by the representatives of the societies I have already mentioned. Y. M. C. A. and Knights of Columbus huts were built and used by the men to the limit of their capacity, and the good ladies of the Y. W. C. A. erected a most attractive hostess house for the use of the families of the men when visiting the post and for the entertainment of the men themselves.

Until the completion of the gymnasium building, however, there was no hall of sufficient size to accommodate the men desirous of attending mass meetings, moving pictures, other entertainments, or the Sunday night religious services. Consequently the opening of the gymnasium was a great event. It occurred on a snowy day in December, 1917. The hall was packed with officers and enlisted men and there were present also a large number of prominent men and women. Bishop Murray, of Maryland, made the opening prayer. Secretary Daniels, General Barnett and Chaplain Niver made brief addresses. I presided, and introduced the speakers. As I stood on the platform and gazed into the shining eyes and eager faces of that throng of men, I felt an electric current or a magnetic force spring from them, which permeated the great hall, and reached my very soul. All the embarrassment which I had hitherto felt on the few occasions when I had faced an audience of men and women completely disappeared, and I felt stimulated and uplifted instead. The remarks I had planned to make were forgotten, and instead I spoke the words which found their way unaided to my lips. Throughout the World War I always experienced the same sensation when I addressed Marines or soldiers, and I hope that they sensed something of the same mystic contact as that which the speaker felt.

All in all, though, it was a heartbreaking winter for

those of us who were left behind.   Unit after unit entrained and departed for the mysterious land where battles raged and between which and us there seemed to be an impenetrable curtain hung.   Always at six o'clock in the morning the detachments left.   What bleak, cold, wintry mornings they were.   Once the thermometer registered 14 degrees below zero.   All of those left behind stood along the railway tracks and shouted three lusty cheers for their departing comrades, while the bands played until their instruments froze.

As we turned away to resume our daily tasks, how heavy-hearted we were!   Colonel Catlin, the headquarters' company and the regimental machine gun company left early in October; then Major Sibley's battalion about a month later; Major Cole's machine gun battalion in December, and Major Holcomb's battalion in January, 1918.   Then, about a month apart, replacement battalions were assembled, trained, and entrained preliminary to the voyage overseas.   Major Keyser, Lieutenant Colonel Snyder and Lieutenant Colonel R. P. Williams were their fortunate commanders.

In this wise the long, dreary winter dragged itself by, and finally springtime appeared.   With it came the appalling reports of Ludendorf's tremendous thrust against the British lines, the defeat of a British army, the almost successful attempt to drive a wedge between the British and the French armies, the temporary cessation of the violent assault, and finally the apparent stabilization of the Allied lines in front of Amiens.   We did not know all, but we knew enough to realize that the situation was a desperate one, and that Field Marshal Haig and his gallant men were fighting with their backs to the wall.   The only bright gleam in the midst of all the inky darkness was the adoption of the principle of unity of command and the appointment of Marshal Foch as Generalissimo of the Allied armies in the field.

The gravity of the situation seemed to make it mandatory that the Marine Corps should give all it had toward helping to win the war.   The officers at Quantico were

strenuous advocates of an additional expansion of the
Marine Corps by fifty or seventy-five thousand men and
the proper proportion of officers, so that at least a Marine
division, complete in all its parts, could be sent overseas,
as well as the necessary replacement units to maintain
it at full strength.   It was in this way only that the artillery, signal corps, engineer and medical units could participate in the active operations of the war.   This was
our constant topic of discussion, and when any of us
visited Headquarters, the question was agitated there.
There seemed to be some opposition to such a large expansion on the ground that the Corps could not maintain
its efficiency under such conditions.   The advocates of
the plan maintained vigorously that the failure of the
Corps to utilize all of its strength, both actual and poten-
tial, in the great emergency then confronting the world
would impair its efficiency to a far greater extent than
would a temporary expansion to the limit of its capacity.
Finally, the Quantico enthusiasm had its effect and estimates for seventy-five thousand men were submitted to
Congress, and appropriation therefor was made in the
naval bill which became a law on July 1, 1918.   This bill
also provided funds for five or six thousand reserves, so
that the total authorized strength of the Corps for the
remaining period of the war amounted to about 80,000
men and 4,000 officers.

The very depths of my soul were filled with an indescribable yearning for the opportunity for service overseas.   I had sent battalion after battalion from Quantico
to France and I felt that I owed it to every officer and
man who had gone to the field of battle to follow them
and share their fate.   The blacker the military situation
from the standpoint of the Allies, the more intense was
my desire to give myself fully to the great cause in which
our country was engaged.   Suddenly, and without warning, one morning in May came the news that Brigadier
General Doyen had been ordered home because of
physical disability.   This news came to me by telephone
from my good friend, Captain Douglas C. McDougal,

who was then on duty at Headquarters. I caught the first train for Washington and went in to see General Barnett. I told him that I had heard that Doyen had been invalided home. He replied that he had not forgotten his promise to send me overseas, but that he rather doubted whether I would want to go under the circumstances described in General Pershing's cablegram to the War Department. He then handed me the message to read. In substance, it stated that Brigadier General Doyen had been ordered home because of physical disability, that Brigadier General James G. Harbord, Chief of Staff of the American Expeditionary Forces, had succeeded him in command of the Marine Brigade, and that if a Brigadier General of Marines were sent to replace Doyen he would not be assigned to command the Marine Brigade, or any other front line unit, but would be detailed to duty behind the lines. I at once said that, while the cablegram was disappointing, I would welcome the opportunity to go under these or any other circumstances, as I would be much nearer to the front in any part of France than I was in Quantico, and that if I got that far I felt sure I would be able to obtain a command at the front. The General then directed Colonel Long to issue my orders to proceed by the first available naval transport. Long stated that the U. S. S. *Henderson*, with a replacement battalion of Marines (Lieutenant Colonel O'Leary's) on board, would sail the latter part of May, and that he would arrange for me to take passage on that vessel.

I then hurried home to tell my wife the news. She faced the situation bravely and unselfishly, saying that she would rather have me go than to have me suffer the disappointment of not going, especially as she knew I would never get over it the rest of my life.

At Quantico there was an elaborate farewell program arranged by Smedley Butler, recently arrived from Haiti. A review of the troops, a great mass meeting in the gymnasium hall where speeches expressing praise and confidence were made, and to which I made reply amid inspiring cheers, and finally a farewell reception at the Officers' Club.

Then, on the following day, came the parting from my dear ones at the railway station. I would draw a veil over this scene. It is too sacred to portray. Suffice it to say that they bade me adieu with smiles on their lips and agony in their souls.

The *Henderson* was lying at the Army docks in Brooklyn and I was taken there by my good friends, the Mowbrays. The *Henderson* cast off her lines from the dock and proceeded to Sheepshead Bay, anchoring off Coney Island. During the night we got under way and headed for the rendezvous, a pre-arranged point in the Atlantic Ocean a hundred miles or so from New York. It was a cloudy, misty day, with poor visibility, but at the appointed time and place the other ships of the convoy appeared one by one, all grotesquely camouflaged, and all laden with troops except a solitary destroyer that accompanied us.

The voyage was uneventful. No storms or heavy seas checked our progress and no submarines or periscopes disturbed the placid surface of the sea. Vigilance, however, was not relaxed, and we greeted with welcoming cheers the appearance of a division of destroyers which escorted the convoy through the danger zone. When near the coast of France, the convoy was divided, a part heading in a southeasterly direction, probably for Bordeaux, and the remainder, including the *Henderson,* continuing in the direction of Brest.

Early in the morning of June 8th land was sighted, and as we steamed up the long, narrow entrance to the inner harbor, a lovely landscape and a busy scene greeted our eyes. Never before had any shore seemed more beautiful, and never before had airplanes and blimps and observation balloons and destroyers and submarines and sub-chasers received more attention from these discoverers of a new world.

Soon the ships were at anchor. Our splendid skipper, Captain Steele, was, I believe, the senior naval officer of the convoy.   At any rate, the aides of Admiral Wilson and General Harries came on board promptly to offer the customary courtesies of the port.

We eagerly questioned them concerning the progress of the war, especially with reference to the garbled reports we had picked up by radio during our voyage which indicated that Ludendorf had been successful in another surprise attack, and that the weak Allied lines on the Chemin des Dames and the Aisne had been overwhelmed by the German masses.   They had little to say, but gave us a file of the Paris editions of the *New York Herald* and *Chicago Tribune* which alluded to the battles in guarded terms, but the names of the towns and rivers mentioned clearly showed the seriousness of the defeat. The German armies had reached the Marne at Château Thierry and to the eastward, and while Rheims was still in the possession of the French, yet it was almost surrounded by the formidable foe; Soissons had fallen; the German forces had crossed the Ourcq; Paris was seriously menaced; the Allies had lost great quantities of munitions, hospital equipment and other supplies; and a large number of cannon and thousands of men had been captured.

I left the ship at once, with Major Ellis and Captain Nelson, my aide, and went to Navy Headquarters to report to my old friend, Rear Admiral H. B. Wilson, before joining the A. E. F. for the remainder of the war. The interview with him was of intense interest.

I asked him about the military situation.   He took me into his inner office and, after closing the doors, said in a low voice, "It is worse that it has been at any time during the twelve months that I have been in France. The defeat of the Allied forces on the Chemin des Dames was a disaster of far greater proportions than the general public has any idea of, and the French officers at Brest are more pessimistic in regard to the outcome of the war than at any time since it began."   He then said that the only rift in the clouds was the fact that the Second American Division, which had gone into position west of

Château Thierry and north of the Marne to fill a great gap in the French lines, had stopped the advance of the German troops in that sector, and that the Marine Brigade of that division had, in a brilliant attack, succeeded in taking the southern part of Belleau Woods and had captured several hundred prisoners. He added that the bitter fighting in Belleau Woods still continued, and that the casualties of the Marines had been very heavy.

The interview ended, I went to Army Headquarters to report to Brigadier General Harries, whom I had known in Washington. He was away for the day, and his Adjutant General, after reading my orders, said he was not empowered to permit me to proceed to G. H. Q., as his instructions were to send all officers not attached to combat units to Blois to await orders from the Commander-in-Chief. He suggested that we return the next morning, when General Harries would be in his office, and that I could then take up the matter with him.

We then went out to Pontanezen Barracks to see Brigadier General Jameson, a classmate of mine at the Army War College, who had arrived with his brigade of the 80th Division in the same convoy as ourselves. There we found Major W. H. Clifford, a former Marine officer, who was Brigade Adjutant. The troops were all under canvas in an open field, but as it hadn't rained for several days the ground was dry and the camp site appeared to be satisfactory. Later on it became a vast quagmire, and its reputation as such was spread far and wide throughout the A. E. F. and at home when the troops began to return there after the Armistice, until a revolution was wrought by Smedley Butler who, after herculean labors, converted it into a model camp.

The next morning (June 9th), we were at General Harries' office at an early hour. To our bitter disappointment he said that he was powerless to help us, as he had positive instructions not to permit any casual officers to go to Chaumont, but to send them to the Officers' Reclassification Camp at Blois to await further orders. Blois was a good place to stay away from, I had been told, as officers sent there frequently awaited orders for weeks, and when the orders did come, they were almost always what one did not want. I appealed to the General for advice and he asked if I knew General Kernan, who was then in command of the Service of Supply, or S. O. S., as it was more generally known. I replied that I did not, but that I had a letter for him from his wife. He said that that gave me a good excuse for calling him up. When General Kernan answered the 'phone, I delivered the messages entrusted to me and told him I had a letter for him. I then told him how necessary it was for me to go to Chaumont to confer with General Pershing about matters of great importance to the Marine Corps. He replied, "There is nothing I can do for you," and hung up the 'phone. I was in despair and had left the office when I suddenly remembered that my friend, Colonel Dennis Nolan, was on duty at G. H. Q. as one of the Assistant Chiefs of Staff. I returned and asked General Harries if I might telegraph to Colonel Nolan. He said, "Certainly, you may. Write out your message and I will mark it 'urgent' and send it along."

I explained my situation fully in the telegram and asked to be authorized to proceed to G.H.Q. overland, with three officers and chauffeur, in the Cadillac automobile which I had brought with me from the United States, and to send Lieutenant Luther Jones and a small enlisted detachment and our baggage by train. Early the next morning orders from the Chief of Staff of the A.E.F. arrived. They were phrased exactly as requested, and in an incredibly short time Major Ellis, Captain Nelson, Captain Geyer and I were burning up the road leading out of Brest toward Paris and Chaumont.

Captain Geyer was our interpreter, as he spoke French perfectly, his parents having migrated from Belgium to the United States. He had been giving me French lessons for a month or more, and while on board the *Henderson* many hours every day were spent in the endeavor to brush up the knowledge of the French language which once I had had, but which I had nearly forgotten, owing to lack of opportunity to use it for nearly twenty-five years.

Beautiful was Brittany, as was all of France outside of the zone of combat. Magnificent highways winding between avenues of great trees, fertile fields every inch of which was under cultivation, communal woods looking like parks, quaint country villages, market towns, cities evidently of great antiquity dominated by the lofty spires of cathedrals, handsome châteaux with lovely grounds about them, scenes of sylvan and rural beauty, rivers, canals, plains, hills, dwarf-like mountains, old men and women bent nearly double and little children laboring everywhere unceasingly, boys of sixteen or seventeen drilling in preparation for their call to arms, and every kind of novel sight that ordinarily would grip the traveller and cause him to loiter by the wayside, were spread like a huge panorama before us as we sped along, never pausing except occasionally to ask our way, or to get a bite to eat at meal time.

We motored half the night, too, and when it became necessary to give the tired chauffeur a rest, we persuaded a friendly gendarme at the entrance to a city to take us to the nearest hotel where we finally succeeded in rousing the sleepy attendant and in finding beds. Inky black were the streets, and the windows of all the houses were darkened. The people had lived in fear of the deadly "avion" since Ludendorf's armies had first thundered at the gates of Amiens, just two months before.

We arrived in Paris late on the second day and took rooms at the Continental Hotel. We had some business to attend to there with our Paymaster, Captain Wills, and at Naval Headquarters, and I had determined, too, to give up a day to visiting the hospitals in Paris where so many wounded Marines were.

That was all the sight-seeing we did in a city which had been famous for its frivolity, its gaiety, its levity, its brilliancy at night, and its pleasure-loving people. Now all was changed. The streets, as dark as Erebus, were empty after dark. No bright lights could be seen anywhere. There were no illuminated night clubs, or cafés, or theaters in evidence. The stained glass windows of the Madeleine had been removed. Historic buildings sought some shelter behind bags of sand. The long-range gun, over sixty miles away, was bombarding Paris each day, and the nights were made hideous by screaming sirens, followed by the din of hundreds of anti-craft guns as they laid a veritable barrage high above and around the city to protect it from the hostile "avions" which visited it periodically. I learned that the Continental Hotel had never been hit by a bomb, so I remained peacefully in bed while the sirens shrieked, and did not heed the warning to take to the "cave," as the French called a cellar, or dug-out. Throughout the continuance of the war I never took refuge in a "cave" because of the bombing of aircraft, as I believed there was more danger to life and limb to be expected when groping one's way about in the darkness trying to find the "cave" than there was in remaining wherever one happened to be.

The morning after our arrival in Paris we visited the Marine Corps Pay Office and U. S. Navy Headquarters. There we were told of the excitement which swept over Paris when the catastrophe on the Chemin des Dames took place and the German armies poured south through the breach they had made in the lines; of the accentuation of the excitement caused by the bombardment of the city by the long-range cannon; of the fear that the hostile troops would extend the breach in the defensive lines and at last be able to lay siege to the capital; of the tens of thousands of its inhabitants who had left the city for other parts of France; and of the sudden rebound from despair to exultation when it became known that the Second Division, A.E.F., had checked the hostile advance towards the Marne west of Château Thierry; that the Marine Brigade had successfully attacked the enemy positions in the fastnesses of Belleau Woods, and that in the bitter fighting which had continued day and night without ceasing, the Marines had established their supremacy and had demonstrated that the endurance, the valor and the determination to conquer of the American soldier were unexcelled. They said that Paris had gone wild and that the rainbow of hope had once more appeared and had remained fixed in the western sky, but that the cost in casualities to the Marine Brigade had been heavy, and that the hospitals around Paris were filled with wounded Marines, and their battlefield carpeted with the dead.

We then turned our faces toward the American hospitals. Villas had been commandeered and volunteer nurses had supplemented the Army and Red Cross nurses. The rooms, the halls, the porches, the corridors—all available spaces—were utilized to the limit of their capacity. Literally, we found battalions of wounded Marines. Such *esprit* I never have seen! These wounded men, when they saw us in our Marine Corps uniforms, spontaneously began to sing the Marine's Hymn, and as we walked through the wards, its sound grew in volume as man after man took up the refrain until it made the welkin ring. There were no signs of downheartedness among those American fighting men, for fighting men and mighty warriors they were! They were certain that the measure of the foe had been taken and that his final defeat was assured. I said a prayer of thankfulness because I was an American and a Marine, even as these men were.

Many officers and men I had known before were there, among them Colonel Catlin, who had been shot through the lungs as he stood on a parapet to observe the progress of the attacking battalions of which he was in command. Powerful physically, he chafed over the confinement to his bed and begged the nurse to let him sit up, insisting that he was nearly well enough to return to his regiment. Poor fellow! He has never fully recovered from his wound.

Major Benjamin S. Berry, with an arm shattered by machine gun fire, was also there. They told me of Major Cole's charge on a machine gun nest at the head of a detachment, of his wounds, and of his death, and of the heroism displayed by both the living and the dead. I wish there were space to put down here all that I heard that day. A veritable Marine Corps "Saga" it was.

The next day after breakfast we were off for Chaumont, going through a beautiful section of France except for the latter part of the ride, when we saw something of the white chalk area, and we were so covered with white dust that we looked like millers when, at dusk, we drove up to the Hotel de France in Chaumont, the capital city of the A.E.F.

Early on the following morning I went to the Headquarters' Building to report to General MacAndrew, Chief of Staff. He saw me at once, and after reading my orders he said, "The Marine Corps has no authority over you while you are on duty with the A.E.F. Your assignment to duty is entirely in the hands of General Pershing." I replied that I fully realized that I was in all respects subject to General Pershing's orders, and that I would not have it otherwise, even if it were in my power to do so. I then added that my chief reason for asking to be ordered to Chaumont to confer with the Commander-in-Chief was to have the opportunity to urge most earnestly the increase of the Marine Corps force in France by a division, complete in all its parts. I then made the strongest plea of which I was capable, using all the arguments in favor of the plan which I believed would appeal both to his head and to his heart. He listened attentively and seemed to be favorably impressed. He then said, "I will bring the matter to General Pershing's attention when he returns to Chaumont this afternoon and will endeavor to arrange for you to see him either tomorrow or the day after. In the meantime, rooms will be assigned to you and Major Ellis at the Guest House."

I then looked up my friend, Colonel Nolan, to thank him for arranging my orders so that I could visit G.H.Q., and to deliver the messages that had been sent him by Mrs. Nolan. I also told him of my conversation with General MacAndrew with reference to a Marine division, and repeated in full all the arguments I had used. He

General Lejeune and Second Division Staff at Marbache.
Colonel Matthews, Colonel Brown, General Lejeune,
Colonel Rhea, Colonel Herbst.

Decoration of French Soldiers at Wesserling, Alsace, July
14, 1918, by General Renouard and General Lejeune.

too seemed favorably impressed. He took me into his inner office and there showed me the great map of the Western Front. The location of every army, corps and division on that front was indicated on the map, not only of the Allied forces, but of the Central Powers as well. He gave me a clear picture of the system in use for gathering military intelligence and explained the reciprocal agreement between the Allies for the exchange of all information gathered by each headquarters. I was amazed at the completeness and the accuracy of the intelligence reports, indicating the existence of thoroughly organized and effective intelligence departments. He also gave me a clear picture of the then military situation, which he regarded with optimism. He was enthusiastic in his praise of the Second Division and of the Marine Brigade, and said that the battle of Belleau Woods already had brought about an immense improvement in the morale of the French people. This I heard everywhere I went, the French vieing with the Americans in praising the fighting qualities of the Marine Brigade.

While at Headquarters I also saw Colonel Fox Connor, who had been an instructor at the Army War College when I was a student there, and who was then the Assistant Chief of Staff for Military Operations. I also met Colonel Eltinge, the Deputy Chief of Staff. Ellis and I took luncheon with Colonel Nolan at his mess, and then we moved to the Guest House, where we found our baggage awaiting us, and where I was never more comfortable during my entire sojourn overseas.

During the afternoon we were invited to take dinner that evening with General Pershing at his Headquarters' mess. The General was then living for the summer months in a delightful château about four miles from Chaumont. In his mess were General MacAndrew and five or six comparatively young staff officers. The General greeted me very cordially and seemed glad to see me. I quote an extract from a letter to my wife written that evening: "We had a very good dinner and the General was most agreeable. He has simple, unaffected manners and was most informal and affable. He looks well, but sad. He bears a great responsibility that no one can share with him, and carries besides a heavy burden of personal sorrow. He said he remembered meeting us at Baguio and seemed to know all about me, including my service with the Army at Vera Cruz and at the Army War College."

Our conversation soon turned to that all-absorbing topic—the war. He spoke in high praise of the conduct and accomplishments of the Marines in Belleau Woods and expressed the deepest sorrow because of the heavy casualties they had suffered. His voice broke and he showed deep emotion, so much so, that one of the members of his staff said, "We must remember, General, that Napoleon said that it is just as impossible to win victories without loss of life as it is to make omelets without breaking eggs;" and another staff officer reminded him that the regiment of the First Division which had captured Cantigny had suffered heavy losses too. The General said, in reply, "Yes, that is true, but the circumstances were different. In the case of Cantigny, it is trench warfare—a set piece attack, thoroughly prepared by artillery fire, and then the holding of the entrenched position against counter attack and artillery fire—while the Marines in Belleau Woods are engaged in open warfare and hand to hand fighting in a dense woods, with little artillery support." The General excused himself at the end of dinner, saying that he had a great deal of work to do and that his Secretary was waiting for him.

After dinner General MacAndrew and I sat in the library while I smoked my cigar. He asked many questions about affairs at home—the attitude of the public, the progress of war preparation, and the reasons for the delay in the manufacture of war material. He then told me that he had spoken to General Pershing about the desire of the Marine Corps to have a Marine division added to the A.E.F. at the earliest practicable date, but that he had not had time to go into the details of the subject, but would do so at the first opportunity.

The next forenoon (Sunday), I went to Headquarters and found that General Pershing was away for the day. General MacAndrew said that the subject of the Marine division would be taken up Monday, provided General Pershing returned by then. He urged me to visit the Staff College at Langres the next day and called up the President to ask him to look out for me. That afternoon Ellis and I drove to Neufchateau, about forty miles distant from Chaumont, to call on my War College friend, Major General Hunter Liggett, who was then in command of the First Corps. He was the same simple, kindly gentleman and warm friend he had been when we were studying the art of war together. He, too, praised the Marines in the highest terms and said he would like nothing better than to command a corps composed of Marine divisions.

The ensuing day we drove in a heavy rain to Langres and had a most interesting and illuminating day with the President of the College, Colonel Smith. He took me everywhere, showed me everything and, with his rare power of lucid expression, made everything plain to me. A gifted man intellectually, and a noble-hearted gentleman he was!

The next morning I went again to see the Chief of Staff. He said the subject of the Marine division had been discussed, but was noncommittal as to the decision reached. It was apparent to me, however, that it was unfavorable. I asked and received permission to see the Commander-in-Chief. He said, "The General will be in his office at 1.30 P. M., or shortly thereafter. If you are there when he arrives, he will give you an interview at once." I carried out his suggestion and had the interview.

I had given a great deal of thought to what I would say, and made the most succinct, the most lucid, and the strongest statement it was possible for me to make. I dwelt on the intense desire of our officers and men at home to take part in the war, and stressed the fact that those who had specialized in artillery and the auxiliary units would be deprived of the opportunity to do so unless a Marine division were organized and assigned to duty with the A.E.F. I stated, too, that the Commandant of the Marine Corps had approved the plan.

The General, in reply, said that no man could appreciate more deeply the splendid service of the 4th Brigade of Marines than he did; that the presence of that brigade in the A.E.F. had been of great benefit to it in stimulating competition and the desire to excel; but that he could not approve the assignment of a Marine division to the theater of operations in France for the reason that its presence there would interfere with his plan for a homogeneous army and would add greatly to the many complications incident to providing replacements. His staff already was burdened with many difficulties, and he did not feel justified in increasing those difficulties unnecessarily. He pointed out that it was scarcely possible to always provide the 4th Brigade with Marine replacements, and a division would require such a large variety of Marine replacements as to make the problem almost or altogether insoluble. He further stated that he would be glad to have individual officers of the Marine Corps detailed to duty with the A.E.F., but that they should be temporarily assigned to or commissioned in the National Army.

I made a brief statement in reply, but without effect. He was very kind and considerate in this interview, and told me that he greatly regretted that the circumstances were such as to make it impracticable to give his approval to my request. Seeing that it would be unavailing to say anything further, I thanked him for giving me the opportunity to lay the matter before him and left his office.

I then returned to General MacAndrew's office, as he had instructed me to do, and told him of the result of the interview. He said he knew what the decision would be, but deemed it advisable for me to hear it from the Commander-in-Chief himself. I asked if he thought there was any possibility of a change in the decision. He said, "No. It is final." I then asked that a cablegram be sent to the Commandant of the Marine Corps, informing him of General Pershing's decision, as it might make necessary important changes in his plans for training, organizing and distributing the personnel. He said that a cablegram on the subject would be sent by Headquarters A. E. F.

I then said, "General, I should like to know what duty I am to be assigned to. I feel that I could render service of greater value in command of the 4th Brigade than elsewhere upon General Harbord's promotion, which I have heard will soon be effected, as I know the officers and men and have served with Marines for thirty years."

He said, "While I cannot make any promises, I can assure you that I will look out for you, and it now seems altogether probable that you will eventually receive the assignment you desire; but, in the meantime, you will be ordered to duty as an observer with the 35th Division, which is now about to enter the front lines, so that you may familiarize yourself with the methods employed in occupying a sector and in training the troops in trench warfare."

I asked and received permission to visit the Second Division en route to the 35th Division, and in a few minutes my orders were handed to me.

I was depressed and disappointed, and could not bear to think of the effect of the news on the officers and men at home. However, I was comforted by the thought that I had done my best, and that a man can do no more than that.

XIII

SERVICE WITH THE 35TH AND 32ND DIVISIONS, A.E.F.

E ARLY on the morning of June 19th, Ellis, Nelson and I left Chaumont by automobile for our visit to the Marine Brigade. During the journey our minds were filled with thoughts of the hardships our men had endured, the dangers they had faced, the losses they had suffered, and the heroism they had displayed. We felt that we were making a pilgrimage to a sacred shrine, and that somehow we would be strengthened and sanctified by the brief association with the living and by our proximty to the hallowed spot where the blood of heroic men had been shed and where their mortal remains had found a resting place.

It was a pleasant summer evening, just before sunset, when we crossed the Marne and met a group of Marines near a château in a grove of trees. They told us that Lieutenant Colonel Wise had his battalion headquarters in the château. He and Major Keyser welcomed us warmly and insisted that we spend the night with them. Wise told us that what was left of his battalion and of the other battalions which had been in Belleau Woods had been relieved a day or two before by the Seventh Infantry so that they might have opportunity for rest and recuperation, as the men had reached the limit of their endurance. It was a wonderful evening we had with him and his staff.

The next morning the companies turned out for inspection. The companies were no larger than platoons. For more than a year he had been with them. He had trained them, taken care of them, commanded them in battle, and had seen them die. We tried to comfort him by telling him that the memory of theirs deeds would live forever, and that they had left a priceless heritage to our country and to our Corps, but our words were unavailing.

From Wise's headquarters we drove to Second Division Headquarters to call on General Bundy, but failed to see him as he was making a visit of inspection. Nearby, however, we found Lieutenant Colonel Harry Lee, who had succeeded Colonel Catlin as the commander of the Sixth Marines, and on our way to General Harbord's headquarters we passed through a wood in which Major Holcomb's and Major Sibley's battalions were in bivouac. We talked to them awhile and then pushed on to Brigade Headquarters.

From General Harbord I learned the story of the attack and gained a clear view of the military situation. It was planned that after the arrival of replacements and a rest of about a week, the Marine battalions would resume their stations in Belleau Woods and drive the enemy from the stronghold which he still held there. The plan as outlined was fully carried out, and Major Shearer, who commanded the attacking force, was able to report at the conclusion of the engagement that Belleau Woods had then become the Woods of the Fourth Brigade of Marines. Immediately General Degoutte issued an order changing its name from Bois de Belleau to "Bois de la Brigade de Marine."

Lieutenant Colonel Harry Lay then accompanied us to Colonel Neville's headquarters.

At the headquarters of the Fifth Marines we found Neville, Feland, Shearer and Waller, and the members of the Headquarters Staff. Neville was in command of the troops operating in Belleau Woods, and Feland's station had been in the woods where he had coördinated the operations of the Marine battalions which had been engaged in the effort to drive the enemy from its confines. Shearer's battalion was at the front and Waller's machine-gun battalion was distributed throughout the sector. They pointed out on the map the location of the German strongpoint near the hunting lodge within the woods, which was known colloquially as the "Hook," and which was supplied with men and munitions by infiltration through a ravine leading into the German lines. Our troops had passed beyond it and held the northern edge of the woods, occupying a crescent-shaped position facing roughly to the westward, one horn of the crescent being north of the strong point and the other south of it. Several days later, after the Marines had relieved the Seventh Infantry, the Marine battalions were drawn back to the southern portion of the woods and a heavy artillery fire was concentrated on the strong point. At "H" hour they moved forward, closely following the advancing artillery barrage. They captured the strong point, a number of prisoners and machine guns, and occupied the entire woods which they successfully held until the Second Division was relieved by the Twenty-sixth (Yankee) Division on July 9th.

It was a thrilling afternoon we spent at Fifth Marine Headquarters listening to the story of the heroic exploits of the officers and men who had stormed machine-gun nests, bayonetted the defenders, made raids by night and by day, and had gained a moral ascendancy over the enemy which they maintained until complete victory crowned their efforts, in spite of hunger, thirst, fatigue, sleeplessness, danger, wounds and death. It is indeed fitting that Belleau Woods should have been converted into a memorial to the great souled men who fought, suffered and died there. Let us trust that the loving hearts of patriotic Americans will maintain it forever, so that the unselfish work of Mrs. James Carroll Frazer and those who aided her in purchasing it, dedicating it, and taking care of it will not have been in vain. At last the setting sun was the signal for our departure, and with reluctant feet and heavy hearts we walked down the road to our automobile, and resumed our journey.

While leaving the area we found Major Hughes' battalion, which was temporarily commanded by Major Garrett during the absence of Major Hughes in the hospital, and in a town on the south bank of the Marne we saw Major Turrill and his battalion which was billeted there. At dusk we left Turrill and again turned our faces toward Chaumont, where we planned to spend the night. Our journey was made in a downpour of rain which continued without intermission until our arrival at the Hotel de France at 2 A. M. There we found every bed taken, so we sat downstairs by a typical French heatless fire. For the sake of economy in fuel, the French made their fires of green wood, which spluttered and only pretended to burn. Heat and light—there were none. In fact, Colonel Preston Brown, the Chief of Staff of the Second Division, once remarked that the most widespread activity in France was frying the water out of wood.

It was indeed a gloomy night, but the sun rose in a cloudless sky and after the good breakfast which Madame the hostess always served to Uncle Sam's wayfarers, we took to the road in search of the 35th Division which was located in the foothills on the western slope of the Vosges mountains in an area nearly west of the Alsatian town of Thann. After stopping en route at Third Corps Headquarters, where I received a most cordial welcome from my old friend, Major General "Billy" Wright, we continued on to 35th Division Headquarters. It was located in the lovely little town of d'Arches, which was almost hidden from view in a forest of fir, pine and spruce trees.

Brigadier General McClure was then temporarily

in command of the Division, and Lieutenant Colonel McCleave, a very able officer, was Chief of Staff. We were invited to join the Headquarters' mess, which we gladly did, and were billeted in the beautiful home of Monsieur Pierregot, a wealthy manufacturer of fine writing paper, and the owner and mayor of the town. The paper mills were still running so as to give employment to the crippled, the maimed, the very old and the very young. Two hundred soldiers had gone out of d'Arches, of whom fifty-five had been killed, five captured, and twelve had been reported missing. (Probably they occupied unknown soldiers' graves.) Of the remainder, a large proportion were maimed or disabled and the others were still fighting.

Monsieur Pierregot had a charming family consisting of Madame and their two daughters. Both daughters had married officers of the French Army and remained at home with their parents; their little children were fascinating, and during the two days I occupied a room in the lovely Pierregot home I made brave efforts to converse with them, with fair success. The entire family was most cordial and gracious to the stranger from a foreign land, and with the delicate courtesy of French gentle folk made him feel that he was a most welcome guest.

I passed the first day at Division Headquarters studying the plan of defense of the sector in the Vosges mountains that one of its brigades was to occupy, while the other brigade continued its training in so-called open warfare. The second day I drove out on the road to the Wesserling, or Thann Valley, and watched the troops moving by "camions" into their new billets in the valley towns preliminary to taking over the sector. Splendid looking men they were—the flower of Missouri and adjacent states. They moved off towards the front cheering, singing and waving their hats. At last their dreams had come true and they were moving to the front. The great adventure was soon to reach its culmination. Like the young men of all the previous centuries, they went to war blithely, for they knew naught of its stern reality. That reality it seems impossible for men to learn except by their own personal experience. In all probability the generations yet unborn will, for this reason, continue to march to war singing and cheering and waving their hats like their forefathers. They will refuse to believe, until they have endured the shock of battle, that the road to war is a *"Via Dolorosa."* Perhaps this is the irrefutable answer to the pacifist creed.

On the following day we left our comfortable château, crossed the mountains, and moved to the town of Wesserling which lies in Alsace near the head of the Thann Valley. On arriving at Wesserling, I called on General Renouard, the youngest Division Commander of the French Army, being then only forty-three years of age. To quote from a letter to my wife, "I was received most cordially, was assigned a room in the attractive home of a dear old French couple, who had endured German rule since 1871 stoically, but who were happy as children out of school to be again living under the Tricolor, and tonight I dined with the General and his staff. A most delightful man he is—courteous, cordial, and simplicity itself." He had been Chief of Staff to Marshal Joffre and was detailed as Division Commander just before the famous old Marshal had been relieved as Commander-in-Chief by General Nivelle.

General Renouard's division was in reserve on the south bank of the Aisne when Ludendorff launched his attack on the Chemin des Dames about a month before, and instead of remaining in place to afford a rallying position for the defeated troops, he marched his division towards the sound of the guns and met the victorious enemy with his own division astride the Aisne. The result was a disaster. He succeeded with great difficulty in extricating the remnants of his division, which had then been sent to this quiet sector for rest and recuperation. Months afterwards, I was told by a French officer that he had been relieved of his command in August, 1918, and had died in September from an attack of pneumonia. Such is the fortune of war! Glory is not always the portion of the brave.

The Valley of Thann was a part of the strip of Alsace which the French had succeeded in holding since 1914. The city of Thann was included in their lines, although the Germans held its eastern outskirts. The eastern section of the city was partially destroyed and its streets were as empty as those of a city of the dead. The western section was still inhabited and the little children, accustomed as they were to the sound of cannon, played about its streets. The valley was densely populated and, in addition, was filled with French and American soldiers. The roads and streets, within easy enemy artillery range, were crowded with pedestrians, camions, and military automobiles, and yet were undisturbed. The same situation, I have been told, existed behind the German lines. Apparently neither side wished to antagonize the Alsatian people, as each hoped to become the permanent possessor of Alsace at the close of the war. Many fierce battles, however, had been fought for the possession of near-by points of vantage in the Vosges mountains. In plain view of Wesserling was battle-scarred Hartmann Weiler Kopf, on which every tree and all other vegetation had been destroyed, and where one hundred thousand men had laid down their lives.

We messed with Colonel McMahon and his staff until he moved the headquarters of his regiment into the sector occupied by it, when we rejoined the mess of Brigadier General McClure which had arrived at Wesserling. We made many excursions to the front lines, going by automobile by a steep and winding road to the top of the mountain ridge, then by a fairly level road along the crest until opposite the Battalion or company strongpoints which were located on mountain spurs jutting out toward the plains of Alsace, when walking on covered trails or in trenches was resorted to. Between these spurs, patrolling was supposed to be sufficient to afford security, and parties unfamiliar with the terrain sometimes wandered into the enemy lines. We were, therefore, always furnished with guides, but even so, on one occasion, General McClure and I, on leaving a French salient position, came near walking into a village held by the Germans, our guide having taken the wrong turn at the junction of two communicating trenches. Fortunately we discovered just in time that we were well on the way to a German prison camp, and hastily retraced our steps. A few days later, an American raiding party received its baptism of fire in a successful attack on that village.

It was interesting to watch the great care with which the French *poilus* instructed the relieving American soldiers. They explained every detail of duty with the utmost precision, including their own unwritten code. The opposing German troops were old reservists, as were many of the French in that quiet sector. They had faced each other for months and had learned to recognize each other across the narrow "No man's land" which separated them. During the relief, a Frenchman stood guard with each American, a French squad, section, platoon, company or battalion with each corresponding American unit. I was told that the morning after the Americans had gone into line, a German soldier climbed up out of his trench and sat on the parapet in full view while he cleaned the equipment of the officer for whom he was probably the orderly. An American soldier promptly brought his piece to an aim and was about to fire when his French comrade knocked it away, saying excitedly, "Do not shoot! He sits there every morning to get the air and to feel the sunshine. To kill him would be murder, not war." I wonder if the American soldiers continued to allow the old *boche* to get his morning air. I fear it is doubtful if they did, for soon the American combative spirit asserted itself and small battles raged here, there and everywhere on that front. On each subsequent visit we were compelled to leave our cars farther and farther away from the outpost positions, and to move very cautiously on foot so as to avoid shell-swept areas and machine gun fire. It was necessary for military activity to be encouraged so that the divisions would be inured to battle and fitted for the terrible strain which they would have to undergo before the war could be brought to a victorious conclusion.

We interested ourselves in the French system of supplying troops in that mountain sector as well as in the front line military activities. The terminus of the French railway was near the foot, on the western slope, of the ridge over which the steep highway climbed. The grade of the road was too steep to be negotiated by heavily laden motor trucks, and all supplies for the troops and the people living in the valley were transported by an overhead endless cable to the railhead on the other side of the mountains, and thence by rail or truck to the valley towns. Similarly, the road from the valley to the top of the mountain ridge to the north was impracticable, and all supplies for the troops stationed there went up to the top by the air express, thence by wagons as far as safely permitted, then by pack animals to the support positions, and finally on human backs to the outpost lines. It was a quaint, rather antiquated, but effective line of supply, and we got quite a kick as we observed the tender care with which the casks of *pinard* (red wine) were handled and the frequency with which they appeared dangling high in the air on their way to the *poilus*.

It was a common saying that *"Pinard, en permission* (leave), *and croix de guerre"* would win the war for France. The French soldiers were granted leave semi-annually to visit their homes. Each man knew to a day when his turn for leave would come. No emergency was allowed to interfere with the granting of that cherished privilege, and just as scrupulously did he observe its termination. Every day *poilus* could be seen with pack and rifle going to or returning from the family reunion. When at home, they did not loaf about the place, but were busily engaged in all manner of chores to help the old people and the children with the farms and livestock.

One day, we drove south along the mountain road known as "le Chemin du Marechal Joffre," a magnificent military road built during the war so as to permit freedom of communication north and south behind the mountain barrier. Our destination was the headquarters of the 32nd Division, where we met General Wright, the Corps Commander, for the purpose of joining him in a tour of inspection of the units of that division. Major General Hahn, a sturdy American of German parentage, was the Division Commander, and Colonel W. D. Connor, a member of the War College staff when I was a student there, was its Chief of Staff. Staunch friends of mine they were, as was General Wright. Needless to say we had a busy and most interesting day visiting the brigades, the regiments, the battalions and the front lines. I went with General Hahn to an observation post and looked out on "No man's land." Not a man, or a gun, or animal could be seen in the German lines. All was hidden from view, yet we knew that keen ears were listening for every sound and that watchful eyes were observing every moving twig or bush. It was a pleasant, rolling country, south of the mountain masses and east of the fortress city of Belfort.

At Suarce, the headquarters of the 64th Brigade, we witnessed an air circus, as the soldiers called it. Suddenly and without warning, a German plane swooped down from the clouds like a hawk and attacked a nearby French observation balloon with its machine gun. Promptly the balloon was aflame, but not before the French observer nonchalantly dropped from it and, with his open parachute, lazily floated to the ground. Anti-aircraft and machine guns opened on the plane from every direction and seven or eight French planes took off from the ground and went in pursuit of it until well over the German lines, when they became, in their turn, targets for anti-aircraft guns. All returned home in safety. The excitement of the day was at an end and the spectators went about their usual tasks.

General Hahn, at the close of the day, said suddenly, "How would you like to command the 64th Brigade?" I replied, "I should like it very greatly indeed, but with the understanding that it would not interfere with my being transferred to the Marine Brigade when General Harbord is promoted." Nothing more on the subject was said until I told General Wright of the interview, when he replied, "Don't hesitate to take the 64th Brigade if it is offered you, for if you command it successfully, as I am sure you will do, it will be an additional reason for assigning you to the 4th Brigade at the proper time."

I returned to Wesserling after dark, tired but much cheered by the prospect of obtaining command of a combat unit. We continued our daily activities and soon felt qualified for membership in the order of the chamois, or the mountain goats. The strenuous exercise was extremely beneficial, however, and our fine physical condition stood us in good stead during the arduous days that were ahead of us.

Wesserling had its air circus, too. One afternoon, a German plane at great altitude was fired on by the anti-aircraft guns and, after a number of shells had burst wide of the mark, one seemed to make a hit. At first the plane was obscured by the smoke, but as it blew away we saw the plane falling slowly as it moved in circles, for all the world like a bird with an injured wing. Finally, it reached the ground and both the pilot and the observer climbed out quickly before it burst into flames. The pilot calmly lit a cigarette, causing much enthusiasm on the part of the crowd of soldiers and civilians who admired his coolness and his nonchalance. The two prisoners were marched off in a few minutes to General Renouard's headquarters and their military activities were at an end for the remainder of the war.

The next day was July 4th, and the French people celebrated it with as much enthusiasm as did the Americans. Everywhere French and American flags were flying, and joint patriotic celebrations were held. General Renouard held a decoration ceremony to which we were invited. He pinned the badges of honor on the breasts of the heroes, saluted them on both cheeks and addressed them in moving terms; the band played the Marseillaise and the Star-Spangled Banner, the troops presented arms and passed in review. The invited guests and the men decorated then adjourned to the General's quarters where appropriate toasts were proposed and drunk, and all the Frenchmen expressed their happiness and gratitude because America was aiding them in their struggle to maintain what their forefathers had aided ours to gain.

As it turned out, this was my last day in the Valley of Thann, as early the next morning we motored over to 32nd Division Headquarters and found awaiting us there my orders assigning me to command the 64th Brigade, and detailing Major Ellis as Brigade Adjutant. We were jubilant, as at last our period of probation had ended, and in less than a month after our arrival in France I had gained the command of a combat brigade at the front, preliminary to being assigned to the command of the Marine Brigade. General Hahn seemed much pleased to have us in his Division, and my old War College friend, Colonel Connor, the Division Chief of Staff, welcomed me warmly.

After luncheon, we motored over to Suarce where the headquarters of the 64th Brigade was located. Brigadier General Boardman received me most cordially, saying he would remain with me for two or three days in order to give me full opportunity to inform myself in regard to all the details of my new command. General Boardman had been for many years the very efficient Adjutant General of the Wisconsin National Guard and had eagerly hailed the opportunity to command the Wisconsin National Guard Brigade when it, together with the Michigan Brigade, was assigned to the 32nd Division. His health, however, was not good, and he realized after nearly two months' service in a quiet sector that he was not physically equal to the demands which would be made upon him in an active campaign. A fine type of officer and gentleman he was! A great pity it was, too, that the natural infirmities of age should have deprived him of the opportunity he had so ardently longed for.

The 64th Brigade, while under the administrative control of 32nd Division Headquarters, functioned tactically under the command of Major General Biese, the commander of the French division which occupied one-half of the southernmost sector on the western front. General Biese, therefore, became my immediate commanding officer, while at the same time I fell heir to the command of the three French infantry regiments of General Biese's division.

The French infantry commander, Colonel Morvaux, had his headquarters in the same building as did the 64th Brigade. Officially he was on duty "near General Lejeune," his orders being so phrased, but actually he was my counsellor, adviser and instructor. Never was an instructor more completely disguised. Never by the slightest chance did he reveal himself in such a capacity. He spent hours, however, in conversation with me. He spoke French beautifully and I found myself becoming skilled in understanding his accounts of his war experiences and in comprehending their application to the tactical questions which they were intended to illustrate. He was striking in appearance, looking for all the world like a Scotchman. A man with brilliant red hair and mustache, pale blue eyes, an English swagger, a tall, powerfully built frame, and a bright, ruddy complexion ought by all the rules of the game to have spoken English fluently; but not one word of it did he know. However, he made up for it, for he surely did speak French volubly, fluently, rapidly and with both hands. I was in a state of exhaustion every day when he left me, but I made great strides in learning how to understand the French language, even if I didn't get much practice in speaking it during his visits.

I also saw General Biese frequently. He had served throughout the war, rising step by step to the command of a division. His greatest opportunity came during Ludendorff's mammoth drive against the British the previous spring, when he almost succeeded in thrusting a wedge between the British and the French armies. General Biese's division was thrown into the gap. The impetuosity of his attack, combined as it was with the element of surprise, brought the enemy advance to a halt temporarily and gave time for the sore stricken Allies to bring up sufficient troops to fill the gap between the two armies and to stop the advance of the hitherto victorious enemy. The casualties in his division were very heavy, however, and it saddened one's heart to see the depleted companies and battalions.

General Biese, as well as the Army and Corps Commanders, were very cordial and friendly. In fact, all the French general officers whom I met were free of what we call "side." ' They seemed to be without conceit, or egotism, and I could observe no evidences of personal ambition among them. All appeared to be entirely intent on driving the enemy army from the soil of their beloved country and in saving *la belle France* from subjugation by their hereditary foes.

They were exemplars, too, of true democracy; their attitude towards the French soldiers being in no sense one of superiority, but always that of a father towards his son. Similarly, there was a delightful atmosphere of camaraderie between the Generals and their aides and other junior officers on unofficial occasions. All seemed to talk at once, and one man's opinion was as good as another's without regard to the rank of the officers engaged in the argument or conversation. Where all were so exquisitely courteous, it appeared to be impossible for anyone to take offense. When a stranger like myself expressed his views, however, there was instant silence, and all listened intently until his flow of language ceased, when the senior, if he differed with him, would reply that the General is right, but that under such and such different conditions, such and such ought to be done.

I was a witness, too, of an impressive scene which

showed the serious side of the Frenchman's character. The Army Commander, accompanied by General Biese and their staff, stopped by Brigade Headquarters to invite me to join them in a visit to the headquarters of each of the regiments in line— two American and three French. The call at the American regimental headquarters was purely one of courtesy, but at the headquarters of the French regiments, General Dubail, the French Army Commander, spoke very seriously about the importance of preparing the second defensive position, as one could never predict far in advance when an enemy blow would be struck.

In reply, one of the French regimental commanders, with deep feeling, expressed the view that his men were insufficient in number to hold the wide front assigned to the regiment, that they were overworked, that he had no available men for trench digging, and that replacements to fill up the depleted ranks were absolutely essential.

The General was greatly moved by the words of his subordinate and spoke with much fervor and eloquence in reply. He said, in substance, "My friend, the high command knows the condition of your regiment. It is the same as that of nearly all French regiments. France has no replacements except the wounded men who have recovered from their injuries. These have been assembled to meet as best they can the needs of the divisions now in readiness to resist the enemy attack in the Champagne and on the Marne. You will hear great tidings from that front in a few days. We are confident of victory. France is doing all in her power. She can do no more. Tell your soldiers what I have told you and appeal to their love for France to continue to give their whole hearts and their whole strength to the defense of their native land—until the last enemy is driven from its soil."

The regimental commander said, *"Mon General,* we will do our best."

Everyone was visibly affected. I felt as if I were a

participant in a holy sacrament. We made the customary farewell salutation, saying, *"Au revoir—bonne chance"* to each other, and then returned to our posts of command.

My conception of my duty as commander of the 64th Brigade involved the gaining of the good will and the affection of the officers and men. I wanted to know them and I wanted them to know me. To accomplish this, I made personal visits to each regimental and battalion commander and impressed on them that it was the desire of Brigade Headquarters to help them in the performance of their tasks in every appropriate way; that they should not hesitate to let us know their troubles or to ask us for what they needed; and that I wanted them to feel that I was their friend.

I then visited each company, and when doing so I not only questioned the company commanders concerning their mission, their duties and their plans of defense, but personally inspected the roller kitchens, observed the men at mess, and made inquiry in regard to their food, their clothing and their grievances. I also went into every front line position and in so doing tramped untold miles through the trenches. I talked to groups of men informally, telling them that they were opposed to a wary foe who by reason of four years' war experience had acquired great skill in the profession of arms; that while Americans were by inheritance as brave as the bravest, yet it behooved them to acquire superior skill in war, and that this could be done only by careful attention to their duties and by unremitting study and training. I also impressed on them the fact that Americans were prone to be careless and to pay too little attention to details; and that they must overcome these defects and always have in mind that ceaseless vigilance is the price of victory. I illustrated my talks by relating instances that I had read of the disastrous results of being surprised by sudden attacks, and told them of an occurrence in their own brigade when the roller kitchen of a company in a support position had been carelessly placed at a crossroads in the open, and while the men were lined up to get their dinner, an enemy battery had opened fire on the crossroads, killing or wounding several men.

To be a successful leader, a commander must not only gain contact with his men, but he must give them the impression of his fearlessness. The soldier looks for that quality in his chief, and if he show timidity his usefulness is ended. I was fortunate in being able to determine the proximity of a shell by the song it sang as it hurtled through the air, and so it came about that I acquired a reputation for courage by lighting my pipe on one occasion as the enemy shell suddenly began to fly overhead while the other bystanders took shelter in a dugout. It wasn't a question of courage at all, but one of knowledge. As a matter of fact, I learned afterwards that those particular shells had found a target a mile or two farther to the rear.

At Suarce, we were not disturbed by enemy shell, but enemy planes frequently visited us. They seemed to have a special grudge against the near-by French observation balloon and the railhead concealed in an adjacent clump of woods. The former they frequently attacked with machine guns and the latter with bombs. Their aim was poor so far as the railhead was concerned and their missiles often fell uncomfortably close to Suarce. It is an ill wind, though, that blows no good. In this case, the French children derived a tremendous amount of pleasure from the bursting bombs, barely waiting for them to explode before they ran screaming with joy and chattering like magpies to see the holes they had made. Early one morning, however, they got a real scare as the bomb was dropped in the outskirts of the town and the shock of the explosion burst some of the window 'panes and shook the houses in a terrifying manner. I thought my particular peasant cottage had received a direct hit, but no real harm was done to it except to frighten the hens, the rabbits, the pigs, the horse, and the cow who occupied one end of it according to the custom of the country.

Another morning, at the break of dawn, I was awakened by a roar of cannon. It was my first introduction to what was known as drum fire. The sound was continuous and awesome. In a few minutes I was at Brigade Headquarters and learned that an attack or raid was being made on a small combat group of the French regiment on the extreme right. I at once drove to the headquarters of the regiment and, finding that the Colonel had gone up to battalion headquarters, I followed him there on foot. He was the same Colonel who had asked the Army Commander for more men. The German artillery had overwhelmed the little combat group with thousands of shell and then the raiding force had succeeded in entering the position and in carrying away with them two or three wounded men. The few unwounded men had made good their withdrawal and were then at battalion headquarters. The Colonel showed his keen distress because of the loss of some of his brave men, but began at once to make preparations for a retaliatory raid.

I gave orders for a raid to be made by one of the American regiments, but before it took place, orders for the relief of the entire Division by the 29th (American) Division were received, and the instructions for the raid were countermanded.

A few days before leaving the sector, I participated in the joint celebration of Bastille Day—July 14th—the great French national holiday. Throughout the war this celebration was held, regardless of circumstances, in all places where troops were located. At Suarce we had a review of French and American troops, at which General Biese and a large delegation of French officers were present. After the review, I invited both the American and French officers to the brigade mess where champagne was served and appropriate healths were proposed and drunk. A national holiday in France without champagne was unheard of, and we necessarily conformed to the custom of the country. At noon I breakfasted with the Prefect of Belfort, the Sub-Prefect, and our ideas were the other guests. After breakfast, we were shown through the fortress and about the town.

Belfort is one of the heroic cities of France, having successfully withstood a siege by the German army during the Franco-Prussian War. To symbolize the heroism of its citizens, Bartholdi, the famous sculptor, had carved a lion of gigantic proportions on the face of the rocky precipice on which the fortress stood. The Prefect took us there, and we were introduced to *un ancien soldat* of France who guarded it against the depredations of souvenir hunters. To my surprise, his name was Lejeune, and to meet a Lejeune there brought home to me very forcibly the fact that my father's forebears were natives of France. Altogether it was a very interesting day and served a useful purpose, affording as it did a little much needed recreation for our war-weary French allies.

It was followed the next morning by Ludendorff's last offensive blow—the attack by powerful forces on the Allied positions in the Champagne and on the Marne. His disastrous repulse was hailed with much rejoicing by the French, and their joy was increased ten-fold by the successful counter-attack on the Marne salient on the 18th of July and the ensuing days. The news of the victorious thrust of the spearhead, consisting of the 1st and 2nd American Divisions and the 1st French Moroccan Division, southwest of Soissons and into the flank of the salient produced immense enthusiasm. All day long we were being congratulated by the French, both military and civilian, on the success of the American troops. They seemed to sense the fact that, after four terrible years, the tide had at last turned. They seemed to leap in one great stride to the heights of joy, and their gratitude to America was exuberantly manifested.

On the second day of the attack our orders came to withdraw from the Suarce sector upon being relieved; that night the relief was effected and the following afternoon our Headquarters was established in the attractive town of Vezelois, a suburb of Belfort. The next day, entraining instructions for the 32nd Division were issued, and on the 22nd, at noon, Brigade Headquarters entrained. Each train section was standardized and consisted of so many box cars for *"huit chevaux ou quarante hommes"* in each; so many flat cars for wagons, guns, caissons, machine guns, or whatever else went on wheels; and one passenger coach for officers. As usual, we had no inkling of our destination. Some thought it was Italy, others a rest area, and others that it was the battle front. Many bets were made and the backers of Italy paid that afternoon when our train followed the track going northwest instead of the track leading towards Italy.

It was a fatiguing, sleepless journey of nearly thirty-six hours, but we were greatly cheered by the enthusiastic greetings the soldiers received as we rattled through the towns. Everywhere the people waved and shouted, *"Vive les Americains!"* In the environs of Paris, there were great throngs who shouted lustily as our band played "Madelon," "The Marseillaise," and other well known airs.

Finally, at 10 P. M. the second day, we reached our journey's end. The train stopped in a woods. It was a very dark night, but in a few minutes the train was unloaded, my automobile drove up, and we were installed in our château ten miles away in half an hour. A remarkably beautiful château it was, but no one was there except the old caretaker and his wife who lit the lights and made up our beds in readiness for use. In the morning I was able to appreciate its magnificence and the beauty of the park in which it was situated. Rare paintings, tapestries and statuary had been left in place in the rooms and in the hallways. The room I occupied had four great mirrors reaching to the ceiling, with elaborately beautiful golden frames, and a huge, four-poster bed of the style of the ancient regime, with heavily brocaded curtains about it. Tiled and marble floors were everywhere, as were lofty ceilings and walls exquisitely decorated with works of art. Table linen, silver and china were at our disposal; all this gorgeousness was left within sight of the observation balloons marking the battle front about Compiegne and with the sound of the cannon always ringing in our ears. War is a great changer as well as leveler and we passed in a few days from humble hovels to a palace.

Immediately after breakfast, I set forth to 32nd Division Headquarters to call on General Hahn. There I found awaiting me orders to command the 4th Brigade (Marine) which would become effective upon the reporting of my relief, and learned that the Second Division was marching from the Forest of Villers Cotterets to the area adjacent to that occupied by the 32nd Division.

The next morning, Brigadier General Winans reported at 64th Brigade Headquarters as my relief, and in a short while I was on the road to 2nd Division Headquarters. The 32nd was a splendid division, composed of first-class fighting men and commanded by a leader of superior ability. General Hahn and the 32nd Division rendered distinguished service during the remainder of the war, and I have always taken great pride in the fact that for three weeks I was privileged to command the 64th Brigade of that Division and to serve with General Hahn.

CHAPTER XIV

THE SECOND DIVISION

OUR drive on July 25th to Second Division Headquarters at Nanteuil-le-Haudouin was a remarkable one. Never before had I seen a road so jammed with traffic. It was a continuous procession of motor trucks, wagons, officers' cars, motorcycle riders dashing ahead at a mad pace, camions filled with men, troops marching, field artillery, guns, caissons, and, most thrilling of all, long trains of captured camouflaged cannon being towed by trucks. Every conceivable variety of driver there was—Americans, Frenchmen, Algerians, Moroccans, Senegalese, Tonquinese—all moving along the road in the densest fog of dust. Owing to the congested traffic conditions, we had to plod along with the procession for several hours until our road diverged from the highway which the traffic was following. It was one of those great panoramas that can only be seen in war. It was a sight to stir a man's senses and to start the blood coursing through his veins, no matter how sluggish it might be.

After reporting to the Division Commander, I located Colonel Harry Lee, whose headquarters had halted for the night at Nanteuil-le-Haudouin. After dinner I found Colonel Neville and 4th Brigade Headquarters, some miles away, and spent the evening with them. Everywhere I went I found old friends among the officers and men. It was good to be at home again, but it was a sad homecoming too, as many of those I knew had made the supreme sacrifice, and the living showed the marks of physical exhaustion and mental strain. I spent the ensuing day visiting each battalion and giving praise and commendation to officers and men, and I issued the following order to the Brigade:

283

"I have this day assumed command of the Fourth Brigade, U. S. Marines.

"To command this brigade is the highest honor that could come to any man. Its renown is imperishable and the skill, endurance and valor of the officers and men have immortalized its name and that of the Marine Corps."

In two days' time the phenomenal resilience of American youth had asserted itself. Springiness had returned to their gait, brightness to their eyes, smiles to their faces. On the afternoon of July 27th I heard tremendous cheering. My first thought was that news of a great victory had been received. I went to the place from whence the cheers proceeded and there I found two battalion baseball teams engaged in a nip-and-tuck struggle, while their partisans cheered them on. I felt certain then that the spirit of the brigade could not be broken and that it would continue to flame forth until the end. The spirit of man springs from divinity. It is the God-like quality in man and through its workings in his heart, a transformation is wrought; buoyancy, courage, determination, forgetfulness of self, and love for comrades, his country and the organization to which he belongs dominates his whole being. In after life, he remembers that period of unselfishness and exaltation. It becomes the most sacred part of his life and he glories in the hardship and the suffering he endured, the dangers he faced, the difficulties he overcame, the sacrifices he made, and the courage he displayed. In these memories, and in these only, lie "the glory of war."

Early in the morning of July 28th, General Harbord sent for me. He had just returned from a twenty-four hour conference with General Pershing at Chaumont. He looked very grave as he told me that he had orders to assume command at once of the Service of Supply of the A. E. F. as the relief of Major General Kernan, and that General Pershing had instructed him to turn over to me the command of the Second Division, inasmuch as I was the senior Brigadier on duty with it.

To say that I was surprised is putting it far too mildly. I was stunned. To become suddenly the commander of a division after only a brief experience as the commander of a brigade in a quiet sector, especially of a division with such a remarkable combat record as the Second Division had, and one whose ranks were filled with officers and men who had already gained fame in battle, brought to me the fullest realization of the responsibility which rested upon me, the keenest sense of my own lack of experience, the most earnest and solemn determination to dedicate myself wholly to the sacred duty which had come to me, and the resolution to seek always the guidance of Almighty God, knowing full well that only by His help could I hope to achieve success as a division commander.

General Harbord concluded by telling me that he was anxious for me to retain command of the division, but that in order to do so it was necessary for me to be promoted to the rank of Major General in the very near future. He then asked if the new Naval Appropriation Bill did not authorize two Major Generals for the Marine Corps, and if it were not generally understood that one of these appointments was to go to me. I replied that two Major Generals had been authorized, and that before leaving Washington I had been reliably informed that I would be promoted. However, four weeks had elapsed since the Appropriation Bill had become a law and I had heard nothing further.

He then asked if I did not know any of the senior officers of the Navy on duty in England or France well enough to inform them of the situation and to ask them to communicate the facts to the Navy Department by cable. I said that I knew Admiral Wilson intimately, and that while I did not know Admiral Sims nearly so well, I felt sure he would be glad to send a cablegram if he were requested to do so.

We discussed and decided on the phrasing of a tentative cablegram, and I immediately wrote letters to Admiral Wilson and to Colonel Dunlap of the Marine Corps who was then serving on Admiral Sims' staff, asking him to bring the situation as I described it in my letter to Admiral Sims' attention. I sent both letters to Major Wills in Paris by motorcycle rider, with the request that he forward them by despatch.

To bring a long story to an end, I received a few days later a cablegram from the War Department, sent via General Headquarters, informing me that President Wilson had appointed me a Major General and had authorized me to assume immediately the title and to wear the uniform of my new rank. A similar message came in regard to Neville's promotion. I learned afterwards that both Admiral Sims and Admiral Wilson sent the cablegrams as requested.

At noon on July 28th, General Harbord invited the senior officers of the Division to luncheon at the château where he was sojourning, and after luncheon he told them of his orders, of the deep sorrow he felt on leaving the Division, of his good wishes for it as a whole, and of his affection for the officers and men. It was a very impressive scene and one I remember most vividly.

He then introduced me to them as his successor, making the kindest of references to me. Each of these officers congratulated me heartily and said that while they deeply regretted General Harbord's departure, they were glad I had been selected as his successor, and pledged me their loyal support. I was deeply touched, especially when Brigadier General Ely, next in rank to me, said in his emphatic way, "I have known General Lejeune for years and I know of no one I would rather have succeed General Harbord." It is a matter of the greatest pride to me that the good will between the Army officers of the Division and myself—which began that day—continued unbroken until the end of our service together.

General Harbord bade each of us good-bye, and then left for his new station. A great soldier he had shown himself to be while in command of the 4th Brigade and the Second Division, and his career thereafter demonstrated that he is also a great administrator and a great man.

I immediately assumed my new duties and found, on going to Division Headquarters, that entraining orders were being prepared and that in a day or two we should be on the road again, moving to a new and unknown area.   Fifty-six standard military trains were required to move the Division, less the motor vehicles which proceeded by road.   Inasmuch as one hour between trains was usually required, the last train was due to leave two days and eight hours after the departure of the first train. This gives some idea of the magnitude of the task of moving troops by rail.   As difficult as it sounds, however, long practice caused troop movements to proceed automatically and without confusion or interruption.

The next morning we proceeded on our journey, stopping at Meaux to communicate with the Regulating Officer who informed us that we should report to the Regulating Officer at St. Dizier for further instructions.   I decided instead to go to Chaumont so as to thank General Pershing and the Chief of Staff for their kindness to me, and to learn there the final destination of the Division. Both General Pershing and General MacAndrew were away, but I saw my unfailing friend, General Nolan, and asked him to deliver my message of thanks and appreciation to them.

After a comfortable night at the Guest House, we motored to Nancy, which I had been informed was to be the destination of the troops, thereby making it unnecessary to go to St. Dizier and to Toul for the purpose of communicating with the Regulating Officers.   The Division, as fast as the trains arrived, was billeted at Nancy and the nearby towns, and settled down for what we thought would be a considerable period of training to break in the large number of replacements which we expected to receive at Nancy.

This, I believe, is a convenient place to pause awhile in my personal narrative and to give a summary of the

Division organization and a brief account of its prior activities so that the reader may be able to obtain a better conception of the events which are to follow and to visualize more clearly the men who played leading parts in its glorious history.

Orders for the organization of the Second Division (regular) were issued by the War Department in October, 1917. In numbers it was the same as all the other American divisions. It differed in organization, however, as a brigade of Marines (8,469 officers and men) was substituted for an infantry brigade. Another difference was the fact that the Division was not assembled in the United States before being sent overseas. Actually, when the order for its organization was issued, the major portion of its infantry units were already in France engaged in training or in guard or provost duty at base ports, depots, headquarters, and in building railroads, etc. By the end of January, 1918, the Division was assembled in the Bourmont training area.

The Second Division was composed of the following organizations:

```
        Division Headquarters
            Headquarters Troop
        1st  Field Signal Battalion
        4th  Machine Gun Battalion
        2nd  Engineers
        2nd  Field Artillery Brigade
            12th Field Artillery (75's)
            15th Field Artillery (75's)
            17th Field Artillery (155's)
        3rd  Infantry Brigade
            9th Infantry
            23rd Infantry
            5th Machine Gun Battalion
        4th  Marine Brigade
            5th Marines
            6th Marines
            6th Machine Gun Battalion (Marines)
```

Decorating Marines of Second Division

General Neville pinning Croix de Guerre *on General Lejeune. Colonel Meyer on the right.*

.

2nd Ammunition Train
2nd Supply Train
2nd Engineer Train
2nd Sanitary Train
Train Headquarters and Military Police

The strength of the Division when its complement was full was:

Commissioned officers 979
Enlisted men 27,080
_____
Aggregate 28,059

Also the following:

6,636 Animals
1,078 Animal drawn vehicles
  676 Motor vehicles
   74 Cannon
  216 Caissons
  260 Machine guns
   48 One-pounders and trench mortars

and the weapons and other military equipment carried by the troops.

I have described the organization in detail so as to convey some idea of the magnitude of a division. To move it was a gigantic task, but this was done without great difficulty, the officers and men having become amazingly expert in handling vast aggregations of troops as well as vehicles, supplies and animals, by night as well as by day.

The Division was busily engaged in intensive training during its stay in the Bourmont area. It was a very severe winter in France, but snow, sleet, rain, slush, or mud were not allowed to interfere with the schedule. A minimum of six hours each day did the steady grind continue, and frequently, by reason of maneuvers or long hikes, six hours in a day were extended to eight or ten hours.   Preparation for modern war is a gruelling ordeal, but the time is well spent as it saves human life and makes victory more probable.

It is not surprising, though, that General Bundy's order for the troops to move to the front was greeted with shouts of joy and enthusiasm. The Division began entraining on March 13th and the last units were on their way to the vicinity of Sommedieu by the 18th. Upon arrival in the new area the tactical command of the Division and the Brigades passed to the French.

The Division occupied the Toulon and Troyon sectors, which were located on the east bank of the Meuse, south of Verdun. They were known as quiet sectors, which signified that no major military operations had taken place there for some time and that none were expected in the immediate future. Much local activity prevailed, however. Each night "No Man's Land" was visited by patrols who harried isolated German detachments, obtained information, and captured prisoners. It was natural for the Germans to react, and frequent interchange of artillery and machine gun fire became the order of the day. Mustard gas shells were used by the enemy and a large proportion of a company of Marines was disabled, some being seriously injured and others only slightly, when finally the 9th Infantry was subjected to a raid by a force of four or five hundred men. The raiding force entered the lines between combat groups and surprised a first-aid station. A medical officer and several hospital corpsmen were captured, also a number of others. A small-sized battle then ensued in which heavy casualties were inflicted on the enemy force, with the result that the raiders were driven off and a large proportion of the 9th Infantrymen who had been captured succeeded in escaping and returning to their own lines. Smaller affairs frequently took place, and our men established their ascendancy in "No Man's Land."

This period of service in the trenches was of very great value to the officers and men. They became habituated to being in close proximity to the enemy and inured to the explosion of the shell, the whistling of bullets, the bursting of grenades, the use of cover, the construction of entrenched positions, the discomforts incident to trench life in the winter months, and the loss of sleep. In addition, as all movements of troops and other military activities were conducted at night, they acquired the sense of direction and the ability to find their way in total darkness. This faculty is of enormous advantage to the soldier, so valuable, in fact, as to be worthy of being designated as the "sixth sense."

While training in trench warfare was of great importance, too long service in fortified positions had the tendency to unfit men for open warfare. General Pershing visualized the vital importance of being prepared for the latter and was insistent in requiring all divisions of the A. E. F. to regulate their training schedules accordingly. With this end in view, the Second Division was relieved about May 10th and proceeded to the Robert Espagne area (near Bar-le-Duc). Here, division, brigade and regimental maneuvers were held until about May 20th, when the Division was moved to Chaumont-en-Vexin (north of Paris), preliminary to relieving the First Division at Montdidier. In fact, preparatory orders to effect the relief were actually issued and early on May 30th the billeting parties proceeded to the area just in rear of the First Division to make arrangements for the arrival of their units, but the catastrophe which had taken place a few days before on the Chemin des Dames was threatening to become a debacle.

A great German army, flushed with victory, had reached the Marne at Château Thierry and to the eastward. Soissons had fallen, Rheims was in jeopardy, Paris was again in danger. Thousands of people were leaving there for southern and western France. At this critical hour, Marshall Foch swept aside the prearranged plans and hurled the Second Division into the breach. The change of orders came on Decoration Day at 4 P. M., and in a few days the number of graves of American heroes to be decorated by loving hands in all the succeeding years had increased by more than two thousand Second Division men.

French camions appeared at early dawn on May 31st, and at once there began the great parade of 28,000 fighting Americans through the outskirts of Paris and the streets of Meaux and over the country roads to the stretch of country lying just west of Château Thierry and north of the Marne. The roads were jammed with French refugees. Mothers with babes in their arms, little children, old men and women carrying their most precious belongings or driving loaded ox-carts, were wearily plodding along. Their numbers seemed unending; their woe seemed indescribable. The hearts of the men of the Second Division were touched as never before, and their will to conquer and their determination to drive the invaders from the soil of France became immutable.

It was with these emotions that they arrived at their destinations early in the morning of June 1st. There had been many changes of orders from the French Corps Commander and rumors were flying thick and fast. The Division was deployed across the Paris-Château Thierry road on a front of about 18 kilometers. Some of the remnants of French divisions were still out in front, but all of these detachments passed to the rear of the Second Division during the ensuing two or three days, and the line to be held was shortened pursuant to the order issued on June 5th, which directed the Division to hold and occupy the line: "Southeast corner of the Bois de la Marrette: Bois de Clerembauts: Triangle: Lucy-le-Bocage: Wood northwest of Lucy-le-Bocage: Hill 142: Point on Champillon-Bussiares road 800 meters north of Champillon" (all inclusive).

The Third Brigade held the right sector of this position and the Fourth Brigade the left. The western limit of the Third Brigade Sector was the line Triangle-Coudru. It was in front of this position of the Second Division that the German advance towards Paris was stopped by rifle fire, and it was from this position that the attacks on Bouresches, Belleau Woods, and Hill 142 were delivered on June 6th.

The attack on Hill 142 was made at 4 A. M. on June 6th by the First Battalion of the Fifth Marines, commanded by Major Turrill. The battalion attacked with very little artillery support and in the face of a withering machine gun fire, but took its objective and held it in spite of very heavy casualties and a series of determined counter-attacks.

In the afternoon, at 5 o'clock, a converging attack on Belleau Woods, combined with an attack on Bouresches, was made under the immediate direction of Colonel Catlin. Major Berry's battalion of the Fifth Marines jumped off from a position a short distance northwest of Lucy-le-Bocage and advanced in an easterly direction against the southern portion of the woods, while Major Sibley's battalion of the Sixth Marines moved up a ravine from Lucy-le-Bocage and then advanced in a northerly direction against the southern border of the woods. At the same time, a company of Major Holcomb's battalion of the Sixth Marines attacked Bouresches.

About twenty minutes after the attacks were launched Colonel Catlin was shot through the lungs while standing on a parapet observing with his field glasses the progress of the attacking forces. Major Berry's battalion was enfiladed by machine gun fire as it crossed the wheat field adjacent to the woods. Major Berry himself was severely wounded and the battalion suffered so severely that only a handful of men were able to reach the woods. Major Sibley's battalion captured the southern portion of the woods after grenade and hand-to-hand bayonet fighting had silenced the machine gun nests which disputed its entrance into the woods. Bouresches was taken and held, but Captain Duncan was killed during the advance of his company to the assault on that town. Simultaneously, the left of the 23rd Infantry moved forward to conform to the new line that was established.

The losses were heartbreaking, but the determination and the valor displayed by these young men electrified the world, when the censorship was lifted for a brief space and it became known to all men that the Marines had made a successful attack on the formidable foe which had a few days before smashed through the Allied lines on the north bank of the Aisne, and had triumphantly swept aside all opposition during his rapid advance to the Marne. The effect on the morale of the Allies was stupendous, far greater, in fact, than that of many a major victory gained in the later months of the war. Suddenly, the blackest of nights was illuminated by the rays of the morning sun. Darkness gave place to light, and despair to hope.

Floyd Gibbons, the war correspondent, told me an interesting story a few years ago of the part he played in causing the censor to raise the curtain on June 6th, thereby allowing the details of the battle to be published. Gibbons stated that he went over the top with Major Turrill's battalion in the early morning and wrote a full account of the attack, giving the designation of the units engaged and the names of a number of the officers and men. This account he sent by a motorcycle rider to the press bureau in Paris, and in the afternoon he accompanied Major Berry's battalion in its fateful advance across the wheat field. He was desperately wounded, having been shot through the head, and lay unconscious on the battlefield. It was generally believed that he was dead and it was so reported. The news reached Paris and that evening, at the moment when Gibbons' story of Turrill's attack was handed to the censor, his telephone rang and he was informed that Gibbons, his best friend and his comrade of many years' standing, was dead. The censor laid aside his blue pencil and said, 'This is dear old Floyd's last press despatch. I will pass it just as he wrote it," and then released it to the press. The curtain remained lifted for two or three days, when it was dropped in obedience to an order from General Headquarters.

The drama continued behind the screen, however. It was a contest of skill against skill, will against will, endurance against endurance, valor against valor, and esprit de corps against esprit de corps. The American Marines won the contest; Belleau Woods was theirs. It was a shambles. It was drenched with the blood of America's and Germany's best. It was strewn with the dead of both nations. Over five thousand Marines were killed or wounded within its borders. It is holy ground.

On July 2nd, the Third Brigade attacked and captured the fortified town of Vaux. The attack was conducted in the most approved manner. Artillery preparation for the attack was thorough and complete. The infantry advanced behind a creeping artillery barrage. It took the town without difficulty, mopped it up, captured a goodly portion of prisoners and many machine guns, dug in, and held what it had gained. The casualties on our side were not heavy. Both brigades had found themselves. They had mastered the enemy. They retained that mastery until the war was ended.

On July 9th, the Second Division was relieved by the 26th (Yankee) Division, and withdrew to a reserve position. On July 15th, Brigadier General Harbord was promoted to the rank of Major General and succeeded Major General Bundy as the Division Commander, the latter being detailed to command a corps which was then in embryo. On July 15th, Ludendorff launched his last great offensive. His attack was unsuccessful. In the Champagne especially, it was repulsed with very heavy losses. It was a ghastly and a bloody failure. Foch's opportunity had come. He seized it with a master hand. He determined to thrust a spearhead in the western flank of the Marne salient and to follow it up by an attack all along the line from Rheims to Soissons. He selected the First French Moroccan Division and the First and Second American Divisions to be the spearhead.

His plan was kept in profound secrecy. The only

occurrence that can now be construed in the light of after-events as an indication of Marshall Foch's intentions was an order issued early on July 14th by the Sixth French Army, which directed the Second Field Artillery Brigade to march at once to Betz, where further instructions would be given by the Tenth Army. Ludendorff's attack was expected hourly. The thoughts of all men were concentrated on a successful defense. There was some unfavorable comment concerning the detachment of the artillery brigade when the whole military situation was in such a state of uncertainty.

At 10 A. M., July 16th, while desperate fighting was still going on from Château Thierry to the Argonne, and while many commanders were calling for reserves to aid them in holding their positions, laconic orders were issued for the movement of the foot troops of the Second Division to a new area by camion, and all trains by marching. That area was in the vicinity of Betz, the objective given the artillery on July 14th. The movement was not toward the sound of the guns. It was away from them. The movement took place during the night of July 16-17, and the destination was unknown to the Division Commander, who had hurried to the new area by automobile. Orders for the attack were hastily dictated and issued at 4.30 A. M., July 17th. It was an almost hopeless task to find the Brigade and Regimental Commanders. It was successfully accomplished, however, and the regiments were assembled as speedily as possible. Then came the long march through Villers Cotterets Forest to the Bois de Retz, where the French and German forces confronted each other. "H" hour was fixed at 4.35 A. M., July 18th.

It seemed impossible for the Infantry and the Marines to arrive in time. The march was on a single road which was choked with traffic. Trucks, tanks, ration wagons, water carts, rolling kitchens, artillery, ambulances, motorcycles, automobiles—all were pressing forward in the blackest of nights in a heavy rain, the only illumination being flashes of lightning. That road was no place for foot soldiers. There were too many and too long delays. So they marched in single file off the road, usually in a ditch, holding one to another so as to keep contact and not lose their direction. The fate of nations hung in the balance. The suspense was heart-breaking, but the regiments arrived and moved into place on time.

Three regiments, the Twenty-third and Ninth Infantry and the Fifth Marines, from right to left in the order named, made the attack on July 18th. The Sixth Marines was corps reserve and the Second Engineers division reserve on that day. The day's objective of the spearhead was Chaudun-Vierzy, both inclusive. The attack was to be made in three phases and involved a decided change in direction to the right after the first phase. The artillery preparation was to continue for ten minutes, and then would come the rolling barrage at the rate of 50 meters per minute, which the leading battalions were to follow closely.

All was quiet on the front. The night passed without the suspicions of the enemy being aroused. Suddenly, at 4.35 A. M., a terrific artillery fire burst forth. The earth shook and the very ground was blasted from beneath the enemy's feet. The great surprise attack was skillfully launched. It went forward swiftly through the thick forest and then into the open. It overran and captured many machine guns and cannon. The enemy forces were in a state of confusion. Beaurepaire Farm fell, as did Chaudun and Vierzy, and when the night came the Second Division occupied a line to the eastward of Vierzy.

The following morning at 9 o'clock, the Sixth Marines, supported by a battalion of Engineers, continued the attack and advanced about two kilometers. Casualties were very heavy. The Division had fought a great fight. The speed and power of its attack were irresistible. Its advance had outstripped that of the neighboring divisions. It was the point of the spearhead and drew on itself the concentrated fire of artillery and machine guns. Its troops had not recovered from the effects of the gruelling six weeks in the Château Thierry Sector when they were required to make the extraordinary effort I have tried to describe. Its attack had been remarkably successful. It had punctured the enemy lines to a depth of over ten kilometers. It had captured 80 cannon and more than 3,000 prisoners.

Immediately the German Army in the Marne sector began its retrograde movement. Its divisions, which had succeeded in gaining a foothold on the south bank of the Marne, recrossed to the north bank and the army retired to the line of the Ourcq River, and then, in spite of stubborn resistance, it was driven back to the Vesle. Foch had seized the initiative and continued to hold it until the end. Thenceforth the war took on its final phase, a phase replete with a series of desperate battles, but with ultimate Allied victory plainly discernible after the spear driven home in the flank of the Marne salient on July 18th and 19th.

The Second Division, less the Second Artillery Brigade, was relieved on the night of July 19-20, and moved into a reserve position, where it remained until after the relief of its artillery brigade several days later. It then marched to Nanteuil-le Haudouin area, preliminary to entrainment, arriving there on July 25th. It was on that day that I joined the Fourth Brigade, and it was three days later that I relieved General Harbord in command of the Division, as previously recounted in this chapter.

At that time, the following officers constituted the Executive Staff and commanded the larger units, viz:

Chief of Staff—Colonel Preston Brown, U. S. A.

Assistant Chief of Staff, G-1—Lieutenant-Colonel Hugh Matthews, U. S. M. C.

Assistant Chief of Staff, G-2—Lieutenant-Colonel G. A. Herbst, U. S. A.

Assistant Chief of Staff, G-3—Colonel J. C. Rhea.

Commander of Second Artillery Brigade—Brigadier General Albert J. Bowley.

Commander of 12th Field Artillery—Colonel Manus McCloskey.

Commander of 15th Field Artillery—Colonel Joseph R. Davis.

Commander of 17th Field Artillery—Colonel John R. Kelly.

Commander of Third Brigade—Brigadier General Hanson E. Ely.

Commander of 9th Infantry—Lieutenant-Colonel Edward R. Stone.

Commander of 23rd Infantry—Colonel Paul B. Malone.

Commander of 4th Brigade (Marine)—Brigadier General Wendell C. Neville.

Commander of 5th Marines—Colonel Logan Feland.

Commander of 6th Marines—Colonel Harry Lee.

Commander of 2nd Engineers—Colonel W. A. Mitchell.

Colonel Leroy S. Upton had served as the Commander of the 9th Infantry from February 24th to July 24th, 1918, and was relieved because of illness.

Colonel Wendell C. Neville had commanded the 5th Marines from January 1 to July 16, when he assumed command of the Fourth Brigade.

Colonel Albertus W. Catlin had commanded the 6th Marines from the organization of the Regiment to June 6th, when he was relieved because of a serious wound received in battle.

CHAPTER XV

NANCY- MARBACHE, COLOMBEY-LES-BELLES

WE arrived in the beautiful city of Nancy on August 1st. It is a miniature Paris and has a wonderful history, having been for centuries the capital of the Duchy of Lorraine. The exquisite palace of the deposed King of Poland, who was also the Duke of Lorraine, is a gem of artistic beauty, and it, as well as the grounds, was kept in the best of condition by the city. The billets of the officers and men of the Division were more comfortable than had hitherto been the case, and all enjoyed their proximity to an interesting city.

My brief stay there was signalized by the visit of Assistant Secretary of the Navy Franklin D. Roosevelt and some six or eight officers of the Navy. He inspected the Marines and directed that the Marine Corps Uniform Regulations be amended so as to authorize the enlisted men of the 4th Brigade to wear the Corps device on the collars of their uniform coats as a special mark of distinction, and he commended the Marines in the highest terms for the heroism and the magnificent fighting qualities of which they had given proof in Belleau Woods and in the attack southwest of Soissons. He was, and no doubt still is, a great friend of the Marines, and a virile, straight-shooting man as well. I always liked him, but my liking and admiration have been strengthened and increased by the courage and the optimism he has shown since he became crippled about nine years ago.

I gave him a dinner at the Cafe de Paris in Nancy and invited the Brigadier Generals, members of the Division Staff and other senior officers. The dinner was also intended partly to celebrate my promotion to the rank of Major General, notice of which had come on

August 3rd, as described in the following quotation from the letter I wrote home that day::

"The great surprise came today. This morning when I went to the office, the Adjutant, Major Pearson, congratulated me and when I asked him what it was about, he handed me a sealed envelope addressed to *Major General* Lejeune. On opening it I found it contained a telegram from General Harbord congratulating me on obtaining the additional star. In the afternoon, a copy of the official cablegram from the War Department to General Pershing arrived. It stated, 'Brigadier General Lejeune, appointed by the President permanent Major General and pending confirmation by the Senate he is authorized to assume the rank and wear the uniform of the new grade.' All the senior officers of the Division came in to congratulate me. Somehow, I don't feel at all elated, but am sobered by the task before me, the necessity of making good, the responsibility for the well-being and the lives of 28,000 officers and men, and, greatest of all, the fact that my acts may in some critical moment have a decisive effect in winning or losing a battle. Every night of my life, I pray God to take from my heart all thought of self or personal advancement, and to make me able to do my full duty as a man and as a General towards my men and my country."

The next day, the French Army and Corps Commanders called at Division Headquarters and held a conference at which there were present, besides myself, General Summerall and the other General Officers and the Chiefs of Staff of the First and Second Divisions. General Gerard, the Army Commander, made a long statement to the effect that he fully realized how greatly the two divisions needed rest and recuperation after their stupendous efforts of the last three or four months, and that it had been intended to give them at least a month in Nancy and Toul and their environs, but that it had become necessary to relieve two French divisions which were in line on our front for use in the theatre of active operations, and that there were no other divisions available except the First and Second. He promised, however, that their stay in line would be brief.

The march to the front began the next day, August 5th, and continued each day until the 9th, when Division Headquarters was moved to a very small, squalid, sad-looking town called Marbache. I took over the command of the Marbache, or Moselle, Sector at 8 A. M. on that day, with the First Division on our left in the Saizerais Sector, both divisions forming a part of the 32nd French Corps under the command of General Passaga. A noble old Roman he was, and the ten days' service under his command form a very happy memory which was vividly recalled a few years ago when he visited the United States.

Just before we went into line, General Gerard gave a luncheon at his Headquarters to General Summerall, myself, and a number of other American officers. He was comfortably located in a very attractive villa where he had spent almost the entire period of the war. When I arrived, his aide said to me, "If you wish to please the General, compliment his flower garden and the plum tart or pie which will be served at luncheon." The flower garden was exquisitely beautiful and furnished a revelation of the aesthetic side of the General's nature. My praise of the garden was spontaneous and needed no prompting. The luncheon too was a work of art and was capped by the most delicious plum tart I had ever eaten. The General beamed when I commended the culinary ability of his cook and the delightful flavor of the plums. He insisted on serving me with a second tart and then discoursed at length on the superior virtues of Lorraine plums and the virtues of every other product of

Lorraine, including its briar-root pipes, presenting me, at the same time, with one of them as a souvenir.

The Marbache sector was uniquely organized, the Division being astride the Moselle River with the 9th and 23rd Infantry and the 5th Marines on the east bank, and the 6th Marines on the west bank. Liaison was effected by the elaborately camouflaged bridge at Point-à-Mousson and by other bridges further south. The front lines extended along the Seille River from Port-sur-Seille to a point near Les Menils and thence in a southwesterly direction to the Moselle, just north of Pont-à-Mousson, and thence to the northern border of Bois Pretre. The real line of resistance, however, lay along the heights of Sainte Genevieve, the northern segment of "La Grande Couronne de Nancy," approximately six kilometers in rear of the extreme front.

The front lines were lightly manned, while the bulk of the infantry and practically all of the artillery were in position on the heights, the infantry being echeloned in depth. It was an interesting sector, and on a clear day, the spires of Metz were plainly visible from the observation tower near Sainte Genevieve. As stated in a previous chapter, this was the very terrain we had studied so diligently on maps during the first few months of the course at the Army War College and as I went about the sector visiting the organizations, I had the uncanny feeling that I had seen it all before and that I was treading on familiar ground. It was indeed historic ground, as on it armies had marched and fought not only during the World War and the Franco-Prussian War, but on many other sanguinary occasions.

On the whole, however, it was a quiet ten days we spent on the Moselle—a quiet that was only broken by desultory artillery fire, active patrolling of No Man's Land by our troops, and a German raid on the combat group of the 5th Marines nearest the Moselle River. Before we relieved the French Division, General Passaga had warned me to be on guard against a German attack on that particular part of the front, saying that it had been their invariable custom to make the raid within two or three days after a new division had occupied the sector, utilizing the "storming troops," which were always under training at Metz, for such purposes. Our men were duly warned and fully prepared, and when the attack materialized, the attacking force was repulsed by our fire, leaving behind a number of dead and one prisoner. The wounded they succeeded in carrying back to their lines under cover of darkness. General Passaga was delighted and immediately went to the front to congratulate the victors and to present them with the prize of 1500 francs which he had offered to the detachment capturing the first prisoner.

A day or two afterwards, the House Committee on Naval Affairs visited the Division. They went first to Sainte Genevieve to view the enemy territory and thence to each town occupied by Marines. The men gathered around them, and patriotic speeches containing much praise were made, and then each Congressman announced his state and district and asked his constituents to come up so he might speak to them. My Congressional friends had a wonderful time talking to the boys from home and made notes of messages to be delivered to their parents when they got back to the United States. They and the senior officers assembled at Division Headquarters for supper, and after supper Congressman Padgett, the Chairman, took charge of the meeting and called on different officers to relate some of their experiences. The last speaker was Colonel Paul B. Malone. He spoke so eloquently and so thrillingly that Congressman Riordan, who had gone to school with him in New York City, said, 'Paul, after having heard your speech, I am mighty glad you went in the Army, for if you had stayed in the district, you and not I would be its representative in Congress."

Another event of interest was the arrival of the noted actress, Elsie Janis. Accompanied by her mother, who never let her get beyond the protecting shadow of her

Secretary of the Navy Daniels and General Lejeune in Germany.

U. S. S. **Henderson,** *which carried a large proportion of Marines to France.*

wing, she went from place to place in France wherever American soldiers were stationed and gave performances each day.   We had built a platform in a natural amphitheatre on the outskirts of a town occupied by two battalions and other units in reserve.   A vast crowd of soldiers and French people sat on the slopes of the surrounding hills and the Division Commander and a group of officers were seated in front of the stage.   I introduced Miss Janis to the audience, and then, within sound of the cannon at the front, she sang, she danced, she acted, she told stories, she engaged in repartee with the soldiers, and finally, just as the sun was setting, she turned handspring after handspring to the great delight of the men. At the end they cheered her repeatedly.   It was a wonderful demonstration of the power of an actress whose heart was filled with love for humanity and whose spirit was imbued with patriotism.

After ten days of duty in the Marbache Sector, the Second Division was relieved by the 78th American Division under the command of Major General Burnham. By August 19th, the relief was completed and we were installed in a training area to the southward of Nancy and Toul.   Division Headquarters was located in the town of Colombey-les-Belles.

Not recreation, but the hardest kind of work, was ahead of us all.   I refer to the training necessary to prepare the newly constituted division for battle.   After the bloody struggle of July 18th and 19th the strength of the Division was reduced to approximately 20,000 men, about 8,000 below the authorized complement.   Nearly all of this shortage existed in the two brigades of infantry, which meant that these combat units were depleted in numbers by nearly one-half.   It was vital to the combat efficiency of the Division that an adequate number of replacements should be received promptly and that there should be a period of intensive training so that the companies and the battalions would be in shape to play an effective part in the approaching attack on the St. Mihiel salient.   When we arrived at Nancy on August 1st, a

replacement battalion of about 1,000 Marines was awaiting us there, but even with this reinforcement the 4th
Brigade was about 2,500 men short and there were no
more Marine replacement battalions in France.

I learned that unless additional Marines became available at once, Army replacements would be supplied. I
knew that the mingling of the personnel in that way
would be disastrous to the esprit de corps of the 4th
Brigade, and I at once wrote to General Harbord and
urged him to transfer to the Second Division all Marines
in France who were fit for duty. I also wrote to Major
Wills and requested that he notify General Harbord of
the whereabouts of all the men whose names were on
his payrolls. Very soon thereafter, they began to arrive
in small details or detachments. Guards from base ports
and supply depots; the company from G. H. Q. at Chaumont; a detachment from England; men detained at
hospitals for use as orderlies, chauffeurs, etc.; individuals
assigned to duties of all descriptions; men who had got
lost—every variety of Marine came home! Very soon
the ranks were nearly full and the menace to the efficiency
of the 4th Brigade disappeared. Thereafter there were
no further difficulties on that score, as ample Marine
replacements began to arrive in France early in September.

The Army units, also, received their replacements,
many of them from the 36th Division which had just
arrived in France. Splendid material nearly all of these
Marines and Army men were, but in need of training
in the use of infantry weapons and lacking in practice in
battalion maneuvers. At Bois l'Eveque, ranges for target
firing were established and constant practice was held
with rifles, pistols, machine guns, trench mortars, 37 mm.
cannon, rifle grenades and hand grenades; also a series
of infantry battalion demonstrations.

From daylight to dark, these preparations for battle
continued unceasingly. Finally, a rehearsal of the approaching attack was held over ground similar to that to
be traversed by the Division. It simulated actual battle

as nearly as possible and was witnessed by officers, including Brigadier General Fisk, from the Training Section at G. H. Q. After its completion the officers were assembled, the mistakes made were pointed out, and I closed the critique with a brief address in which I dwelt on the vital importance of the correct handling of tactical units, and concluded with the statement that tactical errors on the battlefield spelled not only failure, but unnecessary loss of human life; that avoidable ignorance on the part of officers was inexcusable and reprehensible; and that it was their bounden duty so to prepare themselves as to be able to lead their men in such manner as to achieve victory with a minimum of loss.

While interesting myself whole-heartedly in the military training of the Division, I deemed my highest duty to be the welding of all its units into a harmonious whole, and the kindling and fostering of a division spirit, or esprit, which would animate the hearts of all its officers and men.

There is no substitute for the spiritual, in war. Miracles must be wrought if victories are to be won, and to work miracles men's hearts must needs be afire with self-sacrificing love for each other, for their units, for their division, and for their country. If each man knows that all the officers and men in his division are animated with the same fiery zeal as he himself feels, unquenchable courage and unconquerable determination crush out fear, and death becomes preferable to defeat or dishonor.

Fortunate indeed is the leader who commands such men, and it is his most sacred duty to purify his own soul and to cast out from it all unworthy motives, for men are quick to detect pretense or insincerity in their leaders, and worse than useless as a leader is the man in whom they find evidences of hypocrisy or undue timidity, or whose acts do not square with his words.

To be a really successful leader, a senior officer must avoid aloofness, too. He should not place himself on a pedestal and exercise command from a position far above the heads of his men, but he must come down to the ground where they are struggling and mingle with them as a friend and as a father. A word or two of sympathy and of praise spoken to wounded men or to men exhausted from the stress of combat may change depression to exaltation and, being spread about among the men, may cause them to feel that their chief has their welfare at heart and that he is full of human sympathy for them.

I made it a rule never to reprimand an enlisted man, or to censure an officer in the presence of his men. How could a Division Commander correct conditions among 28,000 men by shouting at an individual who might perhaps have his coat unbuttoned, or have on rubber boots under forbidden circumstances; or how could junior officers retain the respect of their men if scathingly rebuked in their presence? Personally, I preferred to see the looks of affection in the eyes of the men when I went about among them than to know that they feared and dreaded my visits. Kindness and justice combined with severe punishment of serious offenders will, I believe, result in a higher state of discipline than can be produced by constant nagging and by unduly harsh punishments for petty offenses.

A Division Commander, too, must stand ready to fight for his men, even at the risk of offending higher commanders. The knowledge that in him they have a champion who is willing to go to the mat, if necessary, to protect them from injustice, to see that they are not imposed upon, and to insist that their creature comforts are looked out for, will cause them to redouble their efforts to gratify him, to give all their strength and all their power to carry out his will, and to do more than is humanly possible to defeat the enemy. It is indeed true that in war the spiritual is to the material as three or even four to one.

In the World War, the division was the largest permanent tactical and administrative unit. The corps was only a temporary tactical unit. It retained its divisions until they were too exhausted and too depleted in numbers to continue the combat, when they were sent to the rear to recuperate and to receive replacements, and other divisions took their places. There was no permanency, either, in the assignment of divisions to an army. In fact, the divisions moved from one part of the front to another and led the lives of nomads. The Second Division, for instance, during its stay overseas, served in not less than nine corps and seven armies.

The divisions, because of their permanence and their sufficiency unto themselves, became more and more clannish and offered the greatest field for the exercise of the powers of leadership on the part of their commanders. In the Second Division, every opportunity was utilized to make officers and men believe that their division was the greatest aggregation of fighting men ever assembled, and that in very truth it was invincible. There was no inferiority complex about the Second Division. We knew not only that we were second to none, but also that we were better than any! So we adopted the star and Indian head as the Division insignia, the Indian head representing its fighting ability, and the star its spirit or esprit de corps. It was, I think, the first division of the A. E. F. to wear insignia. We carried the idea out, too, to its logical conclusion by providing a different background for each regiment, each battalion, and each separate detachment. Not only was this system beneficial to discipline, enabling us to determine at a glance to what organization a man belonged, but it was an aid to building up the esprit of the smaller organizations within the Division.

While in the training area of Colombey-les-Belles, the Division received some seventy-five decorations for officers and men. We determined to award them in the presence of a large body of troops and to make the ceremony a memorable one. At Bois l'Eveque, there was a large maneuver field, and except for being too near the front it was ideally fitted for a "big parade." We arranged for a large force of United States airplanes to be in readiness to drive off any too impulsive German planes that might decide to try to break up our show, and we also warned all the anti-aircraft batteries to be on the alert. Sunday morning and ten o'clock were the day and the hour selected. The troops were formed prior to that time, and very promptly Major General Liggett, who had been designated by General Pershing to represent him, marched on the field to the reviewing point accompanied by Major General Dickman and a number of other officers.

There was a great array of troops. Each regiment of Infantry and Marines was represented by one battalion, each Artillery regiment by a battery, each Machine Gun battalion by a company, the Second Engineers by a battalion, and each separate unit by a detachment of fifty men. The prescribed ceremony was carried out in every detail, and it moved one's soul to see seventy-five stalwarts march to the front and center, followed by all the colors and standards of the Division. Distinguished Service Crosses, Medailles Militaire, and the Croix de Guerre were the awards. General Liggett pinned the appropriate decoration on each man's breast while his citation was being read, and then shook his hand and personally congratulated him, as did each of the accompanying officers. When he had finished, he stood in front of the line and addressed the heroic men. He then faced the troops and received the review of the more than five thousand in line.

In the midst of the review, I saw a German plane flying towards the scene of the ceremony. It was a clear, sunshiny day, and doubtless the aviator had no difficulty in sighting the large assemblage of troops. For a few moments I was disturbed, and then the anti-aircraft guns opened fire. The plane was surrounded by the puffs of bursting shrapnel. Suddenly it showed signs of distress and then began to fall. Faster and faster, until finally it crashed about a mile away. The superstitious declared it to be a good omen. I always believe in good omens, but never in evil ones.

We motored to Division Headquarters for lunch. All were thrilled by the ceremony we had seen, but we were sobered too because the thought was in our minds that in a few days all those gallant men would again be called on to endure the shock of battle and to put their lives in jeopardy.   The period of training at Colombey-les-Belles was at an end.   Orders for the march to the front came the next day.

CHAPTER XVI

BATTLE OF ST. MIHIEL

FOLLOWING the retreat of the German armies from the Marne to the north bank of the Aisne early in September, 1914, and the simultaneous repulse of the attempted advance of the army of the Crown Prince of Bavaria through the gap between Nancy and Epinal, the modified plans of the German high command involved the preparation and the holding of a fortified position to the westward of Argonne Forest and along the Aisne; the advance of the army of the Crown Prince of Prussia in a southerly direction between the Meuse and the Argonne; and an attack from the direction of Metz to the southwest, with the expectation of uniting the two forces on an east and west line running through St. Mihiel, thereby isolating and capturing the French army at Verdun and vicinity. The progress of the Crown Prince's army was stopped without great difficulty a short distance south of Montfaucon and Varennes, but the army operating from Metz was successful in reaching the Meuse river at St. Mihiel and in securing a foothold on the west bank.

This was the tip of the famous St. Mihiel salient. Its southern face ran in an easterly direction across the plain of the Woevre to a point on the Moselle river just north of Pont-a-Mousson, and its western face lay approximately parallel to and several kilometers to the eastward of that river.

The salient I have just described was a thorn in the side of the French throughout the war. It physically interrupted the north and south railway and the highways along the Meuse, and the heavy guns in position within

312

the salient were able with their fire to prevent traffic on the Paris-Nancy railway.

It was this salient which General Pershing selected as the point of attack in the initial engagement of the First American Army.

Colombey-les-Belles was on the highway, and night after night we watched the stream move steadily northward. We knew what it meant. We understood fully that this vast accumulation of men and material was essential to success, and we were determined too that the Second Division, so far as lay within its power, would do its full share towards making that success complete.

We knew of the difficulties our own Commander-in-Chief had had to overcome in order to assemble the American Army; we knew of the strong pressure which had been brought to bear by the Allied commanders in their attempt to retain the American divisions under their control, on the ground that the American commanders and the American staffs were too inexperienced in war to justify their being allowed to control the operations of an army far larger than any which had hitherto served under the American flag; we heard, too, that even partial failure would in all probability spell the redistribution of the American divisions all along the front and the resumption of their control by French, British and perhaps Italian commanders. We also realized fully that the success of the attack would strengthen General Pershing's hands, increase his power, and maintain the honor and prestige of our country and, most momentous of all, we knew that a victory would strike terror into the hearts of the enemy, break down his morale, and bring home to Ludendorff the conviction that inasmuch as the newly organized American Army was capable of delivering an effective and powerful blow, he could not expect any result of the war other than decisive defeat of the German armies, or the conclusion of a peace dictated by the Allies.

These thoughts were continually in our minds during the training period at Colombey-les-Belles and the days that intervened between our departure from that area and the conclusion of the battle.

They were in my mind also when on September 8th the Division Adjutant laid before me for signature the Order of the Day, or *L'Ordre du jour,* as the French called it. It was well expressed and well written, but did not convey clearly the thoughts I have just mentioned. After reading it over, I wrote a tentative order of my own and asked the Adjutant and the Chief of Staff to choose between the two. They unhesitatingly selected mine because it did convey the ideas which had dominated our minds for a month. It was signed and issued to the Division without change and read as follows:

"Headquarters Second Division,
"American Expeditionary Forces,
"France, September 8, 1918.

"The Second Division is again about to attack the enemy. I feel that we should recall the heroic exploits of the Division on the historic battlefields near Château Thierry and Soissons. By these victories the Second Division turned back the invasion of the Hun and immortalized its name and the name of America.

"The approaching battle will constitute a great epoch in our country's history. For the first time, an American army will give battle on the soil of Europe under the command of an American Commander-in-Chief. The prestige and the honor of our country are therefore at stake. I am confident that our division will maintain them proudly and sweep the enemy from the field.

"JOHN A. LEJEUNE,
"Major General, U. S. M. C.,
"Commanding."

During the period of preparation for the attack, its imminence became known to General Fuchs, the commander of the German troops garrisoning the salient. This we learned after the battle from a captured German document which contained his estimate of the local military situation. After analyzing all the elements of the military problem which confronted him, he concluded the estimate with the statement that there were three courses of action available for adoption. These were: first, to make a surprise attack on the American force before it was concentrated and in readiness for battle; second, to stay in place and accept a defensive rôle; and third, to withdraw men and material from the salient and to fall back to the so-called Hindenburg Line, so that the American blow would be struck in the air. He further stated that he preferred the first course of action and would recommend its adoption to the Army Commander provided ample reserves could be furnished, otherwise he would recommend the adoption of the third course of action which, if carried out, would so shorten the front that he could hold it against attack with the force under his command.

The possibility of a German attack must have become known to our high command, because on September 1st we received orders to begin, that night, the movement to a reserve position in the vicinity of Francheville, sending one regiment to the front by motor trucks. So it came about that our stay at Colombey-les-Belles was shortened by about one week.

We were in readiness, however, and the Division was in splendid condition. Every unit was at full strength, and deficiencies in clothing, equipment, etc., were made good before the opening of the battle. My heart swelled with pride as I watched battalion after battalion march by on their journey to the front, singing as they marched, or shouting in stentorian tones, "Where do we go from here?" or joshing each other in the inimitable soldier and Marine fashion.

Again I marvelled at the high spirit of our men.

Nothing seemed to depress or daunt them. They played hard, they worked hard, and they fought hard. They were magnificent!

It was about this time that a change was made in the plan of battle originally furnished us. The change, I have since read, was effected on the initiative of Marshal Foch, who preferred a less ambitious plan than was first proposed as, already, the plan of a great attack to be made the latter part of September between the Meuse and the Suippe Rivers by the First American and the Fourth French Armies had taken form in his mind, and preparations were being made to carry it into execution. The first plan for the battle of St. Mihiel involved not only the pinching out of the salient, but a deep advance through and beyond the Hindenburg Line as well, with the end in view of threatening the Metz-Sedan Railway and the iron district in the vicinity of Briey.

This plan we had carefully studied and discussed in conferences between the general officers and the Division staff. The rôle assigned the Second Division was materially different in its last phases from that assigned in the final plan. Both plans, however, provided for the advance of the Division from Limey to the Rupt de Mad at Thiaucourt. In the first plan, it was the mission of the 89th Division to capture that city, while the Second Division, after assisting its neighbor in the crossing of the Rupt de Mad and in the occupation of Thiaucourt, would proceed in a northeasterly direction through the Hindenburg Line at Rembercourt, and thence almost to the environs of Metz.

The new plan was a much simpler one and the change, therefore, involved but little additional study on our part, as we had already so familiarized ourselves with the terrain by "poring over the maps" that I, for one, could visualize it almost as clearly as if I had spent my boyhood days at Remenauville, Jaulny, or Thiaucourt. Furthermore, there was sufficient time at our disposal after the shift of Division Headquarters to Francheville not only to study the plan of battle ourselves and to prepare all the detailed orders, but also to give opportunity for the officers commanding the brigades, regiments and battalions to do so. Each of these officers knew beforehand the latest information concerning the disposition of the enemy forces and the part his unit would be called on to play in the battle. We could not, of course, predict with certainty what the reaction of the enemy would be, but in all other respects we were, so far as was humanly possible, prepared for the conflict.

Division Headquarters was moved to Francheville on September 3rd. It was the saddest looking village in which we had yet made our temporary home. Our dining room was in the spare bedroom of a French peasant family. Our offices were in a building used for communal purposes. My sleeping place was in an humble cottage—the best in town because it was the cleanest. The proprietress—an old, old lady—was a real virago and screamed and shook her fists at the men who brought in my things. She had a fine supply of rabbits and chickens in the house, and either feared they would be disturbed, or else that her immaculate floors would be soiled. At first, she regarded me with suspicion and watched my every move, but soon I gained her good will by little gifts and friendly words spoken in French, and then she became my staunch friend, and was almost in tears when I said 'au revoir" and drove away, never to return.

General Pershing made the "grand rounds" while we were in Francheville, visiting the headquarters of every division in the First Army. He found everyone at work at Second Division Headquarters. Major Keyser was holding school for the personnel of the Intelligence Department, having commandeered the benches and the blackboards where French children had sat and striven hard to comprehend the mysteries of their three "R's." The General asked many searching questions, all of which we were able to answer to his satisfaction, and on leaving he expressed his pleasure because of our readiness for the approaching battle.

My whole heart and thought went out to our men. The constant, cold, autumn rains had begun and the men in their bivouacs in the woods were wretchedly uncomfortable. Mud—sticky, slimy—was everywhere, and fires were taboo. American airplanes made frequent flights over the woods and villages, and woe it was to the commanders of the units if the presence of the men could be detected from the air. There were many rumors, too, of German spies disguised as American officers riding about the First Army area, and all kinds of restrictions were put on movements of individuals, even Generals. It almost required an Act of Congress to go from the area of one division to that of another.

In spite of the restraints, however, Colonel Rhea and I arranged to go about the areas of the adjacent divisions to observe the troops and to visit the front lines. One day we went to Lironville, where Second Division observers watched the German lines unceasingly in order to detect, if possible, any changes in the disposition of the enemy forces. We drove by automobile up a steep ridge to a point some distance below the crest where all automobiles were required to stop. As we drove up the ridge, we watched the bursting of shell after shell in a ravine about a hundred feet to our left. The Germans were evidently feeling for the road, as the range was slightly shortened after each burst. Just as we reached the crest of the ridge on foot, a shell burst in a group of men who were having kit inspection. Eight of them were either killed or wounded. It was heartbreaking to see the poor mangled and bleeding bodies being carried into a shack which was used as the messroom of the battalion headquarters located there; it was in a woods just behind the crest of the ridge.

We did not linger long at Battalion Headquarters, but went on to Lironville via a deep zigzag communicating trench. Presently we heard sounds of a man's rapid footsteps. He soon appeared and almost knocked us down as he went by at a great rate of speed, shouting, "Run! ——— ——— it! Run! The Germans are shooting at us." His was the only case of a panic-stricken man that I saw during the war, and he didn't belong to the Second Division! The shell were going over in considerable numbers and were striking a hundred or so yards beyond us. It seemed pretty safe to us in that trench. Presently we came to a man, standing on top of the ground, phlegmatically working away with pick and shovel building a ramp across the trench for the small tanks and the artillery to use in the attack. I asked him who the man was who had just gone to the rear. He said, "He is my buddy and was working here with me, but he got the idea in his head that all the guns in Germany were shooting at him, so he beat it." The two men were as opposite as the poles in their behavior under fire, but let us hope that the man who ran soon pulled himself together and made a good soldier later on.

On September 8th, a day or two after this incident, orders preliminary to the attack were issued to the Second Division. These orders involved the partial taking over of its battle sector on the night of September 9-10. The limits of the assigned sector were Limey inclusive to a point one kilometer east of Remenauville. The sector was then occupied by elements of the 89th Division of the 4th Corps, and the 90th Division of the 1st Corps. These two divisions, therefore, were required to narrow their fronts by side-stepping to the left and right, respectively. The 5th Division also entered the front lines, taking position on our right, thereby making necessary a further contraction of the front of the 90th Division. Both the 89th and 90th Divisions, however, left in place the extreme front line elements, so that in the event of German raids being made, any prisoners they might capture would belong to those divisions and the entry of the 2nd and 5th Divisions into the line would not be revealed.

The 3rd Brigade relieved the support and front line battalions, while the 4th Brigade relieved the reserve battalions. The order further provided that the artillery units within the sector would be relieved by similar units of the 2nd Field Artillery Brigade on the night of September 8-9, and that command of the sector would pass to the Commanding General, 2nd Division, at 8 A. M., September 10, at which hour Division Headquarters would be opened "at a point on the Lironville Road." This was the post of command I have previously referred to as having been visited by Colonel Rhea and myself on our way to Lironville.

On the left of the First Corps was the Fourth Corps, with the 89th, 42nd and 1st Divisions in line. These two corps faced the task of breaking through the southern face of the salient by means of a great wheel, or turning movement, to be made on the 82nd Division as a pivot. Facing the tip of the salient and the adjacent portions of its southern and western faces was the Second French Colonial Corps whose task was to follow up the retirement of the enemy. North of the French Corps and opposite to the western face was the American Fifth Corps, with the 26th and 4th American, and the 15th French Colonial Divisions in line. The task of this Corps was to advance its right division to Vigneulles, while the remaining divisions covered its left flank.

The entry of the Second Division into line was accomplished without serious difficulty in spite of the fact that the roads leading to the front were blocked with traffic all of each night, and on the morning of the 10th, as we drove to our new headquarters, the traffic jam still continued. Fortunately, there was such a very low ceiling, to use the idiom of the aviators, that enemy airplane observation during the week preceding the attack was impossible. Our new headquarters was a typical French combat post of command. Deep, bombproof, concrete dugouts, suitably arranged and in readiness for the installation of telephones, electric lights and the meager furnishings which we carried to the front, were at our disposal, but far more inviting were the tiny, one-room "Aladdin" bungalows which the French had erected for occupancy during the state of semi-peace which had existed for a long time in these 'quiet" sectors. Brigadier-General Preston Brown and I occupied one of these flimsy cottages much to the chagrin of my aide, Captain Nelson, who insisted that safety demanded that we should descend into the bowels of the earth. He was partly right, as the enemy, who was evidently of a suspicious nature, shelled the roads and the woods almost constantly, and on the day of our arrival there, one of the many tragedies of war occurred. A shell struck the road within a few yards of our bungalow, killing two men and wounding two or three others of the Second Division Military Police Company.

In war, if a man is to keep his sanity, he must come to regard death as being just as normal as life and hold himself always in readiness, mentally and spiritually, to answer the call of the grim reaper whenever fate decrees that his hour has struck. It is only by means of this state of mind and soul that a man can devote all his thoughts, all his intellect, and all his will to the execution of the task confided to him. Personal fear paralyzes all the faculties, and the attribute of first importance in a commander is freedom from its cold and clammy clutch. Fortunately, a normal man is so constituted that his mind refuses to dwell on morbid ideas, but is ever buoyant, active, and intent on performing the duties assigned him. His thoughts, therefore, turn constantly to the future and do not dwell on the tragedies, the suffering, or the horror of the past. While war is terribly destructive, monstrously cruel, and horrible beyond expression, it nevertheless causes the divine spark in men to glow, to kindle, and to burst into a living flame, and enables them to attain heights of devotion to duty, sheer heroism, and sublime unselfishness that in all probability they would never have reached in the prosecution of peaceful pursuits. Sherman's alleged definition is correct, but thousands, aye millions, of the men who have engaged in war have shown themselves to be truly the children of God.

I must, however, unhitch my chariot from the star and return to the matter of fact subject of the preparation of the orders for battle. There is no more exacting profession or one that requires more painstaking attention to details than the profession of arms in time of war. The preparation of an attack order in the World War required days and nights of the most careful study and analysis on the part of the generals and their staffs, and of junior commanders as well.

The order for the battle of St. Mihiel, for instance, had its inception in a personal interview between Marshals Foch and Petain and General Pershing. General Pershing and his staff prepared the order for the guidance of the four corps constituting the First American Army. Each Corps Commander and his staff worked out the details of the part to be played by his Corps and assigned tasks to each division and to all the detachments of Corps troops.

The Second Division Commander and his staff prepared a tentative plan of attack which was submitted to the Corps Commander on September 8th, and they then prepared and distributed on September 10th the Division order. Brigade and regimental commanders likewise issued written orders for their commands, while the orders of battalion and company commanders were given orally. The Second Division tentative plan and its order for the St. Mihiel attack consisted of thirty-three mimeographed foolscap pages, and included not only the plan of attack, both general and detailed, with reference to each unit, arm and branch, but also full administrative details and ten chapters containing instructions concerning such subjects as the plan of liaison; communication by telephone, radio, telegraph, postal service, balloons, airplanes, panel signals, visual signals, rocket signals, carrier pigeons, couriers and runners; cipher codes and code names; and instructions in regard to the organization of the conquered ground and the distribution of the troops thereon. In other words, the plan of attack and the order were compendiums of information and instruction.

To put the order into final form, the following steps were necessary: a most careful study of the Corps order and plan of attack, particularly that part referring specifically to the Second Division; a detailed examination of the maps; a discussion between the Division Commander and his staff concerning the decisions to be made; the preparation of the tentative order; a careful scrutiny of its provisions; making necessary changes and corrections in its substance, its phraseology, and its arrangement; typewriting the amended order; the examination of the smooth copy and the correction of errors; mimeographing the order; a comparison of it with the typewritten copy (if mistakes were found, a new mimeograph was cut); its distribution by motorcycle riders; and the examination and checking of the return receipts.

This was the procedure followed in preparing the tentative plan of attack and the order for the battle of St. Mihiel, and for other battles in which ample time was available. When the available time was short, it meant sleepless, hectic, and nerve-wracking nights for the Division Commander and his staff in which hours seemed no longer than minutes and the hands flew around the face of the watch, for the element of time was then of crucial importance.

In war, procrastination is a crime, and promptness is a handmaiden of victory.

The Division attack order itself was comparatively brief, detailed information being contained in the tentative plan of attack, copies of which were distributed to the appropriate commanders and staff officers. One hundred mimeographed copies of the Division attack order were distributed, going to seniors as well as juniors, and to commanders of the adjacent divisions and the Fourth Corps. Briefly, it prescribed the following:

"Action: The Second Division attacks on the line Remenauville-Limey; captures Thiaucourt and the line Jaulny-Xammes. By its advance within its own sector, it assists the Fourth Corps in the reduction of the Bois d'Euvezin and the Bois du Beau Vallon."

"Objective: First phase line northern edge of Bois d'Heich-Hill 2442.5."

"First Day's Objective: Northeast corner of Bois

Gerard—northern edge of Bois des Fey—Hill 277.7—
Hill 264.5."

"Army Objective: High ground between Jaulny and
Xammes."

"The Division attacks in columns of brigades, regiments side by side, each with one battalion in front line,
one in support, and one in reserve."

"First line (attacking troops), Brigadier-General Ely,
commanding:

> 3rd Infantry Brigade
> 1st Battalion, 6th Marines
> One Machine Gun Company, 6th Marines
> 2nd Battalion, 12th Field Artillery
> Companies A and D, 2nd Engineers
> Two companies light tanks
> One company medium tanks
> 6—4″ Stokes Mortars
> Company E Gas and Flame Service."

"A combat group of one battalion of infantry (6th
Marines) and one machine gun company will maintain
liaison with the 89th Division on the left."

"Second line (reserve), Brigadier-General Neville,
commanding:

> 4th Marine Brigade (less 1 Bn. and 1 M. G. Co.)
> Companies B, C, E and F, 2nd Engineers
> 4th Machine Gun Battalion
> One company light tanks."

The order further provided that the 2nd Field Artillery Brigade, reënforced by three French artillery regiments, should support the attack, laying down a rolling
barrage preceding the infantry advance at the rate of
100 meters in four minutes to the first phase line, where
a standing barrage would be put down until "H" plus six

hours, when the rolling barrage would continue to the First Day Line at the same rate as previously. The light artillery was also directed to advance by echelon as the attack progressed. "H" hour was fixed at 5 A. M., and the artillery bombardment by all available artillery was to begin at "H" minus four hours, or at 1 A. M. All troops were directed to be in place by 1 A. M.

During the forenoon of September 11th, the senior officers were assembled at Division Headquarters and a final conference was held. Every feature of the attack was discussed and all doubtful points were re-explained and settled. Similar conferences were afterwards held in the minor units.

It poured in torrents all day long and until 3 A. M. September 12th. It was inky dark, and yet the attacking units of thirteen divisions—more than 300,000 men—moved into position and formed for attack over unfamiliar ground, seamed with trenches and pockmarked with shellholes. Lights were forbidden, even at a considerable distance from the front. A senior officer of the Second Division said that in order to get a glimpse of the ground he was traversing, he turned on a flashlight. Suddenly, the sharp voice of an M. P. shouted, "Turn out that light, you —— —— ——!" When asked what he did, he replied, "I turned out the light and then objected to the designation." The men were very sensitive about the appearance of lights, as they did not relish being bombed by airplanes.

We moved into the Second Division post of command after supper and received reports from all of the units as soon as they reached their jump-off positions. All were in place some time before the designated hour. It was a doubly dreary night for them. The cold and clammy feeling that comes to every man on the eve of battle was accentuated by the pouring rain, the darkness, the wet clothes, the mud and water. Trenches were swollen rivulets and low places were miniature lakes. Nothing can be more depressing than waiting and watching under such conditions for the midnight hours to pass. Suddenly, however, silence was banished and the clouds were brightly illuminated. It was the tremendous roar of hundreds of cannon firing simultaneously and the flash of the discharges. There is no sound to which human ears have listened which is comparable to the awe-inspiring continuous crash of artillery fire in preparation for a major attack. There were no intermissions. The sound was not punctuated by a rising or a falling cadence. It was awesome. It was solemn. It seemed to pronounce the doom of all mankind. I left the dugout and walked out on the plateau, in the open. There I could see the long line of flashes of the discharges. It was a continuous blaze of light. The enemy lines were also brilliantly illuminated by our bursting shell, by the blazing fires started by the projectiles of the gas and flame company, and by the pyrotechnics being set off by the German soldiers garrisoning the trenches.

Most weird of all was the song of the shell speeding overhead to find their targets within the enemy lines. Practically all were flying toward Germany; almost none were coming toward us. Each shell sang its own dirge. The notes of the smaller ones were high, like the voice of the tenor, while the notes of the great, monster shell were of the deepest bass. Between the two was infinite variety. The air seemed alive with these missiles of death and destruction. Their flight appeared to be unending. Somehow I was reminded of the migrations of a myriad of wild water fowl flying low at night, each giving its own peculiar cry. Such migrations I had seen and heard in the Louisiana lowlands in my boyhood days. It seemed fantastic to have such a thought then.

Fascinated—almost hypnotized—I stood on the plateau and looked and listened for what seemed an interminable length of time. I could scarcely conceive that there could be a German left living or a tree left standing in the bombarded area, but I knew by what I had heard and read that previous bombardments of even one or two days' duration had not inflicted very heavy loss of life even though the material damage to fortified positions had been great. These bombardments were terrifying and nerve-wracking to the defenders, but they usually found protection in dugouts and held themselves in readiness to emerge in time to meet the advance of the attacking infantry with a hail of bullets.

Before "H" hour, I returned to our own dugout, and a few minutes afterward the reports came in by telephone telling us of the men going over the top, of how they cut lanes through the barbed wire with the wire-cutters, and of how they overtook the barrage, getting so close that they almost leaned on it. As soon as there was light enough, I again took station on the plateau and observed our men going forward resistlessly. I could see them scatter and take cover when a machine gun nest was discovered, and then crawl around the flank until near enough to use their grenades.

Frequent reports were received. All were favorable. They told of overcoming opposition and the steady advance of the attacking forces. Soon, detachments of prisoners began to arrive. They seemed more pleased than otherwise. They told us that for several days their artillery had been going to the rear, that many trainloads of supplies had left Thiaucourt for the rear, and that they had expected the order of withdrawal from the salient within two or three days. When asked if they expected the attack on that morning, some of them replied that in the evening, a few hours before the artillery bombardment begun, most of their officers had been ordered to the rear, and that they then guessed that the attack would soon take place. I had previously read in captured German pamphlets that this precaution was sometimes taken owing to the serious shortage of company officers in the German armies. Its effect, however, was seriously detrimental to the morale of the troops and was, therefore, unwise. It gave me a tremendous thrill to see these long lines of prisoners filing by and to look in their faces in the endeavor to read their thoughts. Altogether it was a wonderful morning.

At 10 A. M., General Ely reported the arrival of his

troops at the first phase line, and at 11 A. M., they went forward as by schedule. By an irresistible rush, his men carried the machine gun positions on the east bank of the Rupt de Mad and, following the retreating enemy closely, crossed the bridges on his heels, and drove away, killed, or captured the detachments detailed to detonate the high explosives which would have destroyed the bridges. By noon they were in possession of Thiaucourt. They then seized the first day's objective without serious opposition and sent patrols forward to the Army objective and the towns of Jaulny and Xammes. A position lying forward of the first day's objective, but somewhat short of the Army objective, was occupied that afternoon and held.

When the report was received that Thiaucourt had been taken, the Chief of Staff and I decided to establish the advance Division Headquarters at Loge Mangin, which was located at the northern edge of the Bois du Beau Vallon, about two kilometers south of Thiaucourt. We started out in an automobile with my aide, Captain Nelson, but were unable to cross No Man's Land and the trench systems, as the road was not then in condition for use. It was a remarkable scene spread out before our eyes. The area which had lain between the two armies for nearly four years was now swarming with men at work on the road. Material for the repairs was being taken from the heap of ruins which had been the village of Remenauville. Guns and caissons, ambulances, tanks and wagons were struggling to get forward through the maze. General Brown and I saw two or three mounted messengers coming to the rear. We stopped them, borrowed two horses, and continued our journey on horseback. So far as I have been able to learn, this was one of the very few instances in the World War when general officers went into action mounted. It was the most thrilling horseback ride of my life.

Everywhere there were evidences of the bombardment—shell holes, broken trees, dead German soldiers, great quantities of military equipment, rifles, machine guns, and all the impedimenta of war. Finally we reached our destination. It looked more like a half-destroyed picnic ground than anything else I had seen. Rustic benches, chairs and tables—even a rustic outdoor altar and gymnastic apparatus were hidden in the woods. Two or three dugouts were near-by, and, going down the steps, we found a dead German soldier lying head downward, just as he fell, with a pool of blood around him. We then walked out of the woods along the crest of the ridge to the Thiaucourt highway, and there we saw some eight or ten of our gallant men in a line, lying where they fell, their faces toward the enemy. They had been killed by machine gun fire as they came over the crest of the ridge. I shall never forget the expressions on their faces. Peace and serenity, and not hate and anger, characterized them. They had died doing their duty.

Before sunset, traffic began to go through and presently Captain Nelson appeared in the automobile. Brigadier-General Bowley and his staff, also my army aide, Captain Brown, with a detachment, soon came and our dugouts were made ready for occupancy by some German soldiers who were found hiding in the woods. They removed the dead German soldier and buried him, and our men buried our own dead. We supped sumptuously on "canned willie" and hardtack, and then General Brown and I moved into the dugout where some candles were burning and where the telephone was in place. We got in touch with General Neville, who was in Thiaucourt, and asked him to come to Headquarters for conference. We went over the situation with him and, finding everything still, peaceful and serene, lay down to get some much needed sleep.

Shortly after midnight I was awakened by my aide, Captain Brown, who handed me a message just received by mounted messenger from Corps Headquarters. I managed to read it by the dim light. It was a hair-raiser—a thriller. In effect, it stated that a wireless message had been picked up far behind the lines which stated that it would not be possible to hold the position if artillery support were not immediately forthcoming. We had sent no such message. We thought perhaps it was German propaganda. Our wires to the rear had gone bad, and the Corps could not get into communication with Division or Brigade Headquarters. Much alarm was therefore felt and stated in the message, and we were adjured to hold until the arrival of a reinforcing brigade. I handed it to General Brown. He read it, and, finding no communication by wire, he went outside and skinned the signal officer alive, figuratively speaking. Major Burr, the Adjutant of the Artillery Brigade, however, had half-hourly reports from the front lines which showed that everything had been quiet during the evening since 5 P. M. when the counter-attack by a German force had been beaten off, of which we had a full report.

Reply to the message of the Corps was sent to the effect that everything was serene; that we didn't want or need any reënforcements, as we had one brigade (the 44th) in reserve; but that we did want a plentiful supply of food and the roller kitchens sent to the front. Weeks afterward, the mystery was solved. A front line unit had sent the message by a little field radio set to stir up the artillery which the infantry thought was slow in laying down a barrage when requested to do so. The message had not been picked up by any near-by radio sets, but it had been received at a point far beyond its normal range. In other words, what was intended for a family secret became the property of the public and, as is customary under such circumstances, a sensation was created. This incident served as a warning. In the future, wire communication within the Second Division and to the Corps could not be improved upon, and no more sensational messages were broadcast over the radio.

The 12th was a glorious day in the history of the Second Division. It broke through the enemy line and pressed forward irresistibly and rapidly, overcoming the opposing force by the power and vigor of its attack. On that day, it captured 3,300 prisoners and 120 cannon of all calibers, also a vast quantity of machine guns, shell, small arm ammunition, military supplies of all descriptions, and several railway trains loaded with heavy guns and valuable material. It attained its final objective in the afternoon some six or seven hours before its neighbor on the left came abreast of it. Apparently the enemy was caught in the act of preparing to evacuate the salient. His procrastination resulted in heavy losses of men and supplies. Our own casualties were comparatively small.

Early the next morning, General Brown and I drove to Thiaucourt, going to 4th Brigade Headquarters. Our reports indicated that there were a number of stragglers from other divisions and some disorder there, so we decided to establish a strong provost guard and to detail Lieutenant-Colonel John A. Hughes, U. S. M. C., to command it. He accomplished his task most successfully, and in a few hours Thiaucourt was probably one of the most orderly cities in the world, and not a straggler could be found thereafter. The town was being heavily shelled and was in rapid progress of disintegration. It wasn't very gay, and cabaret and sidewalk café life was nonexistent.

Nevertheless there was much amusement owing to a laughable happening to General Neville. His heavily braided overcoat was hung outside to dry and was seen by a teamster of the 23rd Infantry who was driving by. The overcoat being very different from the Army variety, the teamster assumed that it had been left behind by an Austrian or a German officer. So he cut off the sleeves at the elbows, proudly placed them on the ears of his mules, and went on his way rejoicing. Very soon Neville discovered the mutilated overcoat and learned the identity of the guilty party. He informed General Ely of the tragedy and the teamster was haled before the two irate Generals. Ely shouted at him, "What did I tell all of you I would do to looters?" He replied in a weak voice, "Shoot them, Sir." The man was very penitent, and as Neville interceded in his behalf, no punishment of any kind was awarded.

During our visit to Thiaucourt, verbal instructions were given both Brigade Commanders providing for the relief of the 3rd Brigade by the 4th on the night of September 13-14, and these instructions were confirmed later in the day by a written order.   Finally, late in the afternoon we returned to Loge Mangin, running the gauntlet in crossing the bridge, as enemy shell were busily seeking to destroy it.   When we reached Loge Mangin we learned that G-2 and G-3, with their assistants, had arrived and that Division Headquarters had been moved to more commodious quarters, about 200 yards away. These dugouts were built on the German side of a hill and were the best I had yet seen, but the pipes for running water had been shot away and the glass panes in the windows were broken.   The papering on the interior walls was still intact, and bunks and other comforts were in evidence.   The apartment was not protected from shell fire from the German direction, however, and after we were relieved I was told they had to be abandoned by our successors owing to the great amount of attention paid them by the opposing artillery.

On the ·14th, orders were received from the Corps to advance our lines two or three kilometers so as to get in close contact with the main enemy position, or Hindenburg Line.   On the right, the 5th Marines succeeded in making the advance without serious opposition.   On the left, however, a battle was precipitated which continued until darkness set in on the 15th.   By then the 6th Marines had cleared the Bois de Montagne of enemy forces, and had repulsed counter-attacks against its left flank, also those launched from "Mon Plaisir Ferme," a strong point in the Hindenburg Line.

It was a stirring scene which we viewed from the high ridge at Loge Mangin.   Not only was the effect of the concentrated fire of our regiment of 155's on Mon Plaisir Ferme plainly visible, but we were also able to see the advance and retirement of the German counter-attacking force by means of the fine German artillery glasses which we had captured.   Although successful in its advance, the 6th Regiment had suffered about 500 casualties.   It was only a minor operation, but to the officers and men of the Regiment it was a severe engagement.

The fighting had scarcely died down before General McRae and his staff of the 78th Division arrived at our Headquarters to make arrangements for relieving the Second Division. They received an unpleasant welcome, as the Germans had got their second wind and had begun dropping gas shell on the woods. Soon the alarm was given and the smell of gas pervaded our dugouts. We had to put on masks, which with the dim candle light made seeing the maps and talking almost impossible. Finally however the odor of gas disappeared and, taking a chance, we removed the masks and were able to give an intelligible description of the situation. Officially the battle had ended, and the 78th Division took over the sectors then occupied by both the 2nd and 5th Divisions. The relief of the 2nd Division was effected that night, and by daylight, the 5th and 6th Marines had recrossed the Rupt de Mad and were sheltered from view by protecting woods, while the 3rd Brigade had marched beyond Limey. Early the next day, Division Headquarters went on its way to its new location in an old medieval stone castle in Manonville. It was very picturesque and quaint, but uncomfortable and cold. It was only a two or three days' stand, however, as very soon we made another move, this time to Toul.

While at Manonville, we lost Brigadier-General Brown, as his promotion to Brigadier-General gave him too much rank for a Division Chief of Staff. He went from us to be Chief of Staff of the 4th Corps. All of us were greatly effected when he said *au revoir*. He has a brilliant, dynamic personality, and a great heart. We learn to understand each other better in a few days spent under the stress of battle than in years of normal, peace-time association, and ties of affection are then formed which endure as long as does life itself.

Fortunately, Colonel Rhea, our G-3, was Brown's successor, and Colonel Hu Myers stepped into Rhea's shoes.

There had also been other important changes among

the Division Staff and senior officers since I had assumed command of the Division.   Major Keyser, U. S. M. C., had relieved Lieutenant-Colonel Herbst as G-2; Lieutenant-Colonel Harry Lay, U. S. M. C., had become the Division Inspector; Colonel Derby the Division Surgeon; Chaplain Jason N. Pierce the Senior Chaplain; and Lieutenant-Colonel Earl H. Ellis the Adjutant of the 4th Brigade.   Colonel Malone had been transferred in August to the 4th Division to command a brigade˙ and had been relieved as the commander of the 23rd Infantry by Colonel Van Horn.   Colonel Van Horn was with us for only a short while, as he was stricken with pneumonia on the eve of St. Mihiel, and the 23rd Infantry was commanded in that battle by Lieutenant-Colonel Stone.   He commanded it so ably and with such distinction that he was retained as its commanding officer until several months after the Armistice, having in the meanwhile been promoted to the rank of Colonel.

In the Artillery there had also been some changes in Regimental Commanders.   Colonel Manus McCloskey had left us to assume command of an artillery brigade, and Lieutenant-Colonel Holabird commanded the 12th Field Artillery until November 12th.   Lieutenant-Colonel Sparks had succeeded Colonel Kelly as the Commander of the 17th Field Artillery and was in turn relieved by Colonel Dunlap the latter part of October.

There were also many changes, too numerous to mention, among the other officers.   In fact, the personnel of the Division was in a constant state of change, but the new arrivals nearly always became quickly imbued with the high spirit of the Division, and the grand old outfit went marching on to victory.

General Pershing sent to the Corps and Divisions copies of the many congratulatory messages he received, and also personally commended each corps of our army for its part in the victory gained.   All of these brought us much rejoicing, but it was the special commendation of the Second Division by General Liggett that touched our hearts.   His message was as follows: "Once more your Corps Commander has had the proud privilege of witnessing the Second Division maintain its splendid standard and fully come up to his expectations."

On September 17th, the Division Commander issued the following order:

> "I desire to express to the officers and men my profound appreciation of their brilliant and successful attack in the recent engagement.
>
> "Our Division maintained the prestige and honor of our country proudly and swept the enemy from the field.
>
> (Signed) JOHN A. LEJEUNE."

St. Mihiel was a great victory for the First American Army, and all of the officers and men of the Second Division were fully convinced that to their Division was due, to great extent, the completeness of the victory. For, on that September 12th, the Second Division was the spearhead that was thrust into the vital spot in the enemy lines.

CHAPTER XVII

THE BATTLE OF BLANC MONT RIDGE

THE Second Division, which arrived at Toul and vicinity on September 21st, presumably for rest and recuperation, was slated to move to another area and to service under changed conditions within a few days. Only a very few of us were aware of the tremendous events that were about to take place—events in which our Division was destined to play a conspicuous part.

Just after our relief from duty in the Thiaucourt sector by the 78th Division, and our march to a position in reserve, I called at First Corps Headquarters to pay my respects to General Liggett. To my surprise, I found that Corps Headquarters had moved to another town and that General Liggett was about to proceed to the same place. In response to my questions, he told me most confidentially of the great attack which was planned to take place the latter part of the month—between the Meuse and the Suippe Rivers—by the First American Army and the French. He said that all available American troops, as well as supplies of every description, were being moved to the combat zone bounded by the Meuse and the western border of the Argonne Forest. He expressed profound regret because of the fact that the Second Division had been assigned to the Fourth Corps, which had taken over the front previously held by the First Corps as well as its own, and stated that the Second Division would be badly missed on "D" day in the big attack.

In view of this information, I was not astonished when a telephone message was received in the afternoon of September 23rd to send a staff officer to Army Headquarters for orders. Major Puryear, who was detailed

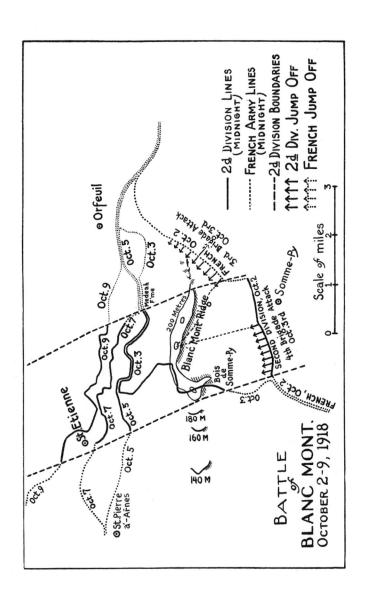

BATTLE
of
BLANC MONT.
OCTOBER 2-9, 1918

Orfeuil

St.Etienne

St.Pierre à-Arnes

Medeah Fme

200 Metres

Blanc Mont Ridge

Bois de Somme-Py

Somme-Py

FRENCH Oct.2
3rd Brigade Attack
Oct.3rd

SECOND DIVISION, Oct.3rd
4th Brigade Attack

FRENCH, Oct.2

Oct.3

Oct.5

Oct.7

Oct.9

180 M
160 M
140 M

Scale of miles
0   1   2   3

2d Division Lines (Midnight)
French Army Lines (Midnight)
2d Division Boundaries
2d Div. Jump Off
French Jump Off

for that duty, returned about midnight, bringing with him instructions for the movement of the Division by rail to an area about ten hours' distant, the entrainment to begin on the 25th and to be completed on the 28th. Many were the conjectures as to our destination.

Colonel Rhea, my aide, and I left Toul in the early morning on September 25th in search of our new home. The secret was in the possession of the regulating officer at Ligney-en-Barrois and was revealed to us when we arrived there. He told us that Division Headquarters would be located at Mairy-sur-Marne, a village not far from Chalons-sur-Marne. We found our billeting party there. It had made all arrangements for us and our belongings had been deposited in our new residence, which was a large château just outside the village. We made a brief inspection of the imposing pile of stone and found that it was strong historically, but weak so far as comforts were concerned. It was not heated and there was no bathroom, but it had been occupied by King James Second after his exile from England, and his face looked down on us from his portrait which, we were told, had been his gift to the French nobleman who had provided him with a home.

I was soon on my way again, this time to Chalons, to call on General Gouraud, the Commander of the Fourth French Army, whose headquarters were located there. He greeted me most cordially and invited me into his private office. I was deeply impressed by his appearance, his face, his manner and his words. Tall, erect, with heavy dark brown beard and hair, and a complexion burnt dark by the blazing sun of Africa where he had seen so many years of army service, he would be a striking looking man in any company, especially as his distinguished appearance was enhanced by an empty sleeve and by a very prominent limp. His gallant service in the Gallipoli campaign was already well known to me as it was to all students of that heroic struggle. I had read, too, of the desperate nature of his wounds which had very nearly resulted in the loss of a leg in addition to an arm.

We had a long and intimate conversation concerning the Second Division, and he displayed much interest in its outstanding achievements, telling me with great pride that he, too, was a Marine, as indicated by the khaki-colored field uniform which he wore, while French officers not belonging to the Colonial Forces wore the sky-blue uniform.

Our conversation then turned to the great battle which would be precipitated the next morning by the attack of the First American and Fourth French Armies between the Meuse and Suippe Rivers, and which would be preceded by an intensive artillery bombardment of the enemy lines along the whole western front from the North Sea to the Swiss border. Hanging on the wall was a relief map of the front occupied by his Army, on which he pointed out the first day's objective—the line of "Buttes," the names of which had become household words during the World War. Everyone who read the newspapers then was familiar with "Navarin Ferme," "Butte Souain," "Butte Tahure," etc. Many bloody battles had been fought for their possession, and the next day they were once again to be drenched with blood and to be the burial place of thousands of gallant men.

He was very calm on the eve of what was to prove *the most tremendous battle in history,* not only from the standpoint of the number of men to be engaged in it, but likewise because of its far-reaching effects, and I ventured to ask him if he were able to sleep the night before the opening of a battle, or if he, like most of us, remained awake and thought and talked about what the next morning would bring forth. In answer, he described briefly his experience on the eve of Ludendorff's great offensive of July 15, 1918.

He said he had the positive information from prisoners captured from several divisions a few days before the battle and also from other reliable sources that the great so-called "Victory Offensive" would begin at dawn on July 15th, and that he had made every preparation to meet it successfully; his artillery and all of his infantry except a small number of machine gun groups were withdrawn from the front, or outpost positions, to the second position which had been carefully prepared in advance for the crisis which was about to arrive. He had information, too, that the enemy's preparatory artillery bombardment would begin at midnight, and he had therefore ordered the counter-preparation bombardment to be opened at 11 P. M. by all the guns under his command, the fire to be concentrated on the areas where the attacking divisions must needs form preliminary to jumping off, and upon the roads leading to those areas. Promptly at 11 o'clock, hundreds of French guns opened fire as ordered. For an hour he nervously walked the floor with every conceivable surmise passing through his mind. Perhaps the enemy had learned his plans; perhaps the attack had been postponed; perhaps his information was a hoax and the attack would be launched on another part of the front. He watched the clock as he walked. The hour seemed interminable. His impatience increased. Finally, the clock begun to chime the midnight hour, and almost simultaneously the telephone on his desk rang. He answered it himself. The voice of the aide he had sent to the front said excitedly that the enemy bombardment had begun along the whole front of the Fourth Army. The General then continued, "My information was correct; the battle was on; everything possible had been done to meet eventualities; my mind was at rest. I went to bed and slept soundly until the dawn."

The interview ended by his insistence that Colonel Rhea, who was with the Army Chief of Staff, and I, should dine with his staff that evening, and by his expression of regret that he could not be present as he had planned to visit his corps and division commanders in accordance with his invariable custom on the eve of battle.

Throughout the interview, his steel-blue eyes seemed to search my very soul. At its end I felt that he had obtained a thorough knowledge of my character, and that he knew what manner of man I was. I was tremendously impressed by this lame, rather taciturn General Gouraud.

I sensed that he was a man of power with a will of iron, but kindly withal. I acquired confidence in his judgment and in his justness. I believed him to be a General whom it would be a delight to follow. This estimate of him was strengthened by everything I afterwards observed. His words were few, but his commands were instantly obeyed. There was real discipline at his Headquarters. He never showed any temper or excitement. He was always calm, placid and unhurried. He showed himself to be a great soldier, a great leader, and a most lovable man.

The dinner was wholesome and ample, but the simplest I had seen at any French headquarters mess. The table appointments, too, were in no way ornate. His staff was small, but a hard-working one we were told. In fact, everything there seemed to reflect the character of the General. We left early for home, knowing that our hosts were under a great tension and needed all the rest they could get.

At one A. M., I was awakened by the roar of cannon. It was a distant repetition of St. Mihiel. I arose and found that Jim Rhea, too, was listening to the man-made cataclysm. Jove hurling his thunderbolts had never produced a mightier sound.

I went to Chalons twice that day to get the latest news from the battle front. General Gouraud was not there but was with his *poilus*. The news was trickling in slowly, as it always did, but every report was favorable. All showed gains; all indicated a considerable success in the initial stages of the battle. *"Ca va bien*. It is always so in the beginning. We will wait and see," the Frenchmen said.

We were impatient for the arrival of the Second Division. We had uncomfortable feelings during a troop movement by rail. For four days we could do nothing but wait. The last train could not arrive until the afternoon of the 28th. Our French Liaison Officer, Captain de Woillemont, was kept busy however in getting us information of the progress of the battle. It looked good

on the 26th.   Both armies were advancing steadily and
numbers of prisoners were being captured.   It has since
been learned that the attack was a surprise to the enemy,
and that his reserves had been massed between Metz
and the Meuse.

On the afternoon of the 27th, a disquieting report was
brought to me by Colonel Rhea, who told me that it had
emanated from Fourth Army Headquarters.   It was to
the effect that owing to the large size of the American
divisions by comparison with the French divisions, it was
planned to divide the Second Division and to assign each
infantry brigade to a French division, leaving Second
Division Headquarters to function administratively only.
I did not take the report very seriously at that time, but
in the light of an actual attempt about two weeks later
on the part of the Chief of Staff of the Fourth Army,
during the absence of General Gouraud from his Headquarters, to so assign the 4th Brigade, I then concluded
that the report in question was founded on fact.   At any
rate, I deemed it wise when the information was furnished me by Colonel Rhea, to take no chances but to
have an interview with General Gouraud with the object
of forestalling any such effort and of establishing definitely the status of the Division.   I therefore arranged
for an immediate interview with the General.

We again went into his private office and, standing in
front of the relief map, he described the progress of the
attack.   The French troops had advanced some distance
beyond the line of Buttes, but their left had been checked
by a strong defensive position running along the Py
Brook from Somme Py to Ste. Marie à Py, and thence
in a southwesterly direction to the Suippe River.   No
infantry attack had been made between that river and
Rheims owing to the location of the enemy line on a
powerfully fortified range of high hills known as "Les
Monts," which it had been decided was too strong to be
carried by direct assault.   The right wing of his army
had been able to make a somewhat deeper advance than

the left, owing to the more favorable nature of the terrain.

Some four kilometers north of the Py Brook, at Somme Py, was a great range of hills in the shape of an arc of a circle, the left of which approached Py Brook near its confluence with the Suippe, and was known as "Notre Dame des Champs." This range culminated opposite Somme Py in a high ridge of which the main feature was designated "Le Massif du Blanc Mont," and thence continued for some distance in an easterly direction via "Medeah Ferme" and "Orfeuil" at a gradually decreasing altitude.

General Gouraud explained that on this ridge was located the enemy main line of resistance on the front of his army, and that up to that time the operations had been confined to a struggle for the possession of outpost positions, no attacks having been made on the main position. He then placed his hand on the part of the ridge lying between Medeah Ferme and Blanc Mont, and said, "If I could take this position by assault, advance beyond it to the vicinity of St. Etienne à Arnes, and hold the ground gained against the counter-attacks which would be hurled against my troops, the enemy would be compelled to evacuate "Notre Dame des Champs and Les Monts," thereby freeing Rheims which he has been strangling for four years, and fall back to the line of the Aisne, a distance of nearly 30 kilometers—as the terrain between the ridges and the Aisne does not lend itself well to defense." He added, "My divisions, however, are worn out from the long strain of continuous fighting and from the effects of the heavy casualties they have suffered, and it is doubtful if they are now equal to accomplishing this difficult task unless they be heavily re-enforced."

I answered, with deliberation, "General, if you do not divide the Second Division, but put it in line as a unit on a narrow front, I am confident that it will be able to take Blanc Mont Ridge, advance beyond it, and hold its position there."

He expressed the greatest gratification because of what

I had said, and added that he had no intention whatever
of dividing the Second Division and that, in fact, it was
not attached to his Army, but was being held at the
disposition of Marshal Foch and Marshal Petain.   He
paused a few moments, and then said, "I will, however,
bring to Marshal Petain's attention what you have just
said."

I was able to understand every word during this rather
long conversation because he was careful to speak slowly
and distinctly, and I also had less difficulty in conversing
with him than with any other Frenchman I met overseas,
chiefly because he encouraged me, at the same time kindly
complimenting me on my accent and my knowledge of
the French language.

The next forenoon, I again repaired to Army Headquarters, this time in compliance with a telephone message from General Gouraud.   When I arrived there, he
met me, saying with great animation, "My General, I
regret so much that you are too late to meet Marshal
Petain, as he left here only a short while ago.   I told him
of your confidence in the ability of the Second Division
to take by assault Le Massif du Blanc Mont.   He was
greatly pleased and has issued instructions for the assignment of the Second Division to the Fourth Army.   You
will receive orders this afternoon to begin the movement
of the Division towards the front."

A few hours later, the order was received.   It directed
the Division to proceed to the Souain-Suippe area, partly
by marching and partly by camions, the movement to
begin on the 29th and to be completed the following day.
Division Headquarters moved to Suippes on the morning
of the 30th, and opened there at 10 A. M.   I shall quote
here an extract from one of my letters which gives a
description of the then appearance of Suippes and the
building allocated to Division Headquarters: "Suippes
has been just inside of the French lines ever since the
first battle of the Marne, four years ago, and during all
that time it has been uninhabited except by troops, and it
is certainly a dilapidated, desolated place.   It has been

shelled frequently and bombed often, and still some of the houses are in fairly good repair. The one we are in, except for the lack of window panes, is a pretty fair house. The old pictures are still hanging on the walls, and the religious images of the Holy Mother and Child, of Jesus on the Cross, and of the Saints are still intact, and there is a great deal of fine old furniture, more or less broken up. The filth of the house, however, and of the courtyard when we arrived was indescribable. But I went off to visit the troops and when I returned a miracle had been wrought. The house had been swept, scrubbed and cleaned; furniture arranged, old beds and bedding put in the attic, electric lights and telephones installed; the courtyard was cleaned up, the kitchen scrubbed and polished, the table spread for lunch, and my room fixed comfortably."

The entire Division was assembled in the Souain-Suippes area by the night of September 30-October 1, and orders were then issued for it to enter the front lines the next night, that of October 1-2. The 4th Brigade took over the front lines with the 5th Marines on the right and the 6th Marines on the left, relieving the 61st French Division (21st Corps), and one battalion of the 21st French Division (11th Corps), the line beginning on the right at a point about one kilometer northeast of Somme Py and thence running in a southwesterly direction to its junction with that of the 11th Corps at a point about two kilometers west by south of Somme Py.

On the right of the Second Division, the French had gone forward about three kilometers the preceding days, while on the left the 11th Corps had been unable to cross the Py Brook, as its advance was held up by the strong position on the north bank of that stream which constituted an enemy outpost line of resistance, and which was connected with the main line of resistance on Blanc Mont Ridge and Notre Dame des Champs by numerous communicating trenches. This outpost line of resistance was also buttressed by many strong points, such as "Essen Hook" on our left, and "Bois de la Vipère" on our front.

The same order provided that the 3rd Brigade should move to a position in reserve near "Navarin Ferme" and that Division Headquarters would open at 8 A. M., October 2nd at P. C. Wagram, at which hour the Commanding General Second Division, would take over the sector.

This order was issued at 5 P. M. on October 1st and was substituted for the previous plan which arranged not only for the 2nd Division to enter the front lines, but also for a frontal attack on Blanc Mont Ridge by that Division and the adjacent French Corps on the morning of October 2nd.

The attack was postponed until October 3rd, upon my suggestion. The postponement was advised principally because the 2nd Field Artillery Brigade could not reach its position in time for the attack, also because I deemed it advisable for the 4th Brigade and the Artillery to have a look at the terrain during the daylight hours before making an attack, and for the additional reason that we believed it to be important that the portion of the trench which lay immediately in front of the Division, and which was then occupied by the enemy, should be mopped up, occupied and utilized as the "jump off" line, thereby avoiding the delay of the assaulting columns incident to an engagement in that complicated system of trenches, while permitting the assaulting troops to follow the artillery barrage closely during the first phase of the attack.

The night of October 1-2 was clear and very cold, which might account in part for the intense activity of the German artillery and air service. I expected a good night's rest in preparation for the sleepless nights and days which I knew we should experience during the approaching battle, and turned in at 1 A. M. Just afterwards, heavy German shell and airplane bombs begun to explode near Division Headquarters. The enemy was evidently searching for the main street through which the highway runs, and which he knew was filled with traffic. The old house shook, pieces of shell fell on the roof, bricks dropped from the chimneys, and I was called

and urged to take shelter in the "caves" in the courtyard, first by the orderly, then by my aide, and finally by
a joint delegation consisting of Rhea, Myers and Keyser.
I yielded to persuasion, got up, dressed and went into
the inky darkness of the "caves," which were jammed
full of our people and poorly ventilated. I didn't stay
there long, but went to the front door of the house and
for the remainder of the night watched the stream of
traffic rolling slowly by. Cannon, caissons, tanks, carts,
wagons, ammunition trucks, supply trucks, troops—on
and on they moved to be engulfed in the seething cauldron of the front.

Night marches when near the front made it possible
for the troops, guns and supplies to reach the battlefields
without serious losses, during the World War, and perhaps night battles will be just as essential and just as
frequent during the next war. Attacks under cover of
darkness may provide both the elements of surprise and
of reasonable security on the battlefields of the future.

On October 1st I prepared and issued to the Division
the Order of the Day:

> "1. The greatest battles in the world's his-
> tory are now being fought. The Allies are at-
> tacking successfully on all fronts. The valiant
> Belgian Army has surprised and defeated the
> enemy in Flanders; the English, who have been
> attacking the enemy without ceasing since Au-
> gust 8, have advanced beyond the Hindenburg
> Line between Cambrai and St. Quentin, cap-
> turing thousands of prisoners and hundreds of
> cannon; the heroic Allied Army of the Orient
> has decisively defeated the Bulgars; the British
> have captured 50,000 prisoners in Palestine
> and have inflicted a mortal blow on the Turk;
> and our own First Army and the Fourth French
> Army have already gained much success in the
> preliminary stages of their attack between the
> Meuse and the Suippe Rivers.

"2. Owing to its world wide reputation for skill and valor, the Second Division was selected by the Commander-in-Chief of the Allied Armies as his special reserve, and has been held in readiness to strike a swift and powerful blow at the vital point of the enemy's line. The hour to move forward has now come, and I am confident that our Division will pierce the enemy's line, and once more gloriously defeat the enemy.

(Signed) JOHN A. LEJEUNE.

I had several thoughts in mind which governed the phrasing of the order. First of all, I knew that the junior officers and men had very little information about the general progress of the war, and that in fact their knowledge was almost entirely confined to the happenings within their own units. Second, I believed that with this information they would fully realize that what they were doing was an important part of the general plan to attack everywhere without ceasing, in order to bring the war to a speedy and decisive conclusion. Third, and chiefly, I wished to make an appeal to their esprit de corps, and this I did in the second paragraph. The order, I was told, had an excellent effect, as it caused each man to feel that he had learned something of the inner workings of the great machine, that he himself was an important part of it, and that the Second Division would do its full share in helping to bring the war to a victorious end.

Furthermore, it had an effect of some importance on the enemy. During the days and nights of constant fighting which ensued, the lines shifted back and forth, especially at night. One of the German prisoners, when captured, had in his possession the despatch case of an American officer which he said he had picked up on the battlefield, and which contained a copy of the order. The prisoner said it had been translated and read aloud to the men of his company by a German soldier who understood English and had been repeated to other companies, so that knowledge of the general military situation had become widespread on that part of the front. He added that information of the desperate state of affairs from the point of view of the Central Powers had not been given to them, but that they had been led to believe that all was going well everywhere.

The relief was effected without incident, and at 8 A. M. I assumed command of the Somme-Py sector. The ride to P. C. Wagram, the new location of Division Headquarters, was through a hideously battle-scarred country. The town of Souain was completely destroyed, and the whole area north of it gave full evidence of the fact that it had been continuously a battlefield for more than four years. It was the white chalk country, and not only was it a perfect maze of trenches and covered with a tangle of barbed wire, but the very soil was desiccated and pulverized. It had been shelled, and bombed and mined so frequently that it had lost all semblance of its former self. Not a tree was standing anywhere near Navarin Ferme, or elsewhere in its vincinity, nor was there even a brick on the site of the farm to show that buildings had once stood there. The debris of battle was still lying about—broken cannon and machine guns, rifles, bayonets, helmets, parts of uniforms, articles of military equipment, and partly buried horses; most grewsome of all, fragments of human bodies were often found. Arms and legs thrust out of the torn soil, and unrecognizable, long-buried human faces, thrown up to the surface of the ground by exploding shell, were frequently visible. The fearsome odors of the battlefield, too, were always present. P. C. Wagram was in the midst of the devastated area. It was not a home, but a horror. A few half destroyed dugouts, entered from a trench, constituted our apartment. Somehow, all seemed to fit well into the scheme of things. A scene more perfectly suited for a place in the tragedy about to be enacted could not well be depicted or imagined.

The task assigned the Second Division and the 21st

(French) Division for the day was the cleaning up of Essen and Elbe trenches. This task was successfully accomplished by the Second Division on its front, but the 21st Division failed in its attempt, which augured ill for its success next day.

While this operation was in progress, I was called to Headquarters 21st Corps for a conference and took with me the Chief of Staff and Brigadier Generals Ely and Neville. There we met for the first time general Naulin, the Corps Commander, and his staff, also other French general officers. General Gouraud arrived during the conference, but took no part in the discussion until a decision had been reached. General Naulin pointed out that the attack of the preceding day by the French Division on our right had created a considerable bulge in the line of which he thought we might be able to take advantage, especially as he feared that the frontal attack would fail owing to the powerfully organized positions before the Second Division.

I replied that I felt no doubt whatever as to the ability of the Second Division to overcome that resistance, but agreed with General Naulin as to the desirability of utilizing the ground gained in the neighboring sector to give us a "jump off" line nearer the objective. General Naulin proposed as the plan of attack that the 3rd Brigade should make an oblique advance from the neighboring sector to the objective—Blanc Mont Ridge—while the 4th Brigade would advance simultaneously to a line about half way between its "jump off" line and the objective. I pointed out that such a plan was impracticable of execution, as some of the fire of the 4th Brigade would probably find a target in the 3rd Brigade, and that it would not be feasible to utilize the artillery rolling barrage in such a complicated maneuver. The Second Division officers then discussed the matter for a few minutes and we arrived at a solution which I then proposed to General Naulin. It consisted of a frontal attack by the 4th Brigade on the left half of the objective, combined with an oblique attack by the 3rd Brigade on its right half. This plan utilized fully the salient position on our right and avoided an attack on the Bois de la Vipere and several other strong points. This plan was approved in full by General Naulin and later on by General Gouraud when described to him.

We returned to P. C. Wagram and worked up the details of the plan of attack, which were then carefully explained and fully discussed at a conference of brigade and regimental commanders and the Division Staff. They, in their turn, described the plan to their unit commanders, so that all understood what was to be done and when. It was fortunate that this precaution was taken, as it was eleven o'clock at night when the written Corps order was received.

The Division verbal orders provided that the 3rd Brigade should march after dark from its reserve position near Navarin Ferme to its "jump off" position. Arrangements were made for French guides to lead it to the selected position, but somehow these guides were not found and the troops made the best of their way through the devastated area. Their problem was further complicated by the fact that at about 6 P. M. a successful German counter-attack had driven the French troops back a distance of about one kilometer on the very part of the front where the Brigade was to form for the attack. The regiments and the battalions, in fact, lost touch with each other during the march, but they reached the appointed place, or rather as near that place as the changed conditions permitted, by the hour set. Under the most difficult and trying circumstances, it was a remarkable display of efficiency.

The orders further provided for a converging attack in line of brigades, the triangular space between the brigades to be mopped up by both brigades after the objective was taken. Each brigade was to attack in column of regiments, the 9th Infantry leading the 3rd Brigade, and the 6th Marines the 4th Brigade, the 5th Marines remaining in place until the 6th had cleared Essen trench, when the 5th would move by the flank and follow in support. The objective—Medeah Ferme (exclusive)—Blanc Mont (inclusive)—was divided into brigade sub-sectors at the point where it was crossed by the Somme Py—St. Etienne Road, the outpost line being about one kilometer in front.

Five-fifty A. M. was fixed as "H" hour, and a preliminary artillery bombardment of five minutes' duration was directed. Artillery barrages to precede both columns were carefully prepared and functioned satisfactorily in spite of the difficult nature of the problem presented for solution.

The 9th Infantry directed its battalions to attack in their natural order. The 1st Battalion having lost touch, however, with the remainder of the Regiment in order to avoid a shell-swept area, the 2nd Battalion was at the last moment directed to lead off. The 1st, not to be outdone, arrived in position just before "H" hour, and both battalions advanced abreast, the 3rd following in support.

The 6th Marines advanced as directed, but with its left flank in the air, as the 21st (French) Division was held up by Essen Hook and the strongly fortified trench position on its front.

To return for a few moments to the happenings at Division Headquarters during the night preceding the attack, it is needless to indicate the fact that it was a hectic night. The late arrival of the Corps order, the considerable length of time required to translate and study it, and the fleeting minutes while the Division order was being written and mimeographed, all tended to keep us keyed up to a state of tenseness which was accentuated by the lack of information in regard to the movement of the 3rd Brigade. Finally, at about 3 A. M., the squadron of motorcycle orderlies sped on its way. Prompt telephone code reports of the arrival of the order were received from all the units except the 3rd Brigade. After waiting for what seemed an interminable time, two other messengers were sent on the quest for the Brigade and regimental commanders, and again, none of the messengers having returned, an officer on horseback was started out to join in the search. It was not until after "H" hour that the report came in that the orders had been received and that the Brigade had jumped off in time.

As soon as it was broad daylight, Colonel Rhea and I went to the high ground at Navarin Ferme, which afforded a good outlook on the battlefield. It was a hazy morning, and the poor visibility was made poorer by the bursting of smoke shell around Bois de la Vipere to prevent the enemy in position there from observing and firing on our advancing troops. We stood and searched Blanc Mont Ridge and the intervening ground with our field glasses, but it was impossible to pierce the mist and smoke. Suddenly, both of us gave shouts of joy. We saw the signal lights being fired on the top of the ridge. They began on the right of the objective, and one by one we saw them until finally those on the extreme left became visible. The objective was taken between 8 and 9 A. M.

Prompt reports were made by telephone from the brigades to Division Headquarters, thence to Corps and Army Headquarters, and to Headquarters A. E. F. Congratulatory messages poured in from Marshals Foch and Petain, General Gouraud, and American G. H. Q. General Naulin was jubilant, and from having been rather pessimistic, he became exultantly optimistic and apparently believed that the German debacle was on the eve of taking place. During the forenoon, he sent a message by telephone suggesting a further advance to the line of Machault-Cauroy, an additional distance of about 10 kilometers. I pointed out that the Corps on our left had not been able to leave its jump-off line, and that the troops on our right were held up by the Medeah Ferme-Orfeuil position and their attacks had been repeatedly repulsed. An hour later, a more positive message was received from the Corps Commander insisting that the advance to Machault be made at once. I replied that until our flanks were supported by the advance of the troops on our left and right, it would be courting certain de-

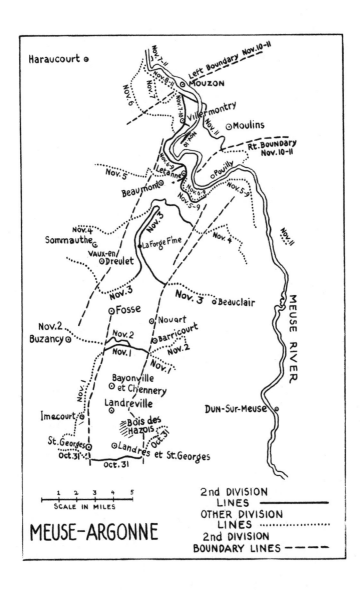

Haraucourt ⊙

Left Boundary Nov.10-11

Nov.7-11

Nov.8-11

⊙ MOUZON

Nov.6

Nov.7

Nov.7-10

Villermontry

Nov.11

⊙ Moulins

Nov.6-9

Di Xon

Rt. Boundary
Nov. 10-11

Nov. 5

Letanne ⊙

⊙ Pouilly

Beaumont ⊙

Nov.6-9

Nov.5-9

Nov.5-9

Nov.6-9

Nov. 3

Nov.4

La Forge Fme

Nov. 4

Sommauthe ⊙

Vaux-en
⊙ Dreulet

Nov. 11

Nov. 3

Nov. 3

⊙ Beauclair

MEUSE RIVER

⊙ Fosse

⊙ Nouart

Nov.2

Nov. 2

Buzancy ⊙

Nov. 2

⊙ Barricourt

Nov. 2

Nov.1

Nov. 1

Bayonville
⊙ et Chennery

Nov. 1

Landreville
⊙

DUN-Sur-Meuse ⊙

Imecourt ⊙

Bois des
Hazois

St. Georges ⊙

⊙ Landres et St. Georges

Oct. 31

Oct.31

Oct. 31

1   2   3   4   5
SCALE IN MILES

MEUSE-ARGONNE

2nd DIVISION
LINES ————

OTHER DIVISION
LINES ··········

2nd DIVISION
BOUNDARY LINES — — —

struction to drive a thin wedge 14 kilometers deep into the enemy lines, and that before carrying out any such order I reserved the right of appeal to General Gouraud. A short while afterwards, the reply came from General Naulin requesting that I consider the order as not having been given, but asking an advance into the foreground of Blanc Mont Ridge. I answered that plans had already been made for such an advance and that orders to effect it were then being prepared. These orders involved an advance to a point about one kilometer southeast of St. Etienne. In the afternoon the 23rd Infantry advanced, but in doing so eased off to the left because of its right flank being exposed to enemy fire, and occupied a position in the 4th Brigade sub-sector.

The 4th Brigade directed that the advance be made by the 5th Marines, but that regiment was facing west in order to cover the exposed left flank and could not be extricated in time to attack that afternoon. Its rear element, the 17th Company, was also engaged in assisting a French battalion to capture Essen Hook. The 17th Company succeeded in entering the Hook and in driving out its defenders. It then turned it over to the French, who lost it when counter-attacked late that afternoon by a German force. The 5th Marines, too, was engaged in mopping up Bois de la Vipere in conjunction with a detachment of the 3rd Brigade. In response to my request, a depleted French division—the 170th—had been ordered to move to our left flank to give it support until an advance by the 11th Corps could be made. It reached a supporting position about 7 P. M., and General Bernard, its commander, reported to me for duty. His division had been relieved from duty at the front the night before, and the order sent to me in regard to it expressly stipulated that it should be used for defensive purposes only, and not under any circumstances for offensive purposes. After the arrival of the 170th Division, the 5th Marines moved farther to the front in preparation for its attack which, in accordance with my approval, had been postponed until early the next morning. Late in the evening, the French 22nd Division, which had been designated as the relief of the 21st, marched into the 2nd Division sector and made preparations to attack in a westerly direction.

In spite of its salient position, I felt that the 2nd Division was secure, although I knew of course that the enemy was bringing up his available reserves to endeavor with all the energy of which he was capable not only to stop the advance of the 2nd Division, but also to crush its flanks. That this effort was made and continued to be made is fully verified by Lieutenant-Colonel Otto's account of the battle from the German standpoint, as recently published in the proceedings of the United States Naval Institute.

At Division Headquarters we were intensely proud of the day's accomplishments. A powerfully fortified and strongly held position had been taken by assault, about 2,000 prisoners captured, and an advance of about 5 kilometers effected—all this in spite of the failure to advance of the neighboring divisions. This feeling of pride was accentuated early the next morning when a telephone message from General Gouraud gave me the information that the prediction he had made was already partly fulfilled, as the enemy had begun evacuating "Les Monts" during the night, that the French had already occupied Moron-Villiers and other villages from which the retreat had been effected, and that at last Rheims was in process of being freed from the deathlike grip which had strangled that historic city for more than four years.

During the night, a German regiment occupied the western portion of Blanc Mont, and considerable enemy forces were concentrated on our front and on both flanks. The reoccupation of Blanc Mont by the enemy was made possible partly by the fact that the leading battalion of the 6th Marines during its advance the preceding day had eased off to the right owing to the heavy fire from its left, and partly to the erroneous understanding of its commander that only the eastern part of the hill was included in the division sector. The enemy built up a formidable strongpoint there which bristled with machine guns and which throughout October 4th proved to be a thorn in the side of the 2nd Division. Similar enemy positions were also established on the right flank, and at Bemont Château, some distance to the right, a strong enemy artillery concentration was effected which bombarded the 2nd Division area night and day as long as the division was in line. On the left front, the town and cemetery of St. Etienne à Arnes were located. This area had been previously converted into a fortress. Cunningly situated machine gun nests were connected by tunnels with the cemetery and with each other, and the ravine through which the Arnes brook flowed was utilized to conceal the movement of troops to and from the cemetery.

It was under these conditions that the attack of the 5th Marines was made in the early morning of October 4th. Advancing in column of battalions through the 6th Marines, it came under heavy machine gun fire from its front, left flank, and left rear as soon as it had crossed the ridge. Its advance was made slowly but surely, and its leading battalion reached a point about one-half kilometer southeast of St. Etienne, when it encountered such heavy fire that a halt was made. At this critical juncture, Major Hamilton, commanding the rear battalion, observed a heavy concentration of enemy troops in the sector on our left preparing to make a counter-attack on the exposed left flank of the leading battalion. Unhesitatingly he moved to his left front and engaged the enemy. It was a sanguinary struggle in which his battalion suffered heavy losses, but effectually prevented the counter-attack. At this crisis, the 21st Corps directed an advance towards Machault. The Division issued the order, but inserted the saving clause that "H" hour, being dependent to a great extent on the progress of the attacks on our right and left would be designated later.

The French division on our left attacked from our sector in a westerly direction and was finally successful in forcing the evacuation of the trenches and strong positions on its front. It eventually took up a position for the day and night south of Blanc Mont Ridge and facing it, with its right in liaison with the reserve regiment (6th Marines) of our left brigade. On our immediate right, the attack of the 21st Corps was again unsuccessful, its infantry regiments beating themselves to pieces against the Orfeuil-Medeah Ferme position.

In the afternoon, after consulting with the 4th Brigade, it was determined that the question of most immediate and pressing importance was the capture of the machine gun nest on Blanc Mont, and the commander of the 6th Marines was directed to prepare the plan, to arrange for coöperation with the French, and to secure the necessary support by the 12th Field Artillery which had been detailed to back up the 4th Brigade. When the report was received from Colonel Lee that all arrangements had been made, it was directed that the attack take place at daylight the next morning, and that during the night the avenues of retreat from the machine gun fortress should be continuously shelled.

Just then my telephone rang, and Colonel Feland, the commander of the 5th Marines, painted a vivid picture of the situation of his regiment, almost surrounded as it was by a ring of machine gun fire, especially from its left rear, supplemented by an intense artillery fire from its front and from Bemont Château. Hanging up the 'phone, I repeated the conversation to General Naulin, who was at my headquarters, and very emphatically pointed out the fact that our troops were being shot up by machine guns located some distance in rear of the location that he had stated the 11th Corps had already attained.

Just at this moment, General Gouraud arrived and asked as to what the discussion had reference. I explained the situation to him and stated that the withdrawal of General Bernard's division had been directed without my knowledge and contrary to my wishes. He said quietly to General Naulin, "Revoke the order. General Bernard and his division will remain in place until released by General Lejeune." (I released it the ensuing afternoon.)

He then highly commended the 2nd Division, expressed regret because of its heavy casualties, stated that the enemy was in full retreat between the Suippe River and Rheims, and that the French army on his left had occupied "les Monts" and was advancing towards the Aisne in pursuit of the enemy forces. He added that the violent enemy reaction against the 2nd Division in particular and the whole Fourth Army was due to the vital importance from the enemy's standpoint of holding that Army's advance in check until its withdrawal from the salient position west of the Suippe River had been completed.

The interview ended, both Generals departed and I again turned my attention to the reports which came in by telephone unceasingly. Both brigades had beaten off counter-attacks which had been ferociously delivered. In fact, throughout the occupation of the Blanc Mont sector by the 2nd Division, it was subjected to frequent violent counter-attacks and was called upon to endure constant machine gun and artillery fire. To its everlasting glory, it should be emphasized that the Division on its part repeatedly attacked the enemy, gaining ground as the result of each of its attacks, and tenaciously held its salient position in spite of heavy losses. Its morale was unshaken, and its flaming spirit burned brightest when the danger was greatest and the fighting hardest.

At 6 A. M., October 5th, Major Shuler's battalion of the 6th Marines captured by assault the Machine gun strongpoint on Blanc Mont, taking 65 machine guns and 205 prisoners—the remnants of the regiment which had originally occupied it. He was voluntarily assisted in the attack by a battalion of General Bernard's division. No casualties were suffered by the attacking force, as it followed the artillery barrage so closely as to surprise the entire garrison in dugouts in which they had taken refuge to avoid the fire of our artillery.

The extinction of this hornet's nest was a great blessing, as it freed our exhausted and sorely tried troops from the harassing effect of a fire from their rear. Incidentally, it made the area in rear of Blanc Mont Ridge within our sector a much safer place for the artillery, trains, roller kitchens, headquarters detachments, troops in reserve, and all the other units which were located there. That area was, however, still a favorite target for the enemy artillery, and going back and forth by automobile or on foot always involved running the gauntlet.

The activity of the enemy was attested by the constant sound of their machine guns in action and by their repeated counter-attacks directed against our right flank, which increased in frequency and in violence when the lull came in their attacks from the left. Their artillery, too, continued its activity, its fire being directed not only against our troops in advance of the ridge, but against the ridge itself and roads in rear of it.

One afternoon, after I had visited the ridge with General Ely and was driving back with him to Division Headquarters for a conference, we saw shell falling ahead of us, and suddenly one struck about a hundred feet away. The chauffeur slowed down almost to a stop, when General Ely shouted at him in stentorian tones, "Step on the gas! Go ahead full speed!" The chauffeur obeyed with alacrity and we shot ahead with almost the speed of an airplane with the result that we passed the danger zone just in time to avoid a shell which struck a few yards behind us. Ely then explained to his chauffeur that in driving over a shell-beaten area, safety lay only in great speed.

Following the successful attack of October 3rd, members of the Division Staff made many reconnaissances in the effort to find a suitable place for Division Headquarters nearer the front than P. C. Wagram. Eventually a location in Somme Py was decided upon and we moved there, bag and baggage, as did Artillery Headquarters. We located ourselves in some "caves" on the German side of a hill, the entrances to which were on the street level. My "cave" had an opening for ventilation purposes through which a huge shell had previously hurtled, but which, being a dud, had caused but little damage. The German Artillery seemed to have a grudge against that hill and the ruined church on its crest, as they were made the targets so frequently, especially at night.

As was the daily custom, a general attack was ordered for October 5th, and no sooner was the successful operation against the strongpoint on Blanc Mont completed, than we were required to give our attention to the preparation of the order directing an attack in the direction of Machault. Again the saving clause was inserted, and "H" hour for each brigade was to be fixed when its exposed flank was supported. The 11th Corps finally succeeded in coming up abreast of our leading regiment on the left, and the advance of the 4th Brigade was directed.

The 6th Marines made the attack and reached the edge of the woods southeast of St. Etienne, where it was in liaison with the 11th Corps which had encountered but slight resistance during the day owing to the retirement of the enemy from its front to the north bank of Arnes Brook from St. Pierre to the westward. On our right, the French attempt to advance was again unsuccessful owing to the strong enemy resistance in the Bois de la Puce and at Orfeuil, Dondon, and the hill just east of Medeah Ferme. The reserve elements of the 3rd Brigade were still in liaison with the left of the 11th Corps front lines at Medeah Ferme, and the 3rd Brigade lines ran thence in a general northwesterly direction to the point of junction with the 4th Brigade, just south of a strong trench system occupied by the enemy.

On October 6th, operations were limited to local engagements. A battalion of the 6th Marines and a battalion of the 23rd Infantry coöperated in an attack on the trench system on their front. Stout resistance was encountered but after about two hours of severe fighting in the trenches they were occupied by our troops, and 40 prisoners and a number of machine guns were captured. The enemy machine gun nests southeast of St. Etienne were still operating actively though, and the guns were so cunningly concealed that their exact location could not be determined until after dark, when the flash of the guns was seen and bursts of fire were delivered by our men with deadly effect, as we afterwards learned when we counted the dead in the underground nests.

On our right, a battalion of the 21st (French) Division during the day extended the lines of that Division in a northerly direction within the limits of the 2nd Division sector, thereby freeing the right of the 3rd Brigade from Medeah Ferme and permitting the Brigade to advance to the St. Etienne-Orfeuil Road. On our left, the right of the 11th Corps advanced to a point just south of St. Etienne where it was in touch, by patrols, with the advanced position of the 4th Brigade.

On that day, the situation of the Division had greatly improved, as only one flank—the right—was then exposed. The men, however, were physically exhausted. Constant fighting, almost no sleep, and the difficulties of supplying food because of the salient position, combined with heavy casualties, caused me to recommend that the Division be relieved. Late in the day, Division Headquarters was informed that the 71st Brigade of the 36th Division would join the 2nd Division temporarily and would take over the front lines on the night of October 6-7. In accordance with the 2nd Division order, its front line battalions were required to remain in place with the front line battalions of the 71st Brigade until further instructions, in order to stabilize those untried troops.

The personnel of the 71st Brigade was excellent, but entirely lacking in combat experience, and it was my hope and expectation that opportunity would be given to accustom its officers and men to front line duty while brigaded with the experienced battalions of the 2nd Division before being called on for offensive operations. This was not to be for longer than one day, however. In an interview with the Corps Commander held on the morning of the 7th, he informed me that a general attack would take place at daylight on the 8th, and that he anticipated that the fresh brigade would achieve a success equal to that gained by the 2nd Division on October 3rd.   I explained to him that he was expecting the impossible of untried troops, and urged that the 71st Brigade be not required to engage in an attack until it had had a few days' training under fire.   He was insistent, however, and on leaving, said, "Tomorrow will be another great day for the 21st Corps!"

The Brigade Commanders, including the Commander of the 71st Brigade, were called to Division Headquarters for conference, and the plan of battle gone over in the utmost detail.   Verbal orders for the attack were given, and the Brigade Commanders were instructed to explain the plan fully to their regimental commanders, and they in turn to their battalion commanders, so that the distribution of the written orders would be a confirmation only.   The verbal and written orders involved a frontal attack by the 71st Brigade and its advance to an objective about 2 kilometers to the front.   A brief preliminary bombardment, followed by a rolling barrage, was directed.

The written orders, as expected, were late in reaching the front line battalions and the attack was made pursuant to the verbal orders.   Each regiment of the 71st Brigade attacked in column of battalions, with the 2nd Battalion of the 9th Infantry as right flank guard and the 1st Battalion of the 6th Marines as left flang guard, and with the additional mission of occupying St. Etienne and connecting up between the 142nd Infantry and the 7th French Division, which had relieved the 22nd French Division on the night of October 7-8.

The initial stages of the attack were successful.   The 141st Regiment and the 2nd Battalion, 9th Infantry, captured the machine gun position north of the St. Etienne-Orfeuil Road, but further progress could not be made as touch had been lost with the artillery barrage, and the two rear battalions, in their eagerness to join in the fight, closed up on the leading battalion, causing an intermingling of units. With all battalions in line, the front stabilized in a position approximately one-half kilometer in advance of the jump-off line.

The 142nd Regiment made a deeper advance, reaching the St. Etienne-Semide Road after cleaning up the machine gun nests in the cemetery of St. Etienne. It organized a line about one kilometer in length, running in a northeasterly direction from St. Etienne, with practically all companies in line and with its right flank in the air. One company of the 1st Battalion, 6th Marines, occupied St. Etienne, establishing a line around the town and holding it for the night against counterattack.

The reports from the 71st Brigade, which early in the day were optimistic, became less so as the day wore on, and finally conditions seemed to be so uncertain at the front that I went to 71st Brigade Headquarters to look into the situation personally. I arrived there just after the area about it had been heavily shelled, causing a number of casualties among the men on duty there. I found the Brigade Commander with a map of the sector spread before him. I listened to his conversation by telephone with his regimental commanders and looked at the line traced on the map showing the positions of the troops. He gave me the latest information he had received, which indicated a lack of contact between the two regiments, also an intermingling of units and no supporting echelons in rear of the front line elements. I told him to endeavor to reorganize his line, echeloning it in depth, establishing liaison between the units, and preparing for counter-attacks. On arrival at Division Headquarters I immediately directed that all orders providing for the relief of the 2nd Division units by the 71st Brigade be revoked, and that the jump-off line be reoccupied immediately by battalions of the 3rd and 4th Brigades. I also personally informed both Brigade Commanders of the situation and asked that they expedite the movement of their battalions to their former positions and instruct them to hold those positions, and reorganize and reform any of the troops that might be driven back by counter-attacks.

Violent counter-attacks were delivered as expected; on the right the line held, but on the left, owing to their more advanced and isolated position, the units of the 142nd Regiment were compelled to retire under heavy artillery fire to the lines held by the 3rd Battalion, 6th Marines. The enemy counter-attack which followed was repulsed or, as picturesquely expressed by Major George Shuler—"We shot the tar out of the Boche." The line of the 142nd Regiment was reorganized for the night to include the patches of woods on the northern slope of Hill 160 about one-half kilometer from the Marines, and the gap between the two regiments of the 71st Brigade was covered by the 23rd Infantry which marched back into its former position pursuant to my instructions.

During the night, the fighting 2nd Engineers were once again called on to fulfill their role of 2nd Division Reserve, the 1st Battalion relieving the 1st Battalion, 9th Infantry, as right flank guard at 9.30 P. M., and two companies of the 2nd Battalion reinforcing the 76th Company, 6th Marines, in St. Etienne at 2 A. M., October 9th.

October 9th was devoted to reorganizing and to readjusting the lines, and to establishing firmer liaison. Company "E," 2nd Engineers, and the 76th Company, 6th Marines, advanced about one kilometer north of St. Etienne, taking possession of a system of practice trenches where they were in liaison with the 7th French Division. On the right, the 73rd French Division attacked and at last came up nearly abreast of our lines, the 141st Infantry participating in the battle.

On the night of October 9-10, the 36th Division took over the 2nd Division sector, the 72nd Brigade relieving all units in support and reserve, and the 71st Brigade extending its front so as to relieve all 2nd Division units in the front lines. Command passed to the 36th Division at 10 A. M. October 10th, and the 2nd Division, with the exception of the 2nd Field Artillery Brigade, the 2nd

Engineers, and a part of the trains, moved to a reserve area. Our Artillery, Engineers and trains remained with the 36th Division and participated in the march to the Aisne.

Before continuing the narrative, I wish to make a few observations concerning several matters referred to in this chapter. In spite of four years' warfare and in spite of their depleted ranks, the French divisions were full of the fighting spirit. I personally examined the area about Essen Hook and Essen Trench and counted over one hundred dead Frenchmen in a two-acre lot, not to mention many more that were locked in the embrace of death with German soldiers in Essen Trench. The place was a shambles, and the number of French dead spoke far more eloquently than words of the desperate attacks by the French troops. I have nothing but praise for them and for the splendid officers and men of the 71st Brigade (American). They displayed fine courage and were lacking only in experience. I am proud to have been their commander during some of those strenuous days.

During the eight days and nights of constant fighting, the conduct of all units of the 2nd Division was superb. My feelings at that time are expressed in an order I issued on October 11th:

"Officers and men of the Second Division: It is beyond my power of expression to describe fitly my admiration for your heroism. You attacked magnificently and seized Blanc Mont Ridge, the keystone of the arch constituting the enemy's position. You advanced beyond the ridge, breaking the enemy's line, and you held the ground gained with a tenacity which is unsurpassed in the annals of war.

"As a direct result of your victory, the German armies east of Rheims are in full retreat, and by drawing on yourself several German divisions from other parts of the front, you assisted the victorious advance of the Allied armies.

"Your heroism and the heroism of our comrades who died on the battlefield will live in history, and will be emulated by the young men of our country for generations to come.

"To be able to say when this war is finished 'I belonged to the Second Division; I fought with it at the battle of Blanc Mont Ridge,' will be the highest honor that can come to any man.

"JOHN A. LEJEUNE."

The conduct of the Second Division and the effect of its successful operations is vividly described in a letter written by General Gouraud to Marshal Petain, of which the following is an extract:

"Because of the brilliant part played by this 'Grand Unit' in the offensive of the Fourth Army during the autumn of 1918, I propose the Second American Division for a citation in 'The Order of the Army' upon the following specific grounds: The Second Infantry Division, United States, brilliantly commanded by General Lejeune * * * played a glorious part in the operations of the Fourth Army in the Champagne in October, 1918. On the 3rd of October, this Division drove forward and seized in a single assault the strongly entrenched German positions between Blanc Mont and Medeah Ferme, and again pressing forward to the outskirts of St. Etienne à Arnes, it made in the course of the day an advance of about 6 kilometers.

"It captured several thousand prisoners, many cannon and machine guns, and a large quantity of other military material. This attack, combined with that of the French Divisions on its left and right, resulted in the evacuation by the enemy of the positions on both sides of the River Suippe, and his withdrawal from the Massif de Notre Dames des Champs."

The following is an extract from General Pershing's report:

"The Second Division completed its advance on this front by the assault of the wooded heights of Blanc Mont, the key point of the German position, which was captured with consummate dash and skill. The Division here repulsed violent counter-attacks and then carried our lines into the village of St. Etienne, forcing the Germans to fall back before Rheims and yield positions which they had held since September, 1914."

Each of the units of the Second Division was cited by Marshal Petain in orders of the French Army in appreciation of its services. About 2,000 French *Croix-de-Guerre* were awarded to officers and men of the Division, and the Division Commander was appointed a Commander of the French Legion of Honor.

CHAPTER XVIII

THE BATTLE OF MEUSE ARGONNE

ALTHOUGH the command of the Somme-Py sector was turned over to Major General Smith at 10 A. M., October 10th, I remained there for twenty-four hours longer so as to be available to furnish any information that might be required, an excellent arrangement which the French always followed.

Promptly at ten o'clock the next morning I left Somme-Py and, after passing through the hideously devastated area, took the highway for Camp Mont Pelier, the new location of Division Headquarters. It lay in a lovely grove of trees and in the midst of a pleasant country which had not been torn and seamed and bruised by war. My room was in a rustic cottage which was immaculately clean. There was an air of peace and quiet everywhere about which was most grateful to our tired minds and weary bodies. Sleep—blessed sleep—fell upon me early in the evening, and blissfully unconscious I was until late the next afternoon.

The following day I motored to Headquarters First American Army and thence to G. H. Q. I missed General Pershing, but saw Brigadier General Drum, the Chief of Staff of the First Army, and several of the staff officers at G. H. Q. To all whom I saw, I made a strong plea for five thousand replacements to fill the gaps in our ranks. Replacements for the Marine Regiments were immediately ordered, but Army replacements were scarce, and I could obtain no definite assurance as to when the vacancies in the Army Regiments would be filled.

On my return to Camp Mont Pelier, I found the birds had flown. Frenchmen occupied my home of only the day before. Presently a Second Division officer who had waited for me gave the information that Division Headquarters had moved that morning to Ferme Vadenay, a great French military post about ten miles away. There we were quartered in brick barrack buildings.

A few days later we were visited by Admiral Mayo and his staff. He was the Commander-in-Chief of the United States Fleet during the entire period of the war and an officer not only of high distinction, but also one who was and is greatly beloved by the personnel of the Navy and Marine Corps. We held a review of the 6th Marines in his honor. The regiment had already been restored to full strength and it made a splendid appearance. The Admiral was tremendously thrilled and said he could scarce restrain his tears as he pondered on the terrible experiences the men had had, the heroism they had displayed, and the heavy losses their regiment had sustained. I also took the Admiral to Somme-Py, Blanc Mont Ridge, St. Etienne, and to the adjacent cemetery.

More than two thousand German soldiers lay buried in that cemetery which had so recently been a battlefield, and standing guard and brooding over their dead was a monstrous stone figure of some god of war. It seemed so incongruous and so grewsome that there flashed across my mind the memory of other cemeteries I had seen, in quiet churchyards in France, where the images of the crucified Son of God and his Holy Mother brought benediction to the scene and comfort to the hearts of the bereaved.

It was a marvelously interesting battlefield, and every foot of it is a sacred memory to me. I trust that, before I die, I may be able once again to visit it and again drink of the holy waters of consecration and dedication which I know must still be flowing there.

On another day I took advantage of our proximity to the half-destroyed city of Rheims and its martyred cathedral to make a pilgrimage there. On my return to Headquarters, I described the journey in my letter home, from which the following is taken:

"I went to Rheims this afternoon. It was a wonderful trip. Our road took us through the old trench system and the area where a battle of more than four years' duration had been waged.

"Such a scene is beyond the power of imagination to describe. There were miles upon miles of trenches, hundreds of dugouts and artillery emplacements; the whole face of the earth torn up by millions of shell; whole forests destroyed; and town after town reduced to piles of debris. It was a pitiful sight to behold, and I pray God that our fair country may never be visited by such devastation.

"And then there is poor ancient Rheims— once a great city, now a ruin. Whole blocks have been completely destroyed, others partly destroyed, but not one house did I see which had escaped unscathed. Many of them still have their household belongings inextricably mingled with the debris of fallen roofs or walls.

"Rheims was a deserted city except for a few French gendarmes guarding the ruins. The noble cathedral was still standing, but bearing many wounds. Several huge shell have crashed through the roof, creating great, jagged holes in the exquisite Gothic arches; the towers and walls have been struck scores of times; the wonderful carvings marred and broken and statues destroyed, but the building still stands erect, heroically like the nation that built it.

"On the east exterior face of the building, high up near the roof, there is a wonderful statue of the Holy Mother. The figures about her have been broken in fragments by shell, but she remains serene, and gazes with pitying eyes on her children.

"The exquisite, tender beauty of her face I

will always carry in my memory. It is typical of this war, for the most heroic thing in it has been the giving by the mothers of their sons to their country. The idealization of motherhood in the person of the Holy Mother of Jesus is to me one of the most beautiful parts of the Christian faith. It appeals to the best there is in every man and woman."

Our peaceful stay at Vadenay Ferme was now at an end, and the day following my journey to Rheims we were once more on the road to a new area, new scenes, and to the age-old shambles which men call a battlefield.

I called on General Gouraud to say good-bye. He was very regretful because of our departure and expressed most feelingly his gratitude for the great service which the Second Division had rendered to France.

A few days before we left Vadenay Ferme, the Division suffered a great loss. Brigadier General Ely was detached and assigned to the command of the Fifth Division with the rank of Major General. I had recommended him for promotion after St. Mihiel, and again after Blanc Mont Ridge. He richly deserved his good fortune, as he had shown himself to be a magnificent troop leader, but I sorrowed over his leaving us, not only because of his fine ability, but also because he was my friend. Colonel Van Horn, who had returned a few days before from the hospital, temporarily assumed command of the 3rd Brigade and led it on its march to the Meuse-Argonne, while the command of the 9th Infantry fell temporarily to Lieutenant-Colonel Corey. The 4th Brigade was recalled just before entering the front lines, and the footsore, weary men were transferred in camions to their bivouacs in Argonne Forest.

Division Headquarters was established at Herpoint on the afternoon of October 22nd, where it remained until the morning of the 24th, when it was moved to Les Islettes. Colonel Rhea and I took advantage of the day's delay at Herpoint to visit First Army Headquarters at

Souilly. As I climbed the stone steps of the Headquarters building, I heard a great, booming voice shouting, "Hello, soldier!" I looked around and saw my old
friend, Rear Admiral Plunkett, who was in command
of the Navy 14-inch guns on railway mounts which
were the joint contribution to the A. E. F. of Rear Admiral Ralph Earle, the Chief of Naval Ordnance, and of
Samuel Vauclain, the head of the Baldwin Locomotive
Works. Plunkett and I had a brief chat, and I then rejoined Rhea and we proceeded to carry out our mission,
which was to induce Army Headquarters to secure the
immediate return to the Second Division of its artillery
brigade, engineers and trains, and to obtain a sufficient
number of replacements to bring the Division up to full
strength. We went first to see Brigadier General Drum.
He told us that the Second Division was being brought
back to the First Army to be the point of the wedge in
the great attack for which preparations were then being
made. He further said the Division had been assigned
the post of honor, and that the whole Army relied on it to
bring the stalemate to an end by breaking through the
center of the German army and thereby forcing it to retreat to the east bank of the Meuse.

When he had finished telling us of the vitally important
task which the Second Division had been selected to accomplish, I replied that if the Second Division were
intact, I felt confident it would be successful in fulfilling
all that the Army expected of it, but that only a part of
the Division was available for the battle, and I was very
doubtful of success under the circumstances. I then
enumerated in detail the units which were then with the
36th Division and told him the number of replacements
that were needed for the 3rd Brigade, urging him to do
all in his power to reunite and rebuild the Division.

He said there were no available replacements in France
and that the Artillery Brigade of the First Division and
a regiment of Engineers would be assigned to support
the Second Division in the attack. I insisted that the
Second Division as a unit could accomplish far more than

could a conglomeration of infantry, artillery and other units hastily thrown together on the battlefield, as it was the *esprit* of the Division which made it such a formidable antagonist. I explained, too, that the Infantry and Marines had perfect confidence in their own Artillery, and that our Artillery, for its part, would overcome insuperable obstacles in order to give effective support to the Infantry and Marine regiments.

He suggested that I see General Liggett, whose office was just across the corridor. General Liggett greeted me warmly, explained in detail the part that we were to play in the approaching battle, and pointed out on the map the then position of the front lines. He also indicated on the map the small advances that had been made during the preceding ten days and painted in glowing colors the results he expected to obtain by the steam-roller attack which he had planned. I then told him the story about the plight of the Second Division which I had just outlined to General Drum. He was deeply impressed and said, "I will go at once to see General Gouraud and endeavor to secure his consent to the return of the Artillery, Engineers and Trains to the Second Division." This he did, and his effort in our behalf was completely successful. The Second Engineers and the Engineer and Supply Trains rejoined the Division at Les Islettes two or three days later, while the Second Artillery Brigade and the horse-drawn ambulances arrived just in time to participate in the great attack of November 1st.

Rhea and I also called on the General Staff Officer having jurisdiction over replacements and repeated to him our appeal for help. He reiterated what General Drum had previously told us about the lack of replacements and expressed great regret that he could do nothing for us. However, in the course of the conversation which followed, he mentioned in the most casual way that 2,500 replacements were then on their way by rail to join the 3rd Division, which would be relieved that night from front line duty. He gave us a significant look which we clearly understood, and without further delay went back to the Chief of Staff's office intent on obtaining those replacements by any means in our power.

We found General Drum had gone to the front, so we stated our case to Colonel Grant, the Deputy Chief of Staff, who at once dictated an order diverting the replacements from the 3rd Division to the Second. We were jubilant at our success, and were much gratified, too, because we had put one over on our dear friend and comrade, Preston Brown, formerly Chief of Staff of the Second Division, and then in command of the 3rd Division. We returned to Division Headquarters feeling that we had done a good day's work.

Thus it came about that the Second Division went into battle on November 1st with its ranks filled and with every unit present and ready to do its full share in making the last great offensive of the First American Army a phenomenal success.

The following day, October 24th, we moved to Les Islettes. As we drove along the road, we were passed by two big limousines going at the rate of about seventy miles an hour. In the leading car we caught a glimpse of General Pershing. He always travelled at full speed and was followed by an emergency car for his use in case anything should happen to the car in which he was riding. The thought of the heavy burden which he carried by night and by day saddened me. It was a burden which he could never lay aside. He had no periods of rest behind the lines such as we had been experiencing. The successful prosecution of the task allotted to his armies, and the honor as well as the security of our country were always in his thoughts, and on his decisions there depended the life or death of thousands of men as well as victory or defeat for our arms. Surely great praise, high honor, and deep affection should be his portion.

A little while after passing General Pershing, we overtook and passed the 4th Brigade, moving slowly in camions toward their bivouacs in the Argonne. We drove past the column slowly so that I could see and be seen by each of the 8,000 men. The thought that in a few days the lives of these men and of many more would be dependent on my acts was enough to banish gaiety or mirth from my soul, and to put in their place seriousness and earnestness of purpose and the determination to do all in my power so to direct the operations of the Division as to achieve victory with the minimum loss of life.

It was a bleak, cold and rainy evening when we reached Les Islettes. Headquarters was located in a large, old-fashioned residence, and at eight o'clock I went to my room, where a blazing fire had been built to take off the chill. Presently Captain Nelson told me that a Private Marine wanted to see me, and I told him to let him come in. My pity was aroused when I saw him. He was a mere boy, very tired and suffering from a bad cough. I made him sit down by the fire to dry his wet clothes and asked him what I could do for him.

He said he had letters for me which had been given him when he left the United States, and which he now handed me. They were from officers I knew who asked me to keep an eye on the youngster and told me that he was actually only sixteen, although eighteen was the age he gave when he enlisted. In response to my questions, he said that his name was Frazier; that he was from Philadelphia; that he had arrived in France in August; and that he had joined the Division a week or two before the battle of St. Mihiel. I then asked, "Why didn't you bring me these letters before?" He said that he was afraid I might keep him at Division Headquarters and cause him to lose the opportunity of going into battle with his platoon. I then said, "Why do you bring them to me now?" He answered, "All my buddies were killed or wounded at Blanc Mont and I am worn out from the forced marches. I saw you drive by us on the road today, so I got permission from our Captain to bring the letters to you."

I called Captain Nelson and told him to see that the boy got a hot supper, a bath, and a cot with mattress, sheets and blankets to sleep on; and I gave Frazier a note for Colonel Lee, in which I asked that he be transferred to Regimental Headquarters for duty so that he could be under shelter, as his youth and his sickness made him unfit to undergo further exposure to the elements.

Several years afterwards, a gentleman called on me at my office in Washington and, introducing himself as Mr. Frazier, recalled to my mind the incident I have just related which he had learned about from his son. He thanked me earnestly, saying that in all probability I had saved the boy from an attack of pneumonia and perhaps death, and that his service in the Marine Corps had made a man of him, so much so that he was then seriously at work in college studying medicine.

I have told this story to illustrate the fact that when my thoughts turn backward, as they have been doing since I began to write my reminiscences, the memory of the little deeds of kindness which I have been able to do for a fellow human being stand out preëminent among the events of my life, and afford me more gratification and more pleasure than does the memory of any contacts I have had with great men, or any prominence I may have achieved. That this is the case with most men during their declining years, I believe to be true, and this statement is recorded here for the benefit of the young men and women who may chance to read these lines.

On the nights of October 25th and 26th, the 3rd and 4th Brigades, respectively, marched into areas near Exermont, taking station in the woods. They were not permitted to use the highway which, as usual, was filled with traffic, but picked their way through the mud on side roads, or "*pistes,*" as such roads were colloquially described by the French. In each case, the troops found their way without guides and without being observed by the Corps Military Police. Our men, by constant practice, had acquired night sight and were able to find their way in the blackest darkness. This faculty was of enormous value to the Division during its participation in the engagements which marked the closing days of the war.

Division Headquarters was moved to Charpentry on the afternoon of October 27th, and on that morning I drove to Fifth Corps Headquarters which was located at Chepy, to report to General Summerall, the Corps Commander, and to make the acquaintance of the staff. The members of the staff with whom we were to deal most were Brigadier General Burt, Chief of Staff; Colonel Emerson, Assistant Chief of Staff, G-3; and Brigadier General Aultman, Chief of Artillery. I took luncheon at Corps Headquarters and joined with the staff in joshing the Corps Provost Marshal because his military police had failed to observe the entry of either the 3rd or 4th Brigades into the Corps Area. None of the staff appeared to be able to understand how sixteen thousand men could march by the M. P.'s without being heard or seen. It was one of the insoluble war mysteries.

I also stopped at First Corps Headquarters and had a talk with Malin Craig, who was still Chief of Staff of that Corps, although Major General Dickman was then in command of it, having succeeded Lieutenant General Liggett when the latter was promoted to the command of the First Army.

All the Generals and staff officers whom I saw at the front showed on their faces the marks of the strain under which they had been laboring during the preceding month. The Corps Commanders and their staffs had remained constantly in line since the inception of the battle on September 26th. There had been no respites for them and they showed the effects of the days and nights of stress and tension.

The impression common among the front line units, that the officers on duty at higher headquarters had an easy time of it, was altogether erroneous. It is true that they were not exposed to physical danger to the same extent as were the men serving nearer the front, and that they had more physical comforts; but it was their lot to bear the heavy burden of responsibility and to suffer the indescribable agony of soul which increased by geometrical progression with increase in rank.

Charpentry, the new capital city of the Second Division, was a sight to behold. It was situated in a flat valley with high, steep hills all around it, and was in a sea of mud. It was a ruined town, having been a target for German artillery since the day it was wrested from German hands by the Americans, and only two or three buildings were in condition to be used. Division Headquarters occupied a two-story building. It was nearly a complete wreck, and promised to fall down as soon as hit again by one of the numerous shells that were being hurled at the town by the enemy.

The German artillery was very active and fired constantly at the rear areas as well as the front lines. Thousands of men had burrowed into the reverse slopes of steep hills and made themselves as comfortable as they could in these holes by putting up their "pup" tents over the entrances. It was a very interesting area, and I could easily have spent a number of days in visiting Argonne Forest, Verdun, Montfaucon, Romagne, and all the Corps and Divisional Headquarters, but it was necessary to concentrate on the plan of the great attack which was due to take place at dawn on November 1st.

Our intensive study of the plan of attack was begun at a conference held at Fifth Corps Headquarters, at which General Summerall presided. He described in detail the happenings since he had assumed command of the Fifth Corps, about two weeks before, and pointed out on the map the small advances which had been made during those two weeks in spite of repeated efforts to go forward. He informed us of the painful necessity which had required the relief from front line duty of several commanders, and then, in illuminating manner, he painted the picture of the plan of attack, dwelling especially on the part to be played by the 2nd and 89th Divisions, which were to be the assaulting divisions of the Fifth Corps and the leaders in the attack. The plan involved an advance on "D" day of over nine kilometers by the 2nd Division, the capture by it of the fortified towns of Landres et St. Georges, St. Georges, Landreville, Chenery and Bayonville; also the powerfully organized Bois des Hazois, Bois l'Epasse, the heights of Barrecourt, and breaking through the Brunhilde and Freya Stellung in front of which the waves of attack had been shattered whenever attempts had hitherto been made to carry Landres et St. Georges by assault.

At a second conference he pointed out on the map the first, second and third (final) objectives for November 1st, told of the enormous concentration of artillery to support the attack of the Corps, and specified that the preliminary bombardment would be joined in by the artillery brigades of the 1st and 42nd Divisions in addition to the 2nd Field Artillery and certain attached French units.

Then, turning to me, he said, "You have no doubt noted that the 2nd Division is to be the point of the wedge. What, in your opinion, is the probability that it will succeed in taking each of the three objectives?" I replied that I felt perfectly confident that it would capture Landres et St. Georges, St. George, Bois des Hazois, and Bois l'Epasse, and that it would reach the first objective, as I didn't believe any force could withstand the vigor, power and speed of its initial attack when backed up by well directed artillery fire; and that I also was of the opinion that it would be able to take and hold the final objective of the day provided one of its flanks was protected by an adjacent division, but that should there be no support for either flank it would be a difficult task for one division to make such a deep advance, especially as the artillery barrage must necessarily dwindle in power during the later stages of the attack.

He expressed his delight because of my confidence that the first objective would be taken, and said that everything that was humanly possible would be done to support the advance of the Division to the heights of Barricourt, the final objective of the day. General Wright, the commander of the 89th Division, then stated that his division, although tired from its long stay in line, would go along with the 2nd Division to the final objective. I then expressed my confidence in and my admiration for the 89th Division and its Commanding General, as I had seen them in action in the battle of St. Mihiel, and I knew of the splendid reputation they had already gained on the Meuse-Argonne battlefield.

Upon the conclusion of the conference at Corps Headquarters, a conference was held at 2nd Division Headquarters at which were present the Colonels and Lieutenant Colonels of all the regiments, in addition to the Brigade Commanders and their adjutants. Again was the approaching battle described in the utmost detail, and copies of the plan of attack and the large army maps were distributed to them, as well as the maps made at Division Headquarters for each battalion, company and platoon commander showing the terrain within the Division Sector and the dividing lines between the regiments.

Further conferences were held within the regiments and battalions, and every commander, down to and including platoon leaders of the battalions which were to lead off in the attack, were sent to the front lines to observe the terrain over which they would be called on to advance, just before dawn, on the crucial day.

In addition, General Summerall and I visited each of the twelve battalions of the two Infantry Brigades, and assembling the officers and men by companies, closely around us, addressed them on the subject of the approaching battle. In each case I introduced the General to the men, telling them who he was, and then made an appeal to their *esprit de corps* and expressed my perfect confidence in them, saying that I was certain that no enemy, however tenacious or courageous he might be, could stop their advance. General Summerall described in detail and at length the immediate and the ultimate objectives to be attained and the strategic effects of victory. He pointed out that a successful assault on the heights of Barricourt would leave the enemy no recourse but to retreat across the Meuse, in which case American heavy artillery could be brought up to the vicinity of Beaumont whence it would be able by its fire to interrupt the operation of trains on the Metz-Sedan railway, thereby preventing intercommunication between the German armies then retreating in Belgium and northern France, and those holding the lines on our front and to the southward as far as the Swiss border. General Summerall then addressed all the Infantry and Marine officers of the Division, and after four hours of tramping through the mud and making speeches in the open air, we drove away together.

The General said as we rode toward Charpentry that he had been compelled to relieve a number of officers from their commands because of their failure to carry out orders, and that he would continue to do so in the future no matter who might be the sufferer. I said, "General, the Second Division officers will carry out orders because of their *esprit,* their pride in and love for their division, and their devotion to the cause for which they are fighting. In fact, we have come to feel that it matters but little what happens to us as individuals, and that the only things which really matter are the welfare of the great Division to which we belong and the speedy and decisive defeat of the enemy." He expressed great gratification because of what I had said and his full confidence that the Division would accomplish on November 1st all that it was humanly possible for troops to accomplish. General Summerall, throughout the war, showed himself to be not only a formidable antagonist, but the hardest kind of fighter for the officers and men who served efficiently under his command.

On the night of October 30-31, the 23rd Infantry and the 5th and 6th Marines, in the order named from right to left, relieved the support and reserve battalions of the 83rd Brigade (42nd Division), while the front line battalions of that Division continued to hold the outpost positions as a screen until 3 A. M. on "D" day. The infantry components of the 42nd Division then assembled in an area near Exermont and passed under the jurisdiction of the First Corps.

The command of the sector passed to the Commanding General, 2nd Division, at noon on October 31st, and

Division Headquarters was transferred to Exermont at 4 P. M. on that day.

At "H" hour minus 10 minutes (5.20 A. M.), a standing barrage was to be laid two hundred yards in front of the enemy line in order to reach the enemy machine gun units, which prior experience had shown usually moved forward into No Man's Land in order to escape the artillery bombardment and to be in readiness to mow down the attacking troops with their fire as soon as they emerged from their jump-off trenches. Our own troops were held back some distance in rear of the front line positions until "H" hour (5:30 A. M.) so as to avoid the effects of the standing barrage.

The attack order further provided that the three regiments in line should move forward simultaneously at "H" hour (5:30), closing up on and following the creeping barrage, the 23rd Infantry on the right, with two battalions in the front line and one in support, being assigned the task of capturing Landres et St. Georges, and of cleaning up Bois de Hazois and Bois l'Epasse, after which it would withdraw and join the 9th Infantry in support of the 4th Brigade.

The 5th and 6th Marines were to move forward in the left half of the sector, each in column of battalions and with a liaison battalion composed of one company of Marines and one company of the 80th Division, to be commanded by Major Stowell, on the left flank.

The 4th Brigade was to expand its front and take over the entire Division sector after reaching the first objective—an east and west line about 400 meters south of Landreville. After a pause of sufficient duration to permit the support battalions to pass through the leading battalions, the Brigade, preceded by the creeping barrage, was then to continue its advance to the second objective—a line about 400 meters north of Bayonville at Chenery, and thence in the same manner to the final Corps objective of the day—the heights of Barrecourt. Beyond this line lay the exploitation line—Fosse-Nouart—towards which strong patrols were to be sent.

The evening before the battle was a quiet one, and I remained at Exermont to keep in touch by telephone with the Corps, with all units of the 2nd Division, and with the adjacent divisions. After dinner I wrote my daily letter to my wife:

"Early tomorrow morning the 2nd Division enters its third great battle since I have commanded it, and all within seven weeks. This battle, we hope, will inflict a deadly blow on the enemy and bring him to his knees. The artillery bombardment begins at 3:30 A. M., and at 5:30 the Infantry attacks. We have a great task ahead of us, and a fight that will try men's souls. I pray God that we may win, and end this horrible war by a decisive victory. Many a poor fellow will give his life to his country tomorrow. The men are brave, strong and determined to beat the enemy. We have large forces attacking and large forces backing us up. I trust we may drive to the line chosen. I am glad to say that I am well and strong; I never felt better in my life and I believe that God will give me the strength to go through the ordeal which is before me. I shall ask His blessing and His assistance before I lie down tonight. I shall go to bed as soon as I finish this and get up at 3 A. M. so as to be about when the artillery opens fire. I feel I must be up then. I could not bear to lie in bed with our men out in the front lines being fired on by the enemy.

"We moved Headquarters this afternoon to the half-destroyed village at Exermont, several miles nearer the front than Charpentry. It is a filthy mud-hole. I have my room and our offices in an old peasant's house, and my room adjoins the stable which is under the same roof; my nearest neighbors are two mules in the stable. We have to be bottled up so as to keep the lights from showing, as our friends the airplanes are forever on the job. They bomb every night, and we have the shelling always with us. We shall make them sick tomorrow morning, though, as we have a tremendous amount of artillery and shall throw tens of thousands of shells into the area the

2nd Division is to attack. I hope each shell may find a suitable target.

"It is a solemn time just before a battle, but it is as if one were in the hands of fate. We do not enter into battle of our own accord. It is always some one in higher authority who gives the order. In our case, it emanates from Marshal Foch, but he is only the servant of the nations allied against the common enemy. One grows to feel that God speaks through the peoples of the world, and that in some inscrutable way it is His command that we fight to the death."

To sleep was impossible, and I was up before 2 A. M. to receive the reports that the troops had occupied their jump-off positions, and that the artillery and machine guns were in readiness for the bombardment.

I was indeed glad that our Artillery Commander, Brigadier General Bowley, had returned. Energy, determination and pugnacity were his dominant traits, and the Infantry and Marines knew they were invincible when they were supported by the 2nd Field Artillery Brigade.

The 2nd Division was lavish in its use of shell, as Bowley and I both strongly believed that the artillery should be utilized to the limit of its capacity in order that victory might be achieved with the smallest possible loss of life among our assaulting troops. Infantry and Marines, on their part, had learned that in order to accomplish this result, it was necessary for them to follow the rolling barrage closely, or to "lean on it" as they expressed it, even to the extent of suffering a few casualties by shell bursting short.

A few minutes after the artillery bombardment opened I walked out to a high ridge and watched the effect of the fire. It was, if anything, more terrific than at St. Mihiel, and seemed as if it were an elemental cataclysm closely approximating the simultaneous eruption of many volcanoes, combined with the continuous lightning and the innumerable reverberations which characterize a thunderstorm in a mountain country.

For two hours the enemy front lines and rear area were overwhelmed with an enormous number of bursting shell, and the air fairly sang with bullets. Two hundred and fifty-five machine guns ground out their hail of death, and the gas company threw into the enemy positions its quota of destruction.

Returning to Headquarters before 5.30 A. M., to receive the reports that the leading batallions were going "over the top," we were thrilled by the news that followed every few minutes, telling us of the successful advance in spite of heavy machine gun fire from the left flank; that the towns of Landres et St. Georges, and St. Georges, and the Bois de Hazois had fallen captive to our resistless waves of attack; and finally that the first objective was reached on schedule time. The rejoicing at Division Headquarters was joined in by Corps and First Army Headquarters.

Colonel Rhea and I could not restrain our enthusiasm and started towards the front to establish our advance headquarters at Landres et St. Georges. At Somerance we found the headquarters of the 6th Marines, and Colonel Lee and Lieutenant-Colonel Holcomb ready to move to St. Georges. Some of the men belonging to the Headquarters Detachment of the 6th Marines were having breakfast, eight or ten being in the mess line. Inasmuch as hours had elapsed since my last meal, I broke out my mess gear and tailed on. The men in line insisted that I go ahead of them, but I declined to do so, saying that they were hungrier than I. I got a liberal helping of good bacon, beans, biscuit and coffee in my regular turn and, naturally, never enjoyed a meal more. This simple story of how a Major-General stood in the "chow line," with his men, spread far and wide, and a year later, long after it had been relegated to the limbo of forgotten things, it was told by Major Bierne, toastmaster at a dinner at the Westmoreland Club of Richmond, Virginia, in introducing me as the speaker of the evening.

As soon as telephone communication with Landres et St. Georges was opened, Rhea and I drove to what was left of that town and established our advanced P. C. there. Enemy shell were still falling on the town, and several men of the 2nd Engineers who were rebuilding a bridge near-by were struck. A few minutes after 11 o'clock reports arrived that the second objective had been occupied after severe fighting at Bayonville, and that several batteries of artillery had been captured as they were limbering up for the purpose of moving back. The reports stated that the enemy was streaming to the rear.

A short while afterwards the advance was resumed and reached the final objective for the day exactly on schedule time. It was a marvelous exhibition of fighting power and efficiency on the part of the Division, and congratulations poured in from Corps, Army and higher Headquarters. Over 1700 prisoners and many cannon were captured, and heavy casualties were inflicted on the enemy. The prisoners seemed stunned by the tremendous power of our attack and the rapidity of our advance. Our own casualties were not heavy by comparison with those suffered by the enemy, but nevertheless many wounded streamed to the rear. First there were the walking wounded, and then a considerable number being carried on stretchers by German prisoners. Each of these seemed greatly to enjoy the experience of being borne in state by four husky Germans, and took great delight in giving them orders. Then there were the seriously wounded in ambulances going back to the field hospitals. Colonel Derby, the Division Surgeon, and his assistant, Lieutenant-Commander Joel T. Boone, were always in evidence directing the removal of the wounded and arranging for their care. The medical department worked smoothly and efficiently under their skillful direction. Chaplain Pierce and the burial parties followed the advancing troops and were untiring in their sacred labor of laying the dead to rest.

Division Headquarters was busily engaged in arranging for the defense of the position that had been taken. We soon learned that the 89th Division had come up abreast of us, so that our right flank was secure, but our whole left flank was exposed, as the advance of the first corps had been held up. As late as sunset we could still hear the sound of many enemy machine guns firing in that sector to the left rear of Landres et St. Georges.

The advance echelons of our artillery regiments were, however, near Landreville, firing vigorously in protection of our left flank, and the 6th Marines and 9th Infantry occupied patches of woods in the neighboring sector to cover the flank. Finally, some hours after dark, a battalion of the First Corps occupied Imecourt and sent a detachment to Sivry.

At 8 P. M. Corps orders for that night and the ensuing day were received. These orders provided that the Division should push forward to the Fosse-Nouart line at daylight, send patrols beyond that line, and at the same time protect and cover the left flank with adequate forces. The brief Division order, prescribing the details of these operations, was prepared and distributed before 9 o'clock, and Colonel Rhea, the Chief of Staff, in compliance with telegraphic instructions received that day assumed command of the 3rd Brigade, relieving Colonel Van Horn who returned to the 9th Infantry.

I detailed Colonel Hu Myers as Chief of Staff, and at 9 P. M. we began what was known at Division Headquarters as the battle of Buzancy. Buzancy was a town in the 1st Corps sector which had acquired prominence along with Boult aux Bois by reason of their frequent mention in communiques and orders. The ridge, known as the heights of Barre-court, ran across the 2nd Division Sector and into the 80th Division sector to the vicinity of Buzancy. The battle of Buzancy was precipitated by an order received from the Corps shortly after 9 P. M. by telephone, and later confirmed in writing, modifying the previous order and directing an attack on Bu-zancy early the next morning, in addition to going forward to the Fosse-Nouart line. Instructions to that effect were issued by Division Headquarters, and the troops were formed for an attack to the westward along the ridge with Buzancy as the ob-jective. Inasmuch as up to 10 o'clock our left flank was still in the air, I represented to General Sum-merall that an advance to Nouart, Fosse and Bu-zancy, while at the same time providing flank pro-tection, would give the Division a front of approxi-mately 16 kilometers to hold, and requested that the 89th Division extend its front towards the left. This was directed, and the reserve troops of that Divi-sion were put in march with that end in view.

About midnight Colonel Myers called up the First Corps and learned that an attack by them was planned to take place at daylight the next morning with Buzancy as the objective. General Craig said there would surely be a mix-up if we attacked across the Corps' front. After hours spent in the endeavor to straighten out the matter the 2nd Division at-tack to the westward was called off about 4 that morning. The battle of Buzancy, so far as the 2nd Division was concerned, was ended, and the order to the 89th Division to take over a part of our front was rescinded.

After communicating with the 3rd and 4th Bri-gades, I decided that it was then too late to reform our troops for an attack to the northward that morning, and directed that the 4th Brigade be re-lieved by the 3rd Brigade, and that arrangements be made to move forward as soon as the relief was completed. In the afternoon orders came prescribing as the task for the ensuing day (November 3rd) an advance from the line Fosse-Nouart early the next morning, with the heights of Vaux-en-Dieulet as the objective of the attack. I then directed the 3rd Brigade to move forward after dark to the line Fosse-Nouart, and thence to jump off at the hour directed.

There was thus begun by the 2nd Division that important series of night operations which was continued until the Armistice. The regiments advanced by the roads in columns of twos, each with an advance party and flanking groups. They moved through the enemy lines, capturing many prisoners, a number of whom they found asleep. Those more alert were surrounded.

The enemy was confused and demoralized, being unaccustomed to such a method of warfare, and the 3rd Brigade had no difficulty in reaching the day's objective early on the 3rd.

The report of the arrival of our troops on the objective was a great relief to Division Headquarters, as prior reports had been vague and uncertain. The Corps, somehow, seemed unable to appreciate the difficulties we had in changing the direction of attack on November 2nd, and was rather impatient because of the delay on that day, but all was well once again as soon as news was received of the success which had attended the night advance.

I insert the commendatory communication from General Summerall in regard to the successful attack on November 1st, also my own order on the subject:

"From: Commanding General, Fifth Army Corps.
   "To: Commanding General, Second Division.
"Subject: Commendation.
   "I desire to add to my telephone message the assurance of my deep appreciation and profound ad-

miration for the manner in which the Second Division executed the missions allotted to it on November 1st.

"The Division's brilliant advance of more than nine kilometers, destroying the last stronghold in the Hindenburg Line, capturing the Freya Stellung, and going more than nine kilometers against not only the permanent but the relieving forces on their front, may justly be regarded as one of the most remarkable achievements made by any troops in this war. For the first time, perhaps, in our experience, the losses inflicted by your division upon the enemy in the offensive greatly exceeded the casualties of the division.

"The reports indicate moreover that in a single day the division has captured more artillery and machine guns than usually falls to the lot of a command in several days of hard fighting. These results must be attributed to the great dash and speed of the troops, and to the irresistible force with which they struck and overcame the enemy.

"The division has more than justified the distinguished confidence placed in it by the Commander-in-Chief when it was selected to take the lead in the advance from which such great results are expected. It is an honor to command such troops and they richly deserve a place in history and in the affection of their countrymen which is not exceeded or perhaps paralleled in the life of our nation.

"I desire that you convey these sentiments to the officers and soldiers of the Second Division, and that you assure them of my abiding wishes for their continued success in the campaigns that lie before it.

"C. P. SUMMERALL."

The above letter was received and issued to the Division on November 4th. On the 2nd the fol-

lowing order of the Division Commander was published:
"ORDER.

"The Second Division yesterday made one of the most brilliant attacks of the war. It drove forward through the enemy's fortified lines to a depth of six miles. The results of this drive are already becoming evident. The First Corps, on our left, has advanced today without opposition to Buzancy and Briquenay, and the enemy is withdrawing all along the line.

"When the history of America's part in winning this war is written, the renown of the Second Division will stand out pre-eminent.

"Let us press on and destroy the enemy!

"JOHN A. LEJEUNE."

On November 2nd it was eminently wise for a single division to drive forward without regard to the neighboring divisions, but on October 3rd such action would have been sheer folly.

It was with this thought in mind that the plan for the remarkable advance of the 9th Infantry during the evening of November 3rd was evolved. About 2 P. M. Colonel Rhea reported that the front line troops were being subjected to a severe trench mortar fire from the woods before them, and suggested the advisability of attacking and occupying the enemy position. The suggestion was approved and a successful attack was made. About this time the 2nd Division order for the night was distributed. It assigned as the mission the operation of driving forward to the heights in the vicinity of Beaumont.

The specific mission assigned to the 3rd Brigade was that of pushing strong reconnaissances, supported by artillery, through the forest of Belval, seizing a position near Beaumont and building up a line of resistance there.

The 4th Brigade was ordered to move forward to the line then held by the 3rd Brigade, Champy-le-Haut—Vaux-en-Dieulet.

At a conference at 3rd Brigade Headquarters, the plan of advancing the 9th and 23rd Infantry through the woods by separate roads was evolved and was approved by the Division Commander. The advance began after dark. Finding that there was only one passable road, that used by the 9th Infantry, the 23rd Infantry followed by the same route. The column, headed by the 3rd Battalion, 9th Infantry, moved forward on the road with Lieutenant-Colonel Corey and a detachment of German-speaking soldiers as point. Enemy parties encountered were quietly taken in charge and sent to the rear. When resistance was encountered, the leading troops halted, while flanking groups surrounded the enemy detachments. This spectacular and remarkable movement was effected in a pouring rain and in pitch-black darkness.

By 11.30 P. M., the head of the column debouched from the woods into the open, took up its position on the line previously indicated, and established outposts. The 23rd Infantry and one Battalion of the 5th Marines followed the leading regiment and gave it support. Due to the cover of darkness and the element of surprise, no losses were suffered by our troops during the advance, while if it had been made during the daylight hours heavy casualties would doubtless have been the price.

Colonel Corey told me the story of the thrilling experience. He said perfect quiet reigned after the advance began, not a word above a whisper being spoken. Many German soldiers were made prisoners while lying asleep on the ground, and at La Forge Ferme the buildings were filled with sleeping men. As the column moved along the road, German guns in the woods on either side continued to fire, the enemy being entirely unaware that his lines were being penetrated. On debouching from Bois du Port Gerache into the open, a farmhouse with all lights burning was surrounded and a number of officers and men were taken prisoners without a shot being exchanged. The prisoners were dumbfounded. They said the Division Commander and his staff had left only five or ten minutes before the Americans arrived.

The night operation I have endeavored to describe was a revolutionary innovation in war, and constituted one of the most remarkable achievements of the 2nd Dision, especially as it involved not only a penetration of the enemy's lines and an advance through a dense woods over an almost impassable road in a pouring rain at night, but also because the position occupied by the troops which had made the advance was six kilometers behind the German lines on the right and left of the 2nd Division.

On the afternoon of November 3rd, 2nd Division Headquarters moved up to Bayonville et Chenery. I shall never forget the hours we spent there. All night long the 1st Division marched through the town. The front window of my room opened on the highway, and I sat there and listened to the marching feet of the troops. Nothing could be seen because of the heavy rain and the inky darkness, but there was much to be heard. The marching songs the soldiers sang, interspersed with their humorous remarks to each other; the picturesque profanity to which some gave utterance when a wagon found its way into a shellhole, as frequently happened, and the nearest platoon was called on to help the mules pull it out; the shouts of command by the officers; the directions as to the route to be followed given by the M. P.'s in stentorian tones in order to be heard above the clamor—to all of these sounds and many more I listened entranced. It was a realistic demonstration of the high spirit of the American troops.

Early the next morning, we changed our home from Bayonville to Fosse. There I saw Brigadier General Marshall, of the 1st Division, who offered the services of the brigade he commanded. Later in the day, a similar offer, so far as his regiment was concerned, was made by Colonel Theodore Roosevelt who, while still suffering from the effects of a wound, had without authority returned to his division. His offer was accepted and his regiment moved to the Forest of Belval to cover the left rear of the division.

Early in the forenoon of November 4th, Colonel Myers and I drove to 3rd Brigade Headquarters, which was located at La Forge Ferme in a clearing. The road through the forest, then almost impassable for automobiles, became completely so for motor vehicles in a short while and for wagons in a few days, making the problem of supply an extraordinarily difficult one until the main highway to Laneuville sur Meuse (opposite Stenay), and thence to Beaumont, was cleared of the' enemy. In the meantime, our forward echelons were on short rations and were partly subsisting on the cabbages which the Germans had cultivated and left behind them in the fields.

Myers and I dismounted from our automobile several hundred yards from La Forge Ferme, as per the instructions of a watchful M. P., and walked along by Major Brainard's battalion of the 15th Field Artillery, which was firing intensively on the enemy artillery positions, machine gun nests, and infantry units which were concentrating their strength in an effort to destroy our regiments that had so valiantly ventured to take up a position behind his lines. A considerable portion of the German artillery, however, seemed intent on doing counter-battery work, as the area in the vicinity of Brainard's artillery battalion and 3rd Brigade Headquarters certainly was being well torn to pieces by bursting shell. Our walk to Brigade Headquarters was similar to passing through a barrage.

Colonel Rhea was waiting to welcome us at the front door of his two-story stone farmhouse, and gave us a succinct account of the operation of the previous night and the hornet's nest into which his brigade had run that morning. Both flanks of the position it occupied were exposed and were manifestly without prospect of immediate support, for while we stood at the second-story window looking out in the direction of the first corps sector, we could plainly see the battle raging just north of Vaux-en-Dieulet and to our left rear. The German rearguard detachments were easily visible, as were the advancing American troops, and the din of machine gun fire was constantly heard. At about the same hour, the 9th and 23rd Infantry, six kilometers farther to the front, made an attack with slight gains, but suffered severe losses owing to the concentration of all available enemy forces in the vicinity on their front and flanks, and the heavy artillery fire from the heights on the east bank of the Meuse.

Realizing the importance of providing flank protection as quickly as possible for the 3rd Brigade in its advanced position, I issued orders for the 4th Brigade, then in reserve, to move forward and occupy the right half of the 2nd Division sector in order to connect with the right of the 3rd Brigade and the left of the 89th Division, which was then advancing towards Landreuville-sur-Meuse and the road leading from that place towards Beaumont. In addition, I called up the Commanding General of the Division on our left and, after describing the situation at our front, I offered to his division the use of the road in the 2nd Division sector, by which he could have marched a detachment without meeting opposition to the farther edge of the woods and from there executed a flank attack which should have resulted in a hasty evacuation of the woods on his front, or else in the capture of the enemy force with which his Division was engaged.

The movement of the 4th Brigade was promptly executed as directed, but the Division on our left, being committed to an advance through the woods on its own front, did not accept my offer of the road in the 2nd Division sector; however, its two right battalions (317th Infantry) reached the northern edge of Bois du Port Gerache within the left limit of the 2nd Division sector about 4:30 P. M., while the remaining front line elements took up positions for the night about 1 kilometer north of Sommauthe. On our way back to 2nd Division Headquarters, we picked up two of the walking wounded men and drove them to the "Tirage." One had his arm in a sling, a bone having been broken, and the other had his head bandaged owing to a severe scalp wound, both injuries having been inflicted by the fire of enemy machine guns during the attack by the 3rd Brigade that morning. The soldier with the scalp wound answered my questions freely, and gave a vivid description of his experience. He said, "I belong to a machine gun company and I am some machine gunner. If those Boche had known it was me they were shooting at, they wouldn't have given me a scalp wound, but would have shot me through the head." He further stated that he was born at Beirut, Syria, and had emigrated to the United States three or four years before. He added that what Syria needed to make it a fine country was a lot of good Americans like himself.

The spirit and the patriotism he displayed were commendable and indicated clearly that the foreign-born soldier was as completely imbued with the unconquerable American spirit as were the men who had been born under the Stars and Stripes. In April, 1929, I attended a Second Division dinner at Boston, Massachusetts, and during my address I told this story. Whereupon one of those present stood up and quietly said, "General, I am the man you have just referred to," and at my request he showed us the scar of the wound he had received. It was a dramatic coincidence, which brought the men to their feet in applause! I wish I could remember his name so that I might chronicle it here.

The orders for the night directed an advance to the Meuse. The 23rd Infantry and the 4th Machine Gun Battalion, which had reëforced the 3rd Brigade during the day, moved forward before midnight. The woods east and southeast of Beaumont were seized during the night, as were the Bois de la Vache, the adjacent trench system, and Hill 241. At dawn, Beaumont and Letanne were mopped up and patrols were pushed up and down the Meuse searching for crossings, while the 4th Machine Gun Battalion occupied positions on the heights of the west bank. The 4th Brigade occupied a position on the right of the 3rd Brigade and joined with the left of the 89th Division.

Following the remarkable advance of the 2nd Division November 2 to 5, inclusive, this order was issued:

> "Headquarters Second Division (Regular),
> "American Expeditionary Forces.
> > "France, November 5, 1918.
>
> "Order.
>
> "During the night of November 2-3, the Second Division moved forward overcoming the resistance of the enemy's advanced elements, and at 6 A. M. it attacked and seized the enemy's line of defense on the ridge southeast of Vaux-en-Dieulet.
>
> "Late in the afternoon, the enemy, having reorganized his line on the border of Belval Forest, was again attacked and defeated. After nightfall and in a heavy rain, the advanced elements of the division pressed forward through the forest, and occupied a position on the heights south of Beaumont, six kilometers in advance of the divisions on our right and left.
>
> "During the night of November 4-5, the division again pressed forward, occupied Beaumont and l'Etanne, and threw the enemy on its front across the Meuse.
>
> "The endurance, the skill, the courage, and the fiery energy of the officers and men of the Second Division are unsurpassed in the annals of war. The victories of the division have been a tremendous factor in bringing near the day of the decisive defeat of the German Army.
>
> > "JOHN A. LEJEUNE."

Both brigades were directed on the 5th to reconnoiter the banks of the river within the limits of the Division sector for crossings, and to seize and hold all undestroyed bridges. In addition, the 4th Brigade was directed to coöperate with the 89th Division in mopping up the Foret de Jaulnay. All bridges across the Meuse on the front of the 2nd and 89th Divisions were found to have been destroyed by the enemy immediately after his withdrawal to the east bank of the Meuse before daylight on the 5th, making it impracticable to effect a crossing of the river until pontoon or improvised bridges could be constructed, as it was nowhere fordable on the front of the 5th Corps.

On November 6th, the sector of the 89th Division was extended to the left to include Pouilly, causing the 4th Brigade to narrow its front, and the 1st Division extended the left boundary of the 5th Corps to include Mouzon. About 6:30 A. M. the 1st Division advanced to Le Faubourg (opposite Mouzon), its right flank during its advance being covered by the 3rd Brigade, the 9th Infantry having moved forward from its support position just after midnight and occupied the heights on the west bank of the Meuse at La Sartelle Ferme, one kilometer south of La Sartelle Ferme, Bois de Hospice, and a point one kilometer west of Villemonterie.

The 1st Division, upon the completion of its advance, held the west bank of the river from Villemonterie to Le Faubourg, both inclusive. Late in the afternoon on the 6th, the 1st Division marched on Sedan pursuant to orders of the 5th Corps.

At about 4 P. M. of the 6th, the Corps Commander visited 2nd Division Headquarters and gave verbal directions for the Division to prepare to march on Sedan. After a discussion of the situation, he decided that the movement to the north would begin as soon as the 89th Division could arrange to take over the front then held by the 2nd Division. Confirmatory written orders were received an hour or two later, and the Division directed the 5th and 6th Marines to assemble preparatory to taking up the march early the next morning via Beaumont, while the 3rd Brigade was instructed to take over the portion of the front held by the 4th Brigade and to remain in position until relieved by the 89th Division, when it would assemble preliminary to moving toward Sedan in support of the 4th Brigade.

During the night, the 4th Brigade was relieved and its concentration was effected as directed. About 1 o'clock in the morning however orders were received from the Corps revoking the previous orders to both the 89th and the 2nd Divisions. The latter was to hold the west bank of the Meuse from Letanne to Le Faubourg (both inclusive), and the former to extend its left to Letanne (exclusive).

No further changes were made in the boundaries of the 2nd Division sector until after the armistice. The boundary lines ran approximately southwest, and included Beaumont, Youncq, La Besace and Sommauthe in the Division area. On its left, the 77th Division, First Corps, held the west bank of the Meuse to the northward.

The 4th Brigade moved into bivouacs on the Beaumont-Sommauthe road in readiness to relieve the 3rd Brigade when ordered. During the evening of the 7th, after completing the above described adjustments of position, active reconnaissances were made with the view of determining the most feasible locations for crossing the river by pontoon or improvised bridges.

On the evening of the 7th, Corps orders were issued directing the 2nd and 89th Divisions to be prepared to cross the river on "D" day at "H" hour and seize the heights on the east bank. The date of crossing, which depended on the time of arrival of the pontoons from some distant point, was first fixed for the evening of the 9th. On that day, however, it was learned that all available pontoons had been assigned to the 89th Division, and it therefore became necessary for the 2nd Engineers to construct foot bridges for the use of the 2nd Division, and the crossing was postponed until the next evening. In the meantime, the 4th Brigade, which I had detailed to make the crossing, had made a night march to positions in readiness, the 5th Marines near Letanne, and the 6th Marines near Le Faubourg, and the 2nd Engineers was busily engaged in the construction at Beaumont and Youncq of a sufficient number of sections to enable that regiment to throw four floating foot bridges across the river, two near Letanne, and two just north of Le Faubourg.

On the evening of the 9th, a conference was held at Corps Headquarters at which the Commanding Generals and Chiefs of Staff of the 2nd and 89th Divisions were present. The whole subject of river crossings in general, and the crossing of the Meuse in particular, was freely discussed. I stated that our reconnaissances clearly indicated that the east bank of the Meuse was strongly held, many machine guns being in place and the enemy artillery being very active, and that, under the circumstances, I deemed it advisable for the 90th Division, which was then across the river, to move north and clear the front of the 89th Division which could then cross without opposition; and that, in its turn, the 89th Division should force the withdrawal of the enemy detachments opposite the 2nd Division. That division would then continue the operation just described and clear the way for the crossing of the 77th Division. This plan was taken under advisement, but on our return to Division Headquarters we were informed that it had not been approved, and we were directed to make arrangements for the two divisions to cross simultaneously on the night of November 10-11.

In general terms, the plan provided for two battalions of the 5th Marines and a liaison battalion of the 89th Division to effect a crossing by the bridges near Letanne, while the 6th Marines and a liaison battalion of the 5th Marines would move across near Mouzon. The 2nd Field Artillery was directed to prepare for the crossing by a preliminary bombardment of the enemy's infantry and artillery positions, and to give effective support to the assaulting infantry with its fire. In addition, the machine gun companies and the 9th Infantry were given instructions to cover the crossing by overhead fire.

The plans were carried out as directed, except that the repeated attempts to throw across the two bridges near

Mouzon were frustrated by intensive enemy artillery fire which swept the approaches to the river bank, and at daylight the troops withdrew to sheltered positions. At Letanne, our efforts were successful. The 2nd Engineers, assisted by other troops, carried the rafts to the river from the place to which they had been hauled by wagon, and after lashing them end to end the bridges were floated across, the men on the up-stream end leaping ashore and fastening them securely to the farther bank. The inky darkness of the night was accentuated by an extremely dense fog, and in order that troops might find the bridges, it became necessary for the 2nd Engineers to form a chain of men to act as guides, from the Bois de l'Hospice, where the men had assembled, to the crossing point. The 1st and 2nd Battalions of the 5th Marines then crossed in the order named, in the face of a heavy artillery and machine gun fire, and were followed some hours later by the liaison battalion of the 89th Division and the 1st Battalion of the 9th Infantry.

In making a lodgement on the east bank, the 5th Marines drove off the enemy machine gun posts and patrols from the flats and moved forward at early dawn. At 11 o'clock its two battalions had reached positions at La Sacerie Ferme and on the ridges near Senegal Ferme and Moulins, with the 1st Battalion, 9th Infantry, in support, and in liaison with the detachment of the 89th Division at Autreville, that Division having crossed near Pouilly during the night.

The night of this last battle of the war was the most trying night I have ever experienced. The knowledge that in all probability the Armistice was about to be signed caused the mental anguish, which I always felt because of the loss of life in battle, to be greatly accentuated, and I longed for the tidings of the cessation of hostilities to arrive before the engagement was initiated; but it was not to be, and many a brave man made the supreme sacrifice for his country in the last hours of the war. The reasons for continuing intensive military activ-

ity until the very end are set forth in an extract from
General Pershing's report:

"At 9 P. M., on November 9th, appropriate
orders were sent to the First and Second
Armies in accordance with the following telegram from Marshal Foch to the Commander of
each of the Allied armies:
" 'The enemy, disorganized by our repeated
attacks, retreats along the entire front.
" 'It is important to coördinate and expedite
our movements.
" 'I appeal to the energy and the initiative
of the Commanders-in-Chief and of their
Armies to make decisive the results obtained.'
"In consequence of the foregoing instructions, our Second Army pressed the enemy
along its entire front on the night of the 10-11
and the morning of the 11th. The Fifth Corps
in the First Army forced a crossing of the
Meuse east of Beaumont, and gained the commanding heights within the reëntrant of the
river, thus completing our control of the Meuse
River line."

Marshal Foch issued the above mentioned order to
force the enemy to accept the Armistice terms which the
German Commission deemed to be harsh and humiliating. No one desired more than he to conserve human
life, but he felt certain that heroic measures, such as
those he directed, would cost fewer lives by compelling
the immediate submission of the enemy than would have
been the case if the negotiations had dragged along for
days and perhaps weeks. At 6:05 A. M., on the 11th,
an orderly from the Division radio station brought me
the following message which had been picked up at
6:01 o'clock:

"Marshal Foch to the Commanders-in-Chief:

"1. Hostilities will be stopped on the entire front beginning at 11 o'clock, November 11 (French hour).

"2. The Allied troops will not go beyond the line reached at that hour on that date until further orders.

(Signed) "MARSHAL FOCH,
"5:45 A. M."

I at once called up the Chief of Staff of the 5th Corps and, after repeating the message just quoted, I asked if it should be carried out. He replied that it might be a German hoax and would be disregarded, adding that no attention should be paid to any such message unless it came officially from Corps Headquarters.

Upon leaving Division Headquarters, the orderly evidently told the men the contents of the message he had delivered, because I heard a great burst of cheering. The cheers were repeated by more distant groups until they died out in the distance. At 8:45 A. M. Brigadier General Burt, Chief of Staff, called me personally to the telephone and gave me the Armistice message officially, with the added instructions to hold all the ground gained up to 11 A. M., and not to permit any unofficial intercourse with the enemy.

I at once called up Brigadier General Neville and Colonel Rhea and repeated the order to them, and I then personally directed Colonel Feland to expedite the sending of the message to Major Hamilton and Captain Dunbeck, who were in command of the two Marine battalions on the east bank of the Meuse. During the last two hours before the Armistice, the enemy's artillery fire was intensified and our artillery sent as good as it received. A few minutes before eleven o'clock, there were tremendous bursts of fire from the two antagonists and then—suddenly—there was complete silence. It was the most impressive celebration of the Armistice that could possibly have taken place. There was a solemn and an earnest joy in the hearts of every man at the front. We were satisfied with the terms of the Armistice. We were happy because fighting, death and destruction had ceased. I offered up a prayer of thanksgiving, to Almighty God.

CHAPTER XIX

AFTER THE ARMISTICE, AND THE MARCH TO THE RHINE

ABOUT 1 P. M. on November 11th, a telephone call from Corps Headquarters caused quite a stir. The message originated with Marshal Foch, and was to the effect that the German High Command had complained that the American troops on the east bank of the Meuse just south of Mouzon were still continuing their advance towards Moulins, and that they had not ceased firing at 11 A. M. The Marshal directed that all military operations cease immediately. We had no information concerning the matter, and on communicating with Brigade and Regimental Headquarters, it was reported that the Armistice orders had been sent to the front, as soon as given, by several runners, and although no acknowledgment had as yet been received it was assumed that they had reached their destination on time.

Officers from Brigade Headquarters were directed to go at once to the front lines with instructions to see to it that the terms of the Armistice were complied with. The Division Inspector was sent on the same mission. When they reached the advanced units, all was quiet and peaceful there, and was so reported. The incident was speedily forgotten, owing to the press of other matters, until some months later, when Major Hamilton, who was in command of the leading battalion on November 11th, called at Division Headquarters. I questioned him about the report that his men had not stopped advancing at 11 A. M. on November 11th, as ordered. He replied that he did not personally receive the message until about 11:30 A. M., and that it was fully noon before it reached all the advanced elements of the battalion, but that as soon as the message was received he had ceased to advance, had drawn back his men to the positions which they had reached at 11 A. M., and had thought no more about the matter, as there had been no casualties on either side after 11 o'clock. So it happened that although the Marines were not the first to fight in the World War, they were the last to stop fighting.

Major Hamilton was a daring and brilliant battalion commander, and although always in the thick of the fighting, he went through the war without a scratch, only to be killed on the battlefield of Gettysburg in an airplane crash in July, 1922, during the maneuvers of the Marines at that place.

Immediately following the Armistice, I visited the wounded in the Division Field Hospitals. It was heartbreaking to see these brave men who had been maimed and mutilated a few hours before the cessation of hostilities. I talked to each one of them. It was marvelous to witness their fortitude, their cheerfulness, and their fine spirit. I asked a man who had been badly mangled by a shell to tell me how and when he had been wounded. He said he was on duty in the telephone exchange of one of the Artillery regiments, and the message came over the wire, "It is 11 o'clock and the war is ——." At this point, he said, a shell landed and burst in the room, killing his "buddy" and seriously wounding him. So far as I have been able to learn, these were the last casualties of the war. The shell was doubtless fired a second or so before 11 o'clock, and reached its mark a few seconds after the clock had struck the hour which brought peace to more millions of people than had any other hour in the world's history.

On a bunk nearby was a Sergeant of Marines whose leg had been so badly mangled by the fragments of a shell that its amputation was found to be necessary. In response to my inquiry, he told me that he had been injured by a high explosive shell just after he had crossed the bridge over the Meuse during the last battle of the war. I asked him if he had heard before the battle that the Armistice would probably be signed within a few hours. He replied that it was a matter of common knowledge among the men. I then said, "What induced you to cross the bridge in the face of that terrible machine gun and artillery fire when you expected that the war would end in a few hours?" In answer, he said, "Just before we began to cross the bridge our Battalion Commander, Captain Dunbeck, assembled the companies around him in the ravine where we were waiting orders, and told us, 'Men, I am going across that river, and I expect you to go with me.'" The wounded man then remarked, "What could we do but go across too? Surely we couldn't let him go by himself; we love him too much for that."

I have always felt that the incident I have just narrated gives one a better understanding of the meaning and the practice of leadership than do all the books that have been written, and all the speeches that have been made on the subject.

It was hard, at first, to realize fully that the war had actually ended, but on the evening of Armistice Day I witnessed a striking demonstration of the men's appreciation of the restoration of peace. I had been to Beaumont on a visit of inspection and was returning after dark to Division Headquarters. The highway on which I drove passed through an area where a division was in bivouac. Thousands of small fires were burning, and standing close to each fire were three or four men, warming their hands and drying their clothes. They had been drenched to the skin and chilled to the marrow over and over again, and now, for the first time in weeks, they were enjoying the comfort of a cheerful blaze. To add to the brightness of the scene, the automobile's searchlights were turned on, and as we drove past the bivouacs, thousands of men cheered from sheer joy, and many of them shouted remarks about the searchlights, "It looks like Broadway," "The lights remind me of home."

Darkness and the lack of fires were the most pronounced characteristics of the World War. The deadly airplane brought about almost a reversion to the primitive days when fire and artificial light were unknown. In previous wars, even the pickets in outpost groups built bonfires and derived much cheer from their warmth and brightness. In the World War, millions of men were deprived of these—the greatest comforts vouchsafed mankind by a generous and merciful Providence.

Armistice evening was celebrated too in another way. The troops of all armies at the front acclaimed the return of peace by a display of fireworks which marked the lines from Belgium to Switzerland. As far as the eye could see, the sky was brilliantly illuminated with the flash of pyrotechnics. All the rockets, stars, etc., in the hands of the front line troops must have gone up in smoke in that greatest of all the celebrations in history.

On my return to Headquarters that night, I wrote the order of the day, setting forth briefly the achievements of the Second Division during the war. It is quoted in full because of its contemporary interest:

"Order.   "France, November 11, 1918.

"1. An Armistice between the Allied Nations and Germany has been signed and hostilities ceased temporarily at 11 A. M. today.

"2. It is fitting that the great part played by the Second Division in bringing about this momentous victory over a redoubtable foe should be recounted at this time.

"3. At the end of May, the enemy broke through the Allied lines on a wide front west of Rheims and reached the Marne near Château Thierry. The safety of Paris and of the Allied Army itself was at stake. At this critical hour the Second Division was deployed to meet the foe. It stopped his advance; it drove him back, and it demonstrated for all time that the American is second to none in valor, in endurance, and in the grim and unyielding determination to conquer.

"4. Again, on July 18th and 19th, during the last great enemy offensive, the Second Division, after a night march of unparalleled difficulty, struck near Soissons the flank of the enemy's salient, penetrated his lines and brought his offensive to a standstill. This was the beginning of the Allied offensive which has continued unceasingly and untiringly until today.

"5. On September 12th to 15th, the American Army fought its first battle in France under American leadership. To the Second Division was assigned the most difficult and the most important task—the capture of Thiaucourt and the Jaulny-Xammes Ridge. It reached its second day's objective on the first day, drove off the enemy's counter-attacks, and clinched the victory.

"6. In the Champagne district, October 2nd to 10th, it fought beside the Fourth French Army. On October 3rd, it seized Blanc Mont Ridge, the keystone of the arch of the main German position, advanced beyond the ridge and, although both flanks were unsupported, it held all its gains with the utmost tenacity, inflicting tremendous losses on the enemy. This victory freed Rheims and forced the entire German Army between that city and the Argonne Forest to retreat to the Aisne, a distance of thirty kilometers.

"7. During the latter part of October, the division was ordered to join the First American Army for the great attack of November 1st. It was given the post of honor, and led the advance. It drove through the enemy's fortified lines to a depth of over nine kilometers, seized the heights of Barricourt and destroyed the enemy divisions on its front. On November 3rd, it advanced to Fosse, and attacked and captured the heights of Vaux. At night, it pressed forward through the Forest of Belval by a single road and occupied the ridge near Beaumont. On the night of the 4th, it again attacked and advanced its lines to the Meuse. Finally, on the night of the 10th it forced its way across the Meuse and seized a commanding position on the eastern bank.

"8. This superb division of fighting men is unsurpassed in valor, in skill, in endurance, in determination to conquer, and in service to the cause of the Allies.

"9. In this great struggle, many of our comrades have made the supreme sacrifice for our country, but their

heroic spirit dwells in the hearts of the officers and men
of the Second Division.

"JOHN A. LEJEUNE."

I also incorporate here extracts from a letter home
written on November 11th, as perhaps it may give a
clearer insight concerning the then state of mind of at
least one of the Americans engaged in the war than
could any narrative written eleven years after the occurrence of the great events referred to:

"November 11th. This has been the day of days, the
day of miracles, the day of peace on earth and good will
towards men. This morning at 6 o'clock, a wireless message broadcast from Eiffel Tower was picked up at Second Division Headquarters. It announced the cessation
of hostilities on all fronts at the eleventh hour of the
eleventh day of the eleventh month, as the Armistice had
been signed. At 8:40 A. M. a telephone message from
the Fifth Corps was received by me, officially confirming
the previous message.

"I breathed a great sigh of relief and thanked God
most earnestly for the great victory which we had
achieved and for the blessing of peace. It was a horrible
task that had to be done to save the world from destruction, and all gave themselves wholeheartedly to the purest
and most self-sacrificing war in the history of mankind.

"Personally, I can never cease to be grateful for the
opportunity which was given me to give all my strength,
all my mind, all my energy, and my very soul to the
carrying out of the great duty with which I was entrusted. It was a tremendous strain and a great responsibility, but a never-to-be-forgotten experience, an experience which I value more highly than great riches, or
pomp, or power.

"I have done my duty to the best of my ability and
have had no thought of pleasure or comfort or advancement, but only the passionate, intense desire to carry
through to a victorious end.

"Last night we fought our last battle. It was the most trying of all battles. Our poor men had to cross the Meuse River by hastily constructed foot bridges in the face of a fearful artillery and intense machine gun fire. They dashed across and defeated the enemy, but at the cost of many lives. To me it was pitiful for men to go to their death on the evening of peace.

"A more gallant, a more skilled in arms division never existed than mine, but it is now much depleted in numbers by casualties, and by illness. I hope we may soon get out of this horrible area and go to some place away from the war-torn zone."

I also incorporate here copies of orders I issued in regard to the crossing of the Meuse, a copy of General Summerall's letter commending the Second Division, and the letter from Lieutenant-General Hunter Liggett to the Commander-in-Chief, recommending that the Second Division receive a special citation because of its outstanding service in the battle of the Meuse-Argonne:

"France, November 12, 1918.

"Order.

"On the night of November 10th, heroic deeds were done by heroic men. In the face of a heavy artillery and withering machine gun fire, the Second Engineers threw two foot bridges across the Meuse and the First and Second Battalions of the Fifth Marines crossed resolutely and unflinchingly to the east bank and carried out their mission.

"In the last battle of the war, as in all others in which this division has participated, it enforced its will on the enemy.

"John A. Lejeune."

"France, November 13, 1918.

"Order.

"In the crossing of the Meuse on the night of November 10th, Companies 'G' and 'H,' Ninth Infantry, assisted the Second Engineers in throwing the briges across the river. The Eighth and Twenty-third Machine Gun Companies (Marines), accompanied the First and Second Battalions of the Fifth Marines in their crossing; the Third Battalion, Three Hundred Fifty-sixth Infantry (Eighty-ninth Division), and Company 'C' of Three Hundred Forty-second Machine Gun Battalion (Eighty-ninth Division) crossed after the above-mentioned organizations; and, at dawn, the First Battalion of the Ninth Infantry, accompanied by Company 'D' of the Fifth Machine Gun Battalion, moved forward to the east bank in support of the advanced force.

"The names of the officers and men of these organizations belong on the roll of heroic men who did heroic deeds in the last battle of the war.

"JOHN A. LEJEUNE,

"Major General, U. S. M. C.,

"Commanding."

"From: Commanding General, Fifth Army Corps.

To: Commanding General, Second Division.

Subject: Commendation.

"Upon the departure of the Second Division from its brilliant service with the Fifth Army Corps, I desire to express to you my admiration for the division; my gratitude for the great service it has rendered, and my profound regret at its separation from the Fifth Army Corps.

"Especially I desire to commend the division for the crowning feat of its advance in crossing the Meuse River in face of heavy concentrated enemy machine gun fire, and in driving the enemy's troops before it, and in firmly establishing itself upon the heights covering the desired bridgehead. This feat will stand among the most memorable of the campaign.

"My good wishes will accompany you in the new fields of activity of the division, where, I am sure, further glory awaits it.

"C. P. SUMMERALL."

"January 16, 1919.
"Headquarters First Army, A. E. F.,
    "Office of the Chief of Staff.
    From: Commanding General, First Army.
    To: Commander-in-Chief, G. H. Q., A. E. F.
    Subject: Citation for Second Division.
    "1. It is recommended that the Second Division be cited in G. H. Q. orders for its excellent work in the attack of November 1-11, 1918, Meuse-Argonne operations.

    "2. After the St. Mihiel operation the Second Division participated in the attacks of the Fourth French Army during the period October 2-10. The remarkable success achieved by this division in these operations has already been referred to in French communications.

    "3. After a short rest the Second Division was again placed in battle for the purpose of taking part in the First Army attack of November 1.

    "4. In the First Army attack of November 1, the Second Division was selected and so placed in the battle line that its known ability might be used to overcome the critical part of the enemy's defense. The salient feature of the plan of attack was to drive a wedge through Landres-et-St. Georges to the vicinity of Fosse. It was realized that if the foregoing could be accomplished, the backbone of the hostile resistance west of the Meuse would be broken and the enemy would have to retreat to the east of the Meuse. Success in this plan would immediately loosen the flanks of the First Army. The Second Division was selected to carry out this main blow.

    "5. The Second Division accomplished the results desired in every particular on the first day of the attack, not only clearing the hostile defenses of Landres-et-St. Georges and the Bois de Hazois, but continuing its advance to the vicinity of Fosse, i.e., about nine kilometers. This decisive blow broke the enemy's defense and opened the way for the rapid advance of the Army.

    "6. Attached hereto is a copy of a letter furnished the Second Division by the Commanding General, Fifth Corps, which is self-explanatory.

"7. In view of the excellent results achieved by this division and the decisiveness of the attack on November 1, it is recommended that the division be mentioned in orders by the Commander-in-Chief.

"H. LIGGETT,
"Lieutenant-General, U. S. A."

It was necessary after the Armistice to turn our thoughts towards the future and to bend our energies towards preparing the troops for their march to the Rhine. The personnel of the Division was exhausted and sick at the close of hostilities. Thousands of men were afflicted with intestinal trouble which our doctors reported was due to exhaustion, lack of hot food, to the cold rainy weather, to lack of shelter, and to their wearing wet clothing night and day for weeks. In addition, the men needed shoes, clothing, and equipment. Our animals too had suffered greatly. The Artillery had had no rest since the latter part of September, many of the horses had died of exhaustion, and because of short forage. A virulent form of mange, too, was prevalent among the animals of the First Army and caused many casualties. Our attention was therefore directed to building up the strength of the men, to obtaining replacements, and to re-equipping and re-clothing the troops.

Our area was a considerable distance from the railroad and the railway was taxed almost beyond its capacity to meet the needs of the vast aggregation of troops which was dependent on it for supplies; and then too, even after the truck trains reached the vicinity of Beaumont, it was necessary to distribute over the villainous roads the huge quantities of supplies to each of the units of the Division. To accomplish all these tasks before November 17th, the date fixed for beginning the march, seemed an impossibility, but fortunately we had a wonderful man in the position of Assistant Chief of Staff G-1. I refer to Colonel Hugh Matthews. Able, conscientious and untiring he was and he succeeded in overcoming the obstacles and in accomplishing the task.

Failure to do so, however, through no fault of his own, was imminent. One evening—I think it was November 13th—I overheard the officer on watch at Headquarters talking over the telephone in the next room. I gathered from his replies that instructions for an immediate march were being given him. I went into the office and asked him what it was all about. He said, "The Corps is giving orders for the Division to march tomorrow morning." I took the receiver from him and said, "This is General Lejeune speaking; what are the orders for the Second Division?" The reply came, "The Second Division is to march south tomorrow morning to Dun-sur-Meuse, and on the following day it will cross the river there and march north to Stenay, preliminary to jumping off from that place on November 17th." I said, "Who is it speaking?" The voice replied, "Clark of Emerson."

It was Lieutenant-Colonel Clark, representing the Third Corps, the code word for that Corps being "Emerson." He explained that Marshal Foch had directed that the troops jump off from Stenay, which made it necessary for the Second Division to march to Dun-sur-Meuse (a distance of nearly forty kilometers) in order to cross the Meuse and then back to Stenay (about twenty kilometers), as all the bridges north of Dun-sur-Meuse were down.

I told him that we had already rebuilt the bridge at Pouilly and could cross there. He explained that the instructions forbade passing through the German lines, which would be necessary in order to reach Stenay if we crossed at Pouilly. I suggested that the bridge at Stenay be repaired, and offered to do the work ourselves if the material were furnished. I then told him my persistence was due to the exhausted and weakened condition of the troops and to the necessity of reëquipping and reclothing them, which could not be done while they were on the march. He answered that he was without authority to make any change in the orders, but was simply repeating them to me as they were given to him by higher authority.

I then asked that the matter be taken up with the appropriate officer with the view of obtaining a modification of the orders. He said that all the higher officers were asleep and he did not care to wake them. I replied, "It is better to wake up one General than to have twenty-five thousand sick and exhausted men march sixty kilometers, and I will do so myself." He then said he would deliver my message.

In a few minutes he called back, saying that he was directed to inform me that the bridge at Stenay would be repaired, that the march to Dun-sur-Meuse would not take place, and that the march to Stenay could be made on the afternoon of November 16th.

I have given the details of this conversation not with any intent to criticize a loyal and faithful officer, but in order to illustrate the importance of sometimes being rather determined and persistent when necessary to protect the welfare of the officers and men under one's command.

The Second Division passed from the Fifth to the Third Corps on the ensuing day. I regretted leaving the Fifth Corps, as eleven days of battle association with it had made our relationship a very close one, and I knew that we were in the house of our friends. On the other hand, the Second Division had never served with the Third Corps, with its Commanding General or any of the members of its staff. I, personally, had never been associated with any of them except Colonel Chaffee, a splendid officer whom I had known as a subaltern in 1910. I therefore feared that we were to be strangers in a strange land.

However, my old friend, Brigadier General Malin Craig, was detailed as the Chief of Staff of the Third Army, the force organized as the Army of Occupation. The Third Army was composed of two corps, the Third and Fourth, each consisting of three divisions of approximately 25,000 men each—a total of 150,000 men, in addition to Army and Corps troops and detachments. During the march to the Rhine, the Fourth Corps, with the First Division in the first line and two divisions in support, was on the right, and the Third Corps, with the 32nd and 2nd Divisions in the first line and the 42nd in support, was on the left.

The Allied Armies were directed to begin their advance towards Germany at 5:30 A. M., November 17th, the Third Army moving through the Grand Duchy of Luxembourg. The Second Division's orders involved an advance in two columns, the right, consisting of the 3rd Brigade, the 15th Field Artillery and attached units, marching via Stenay, Montmedy, Virton and Arlon, and thence into Luxembourg to the Sauer River (the boundary between Germany and Luxembourg), via Mersch and LaRochette; and the left column, consisting of the 4th Brigade, 12th Field Artillery and attached units, via Pouilly, Moery, Etalle, Arlon, and thence into Luxembourg to the Sauer River via Berg and Medernach. The Division reserve, consisting of the 17th Field Artillery, the 2nd Engineers, and attached units, followed the right column.

The march was conducted as though a state of war existed, with flank and advance guards while marching, and with outposts established whenever halted for the night. A schedule prepared by the Allied Commander-in-Chief was strictly adhered to. It prescribed that the march to the Sauer River should be conducted in two bounds with an intervening halt, also a halt of several days' duration was prescribed before crossing that river and entering Germany. The schedule was so arranged as to provide that the Allied armies should follow the retreating German troops closely, but without gaining actual contact with them.

The Second Division, preliminary to the jump-off, sent one regiment to Stenay on November 16th in order to carry out the instructions relating to the advance from that place at "H" hour. The left column advanced via Pouilly, while the remaining units marched from their billets in time to join the right column as directed, the infantry and light artillery moving via the road on the east bank of the Meuse, and the reserve via the road on the west bank. All elements were required to be east of the Pouilly-Stenay road not later than 10 P. M. on November 17th.

Second Division Headquarters moved from Fosse to Stenay on "D" day. I spent the day on the road, taking a look at the troops. They were beginning an arduous and trying march. Each infantryman carried his field kit and clothing roll, and in addition a belt and two bandoliers of ammunition, rifle or Browning automatic, steel helmet, gas mask, overcoat, etc., a total of seventy-five or eighty pounds. The men were still below par physically, and many suffered from sore and blistered feet caused by the English shoes which had been issued them after the Armistice. Our horses and mules were in bad shape also, especially those which had been furnished as replacements by other divisions.

As was the case in all the combat divisions, the appearance of the men, animals, wagons, trucks, caissons and guns was, naturally, not up to the peacetime standard, owing not only to the conditions under which the troops had lived for a long period of time, but also to the fact that stress previously had been laid on battle efficiency, rather than on dress parade and the details of garrison duties.

I did all in my power, by appealing to the Division *esprit,* to win this competition in which personal appearance, military bearing, march discipline and conditions of animals and transportation were now the standards. It was a struggle which required patience and work, but it is with great pride that I say today in all truthfulness that the Second Division finally excelled in peace even as it had excelled in war.

The days were all too short for the marches, which were hard and long, especially those of the Second Division, as we constituted the marching flank in the great wheel which the Third Army executed during its advance to the Rhine. I shall never forget those days of gloom. Even when the sky was cloudless the sun was hidden by the haze and mist until the afternoon, but most often it rained—a slow, misty, but chilling rain it was. Sometimes it snowed gently; sometimes the ground was frozen; but always the mud covered the roadbeds.

It was extraordinarily difficult to supply the troops. The railways had to be extended across No Man's Land and the trench systems, and thence the trains were handled by German railway officials. Delays were frequent, and often the troops were on the verge of having a serious shortage of rations. The supply problem was especially difficult for the Second Division owing to its flank position, which placed it always at the maximum distance from the railhead. Yet again we were successful in overcoming all difficulties without any untoward happenings other than anxiety and worry.

During the march not only the Artillery and Engineers, but all of us greatly missed Brigadier General Bowley and Colonel Mitchell, who had been transferred to higher, but in my judgment not more desirable duty; as I believed then, and I believe now, that duty with a combat division is to be preferred to an assignment with any Corps or Army Headquarters. Certainly it was my belief that to command the Second Division was preferable to any other assignment.

Jim Rhea was also detached, as the Armistice prevented his receiving his Brigadier's stars. A most lovable man and fine leader of troops he was. His friends were much gratified because his last few days on earth were made happy by his promotion to the rank of Brigadier, which came to him less than a month before he died.

The Second Division moved into southeastern Belgium on November 18th, and Division Headquarters was located at Virton until the 20th, when the march was resumed. Our progress through Belgium was a continuous ovation. It seemed as if the entire population of the section of that heroic nation through whose territory we marched, turned out *en masse* to greet their deliverers, as the people acclaimed the Americans. The towns were lavishly decorated, as were many parts of the roads on which the troops marched.

The evening of the 19th, an unusual celebration took place in Virton. The arrangements were made by our energetic senior Chaplain, Dr. Jason Noble Pierce. Promptly at eight o'clock in the evening, the Mayor of Virton called on me at Division Headquarters. We drove thence through a cheering multitude to the City Hall, where we took seats on the portico facing the thousands of Belgian civilians and American soldiers who packed the square. The band then played the Belgian national hymn and "The Star-Spangled Banner," while the great throng stood respectfully at attention and preserved perfect silence. Upon the conclusion of the national anthems, the crowd made the welkin ring with cheers and shouts of *"Vive les Americans!"* and *"Vive les Belges!"*

The Chaplain then introduced the Mayor, who delivered a most eloquent address in French, following which I spoke to the crowd in English. Each of us received an ovation, and the band played the familiar war songs in which the great crowd joined. It was a thrilling experience.

As soon as quiet could be gained, the Chaplain announced in stentorian tones that Mademoiselle Clementine, the famous French danseuse, who was travelling with General Lejeune, would entertain the crowd with her dances. To my horror, the dancer appeared, arrayed in ballet costume, with cheeks well rouged and with head covered with long golden curls. The band played the appointed music, and the dancer did most gracefully the latest steps. The crowd roared its approval and encored the performer over and over again, while I sat there horror-stricken, with cold perspiration running down my back and with thoughts running through my head that my reputation was torn to shreds, that the action of the Chaplain was unpardonable, and that he had certainly secured the services of a most skillful dancer. Finally, to my unspeakable relief, the dancer as a last encore bowed, took off the very pretentious wig, and I recognized the close-cropped black head and smiling countenance of my very masculine soldier cook, who excelled not only in the terpsichorean but the culinary art as well. It was an episode characteristic of our Chaplain, who never failed to grasp every opportunity to bring cheer to the men.

The ensuing day, we were again on the road to Germany. Arlon, a fine Belgian city, was our stopping place for the night. The officers and men were most hospitably received, and my orderly told me afterwards that practically all of the thousands of men billeted in Arlon were entertained at dinner by the people in their houses and provided with comfortable beds for the first time since they had left home.

We were playing at one-night stands, however, and the next day we were off again, this time to the Grand Duchy of Luxembourg. We found it to be a lovely agricultural country, but not nearly so densely populated as Belgium. The people were courteous and friendly, but there was not, of course, the same enthusiasm and boisterous welcome displayed as in Belgium. The inhabitants were neutrals, and looked on us in pretty much the same way as they had regarded the Germans, that is to say, our presence was a necessary or unavoidable evil which was lessened only by the amount of money we spent. They were good bargainers. Long practice as harborers of foreign soldiery had made them so.

My headquarters was located for the night at the little town of Brouch. My room was in the tiny home of the parish priest. He gave me the only heated room, in which were his beautiful potted plants and flowers. He told me there was an old man in the town who had emigrated to America, but had come home many years before. I expressed a desire to see him, so in a little while he hobbled in. He was old and rheumatic, and had forgotten every word of English that he ever knew. His only language was the local German patois. The priest, in common with all the educated people, spoke both French and German. He, therefore, acted as interpreter. The old man said he had served in the Union Army during the Civil

War, and had returned to his native land soon after his discharge. He had expected to see our troops dressed in the blue uniforms that were worn under Grant and Sherman, and was greatly disappointed when they appeared in olive drab. He couldn't seem to understand the explanation of the change given him by the priest. At any rate, he was unhappy about it, as he had been looking forward to seeing himself of the olden time once again in the persons of the American soldiers.

Our march through Luxembourg to the Sauer River was uneventful. The Second Division reached that river on November 23rd and took up a position on its western bank, with strong outposts guarding each bridge on the Division front. When we arrived at the river, our former enemies were in view on the east bank, and stringent instructions were issued forbidding traffic or travel between the area occupied by our army and Germany.

Our troops remained in place from the 23rd to the 30th, inclusive, and advantage was taken of the delay to put the transportation and equipment in apple pie order, and to train the troops in close order drill so as to make a fine impression when Germany was invaded.

Luxembourg is most interesting, as I tried to tell in my letters home:

> "This country is romantically beautiful with its lovely villages, swift running streams, old castles, many forests, and wonderful scenery. Division Headquarters is established in a pretty little town called La Rochette, which is named for the nearby rock hill on which stands the ruin of a castle built in the eleventh century. I am quartered in the Mayor's house, and we have our mess in his dining room, he and his wife being our guests.
>
> "I rode over today to the city of Luxembourg, the capital of the Grand Duchy. It is attractive and romantic looking. The old town is located at the bottom of a river valley, and the

new town on the tops of the surrounging high hills.

"In the afternoon, Captain Nelson and I climbed the hill of La Rochette and went through the ruins of the old castle. It is most interesting. It was built in the eleventh century and was considered to be impregnable until it was destroyed by Louis XIV's cannon when the French conquered Luxembourg. It has never been rebuilt. There are many ruined castles in this country, which were the homes and fortresses of the old Barons in the days of the feudal system."

"November 28th. This is Thanksgiving, and a bleak, rainy, disagreeable day it has been. This morning, however, it stopped raining for a while and we were able to hold the open air services in the square. We had a band which played patriotic airs, and the men sang some hymns and Chaplain Pierce read a psalm. I made a short talk to the men, then there was a prayer by the Chaplain, 'America' was sung, and the meeting was over.

"I am enclosing a copy of my little address which I wrote down later from memory. Similar services were held in every town where Second Division troops were billeted."

My address follows:

"This is the day set apart by our fore-fathers as Thanksgiving Day. Each year the President issues a Thanksgiving proclamation, setting forth the reasons we have had during the preceding twelve months for being thankful, and calling on all our people to assemble in their places of worship and give thanks to God for the bless-

ings which they have received. The President's proclamation is always read at these
services.

"This year, owing to our rapid advance
towards Germany, the proclamation has not
yet reached us, and we are deprived of the
privilege of hearing it read. Our Chaplain,
therefore, has asked me to act as a substitute and to say a few words to you about
this Thanksgiving Day.

"I feel that it is needless for me to tell
you why our Division, our Army, and our
people at home should be thankful today.
All of you know the story of the mighty
miracle that has been wrought. All of you
know the story of how our country has,
as if by magic, been organized for war; of
how our army has been trained, supplied
and transported overseas without loss; and
when, at the end of the month of May,
Germany was at the height of its power
and its path to conquest seemed clear, all of
you know the story of how this splendid
Division of fighting men, with their hearts
inspired with patriotism, filled with burning
zeal, and steeled with divine courage, was
deployed on his front, checked his advance,
and then defeated the enemy. All of you
know the story of how, since those days,
he has met defeat after defeat, and of how,
only a few days ago, he was finally forced
humbly to beg for peace.

"Truly it was the handiwork of God.

"It is, therefore, very fitting that we
should gather together today and give
thanks to the Lord God of Hosts for having given our nation and our cause this
speedy and this decisive victory, and for
having selected us to be among the instru-

ments chosen by Him to carry out His will."

On December 1st the first line divisions of the Third Army invaded Germany simultaneously, the leading elements of the advance guards crossing the frontier at 7:30 A. M. It was an event of great historic importance and one to be always remembered by those participating in it. It was a quiet and peaceful invasion, however. There were no visible signs of hostility. The inhabitants showed no symptoms of unfriendliness, but looked at us curiously as if anxious to discern what manner of men American soldiers were.

It was not a prepossessing looking country, but rocky and rugged and sterile. The towns were shabby, the roads out of repair, and the people were not well dressed. As we advanced deeper into Germany, however, conditions changed for the better, and in the valleys of the Ahr and the Rhine there were many evidences of former prosperity and wealth.

The appearance of the German people in the towns and cities indicated that they were underfed, but in the country districts it was apparent that they were better supplied with food. Everywhere, though, there was complaint that the beer was not fit to drink, as it was a chemical compound and not a brew, no grain being available for use for brewing purposes. There was a shortage of many necessary articles, such as fats of any description, soap, etc., but there seemed to be more discontent among the people on account of the bad beer than anything else. Perhaps it was responsible for the breakdown of the German morale.

Everywhere there was uncertainty. The Communists were trying to gain control of the country. Russian bolshevists were active in Berlin and elsewhere, so we heard, and local soviets had been organized in some of the towns we marched through. I declined, however, to recognize in any way or have any dealings with these soviets, but controlled the population through the Burgomasters and other regular officials. This action was in accord with the policy enunciated by G.H.Q. Our advancing army, therefore, exercised a stabilizing influence throughout Germany, and I believe had much to do with preventing a revolution.

Many Germans, especially the owners of property, were secretly glad to see the American soldiers enter their country. Certainly no defeated people has ever been treated more justly or more considerately by an invading army than were the Germans by the Americans. Implicit obedience to our edicts and our regulations was exacted, but there were no abuse, no tyranny, and no unlawful taking of property. In fact, the most meticulous care was exercised to prevent looting. For instance, in every house occupied by Second Division Headquarters a careful inventory of every article in the house was made by an officer and the owner of the house, and after our departure a similar inventory was again made. The only missing article was a small piece of bric-a-brac, for which the owner was glad to accept a dollar in payment. It was probably worth about a quarter.

Altogether it was a drab, unexciting march, and the men's minds were concentrated more on the large number of kilometers they had to cover during those very short days than on historic or international questions. Sore-footed as many of them were, their general health had nevertheless improved greatly each day after they had left behind the war-destroyed area, and when we reached the Rhine a more hardy, vigorous, ruddy-cheeked aggregation of young Americans I have never seen. They were thoroughly tired, though, by reason of the long marches over steep and slippery roads, and were overjoyed when finally the head of the column reached the Rhine, and a halt of several days was made preliminary to crossing to the east bank of that famous river.

The last stages of the march were made in a single column down the Ahr valley. A picturesque and beautiful valley it is—dwarf mountains, with corkscrew roads leading to ruined castles perched on their peaks; miniature river gorges and palisades; health resorts exploiting springs of every description; hot springs, cold springs, warm springs, Apollinaris springs everywhere—bath houses, too, were plentiful, and full advantage of this luxury was taken by officers and men.

Second Division Headquarters was established at Ahrweiler in what had been a fashionable sanitorium, and during our stay there all the men in the Division had the most comfortable billets which had fallen to their lot since they had left "God's country," as they invariably called the United States.

We arrived at Ahrweiler on December 8th and remained in place until December 13th, the date which marked the crossing of the Rhine, and which somehow stands out more vividly in my memory than any other date connected with the long, epoch-making journey.

XX

SEVEN MONTHS ON THE RHINE

IN the early morning of December 13, 1918, the Allied Armies crossed the Rhine and occupied three bridgeheads on the east bank. British troops garrisoned the bridgehead at Cologne (Koln), the Americans and French the bridgehead at Coblenz, and the French the bridgehead at Mayence (Mainz). The boundary of each bridgehead was a semi-circle drawn from each of the above named cities as a center, with a radius of thirty kilometers.

The American troops occupied the north three-fifths of the Coblenz bridgehead, and the French the remainder. The First, Thirty-second and Second American Divisions, which had led the advance of the Third Army during its march from the Meuse to the Rhine, constituted the garrison of the American bridgehead sector. cach of these divisions crossed the Rhine by the bridges and ferries on its front. Roughly speaking, the First Division crossed at Coblenz, the Thirty-second at Engars, and the Second at Remagen. They took station from right to left in the order named.

Eventually the Second Division occupied the towns along the Rhine from Ehrenbreitstein Castle (opposite Coblenz) to the north boundary of the sector and the valley of the Wied, together with the intervening range of high wooded hills and ridges.

The Headquarters of the Third Army, Third Corps and Second Division were located at Coblenz, Nieuwied, and Heddesdorf (a suburb of Nieuwied), respectively. The three divisions on the east bank were assigned to the Third Corps, while the Fourth,

Third and Forty-second Divisions were assigned to the Fourth Corps, and held the west bank of the Rhine in support of the bridgehead garrison. Three additional divisions took up reserve positions in the Grand Duchy of Luxembourg and along the Moselle in the vicinity of Treves (Trier), the location of the Advance Headquarters of G.H.Q.

The crossing of the Rhine by American troops was a thrilling event to all who took part in it. Our minds reverted to the days nearly two thousand years before, when Julius Cæsar built bridges and marched his conquering army across the river which was the then western boundary of the territory occupied by the Teutonic tribes, and to the many other occasions during the intervening years when armies passed from one bank to the other, some marching east and some marching west, but all seeking either conquest or safety.

Finally a strange flag proudly fluttered to the breeze on the heights and the battlements of the Rhine. It was a beautiful flag, a flag emblematic of freedom and liberty, a flag beloved of more than one hundred million people, a flag brought to the Old World from the New by the most splendid army that had ever marched and fought under any flag, anywhere, at any time! Such were our convictions. It was a proud day for America, not only because of the glorious victory that had been achieved, of which the crossing of the Rhine was the symbol, but also because in none of our hearts was there a vestige of the lust of conquest. None of us coveted one foot of European or any other foreign soil. All of us desired only to do our full share of the task which we had undertaken, and then to return home empty-handed.

That day, and other days, I saw no enmity in the faces of the people. As the long columns of troops marched by, the children waved and shouted with glee, the women smiled, and the men seemed curious or indifferent, but not unfriendly. It was always thus in the towns, but in driving on the country roads I observed that the men doffed their hats and the women curtsied as I passed.

The troops marched at once to their positions after reaching the east bank of the river. The Fifth Marines occupied the valley of the Wied, and the Sixth Marines took station along the Rhine. The 12th Field Artillery was located in support of the Fourth Brigade. The Third Brigade and the remaining units took up positions in reserve. Guards were at once established on the roads at the boundary line, defensive positions located and marked, and a plan of defense prepared and issued to subordinate commanders. Vigilance was prescribed. We were on a semi-war footing until the treaty of peace was signed and ratified by Germany.

It was about noon when Colonel Myers, my two aides and I arrived in Heddesdorf. The billeting officer took us to the large country house in the outskirts of Heddesdorf in which we were to be quartered. As I drove up to the semi-circular steps leading to the front door I saw an old lady of distinguished appearance standing on the landing at the head of the steps. She greeted me with great dignity and with fine courtesy, holding out her hand and saying, as I shook her hand, "You are welcome to my home, General. If you will come in, I shall show you your rooms." She took me into the dining-room and said, "This is your dining-room. The kitchen, too, has been placed at your disposal." Then we went up to the second floor. She showed me the drawing-room and the adjoining sitting-room and then the large library at the end of the hall. She said, "Either of these rooms is yours, but I think you would prefer the library on account of the fine collection of books in English, French, Spanish and German." I told her that I would take the library. We then went up to the third story and, after inspecting three bedrooms, she said, "These rooms are for yourself, your Chief of Staff, and your aides. I think this one (pointing out a very attractive room) is preferable to the others. It is our guest room for my granddaughter's friends, and I feel that perhaps the furniture, the hangings, the ornaments, and the woman's touch would remind you of home. May I ask if you are married?" I replied that I was and that we had three daughters, one of whom was married and the mother of our grandson. She seemed interested and pleased, and then, stepping across the hall, she said, "This is your bathroom." She then wished me good-morning after saying that she hoped I would not hesitate to ask for anything I might need.

Frau Von Ruckel was a very stately but a very kind *grande dame*. A member of a prominent German family, she was an aristocrat to her finger tips and thoroughly loyal to the old regime and to the Kaiser, except that she could not forgive him for having given up his throne and for having fled to Holland. A King, she felt, ought to be willing to die for his country and his dynasty.

Her house was a charming place in which to live. Immaculately clean, and perfectly heated it was. Her corps of servants were well drilled and would have been the envy of any American housewife. There was discipline in that house. Her large garden at the back of the house was beautiful when the Spring came and, like all the gardens of the rich or the aristocratic, was enclosed by a high stone wall so the members of the family and their guests might enjoy it undisturbed by the gaze of the passersby.

Her only daughter had married a gentleman of Spanish lineage, and one of Frau Von Ruckel's granddaughters spent a part of the time with her. I was greatly attracted by a photograph in the library of a gallant lad in the uniform of the Death's-

Head Hussars. One day I asked the granddaughter who it was. She answered that it was her only brother, and Frau Von Ruckel's only grandson, and that he had been killed in Belgium early in August, 1914. She said her grandmother could not speak of him without breaking down, and asked me not to mention him to her.

Nearly two weeks elapsed without any further conversation with Frau Von Ruckel. On Christmas eve, however, my two aides came into my room and delivered an invitation from her to myself and aides to go down to the drawing-room to see the Christmas tree. We were received by our hostess, who showed us the beautiful tree. It was for all the world like the ones we have at home, and looked very gay and Christmaslike. Frau Von Ruckel explained that she had never failed to have a Christmas tree, even during the war and even though Christmas had become a sad and depressing time to her. She handed around cakes and glasses of wine, and rising, she said, "I have two toasts to propose—first, let us drink to a just peace." We joined her in drinking the toast, and then, after refilling the glasses, she said, "Let us drink to your dear ones at home." We were deeply touched by the sentiment, but I managed to reply, "May we not include your dear ones in this toast?" She bowed her appreciation and we drained our glasses. After a few minutes' conversation about the similarity of the Christmas customs of Germany and the United States, we rose, bade her good-night, and went to our rooms.

About two months afterward Myers, my aides and I moved into more commodious quarters in the Landrath's official residence in Nieuwied, where we had at our disposal the large dining-room and kitchen downstairs and the entire second floor, including a reception room and the spacious ballroom. The move was made so that we might be better able to entertain the many guests who visited us, and also in order that the young men could have a ballroom available for their weekly dances and for the theatrical entertainments by our soldier troupes which became the vogue later on.

I did not again see Frau Von Ruckel until Myers and I called to say good-bye a day or two before our departure for home in July, 1919. We found her in her beautiful garden. She was most cordial and expressed deep regret because of our leaving and because of the probability of never seeing us again. She said, "I have learned to like the Americans as individuals, and I hope you will come again to Germany." I replied that I wanted to return to Europe with my wife in a few years so that we might visit together the places I had lived in, and that we would be certain to call on her. She said, "General, I hope you will drive up to my home just as you did that day in December last, ring the bell and say to the servant that General and Mrs. Lejeune have come to be billeted, as it would be a great pleasure for me to have you and Mrs. Lejeune as my guests." I promised that I would do so, but have as yet been unable to revisit the places where I spent those memorable days of 1918 and 1919. Frau Von Ruckel was deeply affected as we bade her good-bye, and assured us that she would always carry us in her memory.

She was the only German with whom I had any but the most formal official dealings during the whole of my stay in Germany. It was no doubt both advisable and desirable that we should not mingle with the people who were subject to our rule, as military government should be not only strict but impartial. Its strength lies in these attributes. We interfered but little in the daily life of the people or in their relations with one another, but where their interests and ours were involved we assumed and exercised control. The Army's

General Lejeune.

edicts were the supreme laws, and as such took precedence over their own laws. The security, the comfort, the welfare and the supremacy of the Army of Occupation were always the first considerations. For instance, every soldier was supplied with a bed before any unmarried German male adult was allowed that luxury. The drinking places were under our control and they were regulated by military order. Severe penalties were inflicted on any civilian selling hard liquor to soldiers, only light wines and beer being permitted to be sold to them. Curfew hours for all the inhabitants were prescribed. Buildings needed for the army, including theaters and other places of amusement, were commandeered. Strict sanitary measures were instituted and persons suffering from contagious or infectious diseases were quarantined or interned. Military police patrolled the streets and roads and exercised control over the military personnel and over civilians too when necessary to prevent disorder, or when found violating the orders of the Army of Occupation. Provost courts were established which took cognizance of breaches of military instructions, or of controversies with officers or men.

On the other hand, no abuse or mistreatment of the inhabitants by the troops was permitted. In consequence of this system we lived side by side with the civil population during the long period before the signing of the peace treaty without any serious disturbances or disorders, and, I believe, left behind us when we departed for home a reputation for justice, honor and fairness that has never been excelled by any army of occupation in the history of the world.

Tremendous efforts were made to build up and to maintain the military efficiency, the discipline, the physical well being, and the morale of the troops. Never have I read of any such campaign being made to prevent the physical, mental and moral deterioration of an army. History, on the other hand, contains many references to the disintegration of conquering armies during the intervals which almost invariably elapse while the statesmen and diplomats quarrel over the details of peace treaties. One of the most recent cases of this kind was the lamentable condition of the victorious Russian army in 1878 after months spent in camp near Constantinople, while the diplomats of the great powers maneuvered to gain advantage over each other in the peace treaty which is known in history as the Treaty of Berlin. Captain Greene's account of the Russo-Turkish War contains a vivid recital of the gradual destruction of that splendid Russian army.

The measures adopted by General Pershing to preserve and protect the American army were the most enlightened and the most effective of any of which I have knowledge. These measures not only involved the active efforts of all his subordinates, but the active co-operation of the great welfare societies as well. While military training continued to be stressed and maintained, perhaps to a too great extent, it was supplemented by a very effective system of physical training and competitive athletics, the creation on an extensive scale of theatrical troupes among the Army personnel, the importation of actors and actresses of well-recognized ability, and the choosing or erection of amusement halls in every town occupied by American soldiers.

Every night, in every town, entertainments of some description were staged. Recreation centers were established. Horse shows, requiring weeks of preparation, were held. Football and baseball leagues were organized, and the rivalry and excitement caused by the games were intense, thousands of men being transported by motor trucks to witness the games. To accommodate them great stands were constructed in every division area. Teams of boxers, too, travelled from place to place, and the manly art taught to thousands of men.

The education of the men was also well cared for. Army and Division Educational Centers were established and the very best teaching talent was employed, while thousands of officers and men were sent to French and English institutions of learning.

The spiritual needs of the men were ministered to on a vast scale. Literally hundreds of religious services were held weekly, and the best obtainable speakers were engaged in the great campaign to elevate the men morally and spiritually. General Pershing took an active, personal interest in the progress of the great program of physical, military, mental and moral training which he had instituted, and made rigorous inspections of all the American divisions and other units.

It was an inspiration to be associated with this great enterprise and to observe its remarkable progress. The Second Division, in fact, threw itself wholeheartedly into all the competitions and achieved unusual success. It won the championship of the Third Corps in football, defeating the teams of the First and Thirty-second Divisions, but finally lost to the Fourth Division owing to the fact that its two star halfbacks were disabled by injuries. It took second place among the baseball teams of the Third Army. It won firt prize in the horse shows of the Third Corps and Third Army.

In rifle shooting it was pre-eminent, its experts winning the majority of prizes in the Third Army rifle matches, and a member of the Fifth Marines winning the championship in the A.E.F.

At Rengsdorf, its college town, were assembled 2,500 students, and thousands more took advantage of the educational opportunities offered by the unit schools.

Its battalions became almost perfect in the execution of military problems and demonstrations, and after witnessing one of these demonstrations, Major General Brewster, Inspector General of the A.E.F., wrote me that it was the best conceived and best executed of all the many demonstrations he had seen in any army while in Europe.

My heart swelled with pride whenever I moved about among the men, which I did each day, sometimes in making informal inspections, sometimes in presenting decorations, when I always made an address, and at other times in attending horse shows, entertainments, religious services, boxing matches, and baseball or football games. As the Division Commander, I became somehow a symbol of the Division *esprit* in the eyes of the men, and they gave spontaneously great cheers for the "Old Indian," or the "Big Chief," as they called me, when I arrived at the games. It is not surprising, under these circumstances, that I never missed a contest.

I felt myself to be the patriarch of the clan, and every officer and man had his own place in my heart. It was for me a marvelous and never-to-be-forgotten companionship; and of priceless value to me now that I am growing old is the knowledge that I still retain the affection and the good will of the many thousand officers and men who served with the Second Division during the period it was under my command. I wish it were possible to enter the names of every one of them in this book.

I had many interesting experiences too, and I was associated from time to time with many prominent men, both military and civil. The visit of Marshal Petain I especially remember. The 17th Field Artillery (155's), commanded by Colonel McCabe, was quartered at Ehrenbreitstein Castle, over which flew the largest American flag that could be found in France. The Colonel not only made the Castle a showplace, but managed to establish there the best Division Motor Transport School in the Army of Occupation. It was so good, in fact, that it was made the Third Corps School also, and then the Third Army School. All distinguished visitors to Third Army Headquarters were sent to Ehren-breitstein. Colonel McCabe always notified me so that I could meet them there if it were practicable for me to do so.

When Marshal Petain arrived at Coblenz in his private train, he of course reviewed the regiment and inspected Ehrenbreitstein. I walked around with him and listened to Colonel McCabe's inimitable monologue which the Marshal's aide translated into French for his benefit. Finally, after an hour or so, the Marshal smilingly said to the aide, "What is Colonel McCabe trying to do—sell me this place?" We laughed at the humor of the remark, but it didn't halt the Colonel. As a special mark of his high opinion of Colonel McCabe, Marshal Petain sent a Croix de Guerre which he requested me to award to him for his services during the war.

I drove with the Marshal to call at Third Corps and Second Division Headquarters, and then, upon his insistent invitation, I dined with him in his private car. After dinner, he presented me with a splendid photograph of himself on which he wrote "Au General Lejeune, Commandant l'une des plus belles Divisions de l'Armee des Etats Unis. Mes tres affectueux compliments. Marechal Petain."

Marshal Foch, too, visited the Army of Occupation and presided over one of the most remarkable ceremonies I ever witnessed.

It seems that General Hoche, a military and administrative genius produced by the French Revolution, who at the age of seventeen was a stable boy at Versailles and at twenty-six was the Commander of the French Army of the "Sambre et Meuse," who led that army victoriously to the Rhine and across the Rhine where he decisively defeated the Allied armies, had, after a two years' successful administration as Military Governor of the Rhineland provinces, died and was buried at Coblenz. After his death, the German forces temporarily regained control of

Coblenz and the provinces, but were subsequently driven out by Marshal Kleber, who erected a granite shaft on the hill where Hoche stood to observe the passage of the Rhine by his army.

After our occupation of Coblenz in December, 1918, the French found Hoche's grave, and Marshal Foch decided to exhume his body and rebury it under the memorial shaft. French and American troops took part in the ceremonies, as did Marshal Foch, General Pershing, General Mangin, and many other French and American generals, including myself. The ceremonies at the cemetery were very simple, the Mayor and City Fathers of Versailles officiating, and the Mayor making an address.

The casket was then placed on a caisson which, with an escort of cavalry, moved slowly between double lines of French and American soldiers for several miles to a point about half a mile from the monument, where the officers who had followed the caisson in their automobiles formed in column of twos and marched behind the casket which was borne by French soldiers to the monument. A large platform had been erected there, on which the officers were seated. In front of the platform was a French military band of over one hundred pieces and two infantry battalions—French and American.

General Mangin then delivered a striking historical address, in which he described the services rendered the French Republic by General Hoche, and in which he eulogized his ability and his character. Upon the completion of the address, Marshal Foch stepped to the front, drew his sword, and gave the words of command, "Battalions attention!" He then read the citation awarding the Grand Cross of the Legion of Honor to General Mangin, commanded "Present arms!" decorated him, gave him the "accolade" with his sword, kissed him on each cheek, and embraced him. He then faced about, brought the troops to "an order," and all stood at attention while the band played the march of the "Sambre et Meuse," the most stirring of all martial music. Upon its completion, the casket containing the ashes of General Hoche was placed in the vault, the band played the Marseillaise and the Star-Spangled Banner, the troops marched off, and we went our separate ways.

As I write these lines, I feel once again the thrill which electrified me when the voice of a great French soldier rang out clear and true in tribute to two other great soldiers of France. Foch and Mangin have since joined Hoche in the happy realm where there are no wars or rumors of wars, but where eternal peace and brotherly love prevail.

In April I had an agreeable surprise in the form of a visit from the Secretary of the Navy and Mrs. Josephus Daniels, who were accompanied by Rear Admirals R. S. Griffin, David W. Taylor and Ralph Earle, also by Captain A. T. Long and Commander Percy Foote. They came at Easter time and spent several days with the Second Division.

A review of the entire Division was held in the Secretary's honor on the heights of Vallendar, a great plateau overlooking Coblenz and the confluence of the Moselle and the Rhine. The review of the Division was impressive beyond the power of expression. Immediately after the review, the 28,000 officers and men gathered close around a platform that had been erected, and I introduced Mr. Daniels, who then delivered an appropriate address.

On the following days we visited all parts of the Division, finally reaching the barrier on the boundary line. A young Marine was on picket post at the bridge. Secretary Daniels spoke to him, and after a few words the Secretary said, "How did you feel when you were in battle?" The Marine replied, "I felt mighty solemn, and I prayed mighty hard." Mr. Daniels then asked if the other men prayed, and he answered that every man he knew prayed, as all felt that God alone could help them.

I relate this incident because it paints a very different picture of the soldier from that portrayed in the books, the plays, and the motion pictures which have been produced since the war. From the knowledge that I have gained of the inner thoughts of many men, I am certain that it is a true picture too. I will tell one story illustrating this conviction of mine. It is about a young man who graduated from the Virginia Theological Seminary only a year or two before we entered the war. His father, Bishop Arthur Loyd, suggested that he apply for appointment as a chaplain in the Army. He declined to do so, but enlisted instead, saying that he was too young to be a chaplain, and that he believed he would have greater influence among the men if he were a private soldier. He went overseas and served with a combat company, and regularly, on the nights before going into battle, he held communion service, and every man in his company, whether he were Catholic, Protestant, or Jew, joined in the service and took communion. Young Loyd came home a physical wreck from the effects of poison gas, but valiantly continued his ministry until the end, which came two or three years after his return from the war.

I often wonder why the religious side of the soldiers' lives is not more often described. Surely it is a theme worthy of the genius of those having the gift of expressing beautiful thoughts in exquisite poetry or in noble prose.

On Easter morning, we attended an unusual service in a theater located in a Second Division town. Every seat was taken by a soldier, a marine, or a welfare worker. On the stage were Secretary Daniels (a Methodist), a Catholic chaplain, a Presbyterian chaplain, and I (an Episcopalian). The Presbyterian chaplain said the prayers, the men sang the hymns, the Catholic chaplain read a chapter from the Bible, and Mr. Daniels preached the sermon.

From the Easter service, we went to Captain Gilder Jackson's company of Marines to dine with the men. It was an excellent dinner and a very enjoyable occasion, as Mrs. Daniels made a very happy, motherly talk to the men.

The next day I joined the party on a journey to

Mayence, where we took luncheon with General Mangin. After luncheon, he took us through the Government palace which he occupied. It had been a temporary residence, more than a hundred years before, of Napoleon Bonaparte and the Empress Josephine. The suite in which they lived had been kept without change throughout all the years which had elapsed. The beds and the coverlets, ornamented with the Imperial arms, were still in place, as were all the articles of furniture which they had used.

A few weeks afterwards, Admiral Benson, the Chief of Naval Operations, accompanied by Mrs. Benson, left the Peace Conference in Paris long enough to pay us a brief visit. The Fourth Brigade was assembled and reviewed by the Admiral who then presented to a number of the officers and men the decorations which had been awarded them for extraordinary heroism by the French and American Commanders-in-Chief. He made them a beautiful address, expressing his high admiration and deep affection for the Marine Corps. It was a real privilege to do Admiral Benson honor, as his administration of the office of Chief of Naval Operations had been characterized by perfect justice. There was no place for prejudice or favoritism in his upright mind.

Among the many other distinguished men who visited the Second Division were the British Duke of York, who with General Dickman reviewed the Third Brigade and witnessed the presentation of decorations, Ambassador John W. Davis, who with General Hines made a visit to the Divisions of the Third Corps, Assistant Secretary of the Navy Franklin D. Roosevelt, who spent a day with us and presented decorations to a regiment of Marines, the House Committee of Military Affairs, of whom Mr. Tilson and several others were our guests, Vice Admiral Gleaves of the United States Navy, and many high ranking officers of our own and allied armies.

General Pershing visited the Division on several occasions, reviewing it and making a detailed inspection of all its units during the month of March. The Division was formed on the heights of Vallendar.

An amusing incident occurred during the inspection. As the general walked by the men, he invariably questioned each one who wore a wound chevron as to where and when the wound had been received. A soldier of the 9th Infantry when asked these questions, replied, "At Vallendar, last night, sir." The General seemed nonplused for a moment, but after looking at the man's face and seeing there the palpable evidences of a fight in the form of blackened eyes and a badly swollen nose, he laughed and said, "I don't mean that. Where did you receive the wound that this represents?" at the same time touching the wound chevron. The man solemnly replied, "At Soissons, sir." Already his recollections of the war had become less vivid than more recent trying events.

Following the inspection, the General with characteristic brevity said to me, "General, your Division is in splendid condition." He never gave praise unless it were fully deserved.

On the occasion of the review, he personally decorated nearly one hundred officers and men. He pinned on my breast the Army Distinguished Service Medal, and fastened about my neck the Cross of a Commander of the French Legion of Honor, while the citations were read by the then Division Adjutant, Lieutenant-Colonel Hanford MacNider, one of the most brilliant of our younger officers, and one whose unfailing friendship I prize beyond words. Following the review, I published the following order to the Division:

From: The Adjutant General, American E. F.

To: Major General John A. Lejeune, U. S. Marine Corps.

Subject: Distinguished Service Medal.

"1. Cablegram number 2414-R received from the War Department January 8, 1919, announces the award to you by the President of the Distinguished Service Medal for exceptionally meritorious and distinguished service as set forth below:

"Major General John A. Lejeune.

"For exceptionally meritorious and distinguished service.

"He commanded the Second Division in the successful operations at Thiaucourt, Massif Blanc Mont, St. Mihiel and on the west bank of the Meuse. In the Argonne-Meuse offensive, his division was directed with such sound military judgment that it broke and held by the vigor and rapidity of execution of its attacks enemy lines which had hitherto been considered impregnable.

"You will be informed later in regard to the time and place for the presentation of the Medal awarded you.

"By commander of GENERAL PERSHING.

"J. A. ULIO."

"With the approval of the Commander-in-Chief of the American Expeditionary Forces, the Marshal of France, Commander-in-Chief of the French Armies of the East, cites in the Order of the Army:

" 'Major General John A. Lejeune, U. S. M. C.,
        " 'Commanding the Second Division.

" 'He commanded his division with great ability in the attack on Blanc Mont (3-9 October, 1918); seizing in a few hours a position of vital importance and capturing 1,800 prisoners and a large quantity of military material.'

"At General Headquarters, 30 November, 1918.
                "PETAIN,
        "Marshal of France,
"Commander-in-Chief of the French
        Armies of the East.

"2. The Division Commander feels that these citations are citations of the Second Division, and that the award to him of the Distinguished Service

Medal and the Cross of a Commander of the Legion of Honor constitutes, in reality, a decoration of the Second Division, and a recognition by the higher command of the splendid services of its officers and men.

"JOHN A. LEJEUNE."

Immediately following the Armistice, the preparation of detailed reports of the military operations of the Division was initiated, and a careful checking up of the casualties suffered, and the enemy prisoners and cannon captured, was made. A summary of the statistics obtained was contained in an order published to the Division on January 1, 1919, of which the following is a copy:

TO THE OFFICERS AND MEN OF THE SECOND DIVISION:

"1. The year that has just ended has been the most momentous of the century. A year ago the military situation was ominous. Russia and Roumania had been crushed, and the enemy was able to mass a greatly superior force on the Western front. In March, April and May he struck powerful and victorious blows in Picardy, Belgium, and on the Chemin des Dames. At this critical hour, the American forces were placed in the battle lines and on November 11th, after an offensive campaign by the Allies' Commander-in-Chief, conducted with consummate skill and characterized by continuous battles of unparalleled activity and violence, the enemy was defeated and the victory won.

"2. The Second Division played a part of great military and historic importance in this tremendous engagement. It fought five pitched battles or series of battles, always defeating the enemy, and it has won the right to have inscribed on its banners the names of the brilliant victories won by it at Château Thierry, Soissons, St. Mihiel salient, Blanc Mont and Argonne-Meuse. Its casualties were 23,218 officers and men. This was about ten per cent of the total casualties of the American Expeditionary Forces. It captured 12,026 prisoners, about one-fifth of the total number captured by the A. E. F. It captured 343 cannon, about one-quarter of the total number captured by the A. E. F.

"3. The officers and men of the Division have earned by their valor, their skill, and their victories, the admiration and gratitude of our Allies and our countrymen.

"4. That the New Year may be a happy one for all members of the Division, their families and their friends is my most earnest wish.

"JOHN A. LEJEUNE."

It may, I believe, be added with propriety that the latest published data show that the number of casualties suffered by the three leading divisions was: Second Division, 23,218; First Division, 22,320; and Third Division, 15,401. Also that the number of prisoners captured by the three leading divisions was: Second Division, 12,026; First Division, 6,469; Eighty-ninth Division, 5,061. And that the number of cannon captured by the three leading divisions was: Second Division, 343; Eighty-ninth Division, 133; First Division, 119.

During the last two or three months of my stay on the Rhine, I had a very interesting and inspiring experience. Colonel Solomon, of Providence, Rhode Island, and several other ardent Freemasons conceived the plan of organizing a Masonic Lodge in Coblenz, and obtained a charter for the lodge from the Grand Master of Rhode Island. It was designated as Overseas Lodge No. 1.

As soon as I learned of its organization, I made application to take the three degrees and to be admitted to membership. I had always desired to become a Mason owing to my father's devotion to the principles of the order and his expressed wish that I should enter Masonry. My application was accepted and I joined the first class—

about thirty officers and men. I was made a Master Mason on May 17, 1919, in an old German Masonic building which was vacated by troops so that it might be restored to its original use. During the comparatively brief period that the Lodge functioned, many candidates—probably seven hundred—were raised to the sublime degree of Master Mason after taking the two first steps, and much enthusiasm was displayed.

Masonry is essentially democratic. Military or civil rank, riches, place, or power do not affect a man's standing in the order. All the brethren are equal, the only distinction being that all must be obedient to the duly elected officers of the Lodge. Love of God, love of country, and brotherly love are the dominant notes of Masonry as practiced among Americans. Pride, hatred and malice do not intrude their ugly heads in the gatherings of the brethren.

After the return of the Army of Occupation to the United States, our lodge was constituted as Overseas Lodge No. 40 of the Grand Jurisdiction of Rhode Island on Armistice Day, 1920, and I went to Providence to take part in the beautiful ceremony. I still retain my membership in that Lodge, which is composed of service men only.

Subsequently, I was initiated into the mysteries of the Scottish Rite in Washington, taking the 32nd degree on April 15, 1921, and walked the burning sands into Almas Temple of the Mystic Shrine on May 25, 1923, in company with Admiral Coontz and Colonel Theodore Roosevelt.

Prior to June, 1919, I stayed close at home during my seven months' residence in Germany, taking no leave of absence and going away from the Second Division for brief trips only, such as to Cologne to attend a dinner given by Colonel Biddle, the American Liaison Officer, to General Plummer, and to Strasbourg to call on my former commander and good friend, General Gouraud. In June, however, I joined a large party of American officers who were sent by special train to inspect the activities of the Service of Supply. Our journey, the third of the kind that had been made, was most interesting and instructive.

Just before our return to Coblenz, the question of whether or not the German plenipotentiaries would sign the peace treaty had reached a crisis, and the troops were concentrated preliminary to a further invasion of Germany. I found on my return that the Second Division had marched into the First Division area, and the two divisions were in readiness to lead the advance, while the Third Division had crossed the Rhine and had taken up a position on the east bank.

The threat of invasion, however, proved to be only a final gesture after all, as the treaty was signed and promulgated as written by the Allied commissioners, and the three divisions returned to their former stations. We rejoiced because the long suspense was at an end, and our long deferred hope for an early return home seemed about to become a reality. There had been much discussion among us concerning the terms of the treaty, especially with reference to the League of Nations. I was from the beginning a staunch advocate of the League, and I have always believed that President Wilson, as its creator, has written his name among the Immortals.

Our hopes for repatriation met their fruition early in July when we received official notification that on July 15th the movement of the Division by rail to Brest, preliminary to embarkation, would begin. At last the long period of waiting was about to end, welcoming hands were beckoning to us. Now there were smiles on the dear faces at home, and happy thoughts of the reunions about to take place filled our minds and hearts.

We were going back with the proud consciousness of duty well performed. We had fought a good fight. We had kept the faith.

CHAPTER XXI

HOMEWARD BOUND

MY thoughts on the receipt of orders for the return of the Second Division to the United States are accurately portrayed in my message to the officers and men which was published in the last number of *The Indian,* the Division weekly:

"The war is ended!

"Victory is ours!

"The Angel of Peace has spread her wings over the stricken fields of France and Belgium.

"The curtain has fallen on the last act of the greatest drama in the history of the world.

"Your task is now finished, and with the proud consciousness of duty well done, you can now turn your faces homeward.

"The events of the past five years have revolutionized the thought of our people. No person living on this earth would have ventured the prediction a little over five years ago that, in 1918, America would place an army in Europe which would engage in battle and decisively defeat the armies of what was then regarded as the most redoubtable military nation in the world; still less would any one have ventured to predict the presence of a victorious American army on the east bank of the Rhine, or that, in 1919, the President of the United States of America would join with the plenipotentiaries of nearly all the nations of the world in writing the most momentous treaty ever penned by the hand of man.

"Yet these things have been done!

"The officers and men of the Second Division have just cause to be proud of the part played by

Division Commander and Staff reviewing Second Division in New York.

them in the historic events which led up to the conclusion of peace. In the prosecution of this great adventure of our nation, the Second Division has won imperishable renown.

"It fought almost continuously from March 15 to November 11, 1918.

"It defeated the enemy in five great battles, or series of battles, and while its casualties were grievously heavy, yet the sacrifice was not in vain, as its victories had the most far-reaching results.

"You have given yourselves completely to the patriotic duty of defending your country's honor, but I believe that you have received much in return. I believe that when you take up once more your former pursuits, you will be better, truer, more unselfish, and more patriotic men, by reason of the hardships and the sufferings you have endured, and the dangers you have faced. I believe, too, that our appreciation of our country, and our admiration for its people and its institutions, have grown greatly during our sojourn in Germany. I believe that until our dying days, whenever we recall to our minds the memory of our glorious flag flying over the Fortress of Ehrenbreitstein and over the cities of Germany, we shall feel a thrill of patriotic emotion in every fiber of our being.

"At this hour we bid farewell to our heroic comrades who lie buried on the battlefields of France. It is meet, right, and our bounden duty to pause for a brief space, say a prayer for them, and promise them that we will never fail our country in its hour of need, whether it be in peace or whether it be in war.

"The Second Division is, once more, moving to another area. We don't have to ask the Regulating Officer what that area is. It is the spot of which we have ever thought and dreamed since we landed in France. It is the place where our hearts have always been. It is HOME.

"There our dear ones are waiting to welcome us with outstretched arms. There we shall begin life anew. I hope that all your fondest expectations may be realized, and I wish for you great success in all your undertakings and much joy and true happiness in the years to come.

"I trust, however, that you will not forget the Second Division, but that you will assemble in great numbers at each of its annual reunions to renew the old ties of friendship, and to keep alive the spirit which inspired it and made it invincible.

"Your friend and commander,

"JOHN A. LEJEUNE."

On July 10th the General officers of the Division who felt confidence in their skill as horsemen were invited by General Pershing to participate in the Victory Parade in Paris on July 14th, Bastile Day. Without hesitation I telegraphed acceptance for the other General officers and myself, and Neville and I, together with our three aides, left Heddesdorf by automobile on the morning of July 12th, going via Cologne, Liege and Louvain to Brussels, where we spent the night. The next morning we proceeded to Paris, going by way of the devastated area in northern France where, for more than four years, continuous battles had been fought. We viewed the Hindenburg Line with interest, especially that portion of it where the American divisions and the Australians crossed the canal. We also rode through the streets of many destroyed cities and towns. The area was deserted, gloomy and depressing. It was overgrown with weeds, while birds and rabbits were nearly the only forms of life in evidence. We flushed many coveys of quail as we drove along the road. They sought safety in an area where a shambles had been only a year before.

We arrived in Paris early, going to the Hotel Continental and then reporting at Headquarters for instructions in regard to the parade. It was a different Paris than when I had last been there, one year before. Its streets now were filled with laughing, light-hearted people. Its cafés and its hotels were crowded with visitors. Flags and pennants fluttered everywhere to the breeze. A holiday—a celebration—was in the air. Men and women had taken up once again the normal ways of peace. The tension, the strain, the suspense, the sorrows, and the horrors of war seemed to be forgotten. Soldiers, though, were everywhere. The streets teemed with men in uniform.

The next day was to be the greatest of French fête days. The destruction of the Bastile symbolized to the French the death of tyranny and the birth of *"Liberté, Egalité et Fraternité."* Thenceforth the day would have a dual significance and would be celebrated in memory also of the reëstablishment of peace, the reannexation of Alsace and Lorraine, and the victory that had finally obliterated the humiliation and bitterness of the defeat of nearly fifty years before.

I quote from my letter home:

"We reached General Pershing's fine residence at 6:45, and a few minutes later the whole crowd of Generals got in their automobiles and rode to the place where the horses were, which was just at the point where we entered the parade. I was uneasy lest a wild horse should fall to my lot, and felt much relieved when I observed that the Sergeant in charge of the horses wore a Marine Corps device on his cap. He brought me a beautiful mount, saying he had selected him for me because he was gentle and accustomed to crowded city streets and military parades. We mounted our horses promptly and formed in the order in which we were to march. The American Generals were just behind the cavalry escort to Marshals Foch and Joffre, who rode at the head of the procession. General Pershing rode alone ahead of the American Generals, and was followed by an orderly carrying his flag; then by Major General

Harbord, the Chief of Staff, and the other members of the staff. Then came the nine Major Generals, including myself, riding in two lines. Behind us were three lines of Brigadier Generals and two lines of Colonels. Following the mounted officers was the picked battalion of American troops with the colors and standards of all the American regiments then in Europe. After the American Battalion came the Belgian and British contingents, followed by about 20,000 French troops with Marshal Petain at their head, then small detachments of Italians, Japanese, Serbians, Portuguese, Chinese, etc.

"The column started promptly at 8:30, passing down the Champs Elysée—probably the most beautiful street in the world—which was splendidly decorated. We marched through the Arc de Triomphe, which had been chained and unused since the conquering German Army marched through it in 1871. The cenotaph, or monument to the dead, was on the left just as we emerged from the arch, and just beyond, but on the right, were President Poincaré and Monsieur Clemenceau. We saluted the cenotaph and then the President. The route of the march was about five miles long, and I have never seen such a mass of humanity. All were cheering like mad and throwing flowers at the marching troops until the street was carpeted. It was a marvelous and never to be forgotten scene that I looked on as I rode along between the masses of cheering people on each side of the space given up to the parade. At the end of the route, the entire column was reviewed by Marshal Foch and Marshal Joffre with their batons in their hands. When we reached the point of dismissal, General Pershing reviewed the American troops. Our men were magnificent and, by common consent, looked and marched better than any of the other troops."

We were deeply impressed by the historic significance of all that we saw in Paris and could easily have spent weeks going from building to building, but I determined instead to spend my last two days visiting some of the battlefields. We rode to Vierzy, driving through the area where the Second Division had made its heroic and decisive attack on July 18 and 19, 1918, thence through Soissons to Belleau Wood and the Champagne country where the Second Division had striven mightily in June and October. Darkness caused us to seek shelter in Chalons-sur-Marne at the hotel known as "Our Lady of Seven Sorrows." The next day we drove to the heroic city of Verdun and spent the daylight hours walking about the bloodiest of all battlefields. Kindly nature, though, had already spread her healing mantle over the torn and bruised ground, for it was covered with wild flowers. There were acres of red poppies, white daisies, and blue cornflowers—the colors of the French tri-color. The people commented on this fact and saw some special significance in it. The "field of the bayonets" we visited also, and heard its tragic story from the guide. Fort Vaux existed in name only, but Fort Douamont was occupied by a French sergeant-major and his family, whom we induced to put at our disposal some bread and cheese and beer, which went to an excellent market. We were fascinated by the sheer horror of this destroyed area, and did not start on our return journey to Paris until the sun was setting.

The following morning I started for Brest and home. I had learned that the Second Division had begun moving out of Germany and I wanted to be at Brest to welcome the men when the trains arrived. We spent the night at Rennes and the next day we reached our destination and were warmly welcomed by Brigadier General Smedley D. Butler, who was in command of Pontanezen Barracks. He and Mrs. Butler occupied a villa a mile or two outside the city and my visit to them was one of unalloyed pleasure. General Butler had accomplished a task of herculean proportions in building, in so short a time, a modern, up-to-date camp of sufficient capacity to accommodate one hundred thousand men in a place where a quagmire had been. Troops were pouring in to camp by thousands, and thousands were embarking daily. The system installed went like clockwork. There was no shouting or confusion, but perfect order everywhere, and ninety thousand men were being fed with the same facility and regularity as a detachment at a small post.

At Brest, a number of French decorations were presented to officers and men by the French Naval Commandant, and the following letter was received:

"President of the Council,
"Minister of War

"Republic of France,
"Paris, July 18, 1919.

"To the Commanding General of the 2nd American Division:

"My dear General:

"Your splendid Division, which is now about to depart from France, leaves behind it imperishable memories of heroism and sacrifice.

"It was one of the first of the American Divisions to cross the seas, and, in March, 1918, your troops, side by side with their French comrades, mounted guard on the heights of the Meuse. When the time of action arrived, the 2nd Division, in one stroke, proved itself to be a 'Corps d'élite.' The name of the Bois de Belleau will be recorded in the annals of France, as well as in those of the United States, as the symbol of audacity, courage and loyal brotherhood in arms.

"Thereafter, the 2nd Division participated in all of the operations of the last great battle. The number of prisoners captured by it is numbered by thousands. At Vierzy, Villemontoire, Thiaucourt, Xammes, Jaulny, Saint Etienne-a-Arnes, and, finally, at Mouzon, it always fully maintained its great reputation.

"I am writing at the moment you are sailing for home to express to you the everlasting gratitude of France. I bow my head in honor of those who, in these fiercely contested battles, have made the supreme sacrifice. I am convinced that the blood poured out in the common cause will strengthen the ties which unite our people.

"Please believe, my dear General, in my most devoted sentiments.

"For the President of the Council and by his order:

"ANDRE TARDIEU,

"High Commissioner of France-American Affairs."

In a few days General Neville and I embarked on the *George Washington* with five thousand other Second Division officers and men, together with some hundred or two casual officers, Red Cross nurses and Y. M. C. A. workers. An hour afterwards we were steaming down the bay, heading for home! We had a pleasant voyage, and I was never so comfortable at sea as I was quartered in the suite which President Wilson had occupied during his historic voyages to and from the Peace Conferences.

When about midway across the Atlantic I received a radiogram from the Secretary of War, Mr. Baker. It referred to my request that the Division be authorized to parade in New York City. The message was to the effect that authority to do so would be granted provided the majority of the men so desired; otherwise the units of the Division would be sent to their regular stations as soon as they arrived at New York. The despatch further directed that I ascertain and report the wishes of the men.

I at once sent for the Colonels and instructed them to have the company commanders confer with their men on the subject, and to let me know the result. An hour or two later, I was informed that the men had expressed a disinclination to parade. I then went below to a large compartment where the afternoon moving picture show was about to begin. The compartment was filled with men. Colonel Snyder, then commanding the 5th Marines, made a brief announcement to the effect that the Division Commander desired to say a few words. I told them of the Secretary's message and of my feeling that the Division should end its career in a manner befitting its distinguished record, and that I felt certain they would regret a failure to do so during all the rest of their lives. I then said, "In your hands lies the decision," and called for the "ayes" and "noes." The two thousand or more men present voted "aye"; there were no dissenting voices The official vote by companies was taken afterwards and again it was unanimous.

I sent a wireless to Mr. Baker informing him that the 5,000 officers and men on the *George Washington* had declared themselves in favor of parading in New York, and urged his approval of the project. In a day or two, his reply, granting the desired authority, was received.

So it came about that the Second Division, as then constituted, closed its career with a great spectacle amidst the plaudits of the multitude who lined the streets through which it marched.

A few days later our straining eyes sighted our native land for which we had striven and fought; the country for which thousands of our comrades had died. Nc greater happiness can any man have than to return from war to those he loves, with a clean heart and the consciousness that he has done his full duty and has served his country honorably and faithfully. It is impossible tc describe our sensations as we steamed up the noble harbor of New York and sighted the familiar landmarks one by one, until finally the marvelous city skyline and the mighty mass of buildings came into view.

We docked at Hoboken, and as quickly as it was possible to get ashore, I was down the gangplank and making my way to the place on the dock where my wife, my sister, my three daughters, my son-in-law, and Admiral and Mrs. Glennon were waiting to meet me. It was the happiest of the many happy reunions which have marked my service career.

Promptly, Second Division Headquarters was established in the City Office Building, which were put at our disposal by Mayor Hylan. The Mayor showed us every possible consideration, and gave us all the assistance in his power, including the valuable services of his Secretary, Mr. Whalen. The ensuing day, a very impressive ceremony was held in the auditorium of the City Hall. The Mayor formally welcomed the Division to New York, making an eloquent address in which he paid a glowing tribute to its brilliant service. Present at the ceremony were a large number of officers and men and the massed colors and standards of the regiments.

Upon the conclusion of the ceremony, Colonel Myers began work on the many details connected with the concentration of all the units of the Division on August 9th, the day set apart for the parade, as well as on the parade itself, while Major Keyser, G-2, installed an up-to-date publicity office which gave out pages of Division news to the press. Headquarters was a busy scene, reminding one of the war-time days and, needless to say, its work was efficiently conducted, as it was under the guiding hands of the able staff officers who had functioned so successfully during the arduous and stirring days and nights of war and its aftermath. No General officer was ever aided by abler, more loyal, or more faithful staff officers than those of the Second Division.

Every arrangement was made, every eventuality was foreseen, every order was executed as directed, and the parade was a brilliant success. Promptly at the hour designated, the Division Commander and the Division Staff rode through Washington Arch and up Fifth Avenue. Each Regiment and each unit followed in its proper place in the mighty column. Over 25,000 fighting men marched with swinging gait despite the intense heat. Each battalion was in mass formation, its companies in columns of squads being closed together so as to make a front of sixteen files, file closers forming squads in the rear of the companies. All were garbed in field uniforms and steel helmets, and all were on foot except the General officers and their staffs. It was a solid phalanx of men which filled the Avenue for a depth of three miles. There were no distances between units, no cannon, no caissons, no trucks, and no wagons to draw out the formation to a weary legth. The entire column passed a given point in exactly one hour.

The Division received an amazing reception. Hundreds of thousands of people jammed the sidewalks, the cross streets, and the windows of the buildings. Thousands of wounded and maimed men in ambulance, in omnibus, and in chairs on the sidewalks greeted us. Great shouts and mighty cheers rose above the din of the great city. Never before or since have I felt such emotions as I did during that ride at the head of the magnificent Division which I had commanded for a little more than a year.

In passing the reviewing stand, where sat many national. state and city dignitaries, my eyes sought out the dear faces of those I loved, while my hand saluted the officials who reviewed us. I recognized many familiar faces as I rode and heard many voices that I knew shouting my name. So it was with all of us. We were at home.

At the upper end of Central Park (110th Street), I turned out of the column and took post in the plaza to review the marching troops. There I was joined by the Division Staff and by each General officer and his staff, as well as by a number of other General officers who had formerly served with the Division and who came back to it on that day. For an hour we watched the serried ranks marching by. Each battalion as it passed gave us three mighty cheers—cheers which sprang spontaneously from their hearts to ours. It was the most exalted hour of my life.

When all had passed, I turned to say good-bye to the

officers who were assembled. On every weather-beaten face I saw the tears streaming down. It was a sacred hour—an hour spent in communion with the living and the dead.

CHAPTER XXII

EIGHT YEARS AND EIGHT MONTHS AS MAJOR GENERAL COMMANDANT

UPON the conclusion of the New York parade, I was granted a leave of absence. In October I assumed command of the Marine Corps Base at Quantico, Virginia, and assigned Brigadier General Butler to duty as Chief of Staff.

After the discharge of the men belonging to the 4th and 5th Brigades in August, 1919, the inevitable post-war reaction had set in and it was our task to restore the morale of the officers and men on duty at Quantico. With this end in view, military formations, reviews, inspections and drills were re-instituted; a Field Officers' School was established; an extensive educational system for enlisted men was created under the immediate supervision of Colonel Harllee; a reorganization of all post activities was effected, and many economies were introduced.

My family remained in Washington until April 1st, when we established ourselves at Quantico in the newly completed house of the Commanding General. We welcomed the change, not only because I was tired of commuting, but also for the reason that we longed for the pleasant social life of a military post.

On June 20, 1920, however, my appointment as Major General Commandant was announced. I assumed my new duties at Headquarters on June 30th, succeeding Major General Barnett and being succeeded as Commanding General at Quantico by Brigadier General Butler. I decided, however to continue to reside at Quantico until the necessary repairs to the Commandant's House at Marine Barracks, Washington, were made. We actually moved into that house on October 1st. It is an historic old house, built by the first Commandant, Lieutenant-Colonel Burrows, in 1804, and having been the official residence of each Commandant since that time. Brigadier General Henderson, for instance, lived there from 1820 until his death in 1859.

When I assumed the duties of Commandant, demobilization had been completed and the entire Corps was suffering from the consequent let-down which invariably follows the return of a military organization to peace-time conditions. Nearly all of the splendid men who had enlisted for the period of the emergency had resumed their civil occupations; many war-time officers had separated themselves from the service; wholesale demotions in rank had taken place; recruiting was slow; the number of enlisted men being only about 15,000, which was altogether insufficient to perform the important duties assigned to the Corps; there was much unrest among the officers owing to their uncertain status; and the lavish expenditures incident to war were to a great extent still prevalent.

My predecessor had successfully carried the Corps through the war-time expansion and the ensuing demobilization, and it became my mission to rebuild the structure of the Corps and prepare it to meet effectively any emergencies which might thereafter confront it.

More men, however, was the most pressing need, and I at once begun an intensive recruiting campaign, opening many additional offices and increasing materially the number of men engaged in recruiting duty. Colonel Porter prosecuted the campaign energetically with the result that by Christmas the Corps had been brought up to the needed strength, and the recruiting service was then reduced to normal proportions.

In the meantime, economy of administration had become the order of the day and many measures in its interest were instituted, such as the resumption of the system of clothing allowances which had been abandoned during the war; the adoption of a simpler method of handling the Navy ration; the elimination of unnecessary expenditures; a material reduction in the number of civil employees; the establishment of a much smaller quota of clerks at Headquarters and other offices; the adoption of tables fixing the enlisted strength of detachments at all Marine Corps posts at the minimum necessary for the performance of essential duties; the reorganization of the 5th and 6th Marines at Quantico, where they were held in readiness for expeditionary or other emergency duty; the increase in the length of enlistments from two to four years; the demolition of a large number of temporary buildings at Parris Island and the concentration of its activities in a small area; the carrying out of a great repair and construction program at Quantico by enlisted men; and many other similar measures too numerous to mention.

It was necessary, too, that efficiency go hand in hand with economy, and I, therefore, bent my energies towards the adoption of policies and the execution of plans which would promote the steady upbuilding of that essential attribute. To succeed in the campaign for economy and efficiency, it was first necessary to obtain the enthusiastic and loyal coöperation of the officers and men. This was obtained, not only by means of official communications and orders and by personel correspondence and personal interviews, but also by frequent conferences which were attended by the officers on duty at Headquarters who occupied key positions there, and by commanding officers. At these conferences, policies and plans were discussed and suggestions were invited; and detailed reports of the conferences were distributed to all posts and detachments and written suggestions from the officers were requested. By these and by other methods, harmony of action was obtained and the Corps stood together as a unit.

I adopted as the guiding principle of my administration the rule that the good of the Corps, combined with the just treatment of all officers and men, was paramount and, therefore, took precedence over all other considerations. The practice of this principle precluded the exercise of favoritism and brought about among the officers and men a feeling of confidence in the administration of Marine Corps affairs. The spirit of unity and confidence which prevailed made it possible to put into effect many beneficial policies in the direction of increased military efficiency.

The military education of its officers is essential to the efficiency of a military organization. The acceptance of this dictum caused the establishment of the Marine Officers' Schools at Quantico, and the school for newly appointed Second Lieutenants at the Marine Barracks, Philadelphia. The Quantico schools embraced both the Field Officers' School and Company Officers' School. Each officer was informed that he would be required to take the course appropriate to his rank and length of service, or else to take an equivalent course at the school of an Army branch. In addition, selected officers were detailed annually to the Army and Navy War Colleges, the Army School of the Line at Fort Leavenworth, and to the Army technical schools.

More important even than military education is practical military training. The adoption of this precept brought about renewed training activity everywhere. This was especially the case at Quantico with reference to the Expeditionary Force which, after periods of intensive training, undertook maneuvers on an extensive scale during four successive summers in Virginia, Maryland and Pennsylvania, and during two winters with the Fleet on the island of Culebra and in the West Indies, and on the island of Oahu in the Hawaiian Islands. Rifle and pistol practice, too, was stressed, and enviable records were made by teams and individuals representing the Corps.

Discipline, however, is the basis of military efficiency. The realization of the soundness of this doctrine not only caused the insistence on the enforcement of a strict and wholesome discipline with reference to both officers and men, but also led the Commandant to encourage the exercise of leadership on the part of officers of all grades by stressing the fact that the major factor of true military discipline consists in securing the voluntary coöperation of subordinates, thereby reducing the number of infractions of the laws and regulations to a minimum; by laying down the doctrine that the true test of the existence of a high state of discipline in a military organization is found in its cheerful and satisfactory performance of duty under all service conditions; and by reminding officers that a happy and contented detachment is usually a well disciplined detachment.

It is proverbial that well dressed soldiers are usually well behaved soldiers. This thought led to the restoration to the Marine Corps of the blue uniform, to the successful endeavor to induce American manufacturers to produce a khaki cloth of high grade both as to texture and dye, and to improvements in the design and the cut of all articles of uniform.

Lord Wellington is supposed to have said that the battle of Waterloo was won on the cricket fields of England. A paraphrase of this saying to fit the needs of the Marine Corps could readily be provided, but it is unnecessary to do so, as I believe it to be almost universally accepted as sound policy that the cultivation of athletics in a military organization is extremely beneficial to the personnel from the standpoint both of improved physique and of improved morale. For these reasons, a comprehensive athletic policy for the Marine Corps was adopted and put into effect, and athletic activity, especially in connection with football and baseball, everywhere prevailed.

It is the clear duty of the military authorities to provide enlisted men with educational facilities for the joint purpose of increasing their efficiency while in the service and of better fitting them for the duties of citizenship when they leave the service. This conviction caused the Commandant to create the Correspondence School which, under the name of the Marine Corps Institute, has functioned successfully since its inception, about ten years ago, until the present time, over four thousand men having been issued certificates of graduation in one or more

Head of column, Second Division review in New York.

of its courses. It evolved from the Quantico school for enlisted men, its staff having been transferred from that post to Marine Barracks, Washington, D. C., in November, 1920.

While the Marine Corps Expeditionary Force, when landed in a foreign country, is primarily intended to protect the lives and property of American citizens residing there during periods of disorder; it is also intended to benefit and not to oppress the inhabitants of the country where it is serving. This altruistic conception of the duties of Marines was constantly impressed on the officers and men stationed abroad, with the result that the good will of the law abiding people with whom they were associated was gained and peace and good order were restored and maintained.

The Marine Corps is dependent on the confidence and the affection of the American people for its maintenance and support. The realization of this fact induced the Commandant to endeavor, both by precept and example, to influence officers and men to so conduct themselves as to gain and to keep the good opinion and the friendship of the good Americans with whom they might come in contact.

The Marine Corps is a part of the Naval Service, and its expeditionary duty with the Fleet in peace and in war is its chief mission. This fact was repeatedly brought to the attention of officers and men and was the controlling factor in deciding questions pertaining to military training, military education, and assignments to duty. It caused, too, every effort to be made to convince officers and men of the soundness of the doctrine that the future of the Corps would be determined by their ability to serve efficiently with the Fleet in the conduct of the shore operations which are essential to the successful prosecution of naval campaigns in war, and which are essential to the successful conduct of the foreign policy of our country in peace.

A few days after I had taken up my new duties, the New York *Nation* published an article which contained an outrageous attack on the conduct of the Marines in Haiti. Our country was then in the midst of a national political campaign and, as is always the case during such periods, the press was prone to be sensational and public officials were more than usually sensitive to criticism.

During the three years which had elapsed since my previous tour of duty at Headquarters, I had, of course, lost touch with the progress of events and the situation in Haiti, and I felt the need of first-hand information on the subject. I therefore requested Secretary Daniels to authorize me to proceed to Haiti and Santo Domingo for the purpose of inspecting the Marines and of familiarizing myself with conditions as they then existed there. I also suggested that it would be desirable for Brigadier General Butler to accompany me because of the acquaintance he had gained with a large number of the Haitian people during his tour of duty as the organizer and the commander of the Haitian Gendarmerie. Mr. Daniels gave his approval to my suggestions and further decided that it was advisable that there should be no publicity attached to our journey other then a brief announcement that we were going to Parris Island, South Carolina, to inspect the Marine Corps training station located there.

On our arrival at Charleston, S. C., we left the train, embarked on a destroyer and sailed for Port au Prince, our trip to Parris Island being postponed until after our return to Charleston some weeks later. Colonel John H. Russell, commander of the Marine Brigade on duty in Haiti, was notified by radio of our presence on the destroyer a few hours before our arrival at the Haitian capital, and was in readiness to receive us.

The necessary formal call on President Dartiguenave was made immediately, the customary good-will speeches were delivered, the customary toasts were proposed, and the customary glasses of warm, sweet champagne were consumed. We then began our informal investigations of present and past conditions, which we continued without cessation during our entire stay in Haiti.

We visited all Marine detachments except the one at

Thomonde, going to Mirebalais, Las Cahobas, Gonaives, Hinche, Cape Haitien, and many other places where Marines or Gendarmerie detachments were located. We not only questioned hundreds of officers and men, but conferred with many Haitians concerning the treatment they had received at the hands of the Marines. French priests and American and foreign civilians were also interrogated, but no real evidence of the mistreatment of the Haitians by Marines was obtained except a few individual cases in which court-martial proceedings had been instituted and appropriate penalties awarded.

Everywhere we were shown every possible courtesy by the Haitian people. Addresses of welcome were made and responded to; school children sang the Haitian national anthem and the Star-Spangled Banner; and the people exhibited towards us all the evidences of friendship. It was manifest, however, that the country was in a state of extreme poverty, which had been accentuated by the depredations of the bands of so-called *Cacos* which, for nearly two years, had devoured the substance of the peaceful inhabitants. One Peralte, after his escape from prison in Cape Haitien, had gathered together a considerable following from among those who preferred banditry or petty warfare to laboring in the fields. A successful campaign against these lawless elements had been waged by the Marines and the Gendarmes.

This campaign had been conducted by Russel (the commander of the entire force), Wise (the commandant of the Gendarmerie), and Little (the commander of the force in the field) in a skilful and humane manner, while the officers and men had endured the severe hardships and faced the extreme dangers always incident to military operations of this nature. For instance, some months before our visit to Haiti, Lieutenant Hannekin, in the disguise of a native, had penetrated Peralte's camp at night and had shot and killed him in the presence of his followers. A panic ensued, and Hannekin escaped unscathed.

The death of Peralte resulted in the surrender of

many of his followers and the dispersal of the remainder. The small bands which still continued their depredations had eventually been broken up, and robbery and violence had been obliterated. In fact, a complete state of peace had been restored after more than a century of disorder, revolution, rapine, assassination and warfare.

As an American I felt an intense pride in our men. They had served their country with fidelity, with energy, and with courage, but no laurels bedecked their brows, and no crowds shouted peans of praise in their honor when they returned home.

From Haiti we went to Santo Domingo, visiting nearly all Marine Corps stations there. Two officers who had served with distinction in important posts overseas were on duty there. I refer to Brigadier General Feland, then in command of the Second Brigade of Marines, and to Major Earl H. Ellis, who was the Chief of Staff. Colonel Dion Williams was in command at Santiago, whence we proceeded to Sanchez, on Samana Bay, where we rejoined our destroyer and proceeded thence to Santo Domingo City and the other ports on the south coast. Thanks to the destroyer's skipper, Lieutenant Brown, our voyage was a delightful experience.

On our return home, however, we found Washington in a ferment and the newspapers filled with great headlines and extracts from General Barnett's report of the conduct of the military operations in Haiti during his terms of office as Commandant. Unfortunately, these extracts when removed from their contexts conveyed an impression different from that intended, as is often the case. Under such circumstances a Naval Court of Inquiry, consisting of Rear Admirals Mayo and Oliver and Major-General Neville as members, and of Lieutenant-Colonel Jesse F. Dyer as Judge Advocate, was convened in Haiti, and after a thorough investigation, it submitted a most commendatory report on the conduct of the Marines who had served in that country.

Following the visit of a Senatorial Committee to Haiti over a year later, Colonel Russell was promoted to the rank of Brigadier General by President Harding, and was appointed High Commissioner in Haiti. He has served Haiti and the United States continuously in that capacity from that time until the present date (May 6, 1930). His administration of the important duties with which he was charged has been characterized by high ideals and great accomplishments.

In fact, the reputation of the officers and men of the Marine Corps and Navy who have served Haiti can well afford to rest on the comparison between conditions as they exist now and as they existed fifteen years ago. In the impartial tribunal of history I am confident that the verdict will be, "Well done, good and faithful servants."

The intervention of the United States in Santo Domingo came to an end more than five years ago by the election and the inauguration of a President there. The Marine Brigade, commanded by Brigadier-General Harry Lee, the wartime commander of the 6th Marines, then returned to the United States. Notable improvements had been effected by American officials, especially during the administration of Rear Admiral Robison. The occupation of Santo Domingo by the Navy and Marine Corps left behind it a tangible or material monument in the form of a fine system of highways and other public works, a schoolhouse in every town and city, a well-trained constabulary, and an intangible or spiritual monument as well in the form of a nine-year record of scrupulous honesty and unquestioned integrity.

A short while after my return from Haiti, Brigadier-General Long was detached from Headquarters and transferred to Santo Domingo as the relief of

Brigadier-General Feland, who was assigned to duty as the Director of the Division of Operations and Training at Headquarters, while Major General Neville succeeded Long as Assistant to the Commandant, in which capacity he served until the summer of 1923, when he relieved Major-General Barnett as the commander of the Department of the Pacific, the latter being due for retirement. Feland succeeded Neville as Assistant to the Commandant and continued on that duty until August, 1925, when Brigadier-General Dion Williams was assigned as his relief. In June, 1928, Brigadier-General Fuller relieved Williams and is still filling that position.

The heads of the staff departments, when I assumed the duties of Commandant, were Haines, McCawley, and Richards, all of whom, except Haines, remained on duty at Headquarters during my terms of service there. Upon the retirement of Brigadier-General Haines, Assistant Adjutant and Inspector Rufus H. Lane was appointed as the head of that Department. Frequent changes in the other officer personnel in the staff departments, the Division of Operations and Training, the Personnel Section, the Recruiting Section, and the Aviation Section were made so that Headquarters might have the benefit of the experience and the ideas of officers fresh from duty with troops serving at sea, at home and abroad.

I also kept in close touch with Members of Congress, especially the members of the Committees having jurisdiction over Marine Corps legislation and appropriations, and established and maintained friendly relations with the officials of the White House, the State, War and Navy Departments, the Cabinet, the Director of the Budget and his assistants, the Diplomatic Corps, the District Commissioners, the American Legion, the Veterans of Foreign Wars, the Military Order of the World

War, the members of the Press, the Gridiron Club, the Sojourners Club, the Board of Trade, the people of Washington, the personnel of the Army, Navy and Marine Corps, the Marine Corps League, the Second Division Association, the churches and the Masonic order. My activities were not confined to Washington, however, but were such as to require many trips to various parts of the country to attend reunions and conventions of patriotic societies, to make addresses in connection with the annual Navy Day celebrations, to inspect Marine Corps posts and stations, to address schools and colleges, and to join in the reunions of the Second Division. It was a strenuous, but inspiring life, and one which I was able to continue without a day's illness, chiefly owing to Captain John Craige's insistence on my taking daily horseback rides in which I traveled a total distance of about 12,000 miles, and to abstemious habits. I was especially interested in church work and identified myself with Epiphany Episcopal Church, serving as a member of the Vestry and as Junior Warden during the ministry of Dr. James E. Freeman, now Bishop of Washington, and that of Dr. Z. M. Barney Phillips.

My service was unique in one respect, in that I was three times appointed Commandant, first by President Wilson, and again by Presidents Harding and Coolidge, with all of whom I was closely associated. My appointment by President Wilson expired at noon on March 4 1921, as none of the important civil, military or naval appointments submitted by him to the Senate at its last session of his second term were confirmed. On Inauguration Day, I was, nevertheless, invited by Congress to be present at the ceremonies in the Capitol. While waiting for the hour, I was taken by Secretary Daniels into the President's room to meet President and Mrs. Wilson. It was sad to see the President's crippled condition, but there was the old look of determination on his face and the same fire burning in his eyes.

Presently we were marched to the Senate Chamber, immediately after the Diplomatic Corps, and the General of the Armies, the Chief of Naval Operations, and the Major General Commandant of the Marine Corps were announced. We took our seats near the President, and I witnessed for the first time the ceremonies incident to the transfer of the Presidency of the Senate from the old to the new Vice President, and the administration of the oath to the newly elected Senators. I was also present at similar subsequent ceremonies on the occasion of the inauguration of Presidents Coolidge and Hoover.

When the ceremonies within the Capitol wese ended, we repaired to the east portico to listen to the President's inaugural address. There was a vast throng present, all of whom were able to hear every word that was spoken owing to the use of loud speakers for the first time on such an occasion. I did not seek a seat, but stood in the fringe of the crowd on the portico. Presently, I felt a hand on my shoulder. I turned and saw Mr. Denby, the new Secretary of the Navy, whose selection for that office had been announced a few days before. He was not a stranger to me by reputation, as he had enlisted in the Marine Corps upon the entry of the United States in the World War and had been promoted grade by grade until he reached that of Major by the end of the war. I had met him personally, too, on the battlefield of Blanc Mont Ridge, where he called on me when that grim battle was at its height. He greeted me cordially on the portico of the Capitol and said, "General, will you do me the honor of serving as Commandant of the Marine Corps during my term of office as Secretary of the Navy?" I replied that I would do so gladly. He then told me to bring him my nomination for that office at nine o'clock the next morning. I did as directed and the paper, after being signed by President Harding, was transmitted to the Senate at noon and my appointment was at once confirmed by unanimous consent without being referred to a committee. My commission, too, was signed by President Harding that afternoon and was delivered to me by Secretary Denby at four o'clock.

At five o'clock, I went through the most trying personal ordeal of my whole career. I had been selected by the National Press Club to be one of four speakers at its so-called "Hobby" party, which took place in Keith's Theater. The other speakers were former President William Howard Taft, Secretary Herbert Hoover, and the British Ambassador. As I walked out on the stage and faced the great audience of distinguished men and women from all over the United States, I must admit that my heart was in my mouth, but a glance at the smiling, friendly faces of President and Mrs. Harding reassured me and I delivered the address I had written and memorized in the two days that had elapsed since I was notified of my designation as a speaker. I told the audience that my hobby was the Marine Corps. It was indeed a friendly audience and it gave me a warm welcome and a hearty send-off.

The key-note of the policy of the new administration was the reduction of governmental expenditures and the balancing of the budget. By Act of Congress, the Bureau of the Budget was established. General Dawes was appointed Director of the Budget, the coördination of governmental activities was instituted, and a rigid control of estimates and expenditures was put into effect.

Because of the pressure that was brought to bear on all departments, especially the War and Navy Departments, to reduce expenditures and personnel and to consolidate activities, there was grave danger that the Marine Corps, being the smaller and weaker vessel, would be crushed between the larger and stronger—the Army and the Navy. So it came about that my major effort during the long period I served as Commandant was directed toward the defence of the Corps. I fought constantly to maintain its organization, its functions, and its semi-independent status; to prevent an undue reduction of its personnel; to secure sufficient appropriations to keep it in an efficient condition and to provide for housing, clothing and feeding its personnel properly; to retain its status as the Navy's expeditionary force in peace and in war; to build up Marine Corps aviation as a vitally important element of the expeditionary force; to erect at Quantico permanent buildings to replace the temporary war time structures; to recreate the Reserve as a constituent part of the war time strength of the Marine Corps; and to secure the enactment of a law providing for a modified form of promotion by selection, combined with an annual, automatic elimination of a certain percentage of non-selected officers.

The fight for every one of these objectives, except the last, was won, as was the fight for a great many less important objectives. I was fortunate, too, in being able to gain my objectives without the creation of ill feeling. If I made any enemies, I am not aware of the fact; rather do my memory and my heart tell me that I made a host of friends. Men prefer a considerate and courteous "No" to a curt and discourteous "Yes." It was made the invariable rule at Headquarters that all telephone calls be answered politely, that all callers be received courteously, and that all letters be replied to promptly and in a friendly manner.

In the drive which came for the consolidation of activities, a number of the Corps Area Coördinators called attention in their reports to the advisability of consolidating the recruiting services of the Army, Navy and Marine Corps, especially the two last named. The subject was considered at the Secretary's conference of Bureau Chiefs, and because of the expectation that pressure would be brought to bear by the Director of the Budget and by Representative Patrick H. Kelly, the Chairman of the House Subcommittee on Naval Appropriations, to force such a consolidation, it was tentatively decided to do so voluntarily, so far as the Navy and Marine Corps were concerned. After the conference adjourned, I asked the Secretary if the decision would be abrogated if I could obtain the approval of both General Dawes and Mr. Kelly to a continuance of the separate recruiting services. He replied affirmatively. I then called on General Dawes and told him I wanted his help in effecting a considerable economy in administration, and explained that the Marine Corps was expending $45,000 per annum for rental of recruiting offices for which we had been unable to secure space in public buildings, and asked him to direct the custodians of such buildings to find space in them for the Marine Corps. He took immediate steps to comply with my request, with the result that the annual rental was reduced to less than $5,000. I explained further that my motives in making the request were twofold, and that the desire to save our recruiting service from virtual extinction, as well as motives of economy, had caused me to seek his help. He replied that he fully understood the situation, as his experience in the A. E. F. had demonstrated the importance in the interests of efficiency for a small military organization like the Marine Corps to retain its semi-independent status. He then, characteristically, offered me a cigar, which he asked me to smoke in commemoration of the fact that I was the first official who had asked his assistance in saving money.

I next called on Mr. Kelly and easily convinced him of the importance from the standpoint of the Marine Corps of maintaining intact, its separate recruiting service. He even went further than I expected, for while I was still in his office, he called up the Secretary of the Navy and told him that the Committee would look with disfavor on the proposed consolidation of the recruiting services. Mr. Denby was delighted when I reported to him the successful result of my efforts and took immediate action to revoke the tentative decision previously described.

In 1922, a much more serious situation confronted the Marine Corps. That was the year signalized by drastic reductions of personnel. The Army was reduced to 125,000 enlisted men, and the House Appropriations Committee had decided to make allowance for only 65,000 enlisted men for the Navy. As was customary, the Marine Corps representatives appeared last before the Subcommittee for their hearings, but in response to Mr. Kelly's request, I called on him several hours before the hour fixed for our official appearance. He took me aside and told me that the Chairman, Mr. Madden, and the members of the Committee had decided to make material reductions in the enlisted personnel of all the services, but had authorized him to inform me that they had such confidence in the Marine Corps that they would accept a proposal submitted by me for its reduction. He asked that I be prepared to submit the new estimates at the hearings.

I made a careful analysis of the personnel situation and decided on a reduction from 22,000 men to 19,500, instead of to 13,000, which would have been proportionate to the proposed Navy reduction, and I had the estimates revised accordingly. Our figures were accepted by the Committee as submitted. In the fight on the floor of the House, which ensued over Naval appropriations, the Navy men succeeded in securing the adoption of a compromise enlisted strength for the Navy of 87,000. The Marine Corps part of the bill, however, passed the House without opposition.

Both Mr. Kelly and Mr. French, his successor as Chairman of the Subcommittee, were among my warmest personal friends, and my collaboration with them, as well as with Mr. Oliver and the other committee members connected with the hearings on our estimates, was always exceptionally pleasant and agreeable, as, in fact, were my relations with Senator Hale, Mr. Butler, Mr. Vinson, and other members of the Senate and House Naval Committees. Later on, the good will of the members of Congress towards the Marine Corps again prevented a reduction in its enlisted strength.

The Navy Department estimates for the fiscal year ending June 30, 1928, as submitted to Congress in December, 1928, provided for only 16,800 Marines, 1,200 less than the number which had been established in 1924 when the Marine Brigade was withdrawn from Santo Domingo. All my efforts to induce the Navy Department and the Bureau of the Budget to allocate a sufficient sum to the Marine Corps proved unavailing, and I was greatly perturbed by the situation confronting the Corps. Twenty-five hundred men were then engaged in guarding the United States mails, and such seriously disturbed conditions prevailed in Nicaragua and China as to cause me to feel certain that the Corps would be called on within a few months to furnish expeditionary forces for duty in both countries. I was strongly of the opinion, therefore, that it was a most inopportune time to curtail the personnel of the Corps. I therefore deemed it my duty to furnish the proper Congressional Committees with full information concerning the situation which would ensue if Congress should fail to appropriate sufficient funds to maintain the Corps at its then enlisted strength. The House Naval Committee took action at its first session after Congress convened, when by unanimous vote it adopted a resolution authorizing the Chairman to appoint five members to call on the Subcommittee on Naval Appropriations, for the purpose of urging it to allocate sufficient funds to the Marine Corps to maintain it without a reduction of personnel. Officials of the State Department, too, lent their assistance, and finally, in my regular hearings before the Subcommittee of which Mr. French was Chairman, I made a perfectly frank statement in regard to the whole matter and urged that the Marine Corps estimates as submitted be supplemented by reappropriating a portion of the unexpended balances of the two preceding fiscal years. This recommendation was complied with by the Subcommittee, and the bill as it was finally enacted into law carried ample funds to maintain the Corps without any diminution of its personnel.

Between January and July of the following year, it became necessary to send a total of approximately 8,000 Marines to Nicaragua and China. My action, therefore, was fully justified by subsequent events, and since then no attempt has been made to reduce the number of Marines.

I came into contact at this time with many foreigners of distinction. This was notably the case during the Washington Limitation of Naval Armaments Conference. My association with Sir Maurice Hankey, the Secretary of the British delegation and a retired officer of the Royal Marines, was especially agreeable. Like every good Marine, his affection for Marines was not limited by nationality, but extended to Marines serving under other flags than his own. He expressed great pride in the record of the United States Marines in the "Great War" and in the many small wars in which they had taken part. He had himself rendered fine service to the British Empire during the war, in recognition of which he had been knighted by the King and had been voted $125,000 by the British Parliament. One day, on his invitation, Mrs. Lejeune and I took luncheon with Mr. Balfour and himself in their apartment. We were the only guests. Mr. Balfour's simplicity and informality were delightful, and his charm of manner made a never-to-be-forgotten impression on us. On rising to leave, Mrs. Lejeune invited them to dine with us *en familee* at two o'clock on the ensuing Sunday afternoon. He said he had made it a rule to attend no dinner parties during his stay in Washington, but that he would gladly accept our invitation with the understanding that only the Lejeune family would be present. He and Sir Maurice arrived at the stroke of the hour. His enjoyment of the dinner, especially of the turkey, which he called "that delicious American bird," was perfectly apparent, and he conversed with our daughters as jovially as would any young man.

He displayed the deepest interest in the history of the Commandant's House and in the portraits of all the former Commandants which hang on its walls. Finally, with much seeming reluctance, he rose to say good-bye, excusing himself on the ground that he must play his daily game of tennis. I then presented him with a walking cane which the Marine forester in Guam had sent me, telling him it was a souvenir of the Conference. He was as pleased as a child with a new toy, and said, "I had never heard of Guam (pronouncing it with a very short *a*) before I came to this conference, but it seems to me I have heard more about it over here than about any other place."

A few days later, I sat entranced as I listened to the most masterly address I had ever heard. It was Mr. Balfour's final summing up of Great Britain's case. He was indeed the finest gentleman and the most skillful diplomat in Europe, and a most lovable man.

The scrapping of battleships from ratification of the treaties negotiated at the Naval Conference caused every Navy heart to be sad. We felt almost as if persons who were near and dear to us had been doomed to die. About a year later, my heart again suffered pangs of grief when my dear friend and chief, Secretary Denby, was pitilessly attacked with the result that he unselfishly resigned his office. In my sixty-three years of life, I have never known a more honorable gentleman than was "Ned" Denby. No man of all my wide acquaintance had a purer soul or a greater heart than he. No American loved his country more than he. God rest you, Edwin Denby!

How well do I remember his keen enjoyment of the maneuvers of the Marines each year while he was Secretary of the Navy. These maneuvers were made notable because, on two occasions, the President of the United States and the First Lady of the Land visited our camp and spent the night there. On the first occasion, General Butler had established the camp in the vicinity of the battlefield of "The Wilderness." President and Mrs. Harding, accompanied by a large company of distinguished men and women, visited our camp. On their invitation, Mrs. Lejeune and I accompanied them on their return drive to Washington. At Gettysburg the following year, the Marines were again honored by the presence of the Commander-in-Chief and his Lady in their camp.

Somehow, though, my memory of the President goes back more strongly to his connection with the funeral of the "Unknown Soldier" than to any other episode with which he was associated. No American can ever forget the unending stream of people who, by night and by day, passed slowly by the mortal remains lying in state under the dome of the Capitol; or the solemn procession from the Capitol to Arlington of the head of the State, the Secretaries of War and Navy, the chiefs of the Army, Navy and Marine Corps, the pallbearers, the soldiers, sailors and marines—all on foot; or, most impressive of all, the enormous crowd standing in perfect silence and with bowed heads as the procession moved by. Then there were the solemnity and the beauty of the service at Arlington; the marvelously beautiful strains of the music rendered by the Marine Band; the exquisite voices of the singers; and the noble addresses.

Not many months afterwards, I took part in another great funeral ceremony. It was that of President Harding. As one of the escort, I marched close to his bier and accompanied his remains to Marion for their burial. Again there were vast outpourings of people—in Washington, in the towns and cities along the railway, and in Marion.

The Coolidge era was then ushered in. It was characterized by unostentatiousness and simplicity, and was made notable by the President's insistence on the exercise of economy and the maintenance of efficiency. General Lord, as Director of the Budget, played an important part in President Coolidge's régime. The era was made delightful by the winsome personality of Mrs. Coolidge. She presided over all social functions at the White House with so much graciousness and charm as to win the hearts of all persons who caught a glimpse of her. It was the good fortune of Mrs. Lejeune and myself to gain the friendship of the Coolidges and of their intimate friends, Mr. and Mrs. Frank Stearns.

On the personal invitation of the President, I accompanied him and Mrs. Coolidge to the American Legion Convention at Omaha. The only guests on the special train were Mrs. James A. Drain, wife of the National Commander of the Legion, the Army and Navy aides,

Officers and two disabled men of Second Division at reunion, St. Louis, Mo.

newspapermen, the regular White House staff and I. Whenever the train stopped anywhere, the President sent for me to join him on the rear platform of his private car. At St. Louis, a man in the crowd came up close to speak to me, saying he was determined to have a word with me as he had served in the Second Division overseas and had never forgotten seeing me one day during the battle of the Meuse-Argonne, when he was one of a group of men who were lying down on the ground, having halted for a brief rest. As I drove up in my car, they rose to salute me, and I said to them, "Sit down, men. It is more important for tired men to rest than for the Division Commander to be saluted." The little story seemed to interest Mrs. Coolidge, who was standing near and overheard the conversation.

It was in the Coolidge era that it became necessary to send large expeditionary forces to China and to Nicaragua. When the orders were issued, I reported in writing to the Secretary of the Navy, Mr. Wilbur, who was my classmate, that a considerable deficiency in appropriations would be caused, and asked him to bring the matter to the President's attention. This he did, and later told me that the President's only reply was, "Go ahead." On one occasion the President said to me, "They may not need those Marines in China, but if they should be needed, we should feel much better with them on the other side of the Pacific than on this side."

Brigadier General Butler was selected to command the Marines in China. He performed his duties in a highly efficient manner. They were distributed between Shanghai and Tietsin, and were in addition to the Legation Guard at Pekin. They provided protection for the Americans residing there, and fortunately it never became necessary for them to fire a hostile shot, but, on the contrary, they succeeded in gaining the good will of the Chinese people. A regiment is still retained at Shanghai and a battalion at Pekin, or Peiping.

The Marines in Nicaragua encountered a different kind of service. At first their activities were confined to garrison duty, but as the revolution increased in violence reinforcements under Brigadier General Feland were hurriedly transported there. Under the terms of the Stimson agreement, the Marines received the surrender of the arms of both factions and then became responsible for the preservation of peace pending the holding of an election under U. S. control. With the defeat of Sandino and his band at Ocotal in July, 1927, the major portion of the Marines was withdrawn, leaving the aviation detachment and a regiment of Marine infantry there under the command of Colonel Gulick.

During the rainy season, Sandino assembled a considerable force in the mountain region in the north, and at the end of December severe fighting ensued in which the Marines, although victorious, suffered rather heavy casualties. I immediately recommended that considerable reinforcements be sent, with Brigadier General Feland again in command, and that I accompany the force for the purpose of making an inspection and of obtaining first-hand information in regard to the situation. This recommendation was approved by the President.

I spent two intensely interesting weeks in Nicaragua, visiting many places in the interior and making a number of flights by plane. I also conferred with President Diaz, Mr. Chamorro, Admiral Sellers, the American Minister, General McCoy, General Feland, Colonel Dunlap (the commander of the field force operating in the north), and many other Americans and Nicaraguans. I returned to Washington via the Pacific Coast and immediately appeared before the Senate Committee on Foreign Relations and made a complete statement concerning the happenings and the situation in Nicaragua.

The campaign waged by the Marines was a remarkable one owing to the large extent of territory covered, the lack of roads and railways, the mountainous nature of the country, and the mobility and wariness of Sandino's force. It was completely successful, however, and the election was held in the autumn under the immediate personal supervision of enlisted men of the Marine Corps and Navy without any disturbances whatever. Subsequently, Sandino went to Mexico and the small remainder of his force disbanded. During all this period, Marines under command of Lieutenant-Colonel Beadle were busily engaged in recruiting, organizing and training the Guardia Nacional dé Nicaragua, which has now to a great extent replaced the Marines in policing the country. The force of Marines in Nicaragua has been greatly reduced and consists of only about 1,200 men.

I cannot bring to a close this brief account of the events which took place in Nicaragua without especial mention of the outstanding service of the Marine Corps aviation detachment under the command first of Major Rowell, and then of Major Bourne. From Managua and a point on the East Coast as bases, our planes kept in touch with every detachment during the period of active military operations and rendered invaluable combat service. In addition, transport planes were utilized on an extensive scale in furnishing the outlying detachments with replacements, food, and other essential supplies. The pilots were both skillful and daring, and the planes gave splendid service.

Aviation, so far as the Marine Corps is concerned, under the able guiding hands of Lieutenant-Colonel Turner and Major Brainard, has demonstrated that it is invaluable. I am, in fact, an enthusiast on the subject of aviation, and I am convinced that it will be of vital importance, both by land and at sea, when war is again precipitated.

I must, however, bring this chapter to an end, even though I leave unwritten many things that I ought to have written, by relating a few incidents connected with the closing days of my service as Commandant. I had determined, when I was reappointed Commandant by President Coolidge, that I would not accept another reappointment, but did not say anything about my plans to any one except my wife until a few weeks before the expiration of my term of office. I then told Mr. Wilbur of my intentions, and gave out the following statement to the press:

> "My term of office as Major General Commandant, U. S. Marine Corps, will expire on March 5, next. On that date I shall still have ahead of me twenty-two months' active service before being transferred to the retired list by operation of law. Many of my friends have urged me to allow them to interest themselves in endeavoring to secure my reappointment. I am exceedingly grateful to them. To be Commandant of the Marine Corps is the highest honor that can come to any Marine. However, I shall have had my full share of service in that office on March 5 and I shall then relinquish it voluntarily and cheerfully.
>
> "I shall always look back on the more than eight years that I have been Commandant as years that have been full of the joy of service, and I shall always remember with much pride the great privilege that has been mine, of being connected with the administrations of President Wilson, President Harding and President Coolidge, and of being associated with the members of the committees of Congress which have had jurisdiction over Marine Corps legislation and appropriations.
>
> "My interest in the great Corps in which I have served my country for nearly thirty-nine years will continue unabated, and I shall keep in close touch with its activities and with its officers and men not only during the remainder of my active service, but throughout the remaining years of my life as well."

I also strongly recommended Major General Neville as my successor. He had served with me in the Second Division as the Commanding General of the 4th Brigade and on several other occasions, and it was my belief that his record was such as to make his appointment desirable. President Coolidge and Secretary Wilbur approved my recommendation, and he was at once nominated and confirmed by the Senate to take office on March 4th, after the inauguration of President Hoover.

Marine officers everywhere expressed the deepest regret because of my leaving the office of Commandant, as did many other friends in Congress, the Navy, the Army, and in civil life. Mrs. Lejeune and I were the recipients of many letters and were given many *despedidas*. Everywhere we received evidences of affection and good will.

CHAPTER XXIII

THE VIRGINIA MILITARY INSTITUTE

WITHIN a day or two after I had made announcement of my desire to relinquish the office of Commandant upon the expiration of my then term, two officers in whose judgment I had great confidence—I refer to Majors Ralph S. Keyser and Joseph C. Fegan—told me they had learned from Marine officers who were alumni of the Virginia Military Institute that General Cocke had tendered his resignation as Superintendent because of ill health, and that there was a strong probability that the Board of Visitors would ask me to accept the appointment. Both Keyser and Fegan strongly advised me to give such an invitation favorable consideration. After discussing the *pros* and *cons* at some length, I told them that to retire from active Marine Corps duty nearly two years before attaining the age of compulsory retirement would be an act of real sacrifice, but that, on the other hand, to be the Superintendent of the Virginia Military Institute would be similar to a change of station instead of retirement, and that I would keep an open mind on the subject.

In the course of a few weeks Congressmen Montague and Moore of Virginia, as well as General Cocke, communicated with me in regard to the same matter, and in March a committee of the Board of Visitors, headed by Captain Massie, the President of the Board, called on me by appointment. They informed me that they were instructed by the governing board of the Institute to ascertain if I would favorably consider its offer of appointment as Superintendent. We spent several hours together, going over the entire situation, and on the ensuing day, at a special meeting of the board in Richmond,

Virginia Military Institute.

Parade.

I was unanimously elected and upon notification of the fact I sent my acceptance.

The Alumni of Richmond gave a dinner in my honor in April, which Mrs. Lejeune and I attended. During our stay in Richmond we were the guests of Governor and Mrs. Harry F. Byrd at the Executive Mansion. The day after the dinner we motored to Lexington with General and Mrs. Cocke and at a reception given us by them we had the opportunity to meet the members of the faculty, their families, and the Cadets of the First Class. Both of us had visited Lexington before, when we were guests of General and Mrs. Nichols, and we carried away with us after each visit delightful recollections of the Institute and of the town of Lexington.

On July 17th Mrs. Lejeune and I returned to Lexington and were domiciled in the Dutch Inn while the Superintendent's house was undergoing repairs. Laura and Eugenia joined us in August, and on September 9th, the day on which the new Fourth Class entered, we moved into the house. The good people of Lexington, and Washington and Lee University, as well as those of the Virginia Military Institute, have taken us within the charmed circle of their friendship, and we now feel thoroughly at home in our new surroundings.

Personally, I greatly enjoy my duties as Superintendent and feel myself growing younger each day because of my association with the Cadets. Fortunately I have been able to keep my youthful point of view and do not, therefore, take my duties too seriously. Neither do I take them too lightly, as I have full realization of the fact that mine is a sacred trust. If I can do anything to help these young men to climb a little nearer to the crest of the heights than they otherwise would do, I shall remember the years I am living here as years that were full of happiness and joy.

This is a school with a great history and wonderful traditions. Since its foundation in 1839, its alumni almost *en masse* have served in every war in which our country has engaged, with fine efficiency and self-sacrificing heroism. They have also been outstanding citizens in the years of peace. I am convinced that the training young men receive here makes them fit for the humdrum struggle of modern life just as the training the Cadets received in the olden time made them fit for the heroic part they played at Newmarket on May 15, 1864, when that little band of gray-clad boys showed to the world that not only did they know how to die like brave men, but that they also knew how to fight like veterans.

The heroic spirit of the Newmarket Cadets, of "Stonewall" Jackson, and of the other "Immortals" who have striven here still exercises a profound influence on the young Americans who receive their education in these halls, and stimulates them to keep their honor unblemished, their courage high and their love of country pure and undefiled.

More than two years have elapsed since the Foreword to this book was written. Since that day nearly all my spare time has been devoted to "The Reminiscences of a Marine." Every word of the book I have written down in longhand, but if perchance my readers find some pleasure in its pages I shall feel fully repaid. There is no rancor in my soul toward any man, and it is my earnest hope that no word I have written will cause any one pain.

I wish it were possible for me so to express my feelings to those who have journeyed down life's pathway with me as to make them know they have my gratitude and my affection; and I wish to repeat, with emphasis, that whatever I may have been able to accomplish was due to them. No man has ever had kinder friends or more loyal associates than have I. Their images are in my heart.